MANAGING
AN INFORMATION
SYSTEM

MANAGING
AN INFORMATION
SYSTEM

James R. Mensching
Associate Professor of Business Computer Systems
New Mexico State University
Visiting Scientist at IBM Corporation

Dennis A. Adams
Assistant Professor of Decision and Information Sciences
The University of Houston

PRENTICE HALL, *Englewood Cliffs, NJ 07632*

Library of Congress Cataloging-in-Publication Data

```
Mensching, James
    Managing an information system / James R. Mensching, Dennis Adams.
        p.   cm. -- (Prentice Hall series in information management)
    Includes bibliographical references and index.
    ISBN 0-13-552746-5 :
    1. Electronic data processing departments--Management.   I. Adams,
Dennis,         .  II. Title.  III. Series.
    HF5548.2.M388  1991
    658'.05--dc20
                                                        90-20505
                                                            CIP
```

Editorial/production supervision and interior design: Maureen Wilson
Cover design: Ray Lundgren Graphics, Ltd.
Manufacturing buyer: Trudy Pisciotti
Prepress buyer: Bob Anderson

Cover photo: VILLON, Jacques.

> *Chess Board.* (1920)
> Etching, printed in black, composition: 7⅞ × 6¼".
> Collection, The Museum of Modern Art, New York. Gift of Ludwig Charell.
> Photograph © 1991 The Museum of Modern Art, New York.

PRENTICE HALL SERIES IN INFORMATION MANAGEMENT
WILLIAM R. KING, Series Editor

 © 1991 by Prentice-Hall, Inc.
A Division of Simon & Schuster
Englewood Cliffs, New Jersey 07632

Printed in the United States of America
10 9 8 7 6 5 4 3 2 1

ISBN 0-13-552746-5

Prentice-Hall International (UK) Limited, *London*
Prentice-Hall of Australia Pty. Limited, *Sydney*
Prentice-Hall Canada Inc., *Toronto*
Prentice-Hall Hispanoamericana, S.A., *Mexico*
Prentice-Hall of India Private Limited, *New Delhi*
Prentice-Hall of Japan, Inc., *Tokyo*
Simon & Schuster Asia Pte. Ltd., *Singapore*
Editora Prentice-Hall do Brasil, Ltda., *Rio de Janeiro*

To D.B. and Melly

Thank you for all your support and understanding.

CONTENTS

5
PHYSICAL ENVIRONMENT   96

6
SYSTEM PERFORMANCE EVALUATION   124

7
HARDWARE ACQUISITION   150

8
LEGAL ISSUES   179

9
FINANCIAL ISSUES   198

10
SOFTWARE ACQUISITION   220

11
SECURITY AND INTEGRITY   251

12
MANAGING END-USER COMPUTING   280

13
MANAGING APPLICATION PROGRAMMING   300

14
MANAGING SYSTEMS PROGRAMMING   320

15
DATA MANAGEMENT   336

16
MANAGEMENT OF DATA COMMUNICATIONS   352

A

REVIEW OF MACHINE OPERATIONS: A BIRD'S EYE VIEW   378

B

REVIEW OF MACHINE OPERATIONS: A WORM'S EYE VIEW   407

INDEX

FOREWORD

William R. King, Series Editor

I am delighted to have the opportunity to include Jim Mensching and Dennis Adams' *Managing an Information System* as one of the early entrants in the Prentice Hall Series in Information Management.

An important phenomenon of the late 20th century is the ubiquity of the management of computer resources. Only a few decades ago, one person, or a few people, in a large organization could be thought of as having this function. Now, in addition to the head of the centralized computing department, business functional managers and work group managers often have significant information management responsibilities.

Even individual knowledge workers using stand-alone personal computers or workstations must share some of these responsibilities. For instance, even if one is the sole user of data and programs, their preservation must be ensured by proper backup procedures and actions must be taken so that company security is maintained.

This book focuses on the management of large systems and discusses the relevance of these management practices to the management of information systems at other levels. It focuses primarily on the perspective of the manager of a large computer installation and the importance and pervasive issues that he or she must face.

A basic premise is that the computer manager is both important to his or her firm and very vulnerable to criticism if computer systems do not perform as expected. These expectations can easily become unreasonable as organizational members learn about the benefits of new technologies and new applications without understanding the limitations that go along with them.

Mensching and Adams' treatment of important information management topics is unique. The book is down to earth; yet, it is not a cookbook. It takes a business perspective; yet, it deals directly and specifically with the "guts" of the information system manager's job. It strikes a useful balance between developing theoretical knowledge, which too often is difficult to apply, and reliance on checklists, which too often are applied without real understanding. The student who studies it will come away with a great deal of useful knowledge and understanding that can be directly applied.

The approach taken focuses on IS as an integral element of the organization. IS is not viewed in isolation, but rather in relation to all of the other business functions, with each having the objective of helping the business to achieve its goals. Similarly, the common IS failure to deliver new systems on time and within budget is viewed not just in IS project terms, but in terms of its impact on the business and its goals.

The approach is top-down in that the book discusses first business goals and IS strategic planning and then the tactical issues that must be dealt with to implement these strategies. Among the most important of these tactical issues is the development of standards and procedures in a wide variety of areas ranging from system documentation to the evaluation of computer professionals' performance.

Mensching and Adams carry a single company case example from chapter to chapter throughout the book. This is an important device for enhancing the reader's understanding. Other complex cases are also used and, in many chapters, students are also invited to observe their own computer environment to help them apply the ideas that are presented in a familiar context.

Managing an Information System deals in depth with many important issues that are often slighted. Among these are computer personnel management, system performance evaluation methods, and legal and financial planning issues.

The reader who gives careful attention to the book will come away with a wealth of in-depth understanding and practical knowledge on how to address the most critical issues of information management as well as how to manage their interrelationships. Mensching and Adams have thereby made a valuable contribution to the information management literature.

PREFACE

At times it is rather astonishing to a professor when a senior level student or a graduate student in information systems comes to the professor's office and asks questions about what they will be doing when they enter the work force as an information system professional. From our experience, the thought that comes to mind is "What has this student been doing for the last two years?" However, this is unfortunately an all-too-common situation. Either the academic courses that the students take in an information system curriculum deal with many technical details of computer languages, computer hardware and software, data structures, and the like, or they deal with high level theory. All of this background is absolutely necessary for an information system professional, but many times the students only see the trees and don't know what the forest looks like. A few don't even have a clue that a forest exists.

The student may not have the proper perspective. The technology involved in computing can be intriguing and very challenging but is not an end in itself. It must be realized that the job market is a business-oriented place and that computers are being used as productivity tools in order to enhance the performance of an organization. This means that the information system professional must have more than just the technical computer background but also must have a knowledge of how the information system contributes to the operation of the organization. In order to do this the student must first understand how the various parts of the information system operate and their interrelationships. In addition, there must be a basic understanding of how a business functions and the principles involved in making solid business decisions.

Information system students take business courses which give them a sound background in business decision making. They also take courses dealing with some of the aspects of how the information system functions, the development of computerized application systems being the most notable of these. The final step is to tie together this knowledge and fill in some of the gaps. We believe that the best way to do this is from the perspective of how to manage the information system. This book has been designed to accomplish that objective.

This text has been written from the perspective of the manager of an information system. In this way we can focus on each of the responsibilities of the manager and examine them in more detail. In addition, using this view allows us both to discuss the strategic issues facing an information system and also to deal with the functional issues involved in running a modern information system. The book is organized in what can be thought of as a top-down manner. We start with the strategic issues and work toward the operational issues.

Since the operational issues demand a certain degree of technical background, we provide two appendices at the end of the text that review the operation of a computer system. Additionally, we provide references at the end of chapters that may help students not having the minimal preparation for the next chapter. These references address either prerequisite business knowledge or technical computer background. These references are labeled "Readings before Next Chapter." In order to supplement the material in a chapter there is a list of "Additional Readings" at the end of each chapter. The instructor may wish to assign some of these readings to emphasize specific topics. We also believe that it is extremely useful for the students to become knowledgeable about what is happening in the computer industry and this course is an opportune place to accomplish this. We personally find that the best way to do this is to have the students subscribe to *ComputerWorld*, a weekly publication. We then assign readings out of this publication.

It is important that the concepts in the textual material be reinforced with real world examples. We try to accomplish this by offering cases at the end of each chapter. Many of these cases have been extracted from actual situations and then altered to make them appropriate for student assignments.

There are many people who have helped us in completing this text. In fact they are so numerous that we no doubt will fail to mention someone who has made a significant contribution. We are truly sorry if you contributed and we didn't thank you.

First on the list to be thanked are the many students who were enrolled in the New Mexico State University Business Computer Systems 445 and 450 classes that used these materials. They made very significant contributions, which are sincerely appreciated. Also among those to be thanked are certain individuals who helped in extraordinary ways, some by contributing problems and cases, others by reviewing the manuscript and making valuable suggestions to improve it. These individuals include Lisa Shade, IBM Corporation; Jeff Mainville, Amdahl Corporation; Arrianne Freeman, IBM Corporation; George Buffett;

Margee Kaye; David Labarge; Ronda Cionco, Hewlett Packard Corporation; and Brian Ormand.

During the manuscript review process valuable suggestions were made to improve the final content of the text. We would like to thank Bob Zmud of Florida State University; Skip Lees of California State University at Chico; Bill King of the University of Pittsburg; William Harrison of Oregon State University; David Paradice of Texas A&M University; and Jerome Kanter of Babson College for their many contributions.

In addition there were many individuals at Prentice Hall who helped to publish this text. Among those that we worked with directly were Maureen Wilson, the production editor; Jenny Kletzin, the supplements editor; Elaine Price, supplements production editor; and Valerie Ashton, the acquisitions editor. No doubt there were many others behind the scenes who were also heavily involved. To all of them we would like to express our gratitude.

JIM MENSCHING

Associate Professor of Business Computer Systems,
New Mexico State University (presently on leave)
Visiting Scientist at IBM Corporation

DENNIS ADAMS

Assistant Professor of Decision and Information Sciences,
The University of Houston

1

INTRODUCTION

IMPORTANCE OF THE INFORMATION SYSTEM

For most organizations the computerized information system has become one of the most important and critical functional areas within the firm. Almost all forms of organizations are dependent on digital computer technology to process information. Firms ranging in size from sole proprietorships to massive multinational conglomerates have become dependent on computers. The activities of the firms using computers cover a broad spectrum including manufacturing, service, government, education, retail sales, and many other economic functions too numerous to list. In addition, the areas of application of computer technology within each firm are widespread and continually expanding.

One of the reasons for this growth rate is the dramatic increase in the cost/performance ratio of all types of computer technology, as shown in Figure 1.1. This decrease in cost has made computer processing economical for more and more firms. Also, it makes the use of computing feasible for more functions within a given firm.

The computer is no longer just a sophisticated accounting machine or a super-fast scientific number cruncher. Computers now control entire manufacturing operations, including functions such as ordering and paying for raw materials, manufacturing the goods, accepting and filling orders, and billing the customer. In addition, the decision-making and communications areas have been heavily influenced by computers. Executives can quickly obtain and ana-

Figure 1.1 *Historic Relative Cost/Performance of Computers*

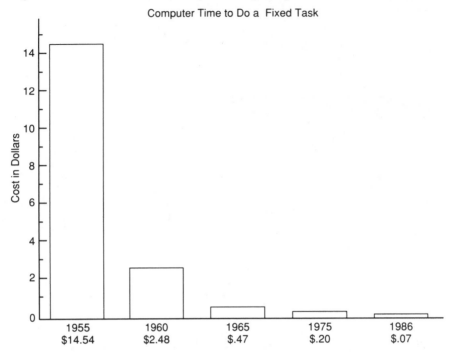

Computer Time to Do a Fixed Task

lyze information using the information system. Then they can easily communicate decisions by using word processing and electronic mail services.

With the tremendous advances in microcomputers, office automation, robotics, telecommunications, and computer aided manufacture and design, computer technology is affecting almost all aspects of business. The role of the computer will continue to grow as these technologies continue to mature and the price/performance ratio of computer hardware continues to decrease. Computers have become so important to some firms that the successful administration of the information system can mean life or death for the organization. Some examples of computerized tasks are shown in Figure 1.2.

When computers are properly managed, they can substantially increase productivity. However, when mismanaged they can lead to disaster. These factors make the various activities involved in the management of an information system very important. In many firms these management functions are scattered throughout the firm. While the major focal point in the information system is usually the manager of the central computer system, there are many others involved in the management of computer resources. Since computers are present in all aspects of business, people generally considered outside the traditional realm of data processing are involved in managing computer resources. These people must also be concerned with issues such as computer security, backup,

Figure 1.2 *Computerized Tasks by Functional Area*

FUNCTIONAL AREA	COMPUTERIZED TASKS
Production	Inventory Control Manufacturing Scheduling Material Requirements Computer Aided Manufacturing
Marketing	Order Entry Sales Tracking Market Analysis
Research and Development	Specialized Engineering Functions Computer Aided Design Experimental Design and Analysis
Accounting and Finance	Financial Statement Compilation Accounts Payable Accounts Receivable Payroll Portfolio Analysis Fixed Assets Control Budgeting
Personnel	Employee Tracking Employee Evaluation Recruiting Government Reports
High Level Management	Summary Reports Ad Hoc Queries Long-range Planning

system compatibility, data integrity, and other issues that are usually associated only with data processing professionals.

For example, the marketing research department may have its own distributed minicomputer. The manager of the marketing research department may actually have to manage a center that is substantially smaller than the centralized system, but one that has many of the same types of problems. With the widespread use of microcomputers, every individual responsible for a micro must be concerned with the proper management of the computer technology under their control. The size and cost of the equipment for the information system under consideration should not determine whether good management principles are to be applied. Mismanagement of any system can adversely affect an organization. However, the general rule is that the magnitude of the damage is usually (but not always) greater for large systems.

Fortunately, the principles of sound information system management can be successfully applied to all levels of the information system. In most cases, applying these principles will consume fewer resources and demand less formal structure in a smaller system than in its larger counterpart. Since the distinction between different size systems is usually unclear, some definitions are offered in Figure 1.3.

For example, protection of corporate data is an extremely important function. Saving backup copies of the data files can be done to help restore lost or damaged data files. On the centralized, mainframe-oriented system data backup is a very formal process. A determination must be made of which files are to be backed up and how often the backup should be done. The backup schedule will affect the availability of the system since users will not be allowed to alter a file while it is being backed up.

On the other hand, for a personal work station the backup process may be as informal as having the primary user copy files from the hard disk to a floppy disk as needed. In either case, improper backup may cause the loss of important data. In the small system case, this could affect only a single user, while for the centralized system this could affect hundreds or even thousands of users.

Understanding the principles of information system management in the complex centralized environment should allow an individual to apply these same principles selectively to smaller systems. For this reason this text will concentrate on managing large systems. Of course, where appropriate we will discuss issues involved in managing departmental and personal systems.

While most managers will have some responsibility for computer technology, the manager of the centralized computer system will have the most responsibility for the proper management of computer facilities. The manager of information systems (or vice-president of information systems or manager of data processing or whatever the chief of computer technology is titled) must not only administer the resources under the control of the information systems area, but must also provide leadership, advice, and direction to others involved in managing computer resources. These factors make the position of manager of information systems of strategic importance.

The manager of information systems is a challenging position with a substantial amount of responsibility. The dynamic nature of computer tech-

Figure 1.3   *Definition of Some Terms*

TYPE OF COMPUTER	INFORMAL DEFINITION OF SYSTEM
Mainframe	Large system that serves many simultaneous users (usually >100) and costs more than $200,000
Minicomputer	Medium-sized system that services multiple simultaneous users and costs between $20,000 and $200,000
Microcomputer	Small computer that generally serves a single user and costs less than $20,000

Note that there really is no firm boundary dividing each of these systems. For example, some micros will serve multiple users and some vendors will call their system a mini while others would refer to the same system as a mainframe.

nology and the complexity of most information systems makes the manager's job quite demanding. The manager must deal with all forms of users ranging from the sophisticated technically oriented user to the casual naive user. In addition, the manager must supervise and plan computer operations and development involving large investments of the firm's capital and extremely complex technology. These activities demand that the manager possess a wide range of job skills including a sound business background, a technical computer background, managerial competence, and a good dose of ordinary common sense.

COMPUTING CONFIGURATIONS

In most organizations some type of computer technology is used in every functional area. The type of computer technology and the way it is organized can be substantially different from one department to another. Some departments may rely entirely on the organization's centralized computer services for their processing. This is usually the case for departments that process very large amounts of data such as accounting and inventory control. Other departments may have their own distributed computer system which usually entails the use of one or more minicomputers. This will occur when the department performs tasks which are substantially different from those of other departments or where geographical distance makes a distributed system more economical. A good example of this situation is the research and development and engineering areas. Other departments may rely almost entirely on single-user microcomputers and microcomputer networks.

The configuration of the computing environment depends on many factors: the managerial style of the firm, the industry, and the size of the firm, to just name a few. In many cases there will be a great variety of technology, some centralized mainframes, some distributed minis, and many microcomputers with some or all of these systems networked together. The present information system is usually the result of many years of growth where different types of equipment were acquired to fulfill various needs. Making these diverse technologies function in a smooth, coordinated manner can be a monumental task.

Each different configuration may present different management problems. However, most of the decision making involving different types of systems will be based on using similar decision tools and thought processes. For example, the acquisition of a mainframe system will entail decisions involving the appropriate central processing unit (CPU), peripherals, systems software, and applications software. These same components would be involved in deciding on the appropriate micro system to acquire. Also, the means of financing the acquisition and the negotiation of the sales contract would be involved in each acquisition. The major difference in these two acquisitions is the magnitude of each decision. Mainframe decisions will usually involve millions of dollars and affect a large number of users.

If the micro decision is for only one individual, then the impact will be substantially less. However, as we will discuss later in this text, even a micro-computer decision must be made relative to the existing technology within the information system. It is important that the information system function as a coordinated set of components and not as a series of unrelated parts. This makes the selection process for the micros very much like that of the mainframe. Again, the specific criteria may be different, but the decision process is the same.

PERSPECTIVE ON THE MANAGER'S POSITION

A few years ago, before computer technology was used by so many areas in a firm, the manager of information systems could hide behind a veil of technical jargon and stay insulated from the rest of the firm. Seldom did upper management know or even care what was happening within the computer center. As long as the processing was "reasonable" and there were no major disasters, the computer center was allowed to seek its own course, virtually independent of the rest of the firm. Upper management had little comprehension of the intricacies of digital computers, hence the information systems area had very little accountability. Few, if any, acquisitions of hardware or software had to undergo cost/benefit analysis, and the total system's performance was an internal concern.

This situation has changed considerably. Now the manager of information systems has one of the most exposed positions in the firm. With such extensive use of computers, almost every department is affected by the information system. Previously, users submitted jobs in a batch mode and received output hours or days later. Most hardware or software failures were effectively masked from the user since only an extremely long delay could be detected.

Now many users process in an interactive mode and expect, or in many cases, demand, almost instantaneous turnaround time. Under these conditions, most system problems become immediately apparent to the users. The user expectations are for the system to be "up" at all desired times and also provide the user with acceptable system response time. These expectations result from both the common notion that a computer in some way represents perfection and the users' lack of understanding of the tremendous complexity of a modern information system.

These factors lead upper management to be sensitive to the smooth operation of the information system. They now realize that decisions within the information system may have significant effects on all other areas of the firm. Also, the computer system requires a significant portion of the firm's resources and now involves all areas, not just the central information systems area. This gives the manager of information systems substantial responsibility, and exposes the manager to a broad spectrum of activity of the business.

SCOPE OF THE TEXT

This text is designed to assist the reader in developing the skills necessary to manage system resources. While we will discuss all aspects of information system management, we will concentrate on the administration of large data centers using mainframe processors. Hence, we will spend a substantial amount of time discussing the functions of the manager of information systems. However, most topics discussed will apply to both large and small systems.

We will examine the role that the manager of the information system plays in the organization and help the reader develop some of the skills necessary to understand the complex operations of a modern information system. The text will emphasize a general understanding of the operation of an information system from a student perspective. We will not be presenting operational checklists and other procedures to run a data center. Instead of being a cookbook, the text will discuss the various functional areas within the information system and the responsibilities of the individuals in these areas. Since the text is designed for a student entering the information systems profession, we will also attempt to orient the student toward the responsibilities and opportunities available. Where appropriate, we will describe a hypothetical employee, the tasks this person performs, and the background this type of person may have. To facilitate this, a hypothetical company, the Major Company, will be used to illustrate specific points.

To develop fully an understanding of the operations of a modern information system, it is necessary to delve into some of the more technical issues. This text will also help students solidify their knowledge of the integrated information system.

The remainder of this chapter will briefly discuss the duties of the manager of information systems and the skills a good manager must possess. The chapter will conclude with a brief description of the rest of the text.

RESPONSIBILITIES OF THE MANAGER

The manager must be able to control both the day-to-day operations of the system and the long-term goals and objectives of the information systems function. The balancing of these two concerns is critical to the continued successful operation of the system. While managers may not be directly involved in all the decisions in these areas, they are ultimately responsible for their successful execution. Hence, the manager must have at least a basic knowledge and understanding of each of the following functional areas:

> *Operations:* This includes scheduling of jobs, allocation of resources to specific jobs, and supervision of the operations staff. Additionally, it is necessary to monitor the performance of the system to determine if service levels are adequate.

Maintenance: The proper maintenance of both the hardware and software is important to assure smooth operations. This would include the negotiation and execution of maintenance agreements, an understanding of systems programming, and the development of a maintenance schedule.

Data Management: For business systems this can be a critical area because of the volume of data and the variety of access needs of the users. Coordination of the database management system and resolution of users' data access and data security problems are necessary in this area.

System Security and Integrity: This is a difficult but important area because of the risk of substantial loss. This would involve data and program backup and recovery, creation of audit trails, and control of access to the machine, data, and programs.

Strategic Planning: Long- and short-term planning and budgeting are key ingredients in any operation. Unfortunately, due to the dynamic nature of computing, these can be difficult to develop and implement.

Acquisition of Computer Hardware and Software: This is a very time consuming but interesting area that demands that the manager and staff remain current as to existing and emerging technologies. Since application software can also be designed in-house, this will include the supervision of the applications programming staff.

It is important that the manager maintains a businessperson's perspective when making decisions. The costs and benefits of any decision must be fully considered. Upper management is primarily concerned with profitability, and the best way to sell ideas is with well-developed and accurate estimates of the impact of a proposed project. A presentation that is too technical will tend to draw opposition from those that do not understand. If this occurs in the upper echelons, it could have devastating results for the information systems area.

SPECIFIC SKILLS THAT MANAGERS NEED

To a certain extent the manager of information systems has to be a Renaissance man (or woman), having knowledge of science to understand the functioning of the computer, knowledge of the business world, and also having mastered the art of managing and dealing with people. The selection of an information system manager can be difficult. A pure technician is not desirable because of the lack of managerial and business skills. Managers with little knowledge of computer technology are usually not successful since they do not have sufficient knowledge to assist and direct the technical staff. Of course, there have been successful managers weak in some of these areas; however, a well-rounded background is becoming more and more a necessity.

Some of these specific skills include the following:

Technical Computer Background: This would include exposure to both application and systems programming with knowledge of hardware and software fundamentals.

Business Background: Experience with accounting, budgeting, finance, economics, operations management, marketing, and other areas of business is essential. The manager should at least be familiar with each of these areas.

Communication Skills: A majority of any manager's time is spent in communication with supervisors and subordinates. Ability to express one's ideas both in writing and orally is critical. This includes the ability to explain technical concepts to noncomputer types without the use of incomprehensible jargon. At the same time, communication with the staff must be at the appropriate technical level.

Managerial Skills: Many think that these skills are acquired only through actual experience. Some of the tasks performed include selection of personnel, delegation of authority, assignment of responsibility, and deciding employee compensation.

The manager of information systems can obtain the preceding skills through a variety of means. The more technical skills are best obtained through formal education (college, university, or professional education seminars), while other skills can only be obtained through job experience. There is no single "best" path to reaching the managerial position. Successful information system managers have come from applications programming, systems programming, operations, and even from the user community. However, they all have acquired the previously mentioned skills through various means.

MAJOR COMPANY

Throughout this text we will use the hypothetical Major Company to illustrate some of the points made in each chapter. To give a little more insight into Major Company, we will briefly give some background on the company.

Major Company is a large, national conglomerate that deals mainly with high-technology products. The corporate headquarters are located in Chicago, Illinois, and there are plants, warehouses, and distributorships throughout the United States (see Figure 1.4).

The computing environment involves a large centralized site near the corporate headquarters and many local computing facilities. While the central site is under the direct control of the corporate vice-president of information systems, most of the decentralized computer operations are managed by the local plant, warehouse, or distribution facility. However, the central information systems area develops and enforces data processing standards that the remote sites must follow. These standards encompass the selection of hardware and software, design of new systems, data custody and integrity, and other issues that have an impact throughout the company. However, many of the local computing decisions are made independently of these centralized standards.

Computing has been growing at Major Company at a steady rate. Because of the high-tech products produced by Major Company, almost every area

Figure 1.4 *Map of Major Company's Operations*

◆ = Corporate Headquarters
▲ = Plant Site
■ = Warehouse

of the firm employs computer technology. All forms of computing, including micros, minis, and very large mainframes, are being used. Higher management believes that the thoughtful application of computers will help to give Major Company an edge over its competitors.

MEET THE BOSS

Vince is the vice-president of information systems for Major Company. He has been with the firm for 10 years and has been in his present position for the last three years.

Like most computer professionals who have been in data processing for more than 20 years, Vince's professional experience and formal education are quite varied. His undergraduate degree is in mathematics with a minor in history. However, during his senior year at college he took a FORTRAN programming course and has been hooked on computers ever since.

Vince's first job was with a large computer manufacturer, where he spent a majority of his first year attending classes and reading educational material dealing with this vendor's hardware and software. His first assignment was as a systems programmer. After three years he decided to go into application programming so that he could deal more directly with people. This involved additional learning, and there were some reasonably frustrating times.

After changing jobs a couple of times, with a substantial increase in pay each time, Vince realized that his lack of understanding of the business world was holding him back. He attended night school and received a Masters of Business Administration after four years.

Armed with a better knowledge of the business environment and having acquired good managerial skills by supervising his subordinates, Vince quickly moved up the management ladder to his present position.

Vince's responsibilities at Major Company are probably more like those of the other executives on the same level as he (such as vice-president of production, vice-president of marketing, etc.) than those of a computer professional. Much of his time is spent in meetings discussing various solutions to problems and setting policy for his area and the company as a whole. The specific work on most projects is done by people reporting to Vince. He will usually make the decision or recommend a solution to the president or board of directors based on a series of options developed by the people working for him.

For example, today Mary, the manager of new systems development, presented a proposal on staffing and scheduling of the major systems to be developed over the next two years. The presentation was made to Vince and the computer steering committee, which has representatives from all the major user areas. With considerable input from committee members, Vince asked Mary to revise the schedule to meet some of the objections raised by certain committee members. On a decision of this magnitude, the process may take many meetings before Vince decides that he has the best schedule. On most matters of this sort, the committee has only an advisory role and the final decision lies with Vince.

Other activities in a typical day for Vince might include a meeting with the managers directly under him. This would involve a report on the status of each department, any impending problems, and a general discussion of the upcoming events and their impact on the information system area. Of course, there are always problems which develop rapidly and need immediate attention. For example, last week Major Company's legal staff made an emergency request to obtain detailed information on Workmen's Compensation claims, employee injuries, and sick leave, in detail, by department, work shift, and type of employee for the last three years. Since this information was to be used as evidence in litigation against Major Company, it became an extremely high-priority problem. After substantial deliberation, certain current lower-priority projects were delayed and two staff members were temporarily reassigned to work with the legal staff.

Last week a violent electrical storm damaged some of Major's dedicated communication equipment. In the early hours of the morning, Vince's staff reconfigured the system so that some users were given reduced service. Because of the possible widespread impact of this type of problem, Vince became directly involved in the decision making. Until the equipment could be repaired or replaced, he decided to purchase temporary services from a common carrier, to maintain the previous service levels. He saw this as an expensive but necessary action to maintain minimum service levels. While a vice-president of information systems will not be immediately involved in all problems of this nature, he or she will usually want to have ultimate decision-making capacity on problems involving major changes in user service and large expenditures.

As you can see, Vince has a lot of responsibility; however, his job is made bearable by the extremely competent people under him. At times Vince regrets that he accepted the position of vice-president because of the responsibility of the position and the large time commitment he must make. He feels that his managerial position does not allow him time to stay abreast of the rapid technological developments in the computer field. However, he feels that if he had it to do over again he would make the same decisions and be in the same position. His job is exciting, challenging, and rewarding. He has been quoted as saying, "I may die of exhaustion but will never die of boredom."

ORGANIZATION OF THE TEXT

This text will examine each of the aspects of managing an information system. The emphasis will be technical in nature. It is assumed that the reader has a general knowledge of business operations. This includes a background (i.e., either practical or classroom exposure) to the areas of accounting, finance, economics, business law, and management. Additionally, the reader should have a basic knowledge of the operation of a typical medium-to-large computer system, including some knowledge (not necessarily extensive knowledge) of applications software design and system software and hardware.

For those readers having deficiencies in the business areas or those wishing to review this material, each chapter will list sources to be read prior to tackling the material in the next chapter and will also list sources for expanding the material covered in that chapter. To assure a minimal background in the basic operation of a complex computer system, Appendix A and Appendix B review basic machine operations. These two appendices present a review of the operations of a typical mainframe system from both the system view (bird's-eye view) and the individual job view (worm's-eye view). Even if the reader has extensive knowledge in the area, this should prove to be a comprehensive review. This knowledge is essential to the understanding of the subsequent chapters that deal with performance evaluation, job accounting, billing, hardware and software acquisition, legal contracts, and other topics.

Chapter 1 has given the reader some idea of the responsibilities of the manager of an information system. Chapter 2 will give the reader an idea of how the information system relates to the other functional areas within a firm. Chapter 3 will continue this discussion by looking at the ways to do strategic planning. The text will then proceed toward the more specific tactical issues. These tactical issues should give the manager the tools necessary to solve problems in all areas of information systems. The issues involved in specialized functional areas will conclude the text.

Most successful organizations develop a strategic plan which outlines the long-range objectives of the organization. The long-range goals and strategic implementation of these goals for the information system are discussed in Chapter 3. This includes the methods involved in developing long-range plans, the structure of the information system within the firm, and the internal structure of the data processing function.

A long-range plan is of little value if it is not properly implemented. Developing standards and procedures for the various areas in the information system is the subject of Chapter 4. This includes developing programming, data access and security standards, and policies regarding employment, retention, and professional education.

Selecting the proper site and the physical environment in which the computer equipment is to operate is discussed in Chapter 5. The proper physical environment is necessary for the continued efficient operation of the information system. This includes the selection of the site, factors involved in the construction of the building, physical security, cooling, electricity, fire protection, and disaster recovery.

The next few chapters discuss the steps that are taken when acquiring additional resources for the information system. As in any problem-solving situation, before you can find a solution, you must define the problem. In computing this involves measuring the performance of the system. This is called performance evaluation and involves measuring, evaluating, and tuning a computerized system. These issues are discussed in Chapter 6.

After measuring the system and determining the desired configuration, it may be necessary to acquire additional hardware. The methods of acquiring this hardware will be discussed in Chapter 7. This includes the determination of the characteristics of the equipment, the solicitation of vendor bids, and the evaluation of the bids made by each vendor. The formal negotiation of the legal contract to acquire this hardware is discussed in Chapter 8. The legal contract is of such importance that we devote an entire chapter to it and other legal issues.

Various financial alternatives in an acquisition must also be considered. These alternatives are discussed in Chapter 9. This includes the various methods of financing (buy, lease, or rent) and the ways of charging internal users of the services.

Acquiring additional computer resources almost always involves acquiring additional software. The acquisition of software is a complex and in many ways a riskier decision than hardware acquisition. Software acquisition is considered separately in Chapter 10.

The important area of computer security is addressed in the appropriate places in Chapters 1 through 10. However, this topic is so important that Chapter 11 ties together the issues covered in the previous chapters and presents additional issues concerning this subject.

The last five chapters (12 through 16) discuss special functional areas in the information system. The areas of end-user computing, application programming, systems programming, database management, and data communications are rapidly growing and have unique characteristics which must be considered. Because of the integration of the various types of computer technology, the

Figure 1.5   *Summary of Text Material*

CONCEPTUAL LEVEL	CHAPTER #	SUBJECT
Introductory	1	Introduction
	2	The Role of the Information System
High-level	3	Strategic Issues
	4	Establishing Standards and Procedures
	5	Physical Environment
	6	Performance Evaluation
	7	Hardware Acquisition
Operating Issues	8	Legal Issues
	9	Financial Issues
	10	Software Acquisition
	11	Security Issues
	12	End-User Computing
	13	Applications Programming
Specialized Areas	14	Systems Programming
	15	Database Management
	16	Communications Management
Review	Appendix A	Bird's-Eye View of a Computer System
	Appendix B	Worm's-Eye View of a Computer System

proper management and coordination of these areas is becoming a necessity for any information system that wants to offer its users quality service.

The contents of the text are summarized in Figure 1.5.

SUMMARY

Computerized information systems are an integral part of most business organizations. This puts the manager of information systems in a position with many responsibilities and high corporate exposure. The manager must have skills in a variety of areas including a technical computer background, good management and communication skills, and a solid business background.

The responsibilities of the manager include the management of machine operations, system maintenance, data management, system security and integrity, strategic planning, and the acquisition of system resources including hardware and software. While the manager is not directly responsible for all of these areas, he or she is ultimately responsible for their proper management.

QUESTIONS

1. Briefly explain why businesses are becoming so dependent on computer technology.

2. In the beginning of the chapter, we stated that office automation is becom-

ing an important computerized function; explain what office automation involves.

3. Explain what communication skills the systems manager must have and why these skills are important.

4. Many people claim that in a typical business computer environment, the two most valuable components of a system are the people and the data—however, the hardware and software may be carried on the books at millions of dollars, whereas the people and data are not given any accounting value. Explain.

5. Some people claim that there is no need to have any technical computer knowledge to be an information systems manager. They claim that managerial skills are the only skills necessary. Defend or attack this position.

6. Give examples of how decisions made in the information systems area greatly affect other areas in the firm.

7. Before companies used computers so heavily, the accounting department was viewed by many as the heart of the organization, and a majority of firms had accountants as their chief executive officer. Why? Do you think this still holds true?

8. For each of the functional responsibilities of the manager (see pp. 7–8) discuss what business skills are most important to carry out each of these responsibilities.

CASE ANALYSIS

Case 1

Describe all of the computer facilities in your school and briefly explain how each is used. Be sure that you include the facilities available to the students, to the faculty, and to the school's administration. How is each of these different systems managed?

Case 2

Observe your local computer center. Watch the activities of the personnel involved. Identify and list at least two situations for each of the four skills needed by a manager of an information system. For each situation, explain which skill would be needed to handle it and why. (This may require checking areas that are outside the computer center but interact with it.)

Case 3

Describe the career path you envision yourself pursuing over the 10 years following your graduation. Be as specific as you can about the job titles, the salary levels, the industry or company with which you wish to affiliate, additional education, any specializations, and other details.

Describe *each* of the 10 years. The best way to do this is in a narrative format with a summary of your position, pay, etc. in each year.

ADDITIONAL READINGS

"Artificial Intelligence, The Second Computer Age Begins," *Business Week*, March 8, 1982, pp. 2–7.

BALZER, ROBERT, THOMAS E. CHEATHAM, JR., AND CORDELL GREEN. "Software Technology in the 1990's: Using a New Paradigm," *IEEE Computer*, November 1983, pp. 39–45.

CRANE, JANET. "The Changing Role of the DP Manager," *Datamation*, January 1982, pp. 96–108.

"Getting Smarter, Spending Strategically," *Datamation*, April 1, 1987, pp. 76–80.

GILLENSON, MARK L. "Trends in Data Administration: 1981–1985," *MIS Quarterly*, Vol. 9, No. 4, December 1985, pp. 317–325.

KANTER, JEROME. "Ten Information Systems Megatrends," *Information Strategy: The Executive's Journal*, Fall 1985, pp. 13–17.

READINGS BEFORE NEXT CHAPTER

None since the next chapter is also introductory in nature.

2

THE ROLE
OF
THE INFORMATION SYSTEM

In the previous chapter we gave you a brief look at some of the responsibilities of a manager of an information system. In this chapter we will look at the ways in which the information system itself can help contribute to the success of a firm. In part, this will be done by giving examples of different ways an information system can be used within a firm.

For an organization to operate at its maximum effectiveness, each of its various functions must be coordinated. This applies to any type of organization—a business, a government institution, a symphony orchestra, an athletic team, etc. The separate components must operate toward a common goal, otherwise they will be working in opposition to each other. For example, an orchestra can be made up of the very best solo players of each instrument, but if these players do not play as a cohesive unit, the quality of the performance will be only mediocre at best.

The same applies to business. If the operations of the individual areas are in harmony, then the firm will benefit. If they work in opposition, ultimately the productivity of the firm will suffer. For example, if the marketing department notifies production and inventory control of its projected sales forecast for the coming quarter, the proper levels of inventory can be stockpiled to satisfy the anticipated demand. This type of communication is particularly important when special sales promotions are planned. Without this communication, the sales items may be quickly sold out. The end result may be directly opposite of what was intended. Instead of producing new, satisfied customers, the sales promotion may result in disgruntled customers.

The information system is one of many functional areas within an organization. However, its position is rapidly becoming a pivotal one. Many times the information system provides the means to coordinate the various organizational units. Most of us have heard the overused phrase that we are living in an "information age." This means that the way in which information is distributed and analyzed within a firm can be an important factor in the success of that firm, and it implies that the information system area plays a vital role in this process.

GOAL SETTING

Any organization must have a series of goals. Sometimes these goals are very formal and written. Other times the goals may be vague and informal. For example, some companies have a statement of goals and code of ethics that employees must ascribe to and sign on a yearly basis. Some of these goals may include having a high level of customer satisfaction, selling a quality product, and adhering to high moral standards. Usually the board of directors or chief executive officer will establish firm-wide goals for a given period of time. These types of stated goals are usually made in a more substantive manner. An example may be to increase the company's share of the market from 12% to 14% or to produce and market a new line of products.

Informal goals can be implied by the type of organization or the working environment. For example, in a government agency one of the goals must be that no agency spends beyond its budget. For a company an unstated goal will be to make a profit. Informal goals, however, may be so vague as to cause confusion. Obviously, this is not a desirable situation. If possible, it is better to establish formal goals.

No matter how the goals are derived or whether they are formal or informal, they help provide guidance by which each department within the organization operates. Well-formed goals will give a manager a stronger basis by which to make decisions and set the direction of a department. The organization-wide goals should be used in deriving subsidiary goals for each unit within the firm. Care must be taken to assure that the goals are communicated throughout the firm and that the subsidiary goals of various areas are not in conflict. This will help to reduce future problems and serve to inform others as to the role each department has within the organization. This process is summarized in Figure 2.1.

As an example, let's assume that corporate management wishes to increase its share of a specific market from 12% to 14% in a given year. The marketing department would have to analyze the present market conditions and predict how best to increase market share. This could entail the development of new products, opening new avenues of distribution, increasing advertising expenditures, etc. The impact of these anticipated changes would then be communicated to the production and inventory control area. Production would have to calculate optimal inventory levels, new production schedules, changes in work

Figure 2.1 *The Goal-setting Process*

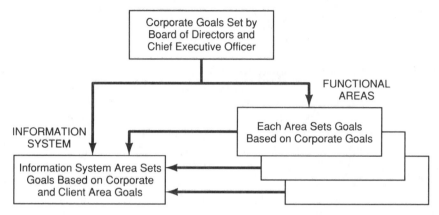

force, changes in plant and equipment, and changes in raw materials to be ordered.

Notice how the broad corporate goal of an increase in market share must become more specific and focused as the plan of implementation is developed. Hidden in this process is the fact that the specifics of the plan will be based on projections primarily derived from historical data. Of course, the information system must provide this data and will also provide the means by which to analyze the data.

THE INFORMATION SYSTEM

The information system is an internal service function. Its primary function is to assist other units of the organization to function in a more effective and efficient manner. Unless the information systems area also sells computing services to external users, it will not produce an end product or generate external revenue. Hence, it is of utmost importance that the managers within the information systems area understand the operations of their client departments and the company as a whole. Without this knowledge of the operations of the client areas, it is difficult for the information system to deliver services that are consistent with the goals of that area.

For example, when dealing with the marketing area, the information system specialist must first understand how marketing functions. Sales could be done by direct mail or by phone or by a salesperson's visit. Each different method of marketing may dictate differences in the necessary information and the way this information is stored, processed, and presented. Information requirements will also vary for different types of goods and services. For example, an automotive manufacturer will have different information needs than a hamburger franchise outlet. It is the job of the information system specialist to identify these information needs and help the users fulfill their information processing needs.

While the preceding may seem obvious, one of the more difficult tasks of the information systems area is in gaining an understanding of the information needs of a client department. Too often, the information system specialist is anxious to implement a highly technical solution to a client's problem without having a thorough understanding of the problem. Usually this results in a dissatisfied customer. The information system specialist will usually have extensive knowledge concerning the technical aspects of data storage and retrieval. However, the employees within a given functional unit are usually intimately acquainted with the operation of that area and the information needs of the area. Only with cooperation between these two groups will it be possible to design an information system that best meets the needs. Of course, the information system needs of an area are directly related to the goals of that area. Let's give some concrete examples.

A bank wishes to install a new system to handle various types of customer accounts, including checking and savings accounts and certificates of deposit. The board of directors of the bank has stated that protection of the bank's assets is of paramount importance. The bank prides itself on the fact that it has never lost one cent of a customer's money through fraud or theft. The bank's advertising campaign is based on the rock solid security of the institution.

How will this reputation for security affect the decisions made by information systems concerning the new deposit system? First, there should be a tendency for the information systems area to advocate the selection of well-proven products. This is especially true for the selection of any product having security implications. In this situation, new technology or more innovative approaches to banking may not appear attractive. The information systems area may see that it is technologically feasible to hook up many local businesses to allow automatic debiting of an account when a customer buys goods. However, if no other banks have done this, then it may be deemed too risky for this bank's stated goals of security.

On the other hand, a bank that is primarily marketing oriented may see the opportunity to allow instant debiting of accounts as an excellent means of increasing market share. In this case the information systems area would be encouraged to pursue this new technology.

Note that in both situations security and marketing are important issues. However, the relative degree of importance for each firm may be quite different. In this case the goals of the one firm dictate that the decisions be more risk adverse than the other firm.

Let's now use the example discussed earlier. Corporate management wishes to increase market share. The information system may not just provide the data to analyze the situation, but may also be employed directly to effect the change. For example, it may be determined that a new computerized customer tracking system will allow the company to identify customers that will generate new or increased sales. As an example, a customer that buys electronic test equipment should be a candidate for purchasing the corresponding repair and replacement parts.

In this situation the information system must deal with all of the departments involved in the process. This would not only include providing marketing with the necessary sales data, but making data available to production, inventory control, purchasing, and the other departments involved in the decision making. Unfortunately, life for the information system personnel is not as easy as it may sound. These and other data requirements must be predicted by the users and the information systems people when the system is designed. Many times unanticipated requests for data cannot be satisfied simply because the system has not been designed to deal with that type of request. So for the information system, meeting the goals of the organization must be a long-term proposition. This involves determining future needs when new systems are designed and installed.

It can be seen that decisions involving the information system are dependent on the goals of the organization and the goals of the various departments affected by those decisions. In fact, the information system should act as a technical consultant in these decisions. The staff should investigate alternative options and evaluate their appropriateness. Except for technical decisions which concern only the information systems area, the final decisions would be made by the client departments and high corporate management.

USING THE INFORMATION SYSTEM AS A COMPETITIVE WEAPON

If used in the correct way, the information system of a firm may be used to differentiate the firm from its competition. Progressive firms have exploited new computer technology to enhance their competitive position. In this situation some of the goals of the information system may become the goals of the company as a whole.

An excellent example of this is the case of American Airlines. Many years ago the company saw that an interactive reservation system was technologically feasible and decided that developing an interactive system would give them a competitive edge. Their flight reservation system made it possible for a prospective customer to determine quickly what flights were available. The other airlines could not provide the same quality of information as rapidly. Not only did this directly increase the number of customers, but it also created a new source of business. Terminals could be installed in travel agents' offices and a usage fee could be charged for this service.

The other airlines were forced to provide the same service to be competitive. They either developed their own systems or were forced to pay American to use its service. Developing a system of this magnitude is a time-consuming operation. Hence, the other airlines were at a competitive disadvantage for a significant length of time.

Using computer technology as a competitive weapon can take many forms. It can be used to increase revenues, open new markets, provide better customer service, or reduce expenses. In all cases the top management of the firm must be enlightened to the possible opportunities for applying new technology. Unfortunately, many top executives only view the information system as an expenditure that is necessary for the company to operate smoothly. This attitude is not conducive to innovative, strategic use of computing.

The perception of the information system is often in the hands of the information system's management. They must be able to promote and market the services offered by the system. It is their responsibility to convince top management that the goals of the organization are tied very closely to the information system. In the same way it is necessary to convince client departments that the information system can be employed to help reach their goals. Too often the information system management assumes that everyone realizes the benefits derived from the information systems function. An internal low-key marketing campaign can help focus attention on the services provided by the information systems area.

One method of enlightening users is to involve them directly in the computing process. The introduction of a user friendly computing environment can be very helpful. This is termed end-user computing and will be discussed at length later in the text.

REALIZING STATED GOALS

It is necessary to align the information system goals with those of the client departments and the firm as a whole. However, accomplishing these goals within the stated resource constraints is the measure of the effectiveness of the information system. Not being able to fulfill promised goals is the single most pressing problem in most information systems. The most frequent failures occur in developing new systems. The failure occurs because the system was not delivered within the cost constraint or within the scheduled period of time or because the system did not perform as promised.

An information system's failure to meet specific goals is usually caused by a variety of factors. Unfortunately, the most convenient explanation is that the staff did a poor job. This problem is then corrected by punishing the individual staff members or reorganizing work teams. This will usually result in only a temporary improvement or no improvement at all or possibly even a complete loss of employee morale. The problem is frequently much deeper. Many times the goals are unrealistic from the start. Or, it may be that the project has not been thoroughly analyzed before cost and time estimates were established.

The resources needed to implement a system properly are difficult to estimate accurately. In most cases the specifications of the system may be difficult to ascertain until the project is partially completed. Some of the problems are caused by poor communication between the future users of the system and the designers. It is critical that these two groups understand each other's responsibilities and be able to communicate their ideas. When the two groups are able to work as a team, realistic goals can be set and hopefully attained.

Let's give an example based on the goal of increasing market share. The information systems area decides that it can redesign the existing marketing information system so that it will provide more current and accurate customer information than is presently possible. Armed with this new information, the sales staff should be able to increase their sales on each sales call. It is estimated that the changes will take a total of six months before the new system is operating in a production mode.

After nine months have passed, the new system is not as yet fully operational. The project manager claims that the vice-president of marketing and his immediate staff have not been available enough to specify what information was needed by the system. Hence, the design proceeded based on certain assumptions about the necessary information and the format of the output. After the system was close to completion, the vice-president reviewed the system and found that it did not entirely meet the marketing area's needs. Reluctantly, changes were made to the system and resubmitted to the vice-president. At this point he decided that certain other changes were absolutely necessary. Presently these changes are being incorporated into the system. It is estimated that it will take at least one more month before the system will be completed.

The various sales managers are not happy because their staffs have not been able to meet the increased sales quotas budgeted for this quarter. They have been grumbling that the new quotas were based on the increased sales potential anticipated by the new information system. Since the new system has been delayed, the sales managers feel bitter about their performance being adversely affected by the failure of the information systems area to meet its schedule. Of course, the systems people feel the entire blame lies with the marketing area. All in all, no matter who is at fault, the situation is not good for the company as a whole.

Again it must be emphasized that the information systems area must be able to deliver on its promises. The friction caused by broken promises can make the relationship between the user and the information system strained to the point of collapse.

ORGANIZATIONAL ISSUES

The goals of an organization may not only dictate the way in which decisions are made in the information systems area, but may also determine the way in which the information system is organized. In fact, it may be more accurate to say that the organizational structure may actually determine the way in which decisions are made concerning information processing.

In the previous chapter we tried to give an impression of how the director of an information system would conduct business. From this explanation it may have appeared that an organization will have but one unified information system that operates as an independent entity under the direction of a single head. Even in highly centralized organizations, there will be many disparate components to the information system. In a decentralized environment, the information system components are even more numerous. Let's look into this a little more deeply.

There are two extremes in organizing any type of entity: totally centralized and totally decentralized. In a centralized organization, decisions are made at the top and are handed down to subordinate units. This does not imply that all decisions are made only by high-level management, but that policy and guidelines are determined by high-level management. Subordinate managers are then responsible for making decisions based on these guidelines.

A totally decentralized organization allows for complete autonomy by the various divisions of the firm. In this case managers of divisions are independent of centralized control and are free to determine the policy of their division.

Very few, if any, businesses are organized as either totally centralized or totally decentralized. Instead they will employ some combination of these two philosophies. Figure 2.2 illustrates some of the possibilities.

The structure an organization chooses is determined by many factors. Primarily centralized organizations function best when there is not rapid change in the industry and when the activities of the various units of the firm are rather homogeneous. Decentralization flourishes when the industry demands rapid responses to changes, when many types of dissimilar activities are ongoing, and when the input and ingenuity of the lower-level managers is valued. Figure 2.3 shows some of the advantages of different organizational structures.

As stated before, the organization of the information system is dependent on the structure of the firm and the individual departments. However, the information system has its own organizational requirements based on its activities. Since the information system deals with all parts of the company, a

Figure 2.2   *Types of Organizational Structures*

STRUCTURE	CHARACTERISTICS	DISCUSSION
Totally Centralized	All policy determined by higher management	Best in static environment with homogeneous products
Centralized with Independent Units	Most policy set by higher management but independent units set own policy	Allows for innovative development in a centralized environment
Decentralized with Broad Central Policy Making	Autonomous operation under high-level guidelines	Allows independent units with high-level coordination
Totally Decentralized	All decisions made by independent business units	Faster response to problems and more innovation possible

Figure 2.3 *Advantages of Centralization and Decentralization*

CENTRALIZATION	DECENTRALIZATION
Higher degree of standardization	Quicker response to unique problems
Less pressure on subordinates	Ideas can come from many sources
Most jobs are well defined	Employees have more control over environment
Well-defined line of command	More conducive to a heterogeneous product line

certain amount of information must be shared between various departments. In fact, the coordination of data sharing is an important function of the information system. The more integrated the information system (i.e. the more data sharing), the stronger the possible lines of communication and the more accessible data will be to other departments in the firm. Remember, data is a resource and its proper management is very important.

The ability to integrate the corporate database is partially gained by having the information system establish certain standards. Standards must also be established in other areas such as system design, program development, and system documentation. Establishing standards means having a certain amount of centralized authority. Thus the information system will have certain functions which will be centralized. However, in a decentralized environment it is important that a manager have control over the information in that area, for this information is used to make decisions.

So the information system has two forces pulling at it. The goal of data integration and standardization cries out for centralization. The goal of servicing a specific department in the way deemed best by that department's management means treating each department independently; that is decentralization. So the process is one of compromise, in which the two forces are kept in balance.

Again an example may help. Assume a company produces high-technology goods which are sold to different types of markets. Top management wants the separate product divisions to be able to react to technological change quickly. Hence, the firm has adopted a rather decentralized organization. High-level management determines the amount of investment capital to be allocated to each division, but the setting of product prices and the controlling of costs is entirely the responsibility of each division manager.

For the information system to service this type of organization, it must be able to deliver current budgeting and performance information to corporate management. For most reports, only summary data will be needed. At the same time, it is necessary to deliver detailed information on the day-to-day operations to each of the individual divisions.

One way to handle this type of situation is to determine which information must be handled in an integrated manner. These systems would then be common to all divisions. The other systems could then be individualized to meet the needs of each division. For example, the financial information such as general ledger, accounts payable, and accounts receivable would probably be common to all divisions. In this way corporate reports could be easily compiled by aggregating the information from each division. Other systems such as the production and inventory control systems may be designed to meet the needs of an individual division.

The organization of the information system in this case could be totally centralized or quite decentralized. It would be possible for each division to have its own information system staff. A small, centralized information system organization could then establish standards and guidelines that would have to be followed for all integrated systems.

THE CHANGING ROLE OF INFORMATION SYSTEMS

The introduction of cheap and powerful microcomputers and distributed minicomputers into businesses has caused a dramatic change in the way in which the corporate information system functions. Previous to the advent of micros and distributed minis, the information system was primarily centralized and was the sole source for implementing computerized systems. If a department needed a system to be designed, the centralized information system would analyze the problem, design and test the system, and install it.

Microcomputers allowed users to develop their own systems. Instead of going to the centralized information system and waiting for a system to be developed, the user could quickly implement a solution on a personal computer. The user friendly tools available on these micros made the solution of certain types of problems very easy for even a novice user.

The perceived convenience of microcomputers caused a revolution within the organization. Control of the computerized information was no longer in the hands of only the information system managers but dispersed throughout the organization. In addition, the funding of acquisitions of computer hardware and software came from many sources within the organization. In fact, a majority of expenditures for hardware and software shifted to the end-user departments.

Some information system managers saw this shift to more end-user responsibility as a loss of their political power base. They feared that a centralized information system would become less important. The more progressive managers saw that in the long run having the end-users more deeply involved was an excellent opportunity for computer technology to be widely employed to help the firm. However, they also saw very serious short-run problems. The microcomputer revolution in many firms was more of an uncontrolled explosion. Departments were purchasing hardware and software with little or no regard for what other departments were doing, with decisions based more on rumor than fact. Since there were no standards for hardware or software acquisition, system development, data storage and exchange, or system maintenance, there were many incompatible systems with a tremendous duplication of effort. An equally serious problem was that the systems were either physically incapable of sharing data between diverse users or the lack of data standards made data sharing impossible.

Many firms had invested heavily in acquiring computer resources. Again, a majority of the funding came from departments not under the control of the information systems area. These funds were spent with expectations of large returns in productivity. Unfortunately, for most firms these returns have not materialized. The problem lies primarily in the lack of established standards and procedures dealing with these diverse information system resources and not in the technological capabilities of the systems.

Let's look at an example. The manager of receiving is responsible for examining all goods that are received to see if they are damaged. To examine thoroughly all goods received has required a large staff. To cut back on this staff, the manager decides to use statistical sampling to check on deliveries. To do this, the manager has a staff member set up a microcomputer system to track the number of defective units in all shipments received. With this information the manager can see what modes of transport and the types of goods which are most likely to be damaged. This system allows the manager of receiving to track more closely the damaged goods and to reduce manpower.

In the same firm the purchasing agent has developed a small computer system to track the various vendors. Information is stored on the goods each vendor sells, prices, quantity discounts, lead time for delivery, shipping costs, and various other information about the vendor.

Upon learning about the system used in receiving to track defective goods, the purchasing agent would like data on the percentage of defectives delivered by the various vendors. The purchasing agent believes that this is important information in choosing vendors. Unfortunately, the receiving system does not store the data so that information about specific vendors can be easily retrieved. If this information is even available, it can only be derived by laborious manual operations. In fact the systems were developed using completely different tools and are not compatible.

One can see that if the two systems were integrated, then this type of data could be obtained easily. The question is, how can these two systems be integrated in this type of environment?

TOP MANAGEMENT SUPPORT

The answer to the integration problem and the incompatibility problems lies in establishing standards for information system activities. This means that a centralized authority, the information systems area, derives the standards which other departments must follow. This does not mean that the information systems area will control the funds or the development projects dealing with computers in other departments, but that a set of rules are derived by which these departments must purchase hardware and software and by which they develop systems.

The only way in which the information systems area will be able to establish and enforce standards is with the support of top management. This means that all the way up to the chief executive officer and the board of directors there must be a strong commitment to a highly integrated information system. Without top management support these standards become only "paper tigers."

This means that it is a fundamental necessity for the chief executives to understand the compatibility and data integration issues facing the firm. Without this understanding there will be no motivation to enforce standards. Without standards the information system will become a series of disjointed parts. As when we were discussing using computing as a competitive weapon, knowledgeable top management makes for a strong information system.

Using the previous example, at a minimum there could be standards involving the hardware and software that each department uses. There could be a company-wide standard for the brand of PC and even for the specific hardware configurations that are acceptable. The software tools used to develop different types of systems should also be standardized. In a strong standardized environment it would be mandatory that the development projects be coordinated to reduce data redundancy and to help eliminate duplication of effort.

This top-level support of the information system is not as straightforward as it may appear. The expenditures within the information systems area are usually classified as either committed fixed costs or discretionary fixed costs. The systems that are operational are classified as committed fixed costs, i.e., necessary for the operation of the business. The projects under development and expansion of existing resources are the types of costs that are perceived as being desirable but not absolutely necessary for the operation of the business. These are usually the first to be cut in hard times.

Because most computerized systems are very complex, they will span a period of years before they are completed. During the time the project is in development, there is a reasonably high probability that the business will experience at least a mild economic downturn. This, coupled with the discretionary nature of the cost, makes these expenditures prime candidates to be discontinued or postponed. This will in turn disrupt the development cycle and hence adversely affect the long-range information system goals. The information system in this type of situation will experience a series of feast or famine cycles. Under these circumstances, resources are wasted and long-range planning becomes impossible.

OTHER PRESSING ISSUES

The modern information system is very dynamic. Within a brief period of time, the problems faced by an information system can change dramatically. However, certain problems seem to be more or less universal. One of these is termed "the applications backlog." This refers to the number of development projects that are outstanding in the information systems area.

For most firms the applications backlog continues to grow at an alarming rate. As more users realize the advantages to using computer technology and as that technology becomes more sophisticated, the demand for more and better systems increases. Many of these proposed new systems are extremely complex. Also as more systems are designed and implemented, it is necessary to assign additional programming staff to maintain these systems.

This increased burden on the development staff forces long delays in implementing many of the proposed projects. Sometimes this delay is indefinite. The delays cause frustration for the users and increased pressure for the system development staff. Add to this pressure the rapid changes that are occurring in computer technology and in many cases the result is high employee turnover. The loss of experienced employees compounds the backlog problem.

Another problem is associated with the applications backlog. Users that are frustrated with the perceived lack of performance by the information system may decide to do their own work. This is now possible with the advances in microcomputers and the associated user friendly software. This is termed *end-user computing* and may appear to be an appropriate solution. In fact, in some situations end-user computing has been very successful. One obvious benefit is the reduction in the applications backlog. However, there is a down side to this type of activity. The end-users are usually not very technically sophisticated. This can lead to a misuse of computing resources and an increased load on the systems staff to train and support these end-users. Again it is a question of balance. Some problems are best solved by end-users; others are best solved by the information system professionals.

In the past, information system managers could decide to limit their company's hardware and software to only one vendor. While this was usually more expensive, it made the management of the information system quite a bit easier. If something went wrong, there was only one vendor to deal with. That era is now history.

Today companies will have hardware and software from many different vendors. As stated earlier, user departments will also be acquiring their own hardware and software. In many cases the various systems are incompatible. It has become a real challenge to the information systems area to allow users to interact with these systems in such a way that it is transparent to the user which technology is actually being employed. This is termed *making disparate systems seamless* and looms as the big challenge of the next decade.

The final problem we will discuss has plagued information system managers from the time computers were first used in business. In the extremely competitive world of computing, how do we attract and retain qualified staff? Computer technology is developing on two separate paths. On the one hand, there are more and better user friendly systems that allow an individual with little computer background to accomplish some rather sophisticated tasks. On the other hand, the large-scale application systems are becoming more and more

Figure 2.4   *Important Information System Issues*

ISSUE	PROBLEM
Organization	How to organize the information system to best serve the users
Goal Setting	Establishing information system goals that are congruent to the company and client department goals
Applications Backlog	How to reduce the applications backlog
End-User Computing	How to manage end-user computing so that both the end-users and the information system benefit
Data Integration	How to integrate data and still allow development of unique applications for different functional areas
Sharing of Resources	Making diverse technologies function in a seamless manner
Skilled Employees	How to attract and retain technically competent employees

complex. The information system expert must be able to access complex database management systems efficiently and interactively distribute this information over a complex network of systems. The complexity of system development is becoming mind boggling. Finding people who can handle these complex tasks and at the same time are able to communicate with unsophisticated users is another challenge.

The important information system issues are summarized in Figure 2.4.

MAJOR COMPANY

Major Company has experienced many of the problems discussed in this chapter. In the following chapters we will discuss these issues and propose ways in which some of these and other problems concerning the management of an information system can be handled. The Major Company will be used to illustrate how specific cases can be handled.

QUESTIONS

1. It is stated in this chapter that the information system is a service organization in which the other departments in the firm are its clients. Explain why this is the case. How will this affect the operation of the information system? Consider the impact on the way the information system may be

organized, the way in which its performance may be measured, and the way in which it is funded.

2. A corporation wishes to project an image of being a leading-edge high-technology firm. How may this goal affect the decisions concerning the information system? Explain and give some examples.

3. How may a university use computer technology as a competitive weapon? Give examples.

4. Why is it stated that the information system's goals must conform to those of the firm and other departments, instead of the inverse—that these other departments' goals must conform to the goals of the information system?

5. Explain why it is necessary for information system personnel to attempt to predict the needs of the user departments and not just meet the current needs when designing systems. Give some examples.

6. Why is it so difficult to estimate the amount of time and money it will take to design and install a new information system for a specific functional area?

7. It is stated that communication between the user and the information system specialist is important for the system to be successful. Describe why communication may be a problem. Describe ways in which some of the barriers to good communication may be overcome.

8. What is meant by the applications backlog? What impact does it have on the information system?

9. A centralized information system may have certain advantages over a decentralized system in certain organizations. However, in another organization these may actually be disadvantages. Explain why this is true by discussing examples.

10. This chapter states that systems are getting easier to use and at the same time much more complex. Explain what this means. Give examples.

11. Discuss how the information system can be used as a competitive weapon in each of the following industries:
    a. Banking
    b. Retailing
    c. Automotive manufacturing

CASE ANALYSIS

Case 1

Examine the computer center(s) that services student computing for your campus. List the important problems you perceive there are in this center(s). Discuss how these problems may be solved. Be sure to include in your discussion the costs involved and how the specific solution may affect other areas of service.

ADDITIONAL READINGS

BENJAMIN, ROBERT I., CHARLES DICKINSON, JR., JOHN F. ROCKART. "Changing Role of the Corporate Information Systems Officer," *MIS Quarterly,* Vol. 9, No. 3, September 1985, pp. 177–188.

BENJAMIN, ROBERT I., JOHN F. ROCKART, MICHAEL S. MORTON, AND JOHN WYMAN. "Information Technology: A Strategic Opportunity," *Sloan Management Review,* Vol. 25, No. 3, Spring 1984, pp. 3–10.

CARLYLE, RALPH. "The Selling of IS," *Datamation,* July 1, 1989, p. 22.

FOSTER, LAWRENCE W., AND DAVID M. FLYNN. "Management Information Technology: Its Effects on Organizational Form and Function," *MIS Quarterly,* Vol. 8, No. 4, December 1984, pp. 229–236.

IVES, BLAKE, AND GERARD P. LEARMONTH. "The Information System as a Competitive Weapon," *Communication of the ACM,* December 1984, Vol. 27, No. 12, pp. 1193–1201.

KERR, SUSAN. "The New IS Force," *Datamation,* August 1, 1989, p. 18.

McFARLAN, F. WARREN. "Information Technology Changes the Way You Compete," *Harvard Business Review,* May-June 1984, p. 98.

READINGS BEFORE NEXT CHAPTER

If you have not had an introductory management course or practical experience in strategic management, it would be helpful to read an introductory management text before reading the next chapter. The topics that should be most helpful are strategic planning and organizational structures. One popular text is *Management,* by Ricky Griffin, 2nd edition, Houghton Mifflin, 1987. At this point it would be best to read Chapters 4, 5, and 9 in that text.

3

STRATEGIC ISSUES

STRATEGIC MANAGEMENT

Strategic management is the process of determining the future direction of an organization and implementing policies that will move the firm in that direction. Without adequate strategic planning, everyday operational decisions will be made without reference to any general guidelines. In this situation, even decisions that appear sound in their specific context can conflict with decisions made in other areas. A strategic plan provides a predictable environment in which to make decisions.

For example, a production foreman decides to produce batches of goods of twice the normal quantity since there will be a substantial savings in fixed production costs. The result of this action is to increase dramatically the carrying cost of inventory. To reduce this inventory, the sales manager decides to decrease the selling price of the goods. While both of these decisions appear sound, they may ultimately reduce net income. If the strategic plan stated that optimal inventory levels be maintained, then these decisions would not have been made.

The process of strategic planning is similar to laying the foundation for a house. The better the foundation, the more solid the resulting structure will be. Strategic planning can occur at various levels of an organization. For convenience of categorizing these levels, we will term the highest l the *corporate level* of strategic planning. This level of planning will be the responsibility of the board of directors and the chief executive officer (CEO).

Goals and objectives at this level involve the direction of the entire corporation. These plans will involve major commitments of resources and will have a substantial effect on the organization.

The next level of strategic planning will be termed the *business level*, and the final level will be called the *functional level*. The business level involves the planning of specific lines of business. The plans at the business level must be congruent with the corporate plans and will be more detailed in nature.

The functional level of planning deals with the areas within a business unit. These would include production, marketing, distribution, etc. The plans at this level must be congruent with the corporate plans and the plans for their specific business unit. Figure 3.1 shows these three levels of planning.

The planning process will be interactive in as much as higher management will involve the lower-level management in the decision process. In this way innovative ideas can be solicited from more individuals. Also, there will be more acceptance of plans that have involved those directly affected by them. In addition, the planning process is an iterative process. Plans will be developed initially and then analyzed and revised as additional input is received. This may involve numerous iterations.

One can see that the planning process involves a series of plans. More restrictions are placed on this process as plans are developed at the lower organizational levels. Also, the amount of detail involved in planning will increase at the lower levels.

Let's give an example. The board of directors and CEO decide that a new product market should be entered. They determine that in three years the firm should capture 10% of the national market in that product line. This new product line is to be handled by one of the existing divisions of the organization. This division begins developing a plan to implement this corporate objective. First

Figure 3.1   *Levels of Strategic Management*

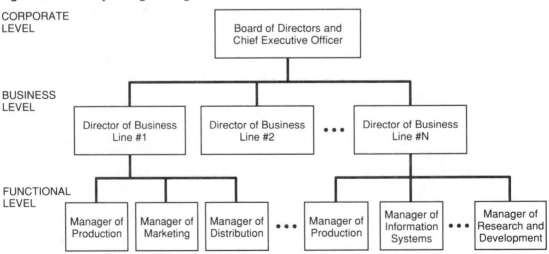

they estimate how many units will be involved in a 10% market share in three years. Then they attempt to estimate the sales of the product in each of the three years. These figures are then given to the production and marketing areas of that division.

The production area examines the anticipated sales figures and calculates production schedules and resource commitments. Their calculations show that the present productive capacity cannot handle this additional load. However, production could be cut on other product lines to make capacity available. This information is passed back to the division planning staff. They determine that cutting other products is not desirable, but that either additional productive facilities can be constructed or that some of the production could be subcontracted to other vendors.

These options are communicated to top management. At this point they could commit to additional capital expenditures for increased productive capacity or to subcontract some of the production with the possible risk of not being able to control the quality of the product. They also have another option of lowering the original objective of obtaining 10% of the market in three years.

This decision-making process would continue in a similar manner until acceptable plans are developed at all levels.

BENEFITS AND COSTS OF PLANNING

As with every business decision, there are benefits and costs associated with strategic planning. For most firms the benefits of strategic planning far outweigh the possible costs.

Following are some of the benefits of strategic planning. The strategic plan establishes a more predictable environment in which decisions can be made. The planning process allows problems to be analyzed and alternative solutions investigated before they become critical issues. In this way the problems can be analyzed in a less emotional environment and more interested individuals can have input into the process. By setting goals the employees will be more motivated, and hopefully this will promote cooperation between the various areas of the firm. Goals will also provide a more objective means of evaluating and controlling performance within the organization. Finally, strategic planning is obviously the logical thing to do.

On the cost side, the planning process can be quite time consuming. This can have an adverse effect on the operations of the organization if those involved in the planning process are not given adequate time. If the resulting strategic plan is not followed, then the planning process will be viewed as a bureaucratic procedure that consumes valuable time. The planning process can also become politicized, in which unworkable goals are set in some areas and too little is demanded of other areas. Of course politics can be a problem associated with all aspects of business. Planners must be alert to what may be deemed political problems. The costs and benefits of strategic planning are summarized in Figure 3.2.

THE PLANNING PROCESS

Within each organizational unit, the planning may be done in different ways. There may be a separate staff function whose sole responsibility is to do strategic planning. This planning staff would report directly to the manager of that unit. Alternately, the planning may be done by a planning committee composed of high-level managers of the unit. Or the planning process may be the responsibility of the unit manager. Usually the more formal the planning staff, the more structured the resulting strategic plan.

Figure 3.3 shows the steps involved in the typical planning process. The first step is to define both the external and internal environment. The external environment can be separated into the direct and the indirect external environments. As the terms imply, the direct external environment includes all factors outside of the planning unit that will directly affect the unit. The definition of these environments depends on the level at which the planning is being done. At the corporate level the direct external environment would include suppliers, stockholders, customers, and competitors. The indirect environment would include the city, state, and national governments, the general U.S. economic conditions, foreign economic conditions, etc. For the information systems area, the direct external environment would include the other client departments within the firm, the overall economic condition of the corporation, and developments within the computer industry.

The internal environment includes all of the resources and activities within that organizational unit. This would include the employees, the physical plant and equipment, the ongoing operations, and the projects under development for a specific planning unit.

Figure 3.2 *Costs and Benefits of Strategic Planning*

COSTS	BENEFITS
Time consuming	Establishes predictable environment
Can be viewed as bureaucratic	Allows analysis of alternative solutions
Process may interfere with normal operations	Reduces amount of crisis management
Process can become politicized	Allows more input from lower level management
	Helps motivate employees
	Helps promote departmental cooperation
	Provides means of evaluating performance

Figure 3.3   *Strategic Planning Process*

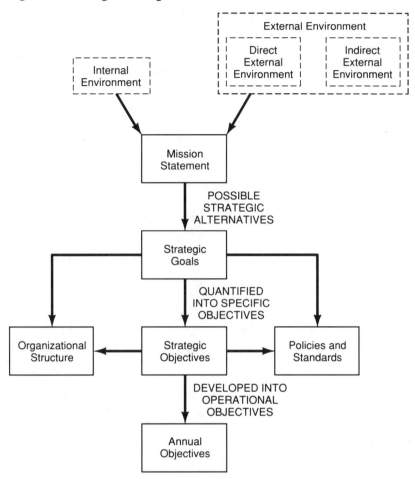

It is necessary to analyze the internal and external environments before any strategic plans are formulated. Otherwise, it would be like trying to plan a trip without knowing the starting point. The process of analyzing these environments is termed *environmental scanning*. We will discuss this in more detail later.

Within the context of the environment, the mission of the unit can be determined. The mission is a broad statement of limits. This may include the types of products and services to be offered, geographic considerations, modes of delivery of goods and services, etc.

From here the process begins to become more specific and detailed. The idea is to develop criteria eventually by which lower-level managers can operate. The next step is still rather broad in concept. It involves developing strategic alternatives within the limits of the stated mission. From these alternatives the strategic goals can be determined. Strategic goals are general statements and are usually not quantitative in nature. These goals are made more exact by forming strategic objectives, and these strategic objectives are then made operational by forming annual objectives. The annual objectives are usually in the form of annual operating and capital budgets.

Again an example may help to illustrate the process. A firm may have determined that its mission was to manufacture high-technology electronic components and only sell in the wholesale market. Within this mission it is determined that a strategic goal is to begin producing electronic medical instruments. This goal is refined to strategic objectives of producing specific products and setting five-year sale targets for these products. The annual objectives are then derived in terms of target sales and production figures for the coming year.

Allied to the preceding planning process is the development of organizational policies and standards. Unlike the objectives, the policies and standards are not quantitative in nature. Instead they dictate the ways in which certain situations should be handled. As Figure 3.3 shows, the policies and standards can be related to implementing strategic goals or strategic objectives. Also allied with implementing strategic goals and objectives is the organizational structure of the firm.

In many ways the organizational structure and the degree of established policies and standards are closely related. The more centralized administrative structure will usually be associated with more established policies and standards. The reason for this is that in a hierarchical organization, policy will be set at a higher level and passed down to the lower organizational levels. Decentralized organizations will allow more independence in the lower organizational units.

If done properly, the strategic planning process should be very comprehensive, involving the entire company. In addition, the strategic goals should be reviewed periodically so that adjustments can be made when conditions in the internal or external environment change.

INFORMATION SYSTEM PLANNING

For any organization to function rationally, it is necessary to have a long-range plan of action. At the highest level this long-range plan is best specified by a series of organizational goals. The attainment of many of these organizational goals will depend on the productivity of the computerized system. Hence, it is critical that any comprehensive business plan include the information system area. This information system plan should serve as a template for future directions of the information system. Like the organization as a whole, strategic planning for the information system involves the same series of procedures as shown in Figure 3.3.

The plan for the information system must be general in nature. The essence of any long-range plan is to give individuals a broad idea of the future direction of the organization without unduly restricting the decision-making capacity of those managing the organization. While a plan would describe the anticipated areas of growth and contraction and the magnitude of these changes, it should not force decisions to be made before the appropriate time.

For example, in the computer area the plan may state the amount of CPU power and the number of work stations connected to the system at some future date, but it should not be specific as to the vendor and model of equipment. It should not even state the type of technology. Most areas of computing are very dynamic and extremely difficult to predict. For example, if external storage is being planned, the capacity and speed of the storage are the necessary units of measure, but specifying the type of device (be it rotating magnetic storage, laser disk, solid state memory, etc.) may unnecessarily restrict future decisions.

Strategic planning is a time-consuming task. This and the fact that many managers feel overwhelmed handling day-to-day operational issues makes it tempting not to develop a strategic plan. Without long-range objectives, decisions will be made considering only the short-term consequences. In data processing this is particularly unfortunate since in many situations a decision today may have an impact well into the future. Buying a particular type of hardware or software may force the firm to support compatible hardware and software for years to come. In addition, reacting to the turbulent environment of data processing technology and methodology could result in a "knee-jerk" pattern of action/reaction. Unfortunately, many managers do not even maintain adequate short-term plans. As the saying goes, "a failure to plan is a plan for failure."

ENVIRONMENTAL SCANNING

The purpose of environmental scanning is to search the internal and external operating environments of the organization for threats and opportunities that could affect its successful long-term functioning. It is normally undertaken by top-level managers and their direct subordinates. In the data processing center, this scanning is useful in assessing the implications of future, perhaps uncertain, events on the operations of the various subunits. We will discuss issues related to hardware, software, personnel, cost, and legal/political matters. There are obviously many areas of which a manager must be aware.

The activities occurring within an organization can often occupy too much of management's attention. With the turbulent events of modern society, we often are caught by surprise by quick, possibly unexpected, changes. The dependence on computer technology is a particularly vulnerable area for an organization. This makes it crucial that the external environment is scanned appropriately. For example, at first pass, it might have seemed like a prudent idea for companies to invest in RCA computers during the 1970s. After all, RCA is one of the world's largest electronic components manufacturers. However, after operating for only a short time in the computer mainframe industry, RCA got out. Firms that purchased RCA systems were essentially abandoned.

Changes in the computer industry itself are only one of the concerns of the external environment with which strategic managers should deal. Changes in hardware and software technology literally happen daily. Tied very closely to these events are the costs of technology. Finding and keeping qualified technicians is another area of concern. Finally, the current attitudes of the legal system should be taken into consideration.

The following sections will discuss how the information system manager should go about scanning his or her external environment. Specific solutions would be of little use here. However, there are several considerations that should be addressed in each instance.

Managing Changes in Hardware Technology

Saying that information technology is rapidly and constantly changing is stating the obvious. However, to the information systems strategic planner, the rates and directions of change contain important clues to future expectations. For example, current direct access storage device (DASD) technology could quickly become outdated in the event of the announcement of another data storage technique.

The strategic plan for an information system should not, in general, include specific system components. However, what should be included here would be a description of a trend or direction in hardware needs for the organization. This plan should then be compared, as often as necessary, to the current state-of-the-art technology. This information can be gathered from several sources.

A primary source of hardware trends is the computer vendors themselves. Because of their objective to sell the organization more equipment and software, these individuals often boast about the developments of their organizations. Even when viewed skeptically, this is valuable information, perhaps giving the manager leading indicators to new technology announcements.

Another source of information is incorporated in various journals and magazines of the industry. Many of these take pride in leaking product announcements to the public and speculating on new technology impacts. Several manufacturers publish scientific and technical reports that can give useful insights into new trends and expectations. Finally, independent organizations, such as the Association for Computing Machinery (ACM), the Data Processing Management Association (DPMA), and Institute of Electrical and Electronics Engineers (IEEE), provide a scholarly format of presentation of current research in specific areas.

A third source of information that should be used in managing the changes in hardware is the various periodicals that describe the condition of the industry in general. Mergers, acquisitions, and relative stock performance provide important clues to the amounts of revenues a particular organization might have available for the development and marketing of a new piece of equipment.

Finally, outside consultants often provide such services. These individuals perform this activity as a profession and would presumably provide reliable information collected from a variety of sources. As often occurs with consultants, fees are high.

Of course, it is not feasible for any single individual within an organization to monitor all of these sources and all of the equipment types within an organization. Consequently, it is necessary to delegate this responsibility to persons with particular competence or interest in each of these areas. To support this effort, the organization must provide access to the various subscriptions and conventions. It should also be remembered that individuals have known and unknown biases that could affect their views of technological change. Several sources should be considered before adopting any single position. The result of this process should be a semiannual or annual report stating the investigator's supported opinions on the trends.

Keep in mind, however, that this information will be used for decisions affecting long-range planning. As a result, particular product announcements are not necessarily of great import, unless they represent significant changes in the current state of technology. What is needed is a determination of industry trends within each of the categories.

For example, the formation of an international committee to propose a standard for office automation data transmission would be regarded as an important event in the area. However, the announcement of an office product that could transmit data between various office systems might not be as momentous.

Information from a variety of external sources can help the organization plan for technological hardware changes. We have by no means developed a complete list of sources of this information. It might be desirable to motivate the entire data processing staff to watch for trends and reward success. However, individual managers must ultimately be responsible for providing upper management with current trend data.

Managing Changes in Software Technology

The environmental scanning of technological software issues progresses much as it does for hardware technology. One consideration is perhaps just as important, if not more so. This is the area of software support. When purchasing software, one of the most critical considerations is that of program maintenance. If the software producer were to go out of business, the support of the software would fall to the purchaser's organization. It might be that certain programs are not even maintainable by the purchaser.

The difference between hardware and software maintenance is that with the plug compatible manufacturer (PCM—produces hardware substantially the same as the primary vendor) market, the support of hardware devices could be handled by other organizations. However, the maintenance of software products normally cannot be handled by other programming staffs.

The danger lies not only in the company going out of business, but in a healthy company deciding to discontinue support for a specific software system. This occurs when it is no longer economically desirable for a firm to continue to market the product. This can occur for a variety of reasons, such as too small a customer product base, maintenance support that is too costly, or simply that the specific hardware that runs that system is no longer supported.

For example, a major computer vendor recently discontinued one of its operating systems and has provided no migration path for the users of that system. The decision by the vendor was prompted by a need to cut costs and the small user base for this operating system. This means that these users may have to endure a costly and time-consuming conversion to another operating system. The other option is to continue to use the present operating system and essentially freeze the level of system software technology. Neither is a very attractive alternative.

This type of change is a major undertaking for a firm. Without adequate environmental scanning, an event like this could be devastating to the data processing area. Most of the resources of the area would have to go into the conversion, with little time or money left for new system development.

Probably the most important consideration when planning for software changes is the user community's wants and needs. Just as it is necessary for the data processing area to have a long-range plan for the corporate information system, it is also necessary for the individual user departments to provide the office of the vice-president of information systems with an estimate of data processing resource growth and needs for their areas.

The areas of standards and procedures, discussed in the following chapter, is also a vital concern to the strategic planner. There is a substantial cost associated with the creation and maintenance of software systems. Consequently, the organization should be sure to develop these systems in such a manner as to insure their maintainability.

Finally, although conceptually there is a difference between programs and data, in computer storage there is really no difference. Consequently, the long-range planner must be sure that adequate facilities for data and program protection are provided. This data is a corporate resource and should be protected and controlled in much the same way as any other in the organization (raw materials, finished goods, office supplies, equipment, etc.).

There is little difference in the methods of environmental scanning used in managing hardware and software change. In each case, we look at external sources of information, such as periodicals and consultants, collect needs and wants of the user community, and form a plan for data processing incorporating the goals and objectives of the organization.

Costs of Technology

The expense of data processing is of concern to many components of the organization. Because the information system is an overhead cost in many organizations, the appropriation of funds for its operation is usually taken from the users' budgets. We have learned that the costs of hardware are decreasing while those of software are increasing. This is hardly an equitable trade-off. In addition, the concept of decreasing hardware costs is questionable. Bigger and faster systems are being developed that offer a lower cost per function (MIPS, meg, etc.), but the overall cost of the system is still more than its predecessor.

Consequently, strategic planning should incorporate the fact that newer systems will inevitably be more expensive. Planners should also be aware of the supply of data processing labor. As long as the demand for programmers and analysts exceeds the supply, data processing personnel costs will continue to occupy a substantial portion of the data processing budget. As we shall see, after acquiring and training these professionals, care must be taken to insure that these individuals do not leave the organization.

Computer usage hardly ever decreases. Strategic planners should always keep in mind that the costs of computing are increasing over the long run, perhaps exponentially. These costs include hardware, software, and personnel. Planners must remember that in the future, the amounts and consequently the expense of computing will probably continue to increase.

Sources of Qualified Technicians

A data processing shop is a complex combination of people and machinery. It is crucial that a sufficient source of qualified professionals be available to the organization to insure the continued operation of the information system. Once a reliable source of technicians has been found, it is economically smart to encourage the productive relationship between the organization and the source. The source might be a trade school, a university, or an extensive in-house training facility. In any regard, the organization should take care to maintain this personnel channel.

After these individuals have been hired, it is important to attempt to keep them within the organization. Industry averages indicate that approximately one-third of a data processing shop will turn over every year. This indicates that every third year the organization will interact with an essentially new data processing department. It is in the best interests of the organization to try to decrease this turnover.

Employees desire different rewards for their work. Often pay is not enough. The data processing professional is an artist whose tools are some of the most technically advanced in the world. The use of adequate and current hardware and software, as well as sufficient training, can be a major motivator and perhaps serve to decrease the turnover problem.

Personnel issues will be discussed further in the following chapter.

Legal Issues

Chapter 9 will cover many of the various legal issues that a data processing manager might encounter. However, the strategic planner must treat the legal climate differently. Organizations are required to maintain more accounting and personnel records today than ever before. Much of this is accomplished with computer technology. Consequently, a planner who is more aware of pending legislation concerning these matters would stand a better chance of being able to meet them successfully.

The various legal and political arenas are not places for the uninitiated. This portion of environmental scanning is best left to those individuals experienced in these fields. Although these persons would not necessarily be data processing professionals, they should have sufficient knowledge of the area to comprehend the implications of events.

For example, if a major change in the tax law appears evident, then the projected impact of this new law must be analyzed. This could have a major impact on both the amount and the way we acquire resources. Maybe some acquisitions should be advanced if they receive more favorable treatment under the existing law. Also, the new tax legislation may require substantial changes in the accounting and personnel software systems. Knowing this in advance may avoid a crisis situation.

LONG-RANGE PLANNING

It is important that top management direct and support the computer activity of the firm. Since the information system services all areas in the firm, it is necessary that the users know what resources are available now and what will be available in the future. Upper management must encourage the information system area to develop both a strategic plan and the standards and procedures that operationalize that plan. This will assure service that is efficient and responsive to user needs.

Once the internal and external information system environments have been scanned, it is necessary for the information systems area to develop a mission statement. This statement will be broad in scope and will usually state how the information system is to deliver services to the organization as a whole and to each of the individual user areas. The statement may generally describe the services to be offered and the overall quality of these services.

The strategic goals and objectives can then be developed. These are usually presented in a formal long-range plan. The long-range plan should describe the anticipated changes in the information system over some fixed period of time (anywhere from three years to ten years). This will allow users to plan their own computing activities based on this long-range computing plan. Of course, this plan will be of little value unless it is fully endorsed and supported by upper management. Major deviations from the plan must be justified to top management and thoroughly communicated to the user community.

The long-term information systems plan will usually be developed by the central information systems area with input from the decentralized units and each of the user areas. This plan should then be reviewed by a computing advisory committee (i.e., steering committee) before being submitted to top management.

The long-range plan should commit the firm to delivering a certain level of service over a specific period of time. The plan must be expressed in user understandable terms. For example, it could state a maximum acceptable response time for online users or a guaranteed minimum number of transactions to be processed daily for specific batch systems. In addition, the plan should also state how many user work stations are projected to be attached to the system, how many simultaneous users the system will support, the level of commitment to user training, and what major projects will be implemented in the future.

Since computer technology is so difficult to predict, long-range plans must be revised periodically. One method is to review the plan annually, make any necessary alterations, and roll the plan ahead one more year. Hence a five-year plan would consist of the revised version of the last four years of the previous five-year plan and a projection of the activity for the additional fifth year. This should not imply that the plan should be approached in a nonchalant manner, because it will be continually revised.

Besides informing the user community of the expected level of service, the long-range plan should also forewarn management as to when large increments of resources will be needed. This includes hardware, software, and manpower projections. When upper management supports a long-range plan, they will be agreeing to provide these resources at the appropriate time.

This planning process is not an easy task. Commitments are being made by both top management and the information systems area. The final plan is usually arrived at by a substantial expenditure of time and much negotiation. Because of the amount of effort, it is tempting to operate without a long-range plan. However, this will usually lead to major confrontations between the information system and both its users and top management.

GOALS AND OBJECTIVES

For any set of plans to be of use, there must exist a set of goals and objectives on which the plans are based. A goal normally implies a result toward which activities are directed, while an objective is an event against which goal success is measured. The distinction here is important. It is not enough to set a goal without establishing a mechanism that can be used to measure the attainment of that goal.

A data processing center must establish goals and objectives for both short-run and long-run performance. However, these are not created autonomously. To provide effective service to the organization, these goals and objectives must mesh well with those of the company. The better the fit, the greater the probability of success.

Those long-term goals and objectives that are external to the data processing organization are usually related to the level of service provided to the user community. An example of an external goal is to make the user population more computer literate. This goal may be partially achieved by setting an objective of offering a series of three-day seminars dealing with computer fundamentals. These courses would be given to the appropriate individuals, and the degree of success of the program would be measured by the level of computer awareness this group has following the course.

Shorter-term goals and objectives are manifest in operating and capital budgets. These budgets involve estimating the expenditures to be made in the coming year to continue the current operations (operating budget) and the expenditures necessary to expand the facilities (capital budget). The annual budgeting process is one of the most important activities of the information systems director. The procedures used in developing operating and capital budgets are discussed in detail in Chapter 9, which deals with financial issues.

For the goals to be embraced by the information systems area, there must be effective communication of purpose and intent from upper management to the data processing group. Hopefully, the staff will then strive to meet the objectives. Setting unrealistic objectives, whether done inside the computer area or outside, is a chief cause of strife between data processing and the rest of the organization. All parties concerned should be consulted in the setting of these criteria. Any deviation from these should be immediately and completely brought to the attention of all parties. Communication is essential.

Goals and objectives which are internal to the data processing department are applicable to the management of departmental resources, such as personnel, hardware, software, etc. These are usually embodied in standards and procedures documentation. This, however, is not sufficient. The goals and objectives must be clear to each individual within the department, and communication must be encouraged to support compliance.

An example of an internal goal is to assure data integrity. This goal may be partially implemented by the objective of backing up all volatile files on a daily basis and storing at least one backup copy at an off-site location. This would insure recovery of the files even in the situation where the main data center is destroyed.

As another example of this, suppose the director of the information system of Major Company determined that one of the goals of the data processing area would consist of providing adequate response to accounting queries. An objective in this case would perhaps include a desire for all normal accounting queries to produce the expected results. (This may seem to be a contrived example; however, very few data processing shops have goals and objectives that are even this clear.) The data processing department would then have as its goal to provide adequate resources for the maintenance of the accounting database to meet this goal. Related to this goal would be the necessity of employing an experienced database administrator. A subsequent objective would then be to provide training and support to interested individuals who might ultimately become database administrators. Standards and procedures would also reflect the desirability for database normalization.

We can see here that the cooperation of management up, down, and across the organization chart is necessary. Without intelligent selection and establishment of goals and objectives and the necessary communication with which to bond these together, this component of strategic planning is of little worth. In addition, these criteria are not static. They must be altered to meet the long-term strategic plan which is supported and guided by external environmental scanning. They must be flexible and realistic enough to be of use, but not so restrictive as to disallow creativity or individual managerial control.

Top management support for this process is crucial. Without this, the plans, goals, and resulting objectives simply become guidelines and carry very little weight. Once these have been established, it is the job of top management to insure that compliance and support is maintained throughout the organization. They must make sure that their subordinates comprehend the importance of individual actions to the long-range operation of the organization.

ORGANIZATIONAL METHODS

We have stressed that the information system's plan must be congruent with the corporate goals. The structure and general management philosophy of the organization will also have a direct effect on how the information system functions. The methods of capture, control, and processing of information must be coordinated with the way in which authority is delegated throughout the organization. For example, if the firm is decentralized, having separate autonomous divisions, it would be operationally impossible to have a highly centralized information system making all data processing decisions. A major function of each division is deciding how to collect, process, and disseminate the information necessary for the operation of the division. Centralizing this function would usurp the decision-making capacity of every division and cause tremendous interdivisional conflict.

For example, one division may find sales reports by product line to be very useful in decision making while another division may find reports by sales region to be most valuable. To dictate one format as the uniform method of reporting will limit the usefulness of the information. Of course, a rational centralized policy may dictate a single reporting standard for corporate reporting but allow the divisions to use other methods for their internal decision making.

Actually, the question of the centralization of the data gathering, storing, and reporting functions is a very difficult one. To have fully integrated systems, where information from various functional areas can be used for decision making throughout the firm, it is necessary to consider data to be a corporate asset. The more a firm tends toward fully integrated systems, the more central coordination is necessary. In actual practice, firms will adopt a policy that some data that is critical to firm-wide decision making be centrally controlled and that the remaining data be dealt with as the property of the originating department.

The structure of both the firm and the information system can have a significant effect on a firm's computing environment. In fact, the organizational structure will in many instances dictate the ways in which the information system interacts with its users. For example, a highly decentralized firm will have significantly different information processing requirements than a totally centralized firm.

Before going into any more detail, it is necessary to give some historical perspective on the role of computing in most business organizations. For the sake of simplicity, we will discuss only centralized systems at this time. The same sort of phenomena was also occurring in decentralized firms.

Brief History

Computers were introduced in most larger firms in the early to mid-1960s. The primary tasks performed by these earlier systems involved either of two activities: those that were well defined, repetitive in nature, and involved large amounts of data, or those that involved a large amount of mathematical computation. For most firms, this meant many of the accounting and engineering functions were the first to be computerized. With the majority of the computer operations involving either accounting or engineering, the manager of the computer center usually reported directly to the comptroller (see Figure 3.4) so that direct control of the financial data could be retained by the chief accounting officer. This arrangement usually gave priority to the accounting functions. However, the other users were generally from engineering and few in number. Communication between the user community and the computer center was good, mainly because almost all of the users were technical computer types who spoke the same jargon-saturated language. Furthermore, while the processing of the accounting transactions primarily involved input/output-bound programs that demanded intensive use of the peripheral devices, the engineers primarily used the machine for programs that demanded mostly computational power. Hence, there was little contention for the same resources. For example, the accountants would run the payroll job which involved reading each active employee record, doing a minimal number of calculations, and printing a check for each employee. This would intensively use the tape drives and a printer. At the same time, the engineer would be running a program on stress analysis that involved very little data entry but took a long time to execute because of all the computations.

As the computer center grew, the user community became more diverse. There was substantially more contention by different user groups for various computer resources. This and the considerable growth in total resources used by the computer center forced an organizational change in computing. The computer center had simply outgrown the accounting department. The manager was probably given a new title, such as manager of computer systems, and reported directly to the vice-president of finance. Figure 3.5 shows the organizational configuration.

This change brought the administration of the computer center slightly

Figure 3.4 *Early Corporate Organization Involving Computing*

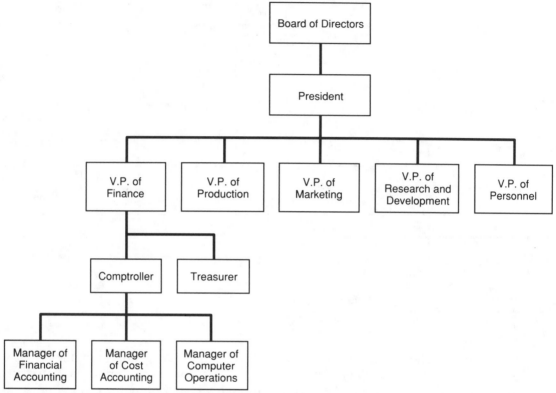

closer to the user, but many of the same problems still existed and there were more communication problems due to the growing variety of users. For example, if the people in the marketing department wanted the computer center to install a sales reporting system, they would have to submit a request for systems analysis to the computer center. All requests of this nature would be examined and the projects prioritized. This priority would determine when and if a given project would be designed and implemented. The vice-president of finance would usually have the final word on this decision. Again, it is possible that the projects under the control of the vice-president of finance would get preferential treatment. In addition, the marketing people who were not technically oriented had difficulty even expressing their needs to those in the computer center. The typical response to this type of request was that "the computer center does not have the resources to implement this project now" (the biggest constraint was usually manpower) and "it will be one to two years until the project can be considered."

One partial solution to this problem was to form a computer steering committee which had members from all functional areas using computer re-

Figure 3.5   *Data Processing Organized Under the V. P. of Finance*

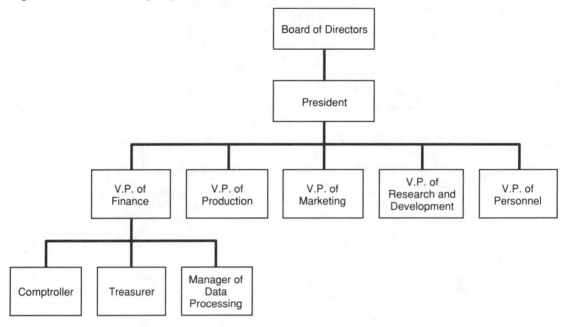

sources. The steering committee would advise the manager of computer systems on a variety of matters. For example, the decision on the priority of projects discussed earlier would have been thoroughly analyzed by the committee, and each representative would be able to argue the merit of the proposals from his or her area. The manager would still make the final decision, but the steering committee would give advice, direction, and recommendations on the matter under consideration.

Even with the steering committee, most firms found that the computer area was not responsive enough to user needs. There were even more users demanding access to computers for a wider variety of uses. In addition, the total number of computer applications running had increased dramatically, resulting in additional commitments to maintain these systems. Even though both application and systems programming staffs were increasing, because of the growing size of the applications and the large amount of software maintenance, the staff available for new system implementation was actually decreasing.

Users, finding the central system unresponsive to their needs, started using innovative approaches to solve their problems. In some cases this meant the acquisition of minicomputers independent of the central site and under administrative control of the user area. This solved some problems, but in many cases it created others even more serious. Some of these additional problems included the inability to access the central data, the incompatibility of hardware and software, and the variety of issues associated with the administration of a computer system such as backup, security, specialized expertise, etc. The explosive growth in the capabilities of microcomputers made this an even bigger problem. The independent purchases of micros by users in an uncontrolled manner caused problems of a larger magnitude. At this point most firms realized that computing had outgrown its organizational structure and management was losing control of the firm's computing environment.

A More Advanced Approach

The logical solution to some of these problems is to increase the authority of the lead position in data processing. This means creating the position of vice-president of information systems or chief information officer (CIO). The vice-president (or CIO) would report directly to the president and be responsible for coordinating all computer-related activities within the firm. While not having direct decision-making authority in all computer-related transactions, the vice-president of information systems will control the central computer facilities, establish company-wide computer policies, and mediate in computer-related disputes between other organizational units.

There are some major benefits to a firm adopting this approach. Each of the user departments will be treated in a more equitable manner. The firm will be able to control the direction of computer technology, assuring compatibility, reducing redundancy, and increasing overall effectiveness. Another important benefit is that the central administration will be more aware of the importance of the information system. This latter point is an important step since it will eventually lead to many of the productivity gains that company-wide computer application promises.

For some firms the creation of the vice-presidential position cannot be avoided. The number of people, the large investment in capital, the strategic importance of the information system, and the large operating budgets in the computer area make this position a necessity. This also forces the computing area to mature in a business sense. Without being controlled by another functional area, the information system area will be totally responsible for its own planning and control. The fiscal health of computing will be directly in the hands of the computer professionals who will have to justify their existence and future growth. These firms may have an organizational structure similar to that shown in Figure 3.6.

Information System Steering Committee

The steering committee can take different forms, with varying degrees of influence. In all cases it has the important function of representing the user community and obtaining its views on operation of the information system. At one extreme, it could consist of all of the vice-presidents of the firm. In this case, the policy-making decisions may be made by this group, with the vice-president of information systems responsible for implementing the decisions.

Figure 3.6 *Organization with V. P. of Information Systems*

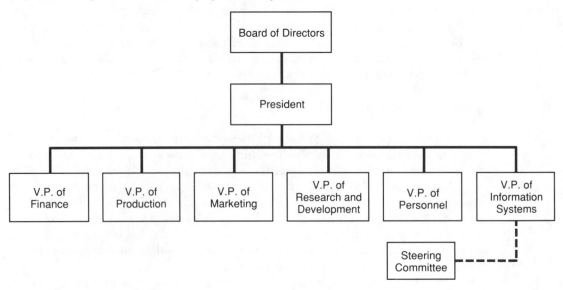

In other circumstances, the committee is comprised of representatives from each of the functional areas with a desirable mix that ranges from the reasonably sophisticated users to the more casual users. In this case, the committee would probably only be advisory, in that the vice-president of information systems is not bound by the committee's decisions. However, each of the members are representatives of their respective vice-president, and most major decisions will be discussed by the steering committee, proposed by the vice-president of information systems, and acted on by the president or board of directors. Of course, there could be forms of the committee between these two extremes.

A committee composed of vice-presidents is attractive since the needs and concerns of the information system are communicated to the top level of the organization. In this way, direct and immediate action can be taken to solve a problem. However, due to the extreme time demands placed on the vice-presidents, the committee meetings may not be as frequent or as comprehensive as needed.

The committee composed of users (sometimes this is called a user review group) may be able to provide more insight into the operational problems of the information system. The reason for this is that these individuals are usually more familiar with the day-to-day operations of the system. Some organizations will have more than one steering committee, where specialized areas such as networking, database management, graphics, etc. each have a steering committee to render advice. One specialized steering committee is the data authority committee. This committee has the task of establishing policies on who will have access to specific data and the type of access that is granted. The duties of this committee are discussed in more detail Chapter 15.

DECENTRALIZED SYSTEMS

So far we have discussed only organizations that have a centralized philosophy. Many firms favor decentralized operations where units of the company act as their own separate businesses. The structure of the information system may be distinctly different in a highly decentralized firm.

To control the independent operating unit properly, it is necessary for the manager of that unit to control the information flow. This does not mean that computer operations must physically reside in the independent unit, although this may be the easiest way of assuring adequate control.

A typical decentralized configuration is shown in Figure 3.7. Note that there are computer facilities distributed throughout the firm, including a com-

Figure 3.7 *Decentralized Computing*

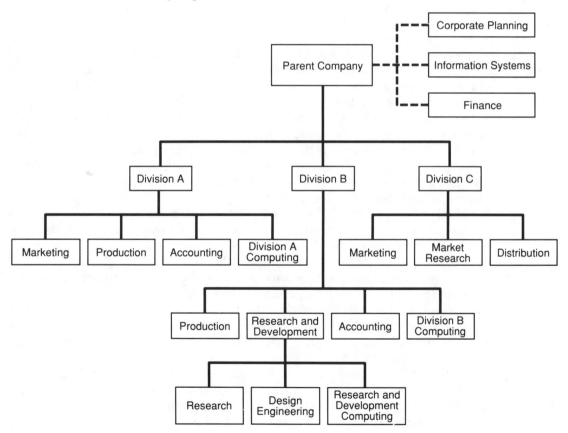

puter complex in the central office. In this case, the independent units have their own small data centers including hardware, software, machine operators, system programmers, and application programmers. Essentially, these data centers are independent of each other and are controlled by the management of the specific unit. They are responsible for processing the data and disseminating the information to the appropriate departments within the unit.

It is particularly important that there is some degree of centralization in the management of the information flow throughout the firm no matter the degree of corporate decentralization. Some data from the various independent units must be aggregated to produce company-wide reports and other data must be shared between units. This means that at a minimum there must be data exchange standards established so that files can be easily transferred. For the sake of economy and efficiency, many firms find it best to establish company-wide standards such as those for hardware and software compatibility. Not only does this allow for the exchange of data but, more importantly, it encourages the sharing of resources and the uniformity of reports.

While to a certain extent these policies restrict the discretion of the unit manager, they can produce dramatic productivity gains. For example, instead of each unit developing its own series of accounting software packages, one common package can be used. Because the systems are identical, it would be very easy to compare unit performances. Furthermore, the data from the various units could be easily consolidated to produce the firm's financial statements. This would also reduce the total amount of software maintenance. If additional standards were enforced, the various decentralized resources could be more easily networked together, producing a very powerful information system.

Even if a firm is decentralized, the computer resources do not have to be physically distributed to the autonomous units. A primarily centralized information system can still effectively service a decentralized organization. In either situation, extreme care must be taken in determining the control and access to the data generated at each independent unit. As mentioned earlier, some of the data must be treated as a corporate asset under centralized control. This allows for highly integrated systems and helps reduce data redundancy and insure data integrity. It is also important that data specific to an independent unit be controlled by that unit and that the policies on the processing, control, and access of that data be made by the management of that unit.

For example, a company may have a firm-wide hiring and compensation policy. While the final decision on who to hire is made by the independent unit, the amount paid new employees and the amount of annual raises and bonuses is determined centrally. This type of policy helps to prevent different departments from bidding against each other when hiring and also helps to maintain equity of compensation for similar positions in different divisions of the firm. In this case, this data must be stored in such a manner that it can be centrally accessed. If each unit were allowed to store the data as it saw fit, the annual review process would be extremely difficult. The policy of the firm should dictate the way data is controlled. Unfortunately, in some firms, the data storage policies dictate the way the firm does business.

END-USER COMPUTING

In a modern company, computer facilities are distributed throughout the organization. The use of computers has become a critical part of the job for many employees. This means that there is a large amount of software and hardware not under the control of the information systems area. Also, a large majority of the users of computer technology are now outside of the information systems area.

The expansion of computing into user areas has opened a new era of information processing. Opportunities abound for the application of computerized systems to increase productivity. However, many problems are associated with the opportunities presented with end-user computing. The acquisition and control of the multitude of computer resources becomes a fundamental problem. User areas cannot be unconstrained in acquiring these resources. A lack of some centralized control will result in incompatible systems, redundancy of effort, and a waste of resources.

An even more irksome problem associated with end-user computing is the efficient education and training of the various users of the systems. Without this training the systems will not be used to their full potential. This training can become very expensive and quite difficult to manage properly.

We have presented only some of the problems associated with end-user computing. Instead of going into more detail here, we devote Chapter 12 to a more thorough discussion of this important topic.

INTERNAL INFORMATION SYSTEM ORGANIZATION

The internal organization of an information system can considerably affect the level of service provided by the system. If an information system is not organized so that it can efficiently handle user problems and new requirements, user dissatisfaction and dissension can result.

The organization of the information systems function is probably as different for each firm as one firm is different from another. In fact, there may be as many different configurations for the computer function as there are companies. We will not discuss specific internal configurations but will discuss some of the basic functional areas.

For most firms the information system will be concerned primarily with the same basic functional responsibilities. (See Figure 3.8.) These include the operation of the data center equipment, namely the running of the machines, the scheduling of jobs, and the proper handling of both input and output. Usually included in the process of operating the system is the systems programming function. This group is responsible for maintaining and installing the system software. The entry and control of data is also one of the functions of the information system; however, in an online environment much of this responsibility lies with the end-user.

Development, acquisition, and maintenance of application software is

Figure 3.8 *Basic Information System Functions*

FUNCTION	DESCRIPTION
Computer Operations	Runs the system; involves starting jobs, mounting the proper input and output volumes, and responding to problem conditions
System Programming	Installs and maintains the operating system and associated system software
Data Entry	Entering data in machine-readable form
Application Program Development	Writing new application systems
Application Program Maintenance	Correcting and updating existing application systems
Data Management	Assuring data security, access, integrity, and useability
Communications Management	Configuring and maintaining the network
End-User Computing	Helping and educating users

one of the largest functional areas in most computerized environments. Because of the amount of work in the application systems area, the function is usually split between the development of new systems and the maintenance of existing systems. Some of this responsibility is also passed on to the end-user. To enhance the effectiveness of the data center staff, some firms have also established information centers which are designed to help solve end-user problems and help the user directly access information from the system without programmer assistance.

The data of the firm is one of the most important assets of the company. Hence, the protection of this data is important. Most firms, especially those with large database management systems, will have a separate area which is responsible for the coordination of these functions. Also, with the rapid growth in the amount and type of data communications, many firms find it desirable to have a separate telecommunications staff to guarantee the integrity and security of all the communication channels.

The size of the information system will dictate the degree of aggregation of these functions. Smaller firms and independent decentralized units may have only a few departments while larger, more centralized information systems may more finely divide the functions. Instead of discussing the different variations in the internal structure of firms, we will look at the organization of our hypothetical company, the Major Company. We will briefly examine the responsibilities of each of the departments. Later chapters will deal with each of the areas in much greater detail.

It is important to remember that the organizational plan for any company is an evolving entity. The structure of an organization should be dynamic enough to handle major shifts in business and industry conditions. This is especially true in a constantly changing environment such as computing.

STRATEGIC PLANNING TOOLS

So far we have discussed only the general procedures involved in strategic planning. It is necessary to discuss also some of the special methods that have been used to aid in the strategic planning process. The following discussions of some specific methods will be simply a brief introduction and will only discuss selected methods. If more detail is desired, other sources of information about these subjects are cited at the end of this chapter.

Delphi Technique

There are many methods of forecasting that can be used. These include mathematical modeling, computer simulation, informal brainstorming, and econometric modeling to name just a few. One technique that you may not be familiar with and is useful in predicting future industry trends is the Delphi technique. The Delphi technique is a set of procedures that can be followed to poll the opinions of a group of experts. This can be a useful technique for doing environmental scanning.

The procedure has a series of steps. The first step involves asking each individual expert to make a prediction or forecast about the subject in question. The experts are not allowed to discuss the subject in question. That is, there is no interaction between the individual experts.

A coordinator tabulates the opinions and determines the consensus opinion. This consensus opinion is then distributed to each of the experts. The experts are then asked if they wish to change their original opinion in light of the consensus opinion. This process is repeated until none of the experts changes opinions.

The strength of the Delphi technique is that it allows experts to use the knowledge of other experts without influencing the original projections. Hence, many sources of opinion can be used to form the first consensus opinion. The task of coordinator is critical to the success of the technique. The coordinator must determine the consensus opinion on each round of the process.

Value-Added Chain

Harvard Business School's Michael Porter has created the value chain model that is intended to help managers meet the trials and opportunities of the future by offering a framework where these managers can assess the role of information systems in their businesses. A firm's value chain is composed of the technological and economical endeavors that it performs to conduct business. These endeavors consist of inbound logistics, operations, outbound logistics, marketing and sales, and service, together with support activities such as human resource management and technology development necessary to conduct business. An IS manager can support the organization by determining those value chain activities that information technology can help improve. Because information pervades the entire value chain, many of the links in the value chain can be supported. It can either be used to support internal operations or external marketplace factors.

The information intensity of a product's value chain is the amount of information processing that is required to acquire, process, and then deliver the product in its final form to the consumer. This information content refers to the amount of useful information contained within that product that is received by its consumers. Executives can use the value chain to pinpoint opportunities for using computer-based systems for these value-added activities. The strength of this model is its reliance on ideas that have been widely accepted by top management; thus top management can be very receptive to the ideas contained in the value chain.

Critical Success Factors

One way of doing strategic planning is to identify the factors which are the most important to the success of the enterprise. This type of analysis is termed *key success factors* or *critical success factors* (CSFs). These factors can then be monitored and strategic goals set pertaining to these factors.

The critical success factors analysis will usually involve determining the CSFs for the organization as a whole and then relating these corporate CSFs to the information resource requirements. The usual method of determining the CSFs is to conduct in-depth interviews of individuals at all levels of the organization. In this way a comprehensive picture can be drawn of the firm, and the CSFs can be derived from that picture. The corporate CSFs can then be used to derive the information system CSFs. These information system CSFs can be used as guidelines for developing the overall information system strategy.

The critical success factors will differ from one company to the next. Hence, the CSFs of each information system will be different. That is the point of doing the critical success factors analysis. It helps to clarify the mission of both the organization and the information systems area.

MAJOR COMPANY

Major Company does its strategic planning on a yearly cycle. It uses the critical success factors analysis to determine both the corporate and information system strategic goals. To obtain a more independent analysis, the CSF study is done by an outside consulting team. Figure 3.9 shows the CSFs for Major Company, and Figure 3.10 shows the corresponding information system CSFs.

Note that Major Company has decided that the quality of the product

Figure 3.9   *CSFs for Major Company*

Produce a consistently high-quality product

Provide a high level of service to the customer

Have adequate inventories to satisfy customer demand

Allow for special orders and modifications to existing products

Increase corporate productivity

Project a positive image to the community and potential customers

Continue to develop new products

and the level of customer service is more important than being price competitive with other vendors. Major Company believes that the information system plays a critical role in delivering both a quality product and quality service. Examining Figure 3.10 shows that some of the CSFs are directly related to the corporate CSFs while other CSFs are not.

Figure 3.11 shows Major Company's higher-level organization chart. The vice-president of information systems (CIO) manages the central information system and sets firm-wide policy regarding computer resources. A steering committee advises the vice-president of information systems. The steering committee consists of representatives from each of the major user departments. The other vice-presidents also control computer resources in their respective divisions; however, they must comply with the computer policies established by the vice-president of information systems. These policies deal with hardware and software acquisition and the development of new application systems. The primary objectives of these policies are to assure a minimum level of compatibility throughout the corporate information system, to reduce costs of acquiring computer technology, to minimize the training of personnel, and to attempt to reduce the duplication of application development effort.

Figure 3.12 shows the internal organization of the centralized information systems area. The information systems function is divided into five areas: operations, application systems, data management, telecommunications, and an information center. We will now describe the functions of each of these areas.

Figure 3.10   *CSFs for the Information System*

Provide quality service to all of the end-users, including user contracts with each department and guaranteed service levels

Improve the marketing information system to serve customers better

Install industrial robots to assure better quality control and to allow for the economical manufacture of special orders

Design a computerized quality control system to track all product failures

Enforce all data processing standards so that higher productivity can be achieved

Increase the number of work stations connected to the company-wide network

Figure 3.11 *Major Company Organization*

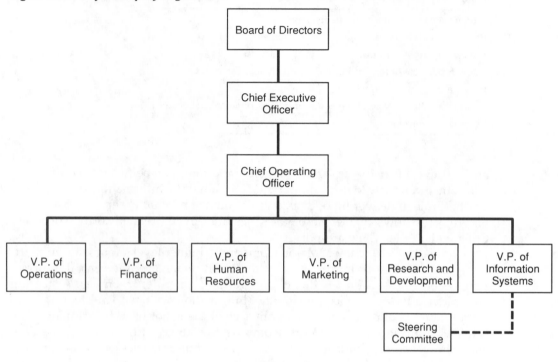

The operations area is responsible for the smooth running of the system. This includes the scheduling and execution of production programs and maintaining a stable environment on the test systems. Most shops separate the production systems, those programs that have been tested and installed and are run on a periodic basis, from the test systems which are still being developed. This increases security by not allowing programmers access to the production systems. Also, it eliminates the chance of a program under development from destroying active data sets or adversely affecting programs which are already in production.

At Major Company, machine operations, systems programming, hardware maintenance, and data entry are all functional areas reporting to the manager of operations. Each of these areas involves the assurance that the computer continues to run efficiently. The system programmers and the hardware maintenance personnel maintain the systems software and hardware. The operators and data entry personnel perform the day-to-day operating tasks.

The application systems area is responsible for the acquisition, development, and maintenance of the software for end-users. At Major Company the system analysts and application programmers are divided by their responsibility as to either system maintenance or system development. Instead of this arrangement, some firms will divide the applications personnel by functional area. This may include financial systems, accounting systems, production systems, etc., each having their own development and maintenance programming staff.

Data management is responsible for custody of the organization's data. This includes establishing policies for access, modification, and security of the data. In many organizations the corporate data can be the most valuable asset of the firm. It is the responsibility of the data management area to protect this data and assure that the data is configured in such a manner as to provide maximum benefit to the firm. This entails the coordination of the development of all application systems so as to reduce data redundancy and to allow for highly integrated systems.

The telecommunications area is rapidly growing in importance. It is the objective of this area to provide access to the system for its many users while using a minimum of resources. Many times this will include designing and installing local area networks and various communication devices and providing access to other networks. This system will not only allow users more flexibility, but will allow the sharing of resources between users and systems.

The final departmental area is the information center. Three years ago Major Company established the information center as a separate department. It is designed to provide assistance and training to the general user community within Major Company. This allows the users to operate in a friendlier environ-

Figure 3.12   *Major Company Central Information System Organization*

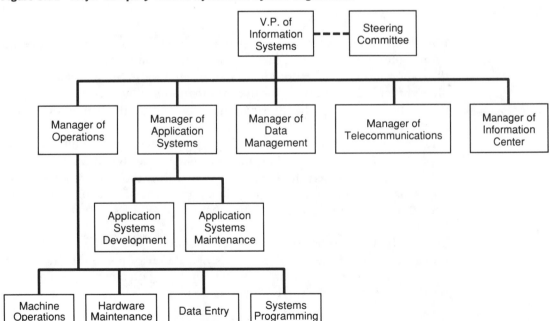

ment and also helps them to develop some of their own application programs. While the information center requires staffing with highly qualified personnel, this investment in staff is justified by the overall benefit to the firm. Besides the increased level of user satisfaction, the users become much more sophisticated and can reduce the application backlog by doing some of the work themselves. Much more will be said about the information center in subsequent chapters.

SUMMARY

Strategic planning involves developing statements of direction for both the firm as a whole and various parts of the organization. These statements of direction are made operational by developing a series of goals and objectives. A goal is a target for expectations, and an objective is a measure by which to determine whether that goal has been reached.

The strategic planning process is important in the information systems area because of the long-term impact of many of the operational decisions. One factor that has a significant effect on an information system is the organizational structure. This includes both where the information system lies within the general organization and the way in which the information system is organized.

Planning is an ongoing process that should take into account many factors. The purpose of this chapter has been to show the importance and some of the components of the strategic planning process.

QUESTIONS

1. Why is it necessary to determine the strategic goals of the corporation before setting the strategic goals of the information system?
2. Why should an organization do strategic planning? Why is strategic planning particularly important for the information system?
3. Why is the position of the information system within the firm important to its effectiveness?
4. Who will usually be on the information system steering committee? Why?
5. Explain the function of the information system steering committee.
6. It has been stated that the computer area within the firm can no longer justify its existence by technical explanations of need, but must use cost-benefit analysis and return on investment to justify additional resources. Explain.
7. Explain the basic duties of a computer operator.
8. Previously, most firms had large staffs of data entry personnel; however, presently these firms have only a small number of data entry people in the computer center. Explain why this has occurred.

9. What is the difference between a systems programmer and an applications programmer?

10. What is the difference between an applications programmer and a system analyst?

11. What skills should information center personnel possess?

12. What is the difference between maintenance and development application analysis, design, and programming?

13. How would decentralization of computing affect the organization of the information system in Major Company?

14. Give some examples of environmental scanning and how it would affect an information system in the long term.

15. Assume one of the goals of the information system is to guarantee "good" response time for all online queries. What objectives might be used to achieve this goal?

16. What does it mean to have a highly integrated system? Why is this desirable? Give an example of an integrated system.

17. Some high-level information system professionals have stated that the position of CIO (i.e., vice-president of information resources) is an academic idea which has found limited success in the business community and that most companies are not ready to accept this concept. Why may this be the case? If this is true, does this mean that the concept of a CIO is a bad idea?

CASE ANALYSIS

Case 1

Analyze the organization chart of computing in your school. Explain why the various functional areas are grouped the way they are and discuss who the director of the computer center reports to and how this affects the effectiveness of the information system. In addition, discuss the decentralized computing operations in your school that are not directly under the control of the director of the computer center. How do these decentralized facilities affect the effectiveness of the information system?

Case 2

For one of the following areas of computer hardware, investigate and predict the changes that will occur over the next three years. Be sure to detail the alternative methods of implementation, the changes in price/performance, and the expected life of the specific media. Also list the reference sources you employed to do this environmental scanning.

a. Central processing units
b. Main memory
c. Fast external memory
d. Sequential external memory
e. Printers
f. Operating systems

Case 3

This case involves using the Delphi technique to determine the five most pressing issues involving academic computing at your institution. Each student (i.e., expert) will independently list the five most pressing issues and submit them to the professor. Your professor will act as coordinator and will determine the consensus opinion. The consensus on the most pressing issues will be presented to the class. Each individual will then be asked to resubmit his or her list of the five most pressing issues. At this point the professor will determine the consensus and discuss how the original opinions differed from the second set of opinions.

ADDITIONAL READINGS

BAKOS, J. YANNIS, AND MICHAEL E. TREACY. "Information Technology and Corporate Strategy: A Research Perspective," *MIS Quarterly,* Vol. 10, No. 2, June 1986, pp. 107–119.

CARLYLE, RALPH EMMETT. "CIO: Misfit or Misnomer?" *Datamation,* August 1, 1988, pp. 50–56.

PORTER, MICHAEL E. "From Competitive Advantage to Corporate Strategy," *Harvard Business Review,* May-June 1987, p. 43.

PORTER, MICHAEL E. "How Competitive Forces Shape Strategy," *Harvard Business Review,* March-April 1979, p. 137.

PORTER, M. E., AND V. E. MILLAR. "How Information Gives You Competitive Advantage," *Harvard Business Review,* July-August 1985, p. 149.

SUMNER, MARY, AND ROBERT KLEPPER. "Information Systems Strategy and End-User Application Development," *Data Base,* Vol. 18, No. 4, Summer 1987, pp. 19–30.

ZACHMAN, J. A. "A Framework for Information Systems Architecture," *IBM Systems Journal,* Vol. 26, No. 3, 1987, pp. 276–292.

READINGS BEFORE NEXT CHAPTER

Again, if you have not had an introductory management course it may be helpful to read about developing and implementing plans and personnel policies. As in the previous chapter, consult *Management,* by Ricky Griffin, 2nd edition, Houghton Mifflin, 1987, especially Chapters 6 and 10.

4

ESTABLISHING STANDARDS AND PROCEDURES

To implement goals and objectives it is necessary to develop a series of standards and procedures. Obviously, different goals and objectives will be implemented by establishing different standards and procedures. Since each organization will have different goals, it is only possible to comprehensively address individual situations. However, there are some information system goals which are common to almost all organizations. We will look at how standards and procedures can be established in order to meet these rather general goals.

PROVIDING QUALITY SERVICE

To be successful, one of the goals of the information system should be to supply quality service to its users. The information system is a service organization and its users are its customers. Thus, providing quality service must be a prime goal. This goal as stated is too broad to be operational. Hence, we must be more specific and discuss what factors lead to quality service.

A successful information system is based on a series of factors. The level of success in meeting user needs is often difficult to ascertain. Unfortunately, the user community often emphasizes gross failures to meet expectations. Varying degrees of success, however, are much more difficult to measure. Hence, there must be good communication between the users and the information system staff. In addition, acceptable performance levels must be established and monitored to guarantee their attainment. We will look at ways to increase communication and methods of establishing acceptable performance levels.

COMMUNICATION

The failure of the information system staff to communicate with its user community can be a serious problem. Historically, the lack of communication has caused friction between the information system area and its users. There are a multitude of situations where poor or even nonexistent communication between the information system personnel and their user community has caused problems. Entire application software systems have been designed that did not satisfy user requirements. Also, users' service-level expectations may be totally different from what the information system can deliver. For example, the sales staff may expect 50 telephone order takers to operate simultaneously, while the system was designed to handle a maximum of 25. In many cases, proper communication would have prevented the problem.

The communication system is made up of a series of both formal and informal channels of information interchange. See Figure 4.1 for a list of some methods of communicating with users. At the highest level, the data processing steering committee provides a medium by which major policy issues can be brought to the attention of the director of the information system. Since this committee meets infrequently (perhaps monthly) and will usually have a full agenda, it only allows consideration of major issues that will have a long-term impact on the organization. More pressing issues and those dealing with a small number of users must be addressed through different channels.

One of the most successful ways of communicating with the user population is for the data center to create an information center. This is a separate

Figure 4.1 *Methods of Communicating with Users*

MEANS OF COMMUNICATION	TYPE OF COMMUNICATION
Steering Committee	High-level issues
User Information Center	One-on-one help Formal classes
Newsletters	Announcements of changes in policy and new products
Online Help	Assistance with problems
Electronic Bulletin Board	Informal communication and notification of changes
Electronic Mail	Direct communication to individual users
User Survey	Determining levels of user satisfaction

department within the information systems area which directly helps users. Its goal is to teach people in other areas of the organization how to use the computer resources available to them. This is accomplished by presenting classes, offering a telephone help service to solve problems, and by demonstrating both software and hardware products to prospective users.

The information center can be a very powerful tool. It allows continuous contact between the data center personnel and its users in a nonthreatening atmosphere. Under these circumstances a free exchange of ideas is encouraged. In this way the information systems area will better understand the users of the system, while the users will have a better idea of the constraints placed on the information system. This will breed a more friendly and open atmosphere that should benefit the entire firm. Design and implementation of an information center will be addressed in detail in Chapter 12.

Another important function of the information center is to offer training sessions for the users. With a well-thought-out and structured series of seminars, a wide range of users can be serviced. These sessions present an excellent opportunity to communicate standards to the user community. This will help to create more uniform approaches to solving problems and leads to the development of more maintainable and longer-lasting software.

While the information center is quite useful, often a significant portion of the user population will not use the information center on a consistent basis. This is particularly true for the more sophisticated users. To maintain contact with all of the users, it is necessary to use other means of communication. These include periodic newsletters describing the activities of the data center, online help facilities which allow users to solve problems when logged onto the system, handy readable documentation describing how to use the various components of the system, online bulletin boards which can be accessed directly by the users, and electronic mail facilities in which messages will only be sent to those individuals involved in that activity.

A useful method of determining the level of user satisfaction is to administer a user survey. The results of this survey should give information system personnel a good picture of the system's strengths and weaknesses. The survey can be given to all users at one time or specific user groups at various time intervals. A properly designed and administered survey can give a comprehensive picture of the status of the information system. Since the results of the survey may be one of the few formal representations of user attitudes, the survey can be used as justification for budget realignment or information system reorganization. A partial user survey is shown in Figure 4.2.

Communication involves more than just talking to a user or distributing documentation. The data processing professional must be able to judge the level of expertise of the user. If the professional uses inappropriate vocabulary, encounters with users can actually be detrimental; not solving the user's problem but instead confusing the situation. Care must be taken so that the individuals interacting with users can communicate on an appropriate level. Also, it is important that specific lines of communication are established so that users

Figure 4.2   *Example of a User Survey*

User Satisfaction Survey

This survey is designed to measure the level of user satisfaction for various services offered by Information Systems. Your cooperation and frankness in completing this questionnaire will help us to supply even higher-quality service in the future.

The first section of the questionnaire deals with a description of your department and your function within that department. The second part of questionnaire deals with services you use and your satisfaction with these services.

SECTION 1: User Information

Department: _____

Function within Department: (check one)
High-level Management   _____
Middle Management   _____
Staff   _____

Use of Information System: (check all that apply)
Data Input   _____
Problem Solving   _____
Program Development   _____
Word Processing   _____
Electronic Mail   _____
Data Inquiries   _____
Other   _____
(please specify)   _____

Type of Computer System Used: (check all that apply)
Personal Computer   _____
Distributed Mini   _____
Mainframe   _____
Other   _____
(please specify)   _____

SECTION 2: Satisfaction Levels

For each of the following questions, check the appropriate area if you use the given facility and then rate the quality of the service for that facility

(continued)

Figure 4.2 *(Continued)*

by circling the appropriate number. The rating system is from 1 to 5, where 1 represents the worst service and 5 represents the best service. There is space at the end of each section for written comments. We strongly encourage you to express your feelings more completely by entering written comments. Do not rate the service if you do not use it.

Do you use the Information Center?   Yes ＿＿   No ＿＿

How do you rate each of the following measures of service provided by the Information Center?

Technical expertise of employees	1 2 3 4 5
Timeliness of service	1 2 3 4 5
Quality of documentation provided	1 2 3 4 5
Overall level of service	1 2 3 4 5

     If you have any comments you wish to add, please enter them here. If the space here is insufficient, attach an additional sheet with your comments.

_____

_____

_____

     (The questionnaire continues by rating all of the services.)

contact the appropriate support personnel. If these procedures are not established, then critical personnel will be unnecessarily interrupted, resulting in a dramatic decrease in productivity.

SETTING AND ATTAINING PERFORMANCE LEVELS

Any successful, service-oriented business must guarantee its customers certain minimum levels of service. For example, a certain parcel delivery service guarantees delivery in 24 hours or your money back. The information systems area must operate in a similar manner. The user must be informed about normal service levels, and the data processing area must conform to these standards. Figure 4.3 presents some performance measures that are important to information system users.

     Following are some of the areas where performance levels should be defined. There must be minimum hours established for when the system will be

Figure 4.3 *Measures of Performance Levels*

MEASURE	UNIT OF MEASURE	GROUP AFFECTED
Response Time	Seconds	All Online Users
Turnaround Time	Hours or Fractions of Hours	All Batch Users
Transactions Processed	Transactions per Hour	Users of a Specific System
System Development Time	Weeks, Months, or Years	Future Users of System

available. Unless an unavoidable failure occurs, the system will always be "up" during these guaranteed hours. The system may also be made available beyond these hours. This dictates that preventive hardware and software maintenance and installation of new equipment be scheduled during the nonguaranteed hours. The productivity of other areas in the firm can be adversely affected by the information system's inability to conform to performance standards. There is no easier way of making a political enemy than to cause people to have their performance judged as unsatisfactory. Frequent system failures can have this effect.

For the online users of modern information systems, the most important measure of performance is the interactive response time of online tasks. The usual measure of response time is the time between when the interactive user makes a request to the system and when the response is received by the user. Many organizations will set goals for response time for production-oriented tasks, such as that 90% of all requests have less than a two-second response time. The ideal response time is considered to be less than one second (usually referred to as subsecond response time). A user that is forced to wait for a significant time between interactive queries will quickly become dissatisfied. The attention placed on response time is well justified, since the performance of the user areas can be adversely affected by poor system response. If the terminal operator must wait an inordinate amount of time when entering transactions, this could limit the number of transactions being processed and reduce the efficiency of the entire area.

The control of response time can be a very delicate matter that entails constant vigilance. Often the operations of the system must be specifically scheduled so that response time can be maintained at an acceptable level even during peak load periods.

Another area of concern to users is the turnaround time of batch production jobs. Turnaround time is usually measured as the elapsed time from submission of a job to the delivery of the output to the user. While turnaround is usually measured in hours for large jobs, it still can be critical to users to have a guaranteed maximum to meet their own deadlines.

In some situations it may be more appropriate to measure performance by the number of specific transactions processed per hour. This is a unit of measure more easily understood by the users and also more easily measured by them. No matter which measures of service level are implemented, it is crucial to detect and correct any degradation of performance before it has an adverse affect on the users. Again, this entails considerable long-range planning as discussed in the previous chapter.

Probably the area of greatest user concern and dissatisfaction regarding information system performance is system development. The application development process in many data processing shops has been plagued by missed deadlines and substantial cost overruns. It is essential that data processing management quote realistic estimates of both the time and cost of developing and installing new systems. Since many shops have a large backlog of system development requests, it may take two or three years before a system will even be considered for development. Under these circumstances the lack of commitment in meeting deadlines of projects can cause tremendous dissatisfaction. Managing the systems development process will be discussed in more detail in Chapter 13.

One way of establishing information system performance standards is to negotiate formal contracts with the client departments. These are usually called user contracts. The user contract will detail the rights and duties of both parties. This not only includes the performance parameters of the system, but it also details what the user department will be paying for these services.

User contracts help to clarify the relationship between information systems and each client department. Just the contract negotiation process can be helpful inasmuch as it can detail any problem areas. Hopefully, any misunderstanding can be resolved before the actual services begin.

PERSONNEL POLICIES

In a service organization such as an information system, the quality of the service rendered is probably most correlated with the knowledge, motivation, and skill of the personnel. For this reason it is very important to hire and retain quality employees. Thus, the personnel policies of a firm can have a significant influence on performance. Good people make for a good information system. Figure 4.4 summarizes some important personnel policies.

Hiring decisions should be made in such a way that the most capable people are hired. This should include the checking of a prospective employee's background and references, determining the level of technical skills, and making sure the person will fit into the firm's environment. For beginning-level employees, factors such as grades in college, the type of degree earned, and the reputation of the educational institution granting the degree will carry more weight. Some firms believe in using standard programming aptitude tests to

Figure 4.4 *Important Personnel Policies*

POLICY	DESCRIPTION
Flex Time	Working hours are variable within a specific range
Dual Career Paths	Allows employees to seek either technical or managerial paths
Lateral Career Moves	Allows employees to change jobs without being promoted
Employee Training	Assures employees of remaining technologically current
State-of-the-Art Computing Environment	Helps reduce turnover by keeping employees marketable

screen potential programming staff. A couple of the more popular tests are the Computer Programmer Aptitude Battery and the Wolfe Computer Aptitude Test.

Carefully screening employees can prevent many serious problems in the future. Significant time and money is expended in orienting and training new hires, and large fees may be paid to employment agencies to hire experienced personnel. If this person must be dismissed or becomes dissatisfied and leaves, this investment is lost.

To attract quality people, it is necessary that the benefits are sufficient and the possibilities for career advancement are present. The professional EDP staff, including application programmers, systems analysts, and systems programmers, often have exceptional demands placed on them. This includes having to work irregular hours and under extreme time pressure. For these reasons it is not uncommon that different personnel policies apply to these professionals. Some firms will allow employees to start work at any time within a certain window and work a full day based on that start time. This is referred to as flex time and allows employees more freedom than a nine-to-five job.

Professional employees are usually not paid for the overtime they incur (they are usually referred to as exempt employees). However, many programming and other related computer jobs demand significant unscheduled overtime. This is particularly true when a major software or hardware failure occurs or when a new system is being installed. These individuals will usually be allowed to take compensation time for most overtime incurred. For example, if significant overtime is incurred at the beginning of the week, abbreviated days could be worked at the end of the week. The personnel system should be designed to reward the conscientious employee without allowing the system to be abused. Some firms do not have a formal policy in this regard. Instead, they allow managers to use their discretion in these matters. However, there are still firms that require employees to work regular hours no matter the circumstances. In these situations, it is not uncommon for a programmer to work through the night and then have to report to work at 8:00 A.M. Obviously, the morale of the staff will plummet if this occurs too frequently.

The primary concern of most professionals is their path of advancement within the firm and their professional development. Computer professionals are also concerned with these two issues. The advancement of an EDP professional is not quite as well defined as in other professions. This is partly due to the rapid growth and relative newness of the profession and also because of the highly technical nature of the work. The lack of a strictly defined career path is not completely negative since it allows for flexibility and provides interesting opportunities.

In addition to the normal vertical promotions, data processing allows for many horizontal moves into new and challenging areas. These horizontal moves produce an employee with a broader experience base and one with a wider perspective of the information system. For example, an individual may move from application programming into database administration. A personnel policy that allows for this type of move can be beneficial to both the individual and the firm.

Most professions involve increased managerial and supervisory duties with advancement and promotion. This is also the case for most computer professionals. However, for those in extremely technical areas, developing managerial skills may be difficult or personally unrewarding. These technicians with their in-depth knowledge of the system and vast experience are critical components of an information system. For this reason many firms have what is called a dual career path for EDP professionals. One path would be a managerial path, which would involve an increasing number of subordinates. The other parallel path would be a technical path, which would involve similar pay raises and promotions but no supervisory responsibility. These people are sometimes referred to as individual contributors. Of course, advancement out of the information system area would be unlikely for someone in the technical track, while it would be a definite possibility in the managerial track.

Most computer professionals are also interested in having a challenging and interesting job. Allowing these people to rotate job responsibilities and to make lateral moves within the organization leads to both keeping the personnel motivated and reducing the impact of the resignation of an individual employee. This is particularly important in the computer area where turnover can be quite high.

The availability of the most advanced tools, both hardware and software, can create an attractive professional environment. This helps to assure employees that the firm is interested in their technical growth and keeps them technically abreast of others in the field. In a highly technical and dynamic area, it is also mandatory that a firm have a well-planned training program. Each employee should be advised about the training activities available, and a comprehensive training plan should be developed for each individual. For larger firms, in-house training may be most economical, but there are many other means of training. These include self-study courses including audio and video tapes, written material, and computerized lessons. Employees can also be sent to vendor-conducted training sessions and other types of seminars. Most larger firms will also contribute toward the employee's attainment of advanced degrees by paying part or all of the tuition. At an initial glance training may appear expensive; however, this should be perceived as a wise investment in the productivity of the staff.

Some firms will also encourage their employees to seek professional certification. The certified data processor (CDP) is an example of one form of certification. Not only does certification assure that the employee has a given level of competency, but it also increases the level of professionalism of the individual. Almost all certification includes a mandatory amount of continuing professional education to retain the certification. This introduces additional incentives for the employee to stay current.

With the rapid developments in the computer field, it is easy for the professional to feel as if he or she is stagnating. Good training programs and state-of-the-art tools can attract and retain high-quality staff. Not only does this increase employee morale, but it also encourages the employees to continue to grow and stay technically competent.

EMPLOYEE PERFORMANCE EVALUATION

A major factor in employees' satisfaction is the feeling that their work is appreciated as a contribution to the firm and that their performance is being evaluated fairly. There must be a set of personnel policies established that is conducive to evaluating all employees fairly. Most firms will have periodic employee evaluations. At these times the employee's performance will be judged and a detailed plan will be agreed on to correct any deficiencies.

Performance of some employees within the data processing function may be more difficult to evaluate than the average employee. The system analysis and application programming jobs are two examples. These positions involve nonrepetitive tasks that demand a high degree of innovation, can be very long in duration, and for which there are few or no performance standards. For example, an applications programming team may spend two-and-a-half years developing a new integrated online inventory control and production management system. The present batch inventory control system was designed over a decade ago, and the demands of the new system are very different from the old batch system. It is very difficult to estimate the time and money it will take to produce this system. The true test of the success of the team comes only when the system goes into production. If it functions the way it was expected, then it is a success. The question is: How can management properly evaluate performance under these circumstances?

In general, positions of this type demand adopting different evaluation policies. Instead of evaluating employees against a set standard, it is necessary to develop a series of individual goals and objectives for each employee. Performance is then compared to these personal goals and objectives. This is commonly termed *management by objectives*. In the data processing area, there may be difficulty in accurately defining the individual goals and objectives, especially when dealing with large application programming projects. This topic will be covered in more detail in Chapter 13, which deals with managing the application programming function.

SOFTWARE DEVELOPMENT STANDARDS

To control the system development and maintenance process, it is necessary to establish and enforce standards. These standards should be designed so that they guarantee uniformity of operations without being so rigid as to stifle creativity. To control program development and maintenance, it is necessary to establish both programming and documentation standards. These should be used to guide the staff in coding and documenting systems. This should enable others to understand more easily and maintain the existing systems. Without standards, each individual developer would be free to operate in a unique manner which may not be easily understood by others. This could lead to major problems when it is necessary to do program maintenance or when someone is analyzing the functioning of that system. Figures 4.5 and 4.6 present some possible programming and documentation standards.

The programming standards should include specifications as to what languages should be used to accomplish specific tasks. For example, COBOL may be used for large batch systems, basic assembly language may be used to implement system programming routines, and a query-based fourth generation language may be used to do ad hoc queries to a database. The standards may also include restrictions on the commands to be used. For example, in COBOL there are certain verbs which are not commonly used by most application programmers. To avoid misunderstanding, the use of these verbs may be forbidden. These restrictions may also be enforced for reasons of efficiency. Probably the most common programming standard is the type of structure to be used during the construction of the program. Most firms find that some variation of structured coding makes for more easily understood and maintainable code. The basic consideration in designing a program is not to have the absolute minimum number of lines of code, but to make that code easy for another programmer to

Figure 4.5 *Possible Programming Standards*

STANDARD	EXPECTED RESULT
Specific Language	Reduces necessary training, improves maintainability
Program Structure	Easier to debug and allows for quicker modification
Restricting Available Functions	Prevents use of possible troublesome procedures
Naming Conventions	Produces uniformity in defining data

Figure 4.6   *Possible Documentation Standards*

TYPE OF DOCUMENTATION	FUNCTION
System Narrative	Written explanation of what the system is designed to do
Document Flowchart	High-level picture of how information is processed
Input/Output Formats	Layouts of both the documents going into the system and those being produced by the system
Procedures Manual	Complete explanation to the user on how to control the system
Operations Flowchart	Diagram showing how each physical input and output is related to the operation of the system
Run Manual	Detailed directions to the operators of how the system should run
Hierarchy Chart	Logical diagram of how all of the modules of the system are related
Data Flow Diagram	Schematic representation of the logical relationships between data files, programs, and users
File Layouts and Data Dictionary	Description of how the data is stored in physical files and the naming conventions for the data fields
Module Logic Flowchart	Detailed description of the flow of control in a complex module of a program

understand and maintain. The programming standards should stress this point. Other standards would include variable naming and field definition conventions.

Documentation standards should detail all of the documentation that must be included with every finished system. The failure to document a system properly cannot only make it difficult to maintain, but may cause the end-users so many problems as to make the system unusable. The objectives of documentation include helping the user understand the functioning of the system, explaining the logical flow and storage of data in the system, and describing the logic of each program in the system. For documentation to be of value, it must be oriented toward the level of the target user. For example, end-user documentation should be worded differently than the documentation designed for the operations staff. In addition, the documentation must be easily maintainable. The latter point means that the documentation must be able to be changed as the system changes. For this reason, verbose documentation can be as much a problem as too sparse documentation.

Most firms will require various levels of documentation (see Figure 4.7) and will limit its distribution to specific groups (see Figure 4.8). One set of documentation will be designed for the end-users of the system. The emphasis of this documentation should be to explain how the user can obtain the desired results from the system. This should include an overview of how the various parts of the system coordinate with each other. The highly technical details of a

Figure 4.7(a–d) *Examples of Types of Documentation*

A. DOCUMENT FLOWCHART: PROCESSING A CUSTOMER ORDER

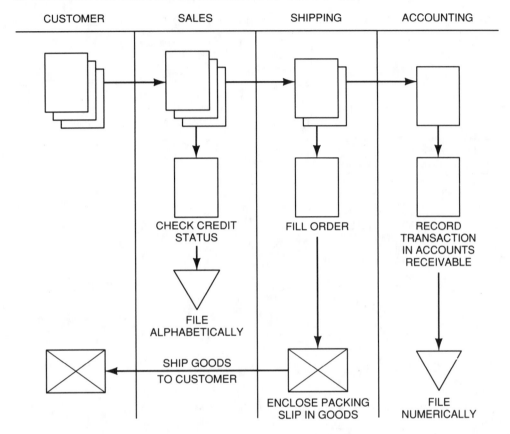

| CUSTOMER | SALES | SHIPPING | ACCOUNTING |

CHECK CREDIT STATUS

FILL ORDER

RECORD TRANSACTION IN ACCOUNTS RECEIVABLE

FILE ALPHABETICALLY

SHIP GOODS TO CUSTOMER

ENCLOSE PACKING SLIP IN GOODS

FILE NUMERICALLY

B. OPERATION FLOWCHART: UPDATING A PAYROLL MASTER FILE

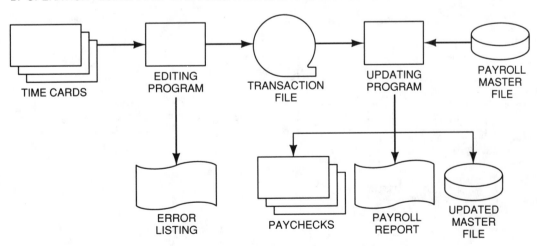

TIME CARDS

EDITING PROGRAM

TRANSACTION FILE

UPDATING PROGRAM

PAYROLL MASTER FILE

ERROR LISTING

PAYCHECKS

PAYROLL REPORT

UPDATED MASTER FILE

Figure 4.7 *(Continued)*

C. DATA FLOW DIAGRAM: A SIMPLIFIED COMPUTING PAYROLL

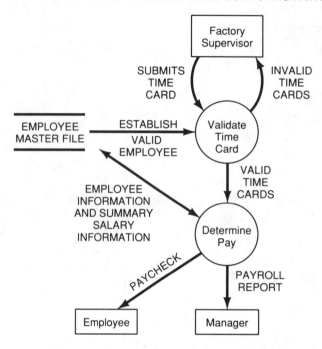

D. HIPO CHART: A SIMPLE ERROR CHECKING PROGRAM

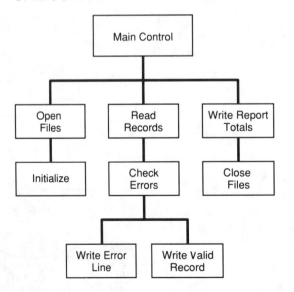

Figure 4.7(e) *Pseudo Code: Simple Error Checking Program*

```
Main-Control
  Perform OPEN-FILE
  Perform READ-RECORDS until last record
  Perform WRITE-REPORT-TOTALS
  STOP-RUN
Open-Files
  Open all files including:
    ERROR-REPORT
    VALID-REPORT
    INPUT-RECORDS
  Perform initialize
Initialize
  Write all report headers
  Initialize all counters
Read-records
  Read a record from the input files
    after last record return to MAIN-CONTROL
  Increment record counter
  .
  .
  .
ETC.
```

well-designed system are usually not of any concern to the user, so these details should not be included in the user documentation.

The user documentation will include a system narrative briefly explaining what the system does and how it does it. This narrative will usually be accompanied by a document flowchart which illustrates how the various input and output documents are processed. It should detail all of the input documents and explain how this data should enter the system and describe any special circumstances that may occur. Also, the format and examples of all output reports must be included. These would be accompanied by explanations of how to interpret each report. Any backup and recovery procedures to be followed must also be fully explained.

The operators involved in running the system should be supplied with a run manual. This manual would document the step-by-step procedures to be followed in running the system. A separate section would detail correct actions to be taken for all exceptional circumstances and error conditions. Unlike the user documentation, which is primarily a narrative and explanation of the functions of the system, the run manual is a cookbook of how to run the system.

The final set of documentation is most complete, and is used by the application and system programmers to maintain and support the system. This documentation will be used to trace and locate any execution problems and will be used when maintenance and changes must be made to the system. This documentation must be much more detailed and technical than that distributed to the users and operators of the system. Of course, the user and operator

Figure 4.8   *Distribution of Documentation*

	USERS	OPERATORS	PROGRAMMERS
Systems Narrative	Yes	No	Yes
Document Flowchart	Yes	No	Yes
Input Documentation Formats	Yes	No	Yes
Output Documentation Formats	Yes	No	Yes
Procedures Manual	Yes	No	Yes
Operations Flowcharts	No	Yes	Yes
Run Manual	No	Yes	Yes
Hierarchy Charts	No	No	Yes
Data Flow Diagrams	No	No	Yes
File Layouts	No	No	Yes
Data Dictionary	No	No	Yes
Module Logic Flowcharts	No	No	Yes

documentation must also be included in the application and system programming documentation, but there will be other more detailed documents also. These may include a structured hierarchical diagram of the system, system flowcharts, data flow diagrams, program pseudocode of each program in the system, file layouts, and logic flowcharts of specific program modules to name just a few of the possible documentation techniques. The combination of techniques to be employed should be fully explained in the firm's documentation standards manual.

Each firm will usually develop its own set of documentation and programming standards. Yearly, these standards must be reviewed and changes made to keep the standards up to date. Entry level personnel should be trained using these standards, and all systems should be reviewed for compliance with these standards before being placed into production.

Other standards which affect the systems development process must also be established. This includes developing a formal procedure for requesting the development of new systems. The procedure should involve a written request initiation form and a set procedure by which this request is evaluated. A separate set of procedures must be established to request changes to any existing system. This again would involve a formal maintenance request form, but it would also include an impact statement concerning the other users of that system. In this way, any changes can be coordinated with all users of a system, reducing friction and ultimately minimizing the total number of maintenance requests.

The quality of the applications software and subsequently the satisfaction of the users depends on establishing and enforcing these standards and procedures. Without proper standards, quality control of the development and maintenance of software becomes almost nonexistent. While some firms have survived in this type of environment, it will eventually have a devastating effect on all aspects of the information system.

OTHER STANDARDS

While setting program development standards is very important, there are other areas in the information system where establishing standards is also desirable. With the substantial application backlog experienced by most firms, departments and individuals have sought other ways of implementing computerized solutions. The acquisition of microcomputers by the user departments has been one approach to the backlog problem. In this way the user can fully control the application development and data processing of the desired function. Unfortunately, this approach will cause other problems if both hardware and software standards are not established immediately to control these acquisitions.

While many micros and minis are first acquired as stand-alone systems, all computing facilities should be perceived as part of an integrated information system. The stand-alone user will most likely want to be connected eventually to the centralized information system. The wealth of data available on the mainframe encourages this. If standards are not set, then connecting diverse technology can lead to many unforeseen problems and be very costly. Establishing a standard hardware and software configuration allows the information systems area to concentrate their efforts, provide higher-quality service, and significantly reduce costs. Having an information center can help enforce these standards. Having the information center provide training, problem solving, and maintenance on only the standard configuration will encourage users to adopt that standard.

So as not to restrict totally users' freedom of choice, some firms will support more than one standard. For example, there may be two or three different types of microcomputers that are considered the company standard. These standards should also be applied to software. In the case of software, the issue is not just a matter of compatibility, but also economics. Many software vendors offer site licenses or bulk purchase discounts. This means that the centralized purchase of multiple copies of software can produce significant savings over individual purchases. The centrally dictated standards may also allow users to acquire technology that is not a supported standard. In this case the user is forewarned that training, debugging, interfacing to other devices, and maintenance will not be supported by the information system staff for this nonstandard equipment. All this would be the responsibility of the individual user. The result of this is to discourage all but the most technical (or foolhardy) user without explicitly forbidding nonstandard technology.

Data definition and usage standards are also an important component of a well-run information system. They must be established to assure data security, integrity, and uniformity. This would include developing a company-wide data dictionary that would uniquely define all data elements in the system. Additionally, COPY libraries (also called macrolibraries) should be established so that programs can fetch data layouts from these predefined libraries. Not only do these libraries introduce standards, but they also reduce the work of the program developer. Establishing and enforcing these standards should be the responsibility of the data management area.

These data standards are so important and sometimes so delicate an issue that a data steering committee (usually called the data authority committee) is established to render advice concerning data standards. Often the data authority committee will be a subcommittee of the information systems steering committee and will report directly to that committee. Their role will also include establishing a set of guidelines on who will be allowed to access specific data and the type of access allowed (i.e., READ only or READ & WRITE).

To paraphrase an old adage: "Information is power." This is particularly true in a computerized information system environment. The ownership and access of data can become crucial issues. This topic will be addressed in more depth in Chapter 15.

BUDGETING

Budgeting is the process by which financial goals are set and funding decisions are made. For the information system's management team, the results of the budgeting process will dictate the rate of growth and the general direction of the entire area for the coming years. There are two major types of budgets: operating budgets, which are short term (usually one year), and capital budgets, which are usually longer term. A majority of the information system's expenses are either discretionary or committed fixed costs. This means that the costs of running the data center stay fairly constant no matter the amount of activity in the center. In addition, the information system is usually considered a service function which does not directly generate revenue. For these reasons, the information systems area must convince upper management of its essential role and the benefits to be derived from the computerization of tasks. The importance of good budget planning cannot be overemphasized.

Budgeting can be a complex and laborious task demanding both good business sense and the knowledge of the political structure of the organization. There are many approaches to budgeting, varying from the incremental approach on one end of the spectrum to zero-based on the other end. Incremental budgeting involves calculating percentage changes to the present or past budget. For example, if the present budget was $2.0 million for operating salaries, we may request $2.3 million based on an expected increase of 10% ($0.2 million) for raises and cost of living increases for present staff and an expected increase in staff size of 5% ($0.1 million). Under the incremental approach, only the increase in staff size and the raises would have to be justified. The present size of the operating staff would not be questioned.

Zero-based budgeting involves the justification of all budget items. This means that any activity, no matter how long it has been in existence, must be cost justified. This can be a very effective management tool that prevents the unjustified continuance of inefficient or ineffective processes. However, the zero-based budgeting process, if done properly, can be very time consuming and demands much of the time of higher management.

Many firms adopt a budgeting system which uses the zero-based approach for all capital expenditures and special projects and uses the incremental approach for normal operating expenditures. For the information systems area, this is very appropriate since the development of new systems and the acquisition of both hardware and software must be preceded by an in-depth cost-benefit analysis. Cost-benefit data can then also be used in the budgeting process.

No matter which budgeting system is used, the manager must be able to anticipate changes in the demand for information system services and the costs involved with providing these services. The managers of each of the individual departments and their subordinates must be fully involved in the budgeting process. They should be the ones who know best the details concerned with their areas. If done properly, the budgeting process will involve communication between the various layers of the organization.

A more detailed discussion of budgeting will be presented in Chapter 9, which deals with financial issues.

MAJOR COMPANY

Following is a description of the ways in which Major Company has implemented some of the information system standards and procedures discussed in this chapter.

Three years ago Major Company established an information center to help users. It was originally intended to deal only with microcomputing. Its original function was to assist users in selecting and implementing microcomputer hardware and software. Management felt that by doing this a de facto standard would be established.

Even with the information center, users were acquiring incompatible hardware and software; hence Major Company management announced the support of only certain hardware and software. Any supported items can be acquired without information system approval. Users can formally request the information center to have new items placed on the supported list. The decision to add or delete items from this list basically lies with the information center area, but all decisions are reviewed by the information system steering committee and approved by the vice-president of information systems. User acquisition of unsupported items must have special approval by this person.

Since its inception, the role of the information center has changed dramatically. It now deals with all forms of computing. Training is one of its biggest duties. Each month a calendar of classes is published. These classes go all the way from the beginner to the advanced user. The classes last from half a day to a full week.

Each functional area with Major Company is assigned a user liaison who works in the information center and monitors the quality of information system service that area is receiving. A computer user survey is also sent out to every user in Major Company in June and December of each year. The results of the survey are compared to previous results and are also used for budgeting purposes.

All system users, including managers, have access to the company-wide electronic mail system. The users associated with a specific product are informed of any changes through this system. For example, some additional functions were added to the SAS statistical package. All SAS users were notified via electronic mail before these functions were added. Since all other users would not be interested, they were not informed of the changes.

In the area of performance levels, Major Company's management feels that this is the key to an effective computer environment. There is a stated policy that subsecond response time is the performance target of the information systems area. Management demands that subsecond response time be accomplished for at least 80% of all online queries and a maximum two-second response time be accomplished 98% of the time. Included in the installation of all new systems is a contract of transaction processing negotiated between the user area and information systems. This contract guarantees the minimum achievable number of specific transactions that the new system will process per hour. The performance of the system is constantly monitored and evaluated. Projections of future system performance are made periodically to anticipate any upcoming performance problems.

In the systems development area, Major Company has historically encountered some rather serious problems. For this reason, the proposal to develop and install a new system must include estimates of minimum, maximum, and expected times and costs of completion. These figures are agreed on by the user, the project leader, and the manager of systems development and are reviewed as the project progresses. The project leader and the other members of the development team are evaluated on their ability to meet these deadlines. This evaluation weighs heavily on their promotions and salary increases.

Major Company believes it is very important to invest in the development of its employees. There are regularly scheduled intensive professional development classes. They are taught by more experienced staff members, local consultants, and vendor representatives. These classes are designed specifically for data center professionals and not the general user community. For more specialized training, employees are sent to either the vendor's training center or national seminars. Each professional data center employee is required to take a minimum of two weeks of professional education a year. During the annual performance review for each employee, the education plan for the upcoming year is established.

Attaining advanced degrees is encouraged by the firm paying all tuition for an advanced technical degree in the employee's area of expertise. For non-technical degrees such as a Masters of Business Administration, Major Company pays only half of the tuition. This policy was established because of the high turnover rate of employees immediately after obtaining this type of degree. To encourage these employees to stay with the firm, the remaining part of this tuition is paid to the employee in equal increments at the end of each of three years after completion of the degree.

SUMMARY

The goals and objectives of the information systems area can be operationalized by adopting a set of standards and procedures. One of the goals of the information system area must be to provide quality service to its users. To accomplish this, it is first necessary to understand the user needs. There must be adequate communication between the information system and its users. There are numerous channels by which the information system personnel can communicate with users. These include using an information system steering committee, newsletters, online help facilities, user documentation, electronic bulletin boards, and user surveys.

Target levels of service should be established and monitored. This should include online system response time, batch turnaround time, minimum number of transactions processed per hour for specific systems, and the development and installation time for new systems. These standards will give the users a set of minimum performance expectations for the information system.

In the long run, the quality of the service provided by the information system is probably most affected by the level of expertise and commitment of the information system personnel. Establishing personnel policies that create a positive working environment and give the individual an opportunity to grow professionally are important to obtaining and retaining quality staff.

Other important standards to establish include programming and documentation standards, hardware and software standards for decentralized purchases, and data definition and usage standards.

The manager of an information system has to use judgment in setting goals, developing standards, and in dealing with the budgeting process. If the standards that are set are too rigid, they may stifle creativity. However, without adequate standards, chaos could result.

QUESTIONS

1. Should different types of communication be used with different types of users? Explain.
2. Describe the ways in which an information system manager may learn that users are encountering problems.
3. Describe what services an electronic mail system offers a user.
4. Sometimes online help facilities may be more helpful than paper documentation. Explain when each is most appropriate.
5. Some departmental managers claim that user surveys often do more harm than good. Why might they believe this?

6. Design an appropriate user satisfaction survey to be distributed to under-graduate students at your school's computer center. Restrict it to no more than three pages in length.

7. Why are online response time and batch turnaround time important to end-users? Which of the two is usually more important?

8. If a computer center has a large applications development backlog, how can this backlog be reduced? Be specific and discuss the advantages and disadvantages associated with each solution.

9. Describe what should be included in an application system maintenance request form. Explain fully.

10. There is a commonly used statement that information is power. Explain the significance of this statement and why it is true. Give an example.

11. Why does an organization do budgeting?

12. What is the difference between zero-based budgeting and incremental budgeting?

13. What is the difference between capital budgeting and operational budgeting?

14. If employees were allowed to work whenever they wanted, it could be possible that meetings would never be fully attended because all of the participants were never at work at the same time. How does flex time solve this problem?

15. Why do programmers and systems analysts sometimes have to work irregular hours? Have you had a similar experience in programming classes? Explain why this has occurred.

16. Studies have shown that many computer professionals do not rank money as the most important component of their job satisfaction. What other factors do you think are important? Explain.

17. Some people claim that in the computer field learning only begins in college and continues throughout a professional career. Describe what you must learn after leaving school and why your college education must be supplemented immediately.

18. Examine professional publications and list five professional seminars that would be appropriate for you to attend. Calculate the cost of each of these seminars. Be sure to include the cost of transportation, lodging, meals, registration fees, etc.

19. What is a user contract? What is the purpose of developing user contracts?

CASE ANALYSIS

Case 1

Assume you are an entry level employee who is to start work for a firm just like Major Company. Design a training program for yourself (and other similar employees) for the first year you are to work for the firm. To make the assignment more specific, you may assume that you will be doing maintenance programming for the accounting system area. The primary tools that you will be using will be COBOL and fourth generation languages (i.e., report writing-type software). These will be running on a large IBM mainframe using the MVS/ESA operating system.

The idea behind the training is for you to become a productive member of the firm in a reasonable amount of time and at a reasonable expense to the firm.

Be specific as to the courses that you would take, the method of delivery of the course, and at what point in the year you would take the course.

Case 2

You have been requested to do a consulting engagement for the Topsey-Tervey Company, a manufacturer of gyroscopes and scientific instruments. Recently the director of information systems for Topsey-Tervey has resigned amidst controversy. It appears a number of the users of the computer system have become very dissatisfied with the service they have been receiving. This and other factors appear to have caused the resignation of the director.

You have been hired to develop a proposal for changes to be made to the existing system and to specify the desired attributes and qualifications of the new director of information systems. This will include specific proposals for changes in all areas of computing including (but not limited to) organization, employment, budgeting, hardware, software, education, user relations, and any other aspect that you deem important. The report should detail the way in which changes should be made, a schedule of implementation, and an estimate of the costs associated with each change. Following is some data concerning Topsey-Tervey and its computer system which may be of help.

Financial History. Topsey-Tervey started as a contractor for the military making precision gyroscopes. It has been in business for over 40 years and has grown steadily since it first started. Presently it still does work for the military and aerospace sectors; however, an increasing portion of its revenues has been coming from the manufacture of precision scientific instruments.

Present Financial Condition. The present financial position is quite sound; however, there is the feeling throughout the company that growth could be greater and income increased if certain problems were solved. There have been some major problems in the following areas and at least some of these problems have been caused by either a lack of good record keeping and information dissemination or an untimely distribution of this information.

> *Sales:* Due to a lack of readily available information, it is very difficult for the sales staff to determine the delivery date of goods to a customer and to track an order once it is placed.
> *Back Orders:* If goods are back-ordered, sometimes the back order is not properly

Comparative Balance Sheets (in millions of dollars)
Topsey-Tervey Company

	19X1	19X2	19X3	19X4	19X5
Assets					
Cash	28	29	30	33	30
Accounts Rec. (net)	85	109	153	184	216
Investments	40	32	42	50	57
Inventory	1,220	1,620	2,080	2,561	2,917
Plant & Equipment (net)	6,082	7,305	8,845	10,109	11,366
Land	834	1,087	1,317	1,576	1,762
Total	8,289	10,182	12,467	14,513	16,348
Liabilities & Owners' Equity					
Accounts Payable	42	52	68	86	102
Bonds Payable	2,085	2,657	3,312	4,333	5,097
Common Stock	1,086	1,312	1,601	1,601	1,601
Paid in Capital in Excess	2,519	2,953	3,640	3,640	3,640
Retained Earnings	2,557	3,208	3,846	4,853	6,010
Total	8,289	10,182	12,467	14,513	16,348

Comparative Income Statements (in millions of dollars)
Topsey-Tervey Company

	19X1	19X2	19X3	19X4	19X5
Sales (net)	18,742	21,288	24,042	26,821	29,321
Cost of Goods Sold	7,807	8,617	9,610	10,511	11,325
Gross Profit	10,935	12,671	14,432	16,310	17,996
Other Expenses					
Selling Expense	1,205	1,566	1,826	2,233	2,454
Admin. Expense	1,481	1,911	2,165	2,540	3,069
General Expense	1,660	2,110	2,781	3,313	3,770
Info Systems Expense	121	126	131	137	143
R&D Expense	3,781	3,731	3,680	3,627	3,568
Total Other Expenses	8,248	9,444	10,583	11,850	13,004
Net Income before Taxes	2,687	3,227	3,849	4,460	4,992
Income Tax Expense	920	982	1,193	1,410	1,587
Net Income	1,767	2,245	2,656	3,050	3,405
Earnings per share	.85	1.10	1.40	1.65	1.91
Dividend per share	.42	.55	.70	.82	.95

filled when the goods finally arrive. The new goods may be used for current sales instead of for filling the back orders.

Inventory: The present system makes it very difficult to determine proper inventory levels. Inventory programs are run on a weekly basis, and the people in charge of this area are certain that this is not adequate. They believe that the firm may be carrying as much as an additional 30% of inventory due to these problems.

Purchasing: The problems in inventory carry over into the purchasing area. There are many times when excess goods or inadequate amounts of goods are ordered. Again, the problem lies in inadequate or untimely information.

Production: Production scheduling appears to be fairly adequate. Production schedules are run nightly on a batch basis for the next day, and any changes are done manually during the day.

Personnel: The personnel people have been having problems producing their federal reports on a timely basis. This is particularly a problem when lawsuits are pending, since the legal staff cannot be given answers to their specific requests as quickly as necessary.

Research and Development: The engineering staff has its own set of minicomputers in which to do their own computer processing. These machines are mainly used to do CAD/CAM work and to run FORTRAN-based simulation programs. For the most part, they are satisfied with this arrangement. Their major problem is dealing with information which resides on computers outside of their area. This is of primary concern when dealing with the scheduling system, which is on the main system.

Accounts Payable: Again, untimely information in this area often results in a substantial loss in discount for quick payment. On more than one occasion, bills have remained unpaid for such a long period of time that the vendor has threatened to deny credit.

Accounts Receivable: The potential for loss of income in this area is substantial. The information system does not handle this area well enough to track overdue accounts and force their collection. Also, the system has difficulty determining whether discounts taken by customers are valid.

General Management: These people are upset over the state of information processing in the organization. They feel that many of their decisions are made using inadequate information which should be readily available from the information system. This problem was probably the major cause for the resignation of the previous director of information systems.

Structure of the Organization. The company is organized in a rather traditional manner. The firm is primarily based on a centralized organizational philosophy. It has the following major areas:

Production: This area employs the largest number of people and has the biggest budget of any department. It coordinates the activities of eight major manufacturing plants in the U.S.

Marketing: This area is responsible for the sales of the products. Its major market is in the U.S. However, it does do some business overseas.

Research and Development: Responsible for the development of new products and the testing of existing products.

Personnel: Responsible for the recruiting of new employees, the evaluation of employees, and employee training.

Finance: The accounting and financial management of the firm is the responsibility of this area. The information systems area is included here.

Information System Organization. The information system is divided into three areas:

Operations: This area is responsible for the proper running of the system, distribution of user output, and collection and processing of user input. There are three departments under this area. They include production and control, computer operations, and systems programming.

Applications Programming: This area contains systems analysis and programming divided into a maintenance area and a development area.

Database and Telecommunications: This group is responsible for the administration of the database and telecommunication facilities throughout the firm. This includes security, integrity, and backup of these systems.

Current Computer Resources. The firm has the following IBM mainframe hardware:

3090 Model 600: Batch production of financial systems
3090 Model 600: Batch production of nonfinancial systems
3090 Model 600: Development and testing systems
3090 Model 400: IMS production systems
3090 Model 200: For user oriented systems, such as DB2 (i.e., SQL)

The firm has the following major software systems:

VM/CMS: For development and testing
MVS/ESA AND JES3: For production systems
IMS/DB: For large database applications
CICS: For interactive systems
DB2: For smaller user oriented database applications
SNA-ACF/VTAM: For networking of systems

Computer Center Personnel. The computer center has the following personnel paid within specific salary ranges:

POSITION	NUMBER OF EMPLOYEES	SALARY RANGE
Operators	44	$16,000–32,000
Production & Control	58	17,000–38,000
Data Entry	21	13,000–22,000
System Programmers	14	32,000–72,000
Application Programmers	78	26,000–45,000
Programmer/Analysts	71	33,000–60,000
System Analysts	52	39,000–66,000
Specialists (Database, etc.)	23	38,000–69,000
Management	56	48,000–123,000
TOTAL EMPLOYEES	417	

The foregoing describes only the personnel at the central site. This does not include computer specialists employed by other departments such as in research and development and other areas.

EDP's Recent Past.   Within the last five years, the computer area has seen an increase in its staff of about 7% per year. In addition, the employee salaries have increased at a rate of about 5% per year. These raises have generally been across the board raises with little or no money going for merit increases. The company as a whole has had average raises of 4% per year, and management feels it has been mildly generous when dealing with the computer specialists.

The employee turnover in the computer area has been quite substantial and appears to be increasing over the past couple of years. Last year turnover was over 25%. A majority of the people who left were considered to be highly skilled, productive individuals. Most the replacements were new college graduates. This high turnover rate has caused the disruption of some major projects. On-the-job training of new people to assume the responsibilities for existing systems has taken a good deal of time.

The workload in the applications programming area has seen a significant shift toward maintenance programming. Presently it is estimated that 90% of programming and analysis time is spent on maintenance programming. Presently the only new system under development is a new employee benefits system. The old employee benefits system is no longer of value since the entire pension plan has changed and federal laws governing this area have changed. The old system was batch and the new system will be online.

Applications Presently Running.   Following is a list of the major computer applications presently running at Topsey-Tervey.

AREA	APPLICATION	DESIGN
Financial	Payroll	Online
	General Ledger	Batch
	Accounts Receivable	Batch
	Accounts Payable	Batch
	Fixed Assets	Batch
	Budgeting	Batch
	Income Tax	Batch
	Portfolio Management	Online
Production	Inventory Control	Batch
	Raw Material Ordering	Batch
	Production Scheduling	Batch
	Work Force Scheduling	Batch
	Long-Range Planning	Batch
	Preventive Maintenance	Online
Marketing	Order Entry	Batch
	Order Tracking	Batch
	Sales Commissions	Batch
	Sales Analysis	Batch

(continued)

AREA	*APPLICATION*	*DESIGN*
	Market Research	Batch
	Sales Forecasting	Batch
Personnel	Employee Benefits	Batch (online under development)
	Equal Opportunity	Batch
	Recruiting	Batch
	Employee History	Batch
	Employee Claims	Batch
	Employee Evaluation	Batch
Research and Development	CAD/CAM	All are run interactively on HP
	Statistical Analysis	1000 computers located in R&D.
	Simulations	

Computer Center Operating Budgets.   Following is a summary of the computer center operating budget for the last five years. Upper management has decided not to increase the budget significantly due to the decreasing costs of mainte-nance, power, and hardware leasing. This budget only includes recurring items and does not include capital expenditures.

Computer Center Operating Budget (in millions)

	19X1	*19X2*	*19X3*	*19X4*	*19X5*
Salaries	46.2	49.7	52.1	55.2	57.8
Maintenance Fees	8.3	8.5	8.9	8.5	8.3
Software Leasing	12.7	14.1	16.2	18.4	19.8
Hardware Leasing	10.3	8.7	6.0	2.9	.6
Outside Consultants	2.6	4.2	6.4	9.4	12.4
Telecommunications	4.2	4.4	4.7	4.9	5.2
Electricity	1.1	1.1	1.1	1.2	1.2
Supplies	2.2	2.4	2.5	2.7	3.0
Travel & Training	1.3	1.3	1.4	1.4	1.5
Other	4.2	7.7	5.1	3.5	2.7
TOTAL	**94.1**	**102.1**	**104.4**	**107.9**	**113.0**

Computer Center Capital Budget.   The computer center has been given a rea-sonably large capital budget in which to purchase hardware. Generally it is a firm policy not to purchase application software. Instead the firm designs its own application software. Only in rare instances, when the software was needed immediately, was any software purchased. This type of activity is usu-ally not budgeted for, but funds are allocated on an emergency basis.

Data Processing Capital Budget (in millions)

	19X1	*19X2*	*19X3*	*19X4*	*19X5*
Central Processors	5.3	5.0	6.7	8.2	7.3
Peripherals	8.7	10.9	13.1	14.4	16.4
Renovation	8.3	2.3	1.9	1.0	1.3
Other Hardware	4.5	4.9	5.3	5.9	6.4
TOTAL	**26.8**	**23.1**	**27.0**	**29.5**	**30.4**

Note: Other Hardware includes microcomputers.

The amount being spent on equipment is increasing because of the tremendous increase in demand for computer services. The per unit hardware prices have been decreasing rapidly, but the total amount of CPU power needed has increased at an even faster rate.

CPU Utilization. Following is a very crude examination of the utilization of the five main processors that Topsey-Tervey owns.

Average CPU Utilization Performance Statistics by Shift

PROCESSOR	*SHIFT 1* *(8:00–4:00)*	*SHIFT 2* *(4:00–12:00)*	*SHIFT 3* *(12:00–8:00)*
3090 Model 600–Batch Prod. Fin.	89%	84%	81%
3090 Model 600–Batch Prod. Non-Fin.	84%	82%	93%
3090 Model 600–Test	88%	23%	19%
3090 Model 400–IMS	28%	11%	9%
3090 Model 200–DB2	12%	3%	1%

Other Computing in the Firm. Due to the lack of responsiveness by the data center, many areas in the organization have begun to acquire their own computer facilities at their own expense. Besides the minis in research and development, these computers have been limited to single-user micro systems. Following is a summary of the micros that central management is presently aware of.

Micros by Area by Vendor

	PRODUCTION	*MARKETING*	*R & D*	*PERSONNEL*	*FINANCE* *(NON-DP)*	*DP*
IBM/PS2	226	0	0	18	118	110
IBM/PC	184	0	124	13	68	322
AMIGA	3	167	0	8	25	0
APPLE MacIntosh	3	167	0	30	8	32

(continued)

	PRODUCTION	MARKETING	R & D	PERSONNEL	FINANCE (NON-DP)	DP
HP Vetra	0	0	221	30	4	0
DEC PRO	0	57	0	10	38	0
COMPAQ 486	0	0	162	2	8	85
Others	116	214	40	19	87	0
TOTAL	**610**	**615**	**547**	**130**	**356**	**549**

These machines are used for various applications developed by non-data processing individuals. Some of these micro applications extend the results of the main system while others have no relation to the mainframe applications. At present none of the micro users is connected to the mainframe, and the information system area has not been encouraging them to be.

Company Educational Policy.   The company's policy on employee education is that each individual is responsible for his or her own education. While an extension of skills is encouraged by the company, it will not pay for training classes, professional seminars, or the seeking of additional college education. The company does make available self-instruction courses which the employees can study on their own time. The computer center trains its employees by on-the-job experience. This means that a less skilled employee is assigned to a more advanced employee. The advanced employee will direct the newer employee and answer questions when necessary.

General Feeling In and About Data Processing.   The general feeling of the employees in data processing is that there is too much work for the staff. The high turnover rate causes a constant shuffling of assignments. Some people complain that as soon as they learn a system they are taken off of that system to fix a major disaster on some other unfamiliar system. Also, many people who were previously working in new systems development are now doing maintenance, which does not appeal to them.

The systems that are in place are quickly becoming very difficult to maintain. Some blame this on the pressure to do more than is possible, while others blame this on the lack of consistent standards caused by the large number of new employees.

The users tend to perceive the data processing area as a nonresponsive group that does whatever it pleases, whenever it pleases. A few of the more knowledgeable users realize the problems that data processing is having and are understanding. However, these people still need to get their work done and they are becoming frustrated.

The average user has been told that there will be at least a four-year delay before any new request for system development can be undertaken. The data processing personnel think that this estimate is much too optimistic. They estimate a minimum of six years.

Summary of Your Responsibilities. The preceding has presented much material. However, no case study can substitute for being in a situation to ask questions and judge the circumstances for yourself. If you feel that there are areas where additional information is necessary, describe what you need to know and how you would go about getting it. If you make assumptions, state what the assumption is and attempt to justify the assumption.

In summary, you are to analyze this company and make specific recommendations for changes to be made involving data processing. These recommendations should be accompanied by convincing documentation as to why the change should be made, the cost to implement the change, and the timetable for implementation. In addition, you are responsible for developing guidelines for the hiring of a new director of information systems. Probably the single most important thing to remember in a situation like this is that your plan be realistic enough for upper management to accept. A plan that is too radical (for example, immediately increases the data processing budget tenfold) will be dismissed without any reasonable consideration.

ADDITIONAL READINGS

BALENSON, D. M. "Automated Distribution of Cryptographic Keys Using the Financial Institution Key Management Standard," *IEEE Communications Magazine*, Vol. 23, No. 9, September 1985, pp. 41–46.

BARTIK, JEAN. "MAP: A User Revolt for Standards," *Data Communications*, Vol. 14, No. 13, December 1985, pp. 147–156.

CHIEN, J. Y. "Detailed Tests Show How Well Industrial Local Network Performs," *Data Communications*, Vol. 14, No. 9, August 1985, pp. 119–131.

GREENLEE, M. B. "Requirements for Key Management Protocols in the Wholesale Financial Services Industry," *IEEE Communications Magazine*, Vol. 23, No. 9, September 1985, pp. 22–28.

KERR, SUSAN. "User Group Chiefs Lukewarm about the Impact of OSF," *Datamation*, July 1, 1988, p. 19.

READINGS BEFORE NEXT CHAPTER

Be sure that you have read Appendix A and Appendix B; otherwise the previous chapters should be adequate preparation.

5

PHYSICAL ENVIRONMENT

IMPORTANCE OF PHYSICAL ENVIRONMENT

The physical environment in which the information system operates is an important factor to the successful operation of the system. Many of the matters to be considered in this chapter may appear to be rather mundane, such as the layout of the computer center or the source of electrical power for the system. However, these considerations can be critical no matter how small the computer installation. Failure to deal with potential problems properly could result in a catastrophic failure of the system with an extended period of down time.

We will discuss the factors that should be taken into consideration when designing the physical environment for computer equipment. While this discussion will be concerned mainly with the design of large data centers, these factors are important no matter the size of the computer installation. Even with a single stand-alone micro-computer, the physical environment should be carefully considered.

While the manager of information systems is usually not responsible for making most of the decisions with respect to site selection and building design, the manager must be closely involved in the process. Architects, engineers, and contractors will usually not be aware of the special resource demands of a computer center. The data center personnel must communicate these needs to the people making the selection and designing the facility.

In this chapter, we will consider many of the controllable factors involved in the physical environment of the system. We will discuss site selection, building construction and modification, machine room layout, heating and cooling, electrical power supplies, physical security, and other related issues.

DATA CENTER SITE SELECTION

The geographical location of a data center will have a significant effect on the usefulness of the system. For some firms, this may not be a difficult decision if all of its facilities are centralized in one geographical area. The choice is obvious. Many firms have a substantially more difficult decision. The decentralized nature of a firm may not make the data center location an easy decision.

The first decision of site selection is the geographical area in which to place the new center. There are many factors that must be considered. Figure 5.1 lists some aspects of location selection that should be taken into consideration.

The location of choice should be close to other company facilities, allowing for better and cheaper communications. The area should have a pool of qualified personnel from which to hire or at least be in an area which is an attractive place to live. It is particularly important to recruit and attract highly qualified individuals. The more attractive the living conditions (including a quality local transportation system, a low cost of living, educational opportunities, and a desirable social environment), the higher the probability of hiring or transferring quality employees and then retaining them.

The quality of the public services in the area is important. An adequate transportation system is required for access to the facilities by staff, vendor personnel, and others. This would include both good, convenient highways and an airport having regularly scheduled service. These public services must also include reliable utilities. Quality electrical power and telecommunications are particularly important because these resources are the lifeblood of a computer center. Electrical power provides the energy to drive the computers and environmental control systems. The telephone system allows users and computers in other locations to communicate with the data center.

Figure 5.1 *Selecting Geographical Location*

Things to look for in an area:
   Close to other company facilities
   Pool of qualified personnel available
   Attractive location to live
   Good transportation facilities
   Reliable public utilities—especially telephone and
      electrical power
   Vendors supply service in this area
Things to avoid in an area:
   High probability of natural disaster—earthquake,
      flood, hurricanes, etc.
   Hazardous industries in area
   Areas of urban unrest

It is also important that the computer vendors with which the company deals provide high-quality and timely remote service and maintenance to the area under consideration. This is an important issue to the continuing smooth operation of the data center. If a failure occurs in the computer system, the quick diagnosis of the problem and replacement of parts is critical.

There are certain conditions to avoid when selecting the geographical area. Natural hazards should be minimized, if possible. Earthquakes, floods, mud slides, forest fires, hurricanes, and other potential dangers must be considered. Besides natural hazards there are also man-made hazards to be avoided. Locations near potentially dangerous industries such as chemical plants, refineries, or other facilities which have a higher probability of fire or explosion are undesirable. This also includes airport landing paths which have an increased chance of disaster. Not only should the present potential for disaster be considered, but also the future potential. Zoning of adjacent open land should be taken into consideration. The construction of potentially hazardous facilities on this adjacent property must be of concern. Of course, the easiest way of protecting against undesirable development is to acquire this land and hence control the future development. For most firms this is an option that is too expensive to pursue.

No area is free from all hazards; however, with proper planning it is possible to minimize these risks or design the facility to withstand them. After the geographical area is chosen, it is necessary to select the specific site on which to locate the data processing center.

SITE SELECTION AND BUILDING SECURITY

When choosing the building site, it is important to find property which has enough space for future expansion. Many firms attempt to make the facility as attractive as possible to their employees. This means having adequate parking, convenient access to public transportation, recreational facilities, and a generally attractive atmosphere.

If the firm is to build a new building to house computer facilities or is using an existing structure which will be renovated, many factors have to be considered to make the center functionally efficient. The facility must be designed for efficiency of operations, protection from physical hazards, ease of use, and at the same time be economical.

The physical security of the data center is a crucial issue. The data center is a critical component in the operation of any business. The temporary failure of the computer facilities will result in a major disruption of the business. A disaster which results in the destruction of a substantial portion of the computing facilities could result in problems so serious that the future existence of the firm can be jeopardized.

The building site should be surrounded by a fence or walls which are high enough to discourage intruders. The number of entrances should be limited, and guards or at least television cameras should monitor these entrances. During nonpeak hours some of the gates can be closed and locked. This reduces the responsibility of the security staff. Proper building design would make access of the center restricted to authorized personnel. This can be accomplished by a wide range of options. First, the building should not be conspicuous as to its function as a computer center. The sign on the building may not even state that this is a computer center; there may just be a building number. All trash that would indicate the presence of a computer center should be placed in trash bins that are not easily visible. Also, the computer hardware should not be in a high-traffic area in the building or be given a high degree of visibility.

When firms first became involved in computing, they placed their computers in highly visible locations with the equipment usually displayed behind all-glass partitions. Companies were proud of their computers and wanted to project a high-tech image. This changed with the terrorism of the late 1960s, when computer centers suddenly became primary targets. The present trend is to place computers in highly secure areas with limited access and few if any windows.

Access can also be controlled by using identification badges or cards for each employee and by having doors that can only be opened by authorized personnel. A low-cost solution is to have push-button combination locks on the critical doors (Figure 5.2). The combination would only be given to authorized employees and would be changed periodically. This system has the major flaw that the combination can usually be obtained by casual observation. A better, but more expensive, method is to have magnetically coded identification cards for each employee. Access through a specific door can only be gained by inserting the card (see Figure 5.3). A computer reads the card, determines whether that individual is allowed access, and then releases the door lock. The information on who entered a specific area and at what time can be saved for future analysis. If personnel are required to use these cards for both entrance and exit of all secure areas, then a comprehensive record of activity can be obtained. For extreme security, a double door system can be employed in which an intruder can be

Figure 5.2 *Push Button Combination Lock*

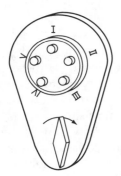

Figure 5.3   *Magnetic Card Reader*

allowed to pass through the first door but is trapped in the passageway between the two doors while the computer alerts security personnel.

It is easier to observe and detect violations of physical security than it is to protect the data, monitor the access to the system, and control the communications. While physical security is important, the protection of the data and access to the system may be even more important because of the difficulty of discovery. The building must be designed to help prevent electronic eavesdropping and interference from external power sources. For example, a radio system close to your site could generate radio waves that would interfere with your processing. To protect against this and also for highly classified operations, the computer room could have a fine wire mesh imbedded in the walls. This would prevent the penetration of external signals and also prevent unauthorized monitoring of electronic impulses generated by the system. The phone lines entering the bulding should terminate in a secure location, and there should be the option of monitoring these lines for wiretaps and, if necessary, encryption of the data being transmitted.

BUILDING DESIGN

A building that is to house a computer center will have different design considerations than a typical office building. The building must meet the special needs demanded by computers, including heating and cooling, electrical power, access control, load bearing capacity of floors, height of ceilings to allow installation of false floors, communication lines, lighting, and other factors.

One of the more difficult problems involves the wiring of the building. The technology in data communications is changing so fast that it is difficult to predict the wiring needs in the near future. Many firms routinely reconfigure a large percentage of their terminals and micros each year. Also, computer use is growing so fast that new devices are added to the system almost daily. The best wiring scheme will allow for flexibility. Being able to change the system quickly and inexpensively will promote smooth transitions in technology.

A good approach is to use covered raceways which allow for all voice, data, and video transmission media to be located in one raceway. Wiring raceways are usually placed in the ceiling and can be either covered or open depending on local fire codes. Raceways are designed so that additional wire can be strung simply by placing it in the raceway with no need for installing additional conduit or for doing major renovations to the building. Because of the flexibility of installing new cables, raceways will easily allow companies to merge voice, data, and video media as this technology becomes available.

Most local fire codes do not allow common types (vinyl coated) of unprotected wire (wire not in conduit or raceways) in the ceiling and between walls (called the open air plenum). The reason for this is that common types of wire will produce deadly fumes when the coating melts. Since laying conduit can be quite expensive and very inflexible, an alternative to raceways is to use Teflon®-coated wire in the open air plenums. Wire coated with Teflon is allowed in these spaces since it will not produce toxic gases during a fire. Even though the wire is more expensive, in most cases this is a better alternative than standard PVC coated wire in conduit.

Air conditioning and heating in the building is a major consideration. While the air conditioning of the machine room will be handled by special equipment, it is also necessary to have sufficient capacity and controllability of the system to handle areas that have clusters of terminals and also to provide temporary backup in case there is a failure in the machine room cooling system. Thus, many new buildings will have a computer-controlled system that circulates the heat from the machine room to the rest of the building. Even in colder climates, offices using this type of system may be able to heat the entire building using only "waste" heat. The cooling requirements can be determined by the total number of British Thermal Units (BTUs) generated by the equipment. The manufacturers' specifications will supply the number of BTUs generated by specific pieces of equipment.

The electrical power coming into the building is an important consideration. There must be a separate power source for the main computers and isolated power supplies for terminals and microcomputers. Heavy equipment on the same circuit will cause power fluctuations which will adversely affect the terminals and especially micros. Additionally, the building should be properly grounded to prevent disruption due to lightning strikes.

COMPUTER ROOM DESIGN

The computer room should be configured for safe and efficient operations and be large enough to allow for future expansion. A raised floor is a mandatory item in any machine room that contains mainframe processors. This type of flooring has many benefits. It allows all cabling to be routed under the floor. It prevents small accumulations of water from damaging the equipment and allows the chilled air to circulate under the floor and to be blown through the equipment to cool it (see Figure 5.4). The false floor is supported by an open framework of supports, and no floor panels are placed under machinery. Instead, the machinery rests on the pillars that support this framework. The machinery is open on both the bottom and top, allowing cold air to pass through the equipment, dissipating the heat. To prevent water damage to equipment, water detectors should be placed under the false floor.

The environment within the center should be controlled to prevent damage to the equipment. Heat and moisture are two of the worst enemies of computers. The temperature of the computer room should be between 65 degrees and 75 degrees Fahrenheit and relative humidity should be held between 45% and 55%. Extremes in humidity can be harmful; when too high, moisture condenses, and when too low, static electricity becomes a problem. Either of these can cause damage to or disruption of the system. It is important that rapid fluctuations in either temperature or humidity also be avoided.

The computer room should have its own cooling system, which could be augmented by the main system in case of failure. The system in the computer room will precisely control both temperature and humidity and provide necessary documentation for maintenance contracts. Most vendors demand that a permanent record of both temperature and humidity be kept to validate maintenance contracts. If a device failure is caused by insufficient cooling or humidity control, then the maintenance contract could be void. The air conditioning sys-

Figure 5.4 *Air Circulation Through Equipment*

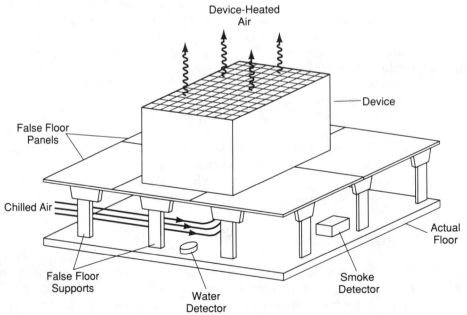

tem must also control dust and other airborne particles. The system will have filters to trap these particles and maintain a positive air pressure differential in the machine room to prevent airborne particles from entering the room when a door is opened. If you have ever been in a computer center, you may have noticed that doors that open inward take much effort to open, while those that open outward literally fly open. Another way of controlling dust is to place "dirty" machines (those that produce airborne particles), such as printers, in a separate controlled area. This will reduce the amount of potentially damaging paper dust in the machine room. Figure 5.5 shows the relative sizes of various particles.

In larger computer centers the devices that do not need human intervention, such as CPUs, disk drives, and controllers, will be placed in a one area, while the remaining equipment will be in a separate area. This allows the environment to be tailored for a specific device. Both CPUs and disk drives generate a lot of heat. By isolating these devices, the temperature in areas where people work can be more easily regulated for the comfort of the people and not the machines. Some computer centers are kept so cold that the operators are in constant discomfort.

Other considerations in room design include installing a vapor barrier in the walls and ceiling of the computer room to help retain room temperature and humidity. Also, any carpeting in the computer room should be static proofed and grounded to prevent buildup of static electricity.

Figure 5.5 *Particle Sizes*

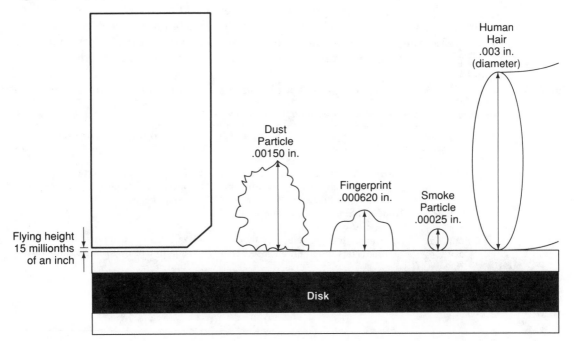

To protect the equipment and personnel, a high-quality fire protection system is mandatory. This would include both smoke and ion detectors, a fire extinguishing system, and a master environment control panel. The detectors should be placed both on the ceiling and beneath the false floor. The master environment control panel should also be able to indicate the exact location of the detector sounding the alarm. In this way the source of the fire can be easily located.

Due to the delicate nature of computer equipment, standard fire extinguishing systems are not acceptable. Both liquid-based and carbon dioxide-based systems can severely damage the equipment. The problem with water is obvious. Water and electrical systems are not compatible. Dry powder methods will leave harmful residues that will damage delicate computer components. The extinguishing of a fire by these means could result in more damage than the fire itself. Carbon dioxide, while being reasonably inexpensive, can cause condensation to form on the electrical equipment. More importantly, a room flooded by carbon dioxide can result in the suffocation of personnel trying to exit the area. The best form of fire control is to use halon gas. This gas will not damage equipment and gives personnel adequate time to leave the site safely since even though it is mildly irritating, it will not suffocate people. However, a halon gas system can be expensive, but when compared with the cost of the computer equipment, this is easily justified.

Unfortunately, halon gas contains chlorofluorocarbons, which have been found to destroy the earth's protective ozone layer. There is an international agreement to limit the use of these products. This means that halon gas will not be an acceptable option in a few years., At present, there is no acceptable alternative to halon. However, the U.S. Environmental Protection Agency is investigating environmentally safe ways to deal with fire protection of delicate equipment. Figure 5.6 summarizes the different computer room fire protection methods.

The fire alarm system should have a direct connection to the local fire

Figure 5.6 *Computer Room Fire Protection Methods*

METHOD	ADVANTAGES	DISADVANTAGES
Water	Inexpensive, can be used in areas with no computer equipment, not harmful to humans	Seriously damages electrical equipment, can damage equipment on floors below
Dry Powder	Totally unacceptable for computer room use	
Carbon Dioxide	Reasonably inexpensive, rapidly extinguishes fire in an enclosed area	Hazardous to personnel, can damage equipment by forming condensation
Halon Gas	Not harmful to humans, does not damage computer equipment, rapidly extinguishes fire in an enclosed area	Expensive Environmentally harmful

department and should automatically shut down the environmental control systems to prevent spreading the fire. The alarm system should have a delay before the halon is activated. This will allow manual override of the system in case of a false alarm or for fires that can be easily extinguished by other means.

As stated earlier, the electrical power entering the system is the lifeblood of a computer. Even small fluctuations in the power can cause major problems. Information can be lost and components destroyed when "dirty" power enters the system. Due to the delicate nature of modern computer circuitry, the power supplied by the public utility is not of high enough quality to use directly by a large system. The variations in the public power supply cause computer professionals to denote this as "dirty" power. For such power to be useful in the sophisticated computer environment, it must be conditioned.

There are four general hazards associated with power supplied by the local utility (see Figure 5.7). There are surges and sags in power which involve sudden increases or decreases in voltage. These can be caused by a malfunction in the electric utility's equipment, the starting and stopping of heavy equipment on the same circuit, or by a lightning strike on or near a local line. The possibility of damage due to an uncontrolled surge is extensive; computer hardware can be "fried" with all or part of the components destroyed. Sags can cause data to be lost or programs to terminate abnormally.

The third major problem with power is the possibility of a brownout. This involves a lowering of the line voltage for an extended period of time. Usually this is caused by an overdemand for electricity by consumers, with the utility forced to reduce voltage to conserve power. These are most common in large metropolitan areas during abnormally high periods of usage, such as during a prolonged heat wave when air conditioners are used almost continuously. This can cause overheating in the equipment and will eventually lead to early component failure.

A blackout, which is the complete loss of power, is the most serious power problem. This can cause the loss of all data currently running on the system and could also destroy permanent data files. More importantly, a black-

Figure 5.7 *Electrical Power Problems*

PROBLEM	DESCRIPTION	POSSIBLE CONSEQUENCES
Surges	Sudden temporary increase in voltage	Serious damage or destruction of equipment
Sags	Sudden temporary reduction in voltage	Loss of data and/or abnormal termination of program
Brownout	Prolonged reduction in voltage	Overheating of components with corresponding decrease in component life
Blackout	Interruption of electrical power	Short term: "crash" of system with necessity of restart (IPL)
		Long term: complete loss of system until power is restored

Figure 5.8   *Power Protection Methods*

METHOD OF PROTECTION	COST	HAZARDS ELIMINATED
Line Regulators	Inexpensive	Surges and sometimes sags
Motor Generator	Moderately Expensive	Surges, sags, brownouts, and sometimes extremely short-term blackouts
Uninterrupted Power	Expensive	Surges, sags, brownouts, and blackouts

out could cause a serious disruption of the computer services for an extended period of time.

All of these hazards will have an adverse effect on the computing environment. The degree of protection a firm seeks from these hazards will be determined by the probability of that specific hazard, the expected loss from the occurrence of that event, and the cost of protecting against that specific hazard. There are three types of power protection (see Figure 5.8).

The lowest-cost power protection is to use line regulators. These devices simply eliminate power surges and sometimes sags from reaching the machine. They are very inexpensive compared with other forms of power protection; however, they do not handle brownouts or blackouts.

A more expensive protection method is to use a motor-generator. This device is exactly what its name implies. It is a motor which turns a flywheel that generates the electrical current. This will clean up the power so that only smooth power will reach the computers. A motor-generator will handle surges, sags, and brownouts but will only handle instantaneous power disruptions.

The most expensive form of power protection is an uninterruptable power supply (UPS). There are various configurations of UPS; however, they all have the same function—to keep the system running even in the event of a power outage. These systems involve the use of storage batteries and a backup generator that will continue to supply power to the computer room despite the interruption of service supplied by the public utility. Because of the large cost, UPS is usually found in firms that have a critical need to keep their systems operating on a continuous basis. Firms that are heavily committed to online processing will usually be in this position. Besides handling blackouts, UPS will handle all the other hazards associated with electrical power.

COMPUTER ROOM LAYOUT

The emphasis in computer room layout should be on convenience, efficiency, and ease of access. Equipment of like function should be placed in the same vicinity. For example, communication equipment should be placed in one area.

Adequate room for proper ventilation, machine access, and traffic flow should be allowed. The usual method of determining the placement of machines is to lay out the machine room on a reduced scale grid. The various pieces of equipment, drawn to scale (see Figure 5.9), can then be arranged on this grid until an acceptable configuration is achieved. Some manufacturers will supply scale drawings of their equipment specifying machine clearances. This would include sufficient room to maintain the devices, to allow operator access to the devices, and to assure that adequate cooling can occur. When placing equipment, it is also necessary to consider vendor cabling restrictions. For some types of equipment, there is a maximum cable length that cannot be exceeded.

Some equipment needs special consideration. Tape drives and tape controllers should be placed close to the tape library and in a location easy for

Figure 5.9 *Scale Drawing*

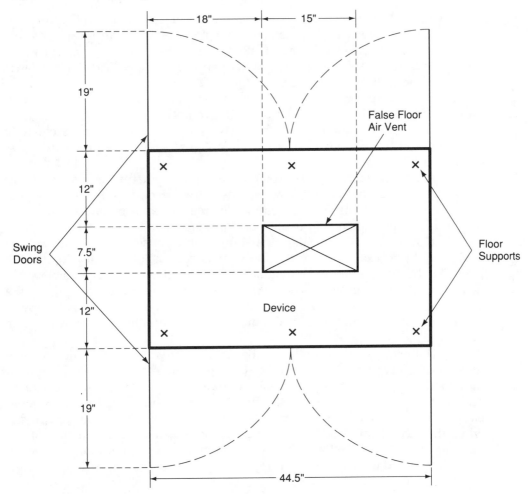

operators to access. Operator consoles, mountable disk drives, and other devices needing operator intervention should also be placed near operators. As stated earlier, dirty devices such as printers and punched card equipment should be placed in a location environmentally separate from the other hardware to reduce the hazard of airborne particles damaging other components of the system. Communications equipment should be placed near the communication patch panels.

If the computer room is properly configured, the cooling of the room, the servicing of the equipment, the access to the devices, and the protection of the system will be made easier. Also, in a room properly designed and configured, future expansion can be done with a minimum of inconvenience.

DISASTER RECOVERY PLANNING

Along with planning for the successful operation of the computer, the information system staff must take a more pessimistic view and plan for all possible contingencies. Examples of some of the questions that should be asked when doing this type of planning include: What happens if a specific disk drive fails? How will the information system operate in the event of a strike by all non-management personnel? How can the information system continue to function if disaster completely destroys the computer center?

Disaster planning is a comprehensive subject that cannot be adequately dealt with in this text; however, we will highlight some of the procedures that should be followed.

The best disaster recovery plan is preventive in nature and helps to spot areas of vulnerability before recovery procedures become necessary. The first step in developing a plan is to inventory all areas of exposure and evaluate the magnitude and likelihood of possible losses. Generally, the areas to be examined include hardware, software, data, personnel, and physical site. Each of these areas should be examined by the individuals responsible for developing the plan. At the same time an individual should be given the responsibility for determining when a disaster is occurring, the magnitude of the disaster, and the plan of action that should be implemented. For a plan of this type to be operational, centralized authority is necessary to reduce response time and mitigate damages.

Following are some of the standard procedures that are included in most disaster recovery plans. Data should be backed up on a periodic basis. Important files should be backed up daily; less important files weekly or monthly, determined by the level of activity in the file. More active files need more frequent backup. There should be at least two backup copies. One should be kept on-site while the other should be kept off-site in case of complete destruction of the facilities. In addition, all software (both systems and applications software) should be copied with at least one copy retained off-site. Again, periodically new copies should be made of software to incorporate any modifications made in the interim.

Proper file backup takes a commitment by the data center staff. It is very tempting to ignore backup when the system is extremely busy. However, this is usually the time when backup is most important, since the files will experience more activity during peak times. The cost of improper backup is difficult to calculate, but the loss of critical data can be monumental.

Personnel should have training in more than one specific area, so that the incapacitation of a key employee will not result in the disruption of the system. This cross-training is of particular importance to supervisory and managerial personnel. They should be able to continue the operation of the data center at a reduced service level in the event of the loss of a significant number of employees. An added benefit of this is that employee turnover will have less effect on the operations.

The loss of a significant portion of the physical facilities is another important consideration. The backup of data and software is of no value if there is no hardware available to process the programs. There must be alternative data processing facilities available within a brief period of time to avoid a catastrophic disruption of services. This can be arranged by having a reciprocal agreement with a firm that has a similar system, by purchasing time from a service bureau, or by owning an alternative compatible facility.

Reciprocal agreements involve the promise of two parties to allow the other to use their system in the event of the destruction of the other's facilities. The two systems must be similarly configured and have excess capacity. While agreements of this type appear attractive because of their low cost, they are usually unworkable due to the possibility of disruption of service caused by problems in the other firm. For the level of service to be barely adequate for the firm experiencing problems, the other firm would usually have to reduce drastically their own service levels. To most firms this is unacceptable.

Another alternative is to sign a contract for emergency services with a firm specializing in disaster recovery. This usually entails the payment of a monthly contingency fee which allows for periodic access to a system for testing purposes. The company will then pay a daily fee when an emergency occurs, and the system must be used on an operational basis. This is a reasonable cost option; however, it is usually only available in very large cities.

The firm can also have an auxiliary data center. There are three ways to configure this center. A cold site is prepared for the installation of equipment by having the proper environment, power, etc. but none of the hardware installed. A warm site is similar, except that everything but the very expensive hardware, such as the CPU, is installed. A hot site entails a fully operational data center.

The hot site can be immediately available for operation but can be very expensive to build and maintain. If the continuous operation of the system is of utmost importance, the high cost may be justified. A cold site and warm site both have the problem of ordering, installing, and testing additional hardware

Figure 5.10 *Disaster Recovery Alternative Site Arrangements*

ARRANGEMENT	COST	FEATURES
Reciprocal Agreement	Low	Coordination and capacity problems with other user may make this unworkable
Service Bureau	Moderate	Most specializing in providing disaster recovery services are geographically limited
Additional Site:		
Cold Site	Low	May take a substantial period of time to obtain and install system
Warm Site	Moderate	Must work closely with vendor to guarantee quick delivery of critical components
Hot Site	High	Great if company can afford it

before operations can resume. Of course, there must be close coordination with the vendors to assure minimum delay in delivery.

No matter which method of recovery is selected, it is necessary to test the plan thoroughly on a periodic unannounced basis. All critical components including the hardware, software, and data should be tested. The various disaster recovery arrangements are summarized in Figure 5.10.

SMALLER INSTALLATIONS

When designing a site that will house only mini- and microcomputers, many of the issues previously discussed are still important. However, usually lower-cost solutions will be sought. Many minicomputers do not need the extensive cooling and environmental control of larger systems. Also, these systems are designed so that a false floor is not necessary. Commonly, these types of machines will be placed in a room without a separate air conditioning system but with a substantially increased air flow from the main system. Also, instead of having a false floor, special wiring channels will be cut in the floor.

Security, electrical power, and fire protection must be considered for all types of computers. Security is an especially big problem with microcomputers. Since there is such a large market for these machines and they are so easily moved, the theft of the hardware and software are very real problems. The cost of such a loss may exceed the purchase price of the machine and its software. For example, if the micro has a hard disk and either this disk is not properly backed up or the backup copies are stolen with the machine, then thousands of hours of work and possibly irreplaceable data will be lost.

To protect against electrical power and fire problems, usually a lower-cost solution will be implemented. For minis and micros, line regulators could be used to eliminate sags and surges. Hand-held halon gas units can be used to extinguish fires.

When considering microcomputer installation, it is important to reduce the risk of electromagnetic interference. Strong magnetic impulses are generated by electric motors. These impulses can damage or destroy the contents of both floppy and hard disks. Storing these media next to a device having an electric motor can have disastrous consequences. For example, storing diskettes right next to a telephone could result in the loss of all the data on the diskettes if the phone bell has a strong electromagnet.

MAJOR COMPANY

Major Company has its headquarters in Chicago, and because of this, the availability of qualified personnel, the company's location near major transportation, its geographically central position, and other factors, Major Company selected the Chicago area as its data center location. The specific choice of site is in the Chicago suburb of Oakbrook. This is an attractive location for business, being conveniently located near major expressways and within a reasonable distance of O'Hare International Airport. Additionally, it is easier for employees to commute to work in Oakbrook than to the Chicago downtown area.

Figure 5.11 shows how the data center site is configured. Access is controlled by having only three entrances to the grounds. During prime times all three entrances are kept open. At all other times only the main gate is open. The entire area is enclosed by a 10-foot brick wall and chain-link fence. Closed circuit television cameras controlled by a security guard, sweep the grounds to detect intruders and vandals. Security guards are located at each open gate to check identification of all people entering the grounds. Also note that there is ample employee parking and sufficient open area for expansion.

Figure 5.12 shows the design of the building. There are some points to note on the design of the building. The computer room has no exterior building walls and is on the second floor to reduce access to the system. All entrances are either controlled by computer-read magnetic cards or are emergency exits which sound alarms when opened. The first floor is constructed in such a manner that all interior walls are nonstructural, temporary walls that can be reconfigured so that an additional computer center can be constructed on the first floor if growth dictates. All hallways and entrances are monitored by closed circuit television. Visitors to the building must be escorted by authorized personnel.

Figure 5.13 shows the layout of Major Company's computer room. This particular installation scheme was developed to facilitate access to the various components of the system, to provide for future expansion, and to assure the best possible environment for the machinery. The tape drives are located near both the tape library and the operators. The communication controllers are all located near the tie lines (patch panels) of the telephone system. The printers are all located in a separate area to prevent the generation of airborne paper dust particles. Notice that there is plenty of room for expansion for each one of the major system components.

Figure 5.11

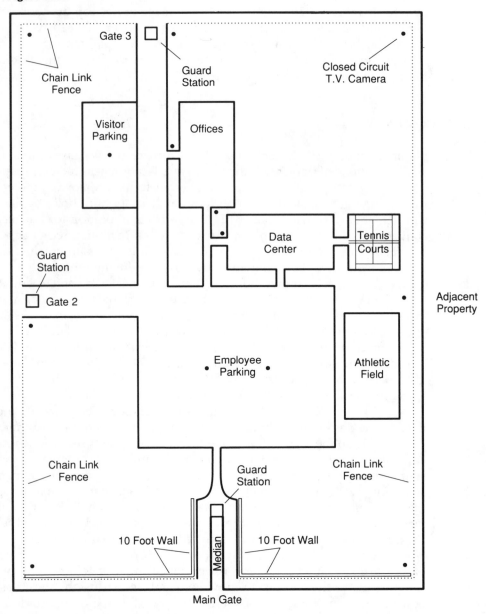

Figure 5.12

Floor 1

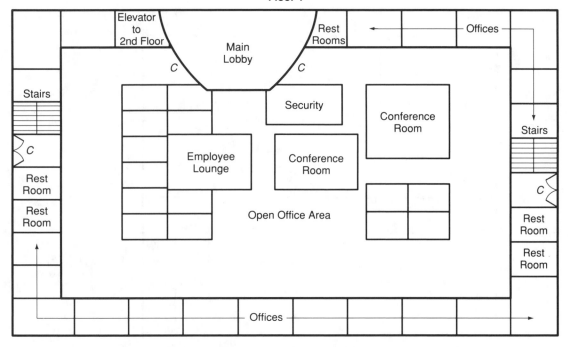

Floor 2

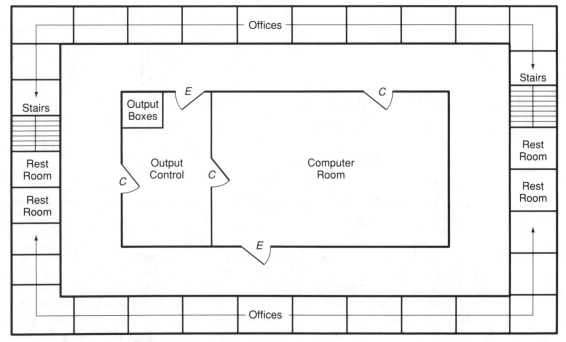

C: Controlled Entrance / Exit
E: Emergency Exit

Figure 5.13

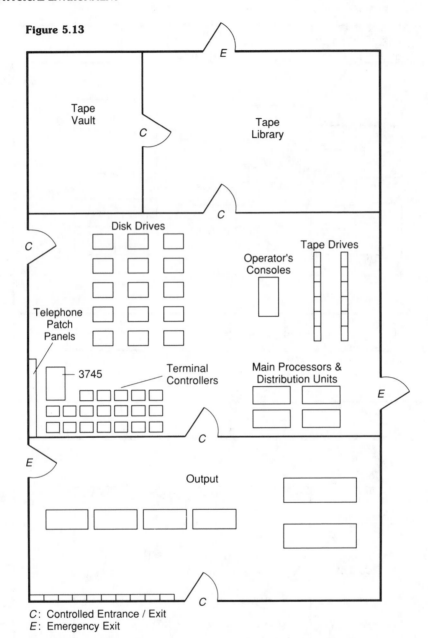

C: Controlled Entrance / Exit
E: Emergency Exit

Due to the heavy use of online/realtime applications, Major Company has decided that the continuous machine operation guaranteed by an uninterruptable power supply was cost-justified. Both the air conditioning units and the uninterruptable power supply are located on the roof penthouse. This saves space in the computer room, allows for easier maintenance access, and also reduces the threat of damage to the computer equipment if this heavy equipment experiences serious problems.

Major Company has developed a very strong disaster recovery plan. The assistant to the vice-president of information systems is responsible for coordination and implementation of the plan. While we will not go into the details of the plan, we will discuss some of its major points.

The backbone of the plan involves continuing computer operations if the data center is destroyed or disabled. Major Company has signed a contract with a regional disaster recovery service center having compatible equipment. This center is located in Chicago's downtown area. The agreement gives Major Company the ability to use the recovery facilities on a first-come-first-served basis upon an initial payment of $50,000 and continuing payments of $20,000 per day. This entitles Major Company to use one of the four mainframe processors and associated peripherals. Also, the contract allows for one day of test time four times a year. In addition, Major Company owns an office complex in Northbrook, Illinois, a northern suburb of Chicago. When the building was constructed, it was designed to be a disaster recovery cold site. It has the proper environment, raised floors, electrical power, and wiring ready to accept computer equipment. The building is presently being used as an office building; however, it is expected to take a minimum of two weeks and a maximum of four weeks to order, deliver, and install the equipment necessary to resume some in-house computing.

Backup of data files, systems software, and applications software is done on a periodic basis. Backup copies are stored at both the Northbrook office site and the downtown service center in fire-proof vaults.

SUMMARY

The physical environment of an information system can be important to the successful operation of the system. The geographical location is one factor. The data center must be close to other company facilities, be in an attractive place to live, and be in an area having a low probability of natural disasters.

The building and associated site should be designed so that the computer center can operate efficiently while adequately protecting the facilities. Some of the major considerations include the physical security of the computer center, wiring the building, air conditioning and heating, fire prevention and control, and electrical power supply.

A comprehensive disaster recovery plan should be designed to allow the computer operations to continue despite major failures of the computer system. This plan must consider the loss of data, hardware, personnel, and software.

QUESTIONS

1. What factors must one consider in the selection of the general geographic area to install a computer center? Which of these factors are the most important? Why?

2. Sometimes the selection of the geographic area for the location of the computer center is quite easy. Can you give some examples?

3. What factors would you be concerned about in selecting a particular site if the firm decided to build a new data center?

4. What factors would you be concerned about in selecting a particular site if the firm decided to buy and renovate an existing structure?

5. What renovations do you think may be necessary to make a typical office building into a data center? What if the original building was a warehouse?

6. What would be the difference in acquiring a building which is leased and one which is purchased to use as a computer center?

7. As data center manager, what points would you discuss with the architect if your firm was constructing a new building which was to contain a large data center?

8. Explain why a false floor is necessary for a computer room.

9. Why is it that the plan for wiring and building for data communications must allow for rapid and frequent reconfiguration?

10. What are the electrical power hazards to computers, and how can you protect against them?

11. In what ways can a computer center help prevent and extinguish fires?

12. Explain why a disaster recovery program is necessary for all computer centers.

13. When dealing with a disaster recovery service center, why is it important to know the number, location, and type of other firms contracting with this service center for recovery facilities?

14. Describe all the physical security measures your school's computer center takes to protect its computer system.

CASE ANALYSIS

Case 1

You are employed by the Columbia Manufacturing Company, which produces high-tensile-strength plastic products for industrial use and specialty alloy metal products. Columbia services customers in all states west of the Mississippi River. It has the following company locations:

TYPE OF FACILITY	*NUMBER OF FACILITIES*	*LOCATION*
Corporate Headquarters	1	Colorado Springs, CO
Manufacturing Plants	4	Ogden, UT
		Sacramento, CA
		Tucson, AZ
		Omaha, NB
Warehouses	8	At all four manufacturing sites plus:
		Fort Worth, TX
		Colorado Springs, CO
		Kansas City, KS
		Portland, OR
Sales Offices	20	At all eight warehouse cities plus:
		Albuquerque, NM
		Las Vegas, NV
		Los Angeles, CA
		Boise, ID
		Sioux City, SD
		Des Moines, IA
		Seattle, WA
		Houston, TX
		Tulsa, OK
		St. Paul, MN
		Cheyenne, WY
		St. Louis, MO

Over 40% of all sales go to aerospace firms. The remaining sales have no specific clustering pattern by industry or region. Next year Columbia expects to break into the *Fortune* 500.

Columbia presently has minicomputers (a mix of Hewlett-Packard, DEC, and IBM minis) installed in each of its manufacturing sites, each warehouse, and the corporate headquarters. It also has microcomputers (mainly IBM PCs) and terminals (mostly ASCII terminals with modem access via telephone lines to other sites) in each of the sales offices. Intermachine communication is accomplished through a clumsy arrangement of dial-up modems and the shipment of tape files. A study has shown that inventory and manufacturing control are very poorly coordinated between the various sites, and that a significant dollar amount of sales has been lost because of this. Record keeping and cost control are also very poor because of a lack of coordination.

Columbia has decided to purchase mainframe equipment to centralize corporate records and allow for efficient, up-to-date communication and retrieval of information between the various parts of the firm. Your team has been requested to develop a site plan for the construction of this computer center and a plan for installation of the preliminary equipment. You have been given a free hand at the selection of the site, the floor plan of the building, and all other details. The following is a list of computer equipment that Columbia wishes to install initially:

TYPE OF EQUIPMENT	NUMBER OF ITEMS
IBM 3090 Model 100 Computer with 16 meg of main memory and 16 data channels	1
IBM 3990 Controller	3
IBM 3390 Disk Storage Device	12
IBM 3800 Laser Printer	2
IBM 2303 Impact Printer	2
IBM 3725 Communications Controller	1
IBM 3490 Cartridge Tape System	6
IBM 3803 Tape Controller	1
IBM 3178 Terminal	220
IBM 3174 Terminal Controller	10
IBM 3820 Laser Printer	5
Communication Lines to All Sites	
The machine will run the VM/CMS operating system with the MVS/JES3 operating system running under VM.	

This plan is to be a formal document which will first be presented to the vice-president of information systems and then to the board of directors. Since this is only a preliminary plan, architectural drawings and other extreme details are not necessary. However, it is necessary to select the site and justify this selection. In addition, estimates of costs and a schedule of completion times should be included.

Case 2

Rio Dark is the world-respected beer produced by the two famous New Mexicans, Adolph Dirty Water and Andhiser Bigbush. The company is named the Adolph and Andhiser Brewery, Inc. The beer gets its distinctive flavor from the sparkling waters of the Southern Rio Grande. To show the true dark color of the beer, it is packaged in a clear plastic baggie with a handy zip-lock seal. The company's corporate headquarters is located at Radium Springs, New Mexico, and their two breweries are in Radium Springs and Anthony, Texas. The company has corporate-owned distributorships (which are referred to as class A distributorships) in the following places:

Austin, TX	Augusta, GA
Anaheim, CA	Akron, OH
Arlington, VA	Ankeny, IA
Auburn, AB	Allentown, PA
Anchorage, AK	Astoria, OR
Amherst, MA	Atchison, KA
Amakup, WA	Atown, SD

The company also has regional warehouses at the Austin, Anaheim, Akron, and Augusta locations. In addition there are 15 independent distributors scattered throughout the U.S. (These are referred to as class B distributorships. You can guess what letter these cities start with!)

All company-owned distributors, breweries, and warehouses, for obvious reasons, should be tied into the company computer network. Currently this is not the case. Although the remote locations all have computers, none of them are connected to the computer at headquarters. It is realized that these connections are desirable in the new configuration. The company is very centralized—as Adolph always said, "The world should center around Radium Springs"—so all ordering, inventorying, and production scheduling, among other things, are done on the computer at headquarters. Figure 5.14 shows the Rio Dark site plan.

The current computing and communications situation at Rio Dark is shown in

Figure 5.14 *Rio Dark Site Plan*

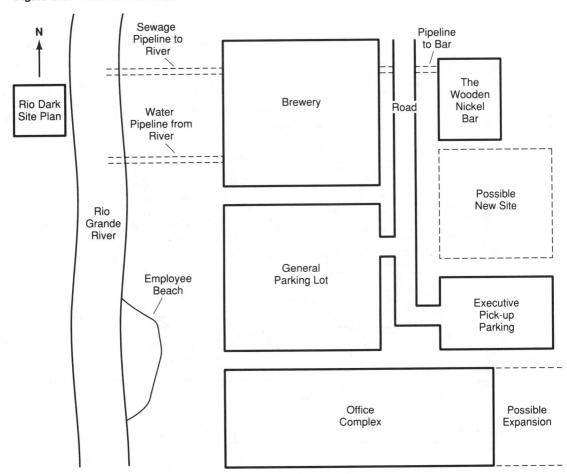

Figure 5.15   *Rio Dark Computer Room*

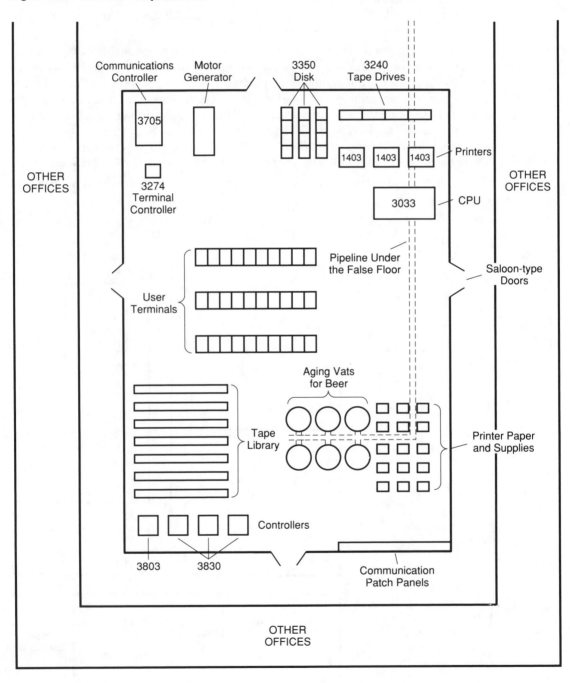

Figure 5.15. All computer equipment, including terminals, is located in an 8,000-square-foot room at the center of the building. Everyone walks from their desks to the computer room, so they all have the same distance to go to have access to the terminals. The computer is not actually hooked to the other locations throughout the nation. Inquiries and output must be either mailed or telephoned through the computing secretary.

The current computer equipment is all IBM and is as follows:

QUANTITY	ITEM
1	3033 Processor
12	3350 Disk Drives
3	3830 Disk Controllers
4	3420 Tape Drives
1	3803 Tape Drive Controller
3	1403 Printers
55	3278 Terminals
1	3274 Terminal Controller
1	3705 Communication Controller

The present center has a raised floor, a motor-generator to protect the electrical supply, and an extensive sprinkler system to protect against fires.

Rio Dark's IBM salesperson has determined that a new computer system is needed, and the company has decided to purchase the following IBM equipment:

List of Equipment

QUANTITY	ITEM
1	3090-Model 200 Processor (32 meg, 32 channel)
1	3725 Communications Controller
20	3174 Controllers (16 running at remote sites)
9	3390 Hard Disk Drives
3	3990 Disk Controllers
2	3800 Printers
2	3203 Impact Printers
16	3490 Magnetic Tape Subsystem
1	3278-A02 Display Console (for machine room)
1	3287-2 Printer Console (for machine room)
1	3178-1 Terminal (for machine room)
250	3179-1 Terminal

The new equipment will come with all the necessary software for the company to have interactive applications in the following areas: inventory control, scheduling, accounts receivable and payable, payroll, etc. IBM has assured Rio Dark that the hardware and system software will take between two and three weeks to install and get running. It has also been decided that the old 3033 processor and 1403 printers will be the only equipment that the company will get rid of; the rest of the equipment will be incorporated in the new computer center.

You have been hired to design the new facilities for the new computer center. Rio Dark has given you the following options:

1. *Addition:* An addition can be made to the current offices at Radium Springs. The addition would be on the east of the building and be a 16,000-square-foot project costing between $18.75 and $20.00 a square foot.
2. *New Facility:* A new facility can be built, on the other side of the executive pickup parking lot to the north of the present offices. This building would be between 25,000 and 35,000 square feet and cost between $25.00 and $27.00 a square foot.

Either building that is built is required to have restrooms, an employee lounge, and as much office spaces as can be allocated without sacrificing any of the needs of the actual machine room. There should be a minimum of two fire exits.

Your mission is to give a detailed report to which site you believe Rio Dark should build along with the internal design of the building. Any nonstandard building specifications should be described and their cost estimated and justified. If you decide no longer to use the present computer center, specify how to use the old computer room in the old office. Develop a detailed schedule for the entire project, including finishing construction, installing new equipment, moving old equipment, deinstalling old unusable equipment, connecting to remote locations, any testing, remodeling any facilities, and final completion of the project.

Be sure that your recommendations are reasonably complete. They should include rough plans of the new site and the configuration of the new center, cost estimates, and an explanation of the basis for your recommendations. You should also provide a diagram with full explanations of how the equipment would be arranged in the data center(s).

Explain in detail why you made the specific recommendations. These must be justified to management before management will accept the project. Neither Adolph nor Andhiser will accept any shoddy work.

Case 3

Congratulations! The Columbia Manufacturing Company has selected you to develop a disaster recovery plan for their firm.

The president of the corporation has recently read about the problems in several major companies caused by computer center disasters. Now that he is alert to these problems, he is more aware of the problems other firms have encountered. Because of Columbia's dependence on computing, he does not feel comfortable with the lack of a formal disaster recovery plan. He is primarily concerned that

Columbia's new data processing center is vulnerable to extended down time or a full-scale disaster caused either by natural or human forces.

Columbia has retained your consulting firm to prepare a report to the vice-president of computer operations concerning steps that could be taken to insure that Columbia would be able to recover from a major disaster in a reasonable amount of time. A reasonable amount of time in Columbia's case, due to the nature of the business, would be a matter of a day or two. This should only be a preliminary report covering all central computing facilities. A full-scale disaster recovery plan will be implemented in the near future based on your ground work here. You should review as many viable alternatives for disaster recovery as are possible, discussing the advantages and disadvantages of each. The report should also include a relative price level associated with each alternative (high, medium, or low cost), as well as a discussion of other factors related to disaster recovery planning.

The Columbia Manufacturing Company was described in Case 1 in this chapter. Please refer to that Case for more details.

ADDITIONAL READINGS

BEAVER, JENNIFER E. "Growing Pains: When You Have to Expand," *Computer Decisions*, July 1983, pp. 88–102.

DEVRIES, DOUG. "A Moving Experience," *Datamation*, August 1982, pp. 131–136.

MEHLER, MARK. "UPSs Flourish as LAN Protectors," *Datamation*, July 15, 1988, p. 69.

MOAD, JEFF. "The Storage Threat," *Datamation*, July 15, 1988, p. 54.

SYMMES, MAINE AND MCKEE ASSOCIATES, INC. "Designing a Data Center," *Modern Office Technology*, December 1983, pp. 86–90.

WALLER, MARK. "Planning Data Center Design," *Datamation*, November 1, 1989, p. 73.

READINGS BEFORE NEXT CHAPTER

If you are not already familiar with the procedures used in statistical simulation and modeling, it may be helpful to do a little reading in this area. A possible reference is *Computer Simulation in Business,* by Hugh Watson, John Wiley, 1981. The first two chapters should give you a good idea of how the process works.

6

SYSTEM PERFORMANCE EVALUATION

WHAT IS PERFORMANCE EVALUATION?

It is not at all unusual today for the data processing department of a large corporation to invest hundreds of millions of dollars in equipment, software, and training. This investment, if poorly managed, could easily become a liability rather than a productive element of the organization. Current trends in data processing suggest that even with the decreasing costs of hardware and the strides made in new technology, computing costs continue to rise. This can be attributed to the increased need for information inside and outside of the organization. The costs of developing new software and maintaining existing programs are increasing. It is also misleading to think that with the decrease in hardware costs many data processing problems could be solved with more hardware. Generally, hardware costs are seen to be decreasing in terms of their processing cost to power ratios. The actual investment in the hardware may not in fact be declining. As a result, it would seem prudent to maximize the usefulness of the resources at hand rather than spend more money.

In some installations, changes are made to the system in a hit-or-miss fashion. When doing this, the computer system is altered without sufficient prior consideration of the effects of the changes. Just as a physician should not go about curing an ailment without a reasonable idea of the causes of the symptoms, a computer system should not be changed to alleviate an undesirable response without first ascertaining the cause of the problem. This could be costly. For example, the seemingly small change of adding an additional DASD to a channel could have a substantial impact on the response time of programs using data stored on the other DASD on that channel, causing online system response to be degraded. Without an organized and intelligent method of measuring and evaluating the performance of the data processing system, even a small change to a system could have devastating results. Performance evaluation is an essential element in the effective management of a data processing shop.

Performance evaluation is simply the systematic determination of the productivity of an object. In this chapter, the objects considered will be hardware, system software, application software, and the programming staff themselves. One should not confuse performance evaluation here with that normally taught in a personnel management course. The emphasis here is strictly from the data processing manager's point of view—that is, how to increase the productivity of the data processing system. First we will discuss in detail the reason for performance evaluation. Then we will discuss the evaluation process. Finally, we will cover specific performance evaluation problems in comparing the performance of competing vendor's products, which is usually referred to as benchmarking, and the special problems involved in database/data communication systems.

WHY PERFORMANCE EVALUATION?

As previously mentioned, performance evaluation is simply a tool which can be used to measure the productivity of hardware, software, and programmers. For example, one of the most important criteria in determining the effectiveness of a transaction processing system would be the system response time. This might be the case when using an ATM (automatic teller machine). Recall that response time is affected by the speed of the processing hardware, the effectiveness of the software, and the number of users on the system. To improve the performance of the system, we will need much more information. With this evaluation, we could determine that the software is needlessly manipulating some of the data, or perhaps the hardware used cannot handle the peak demand.

In any event, system planning is facilitated by knowledge about how the system is currently performing. Without this information, intelligent decisions cannot be made. To plan the usage of the corporate data processing resource, management must know how the system is functioning and compare that to how it is supposed to operate. Performance evaluation can help the manager decide whether equipment should be acquired or the current system should be reconfigured. This type of decision is made based on the objectives of the organization.

Often, as with the performance of an automobile, system response can be improved by tuning, or reconfiguring, rather than acquiring new equipment or software. System tuning is the process of evaluating the actions of a system and optimizing that performance under the current processing loads and system configuration. This simple definition requires extensive research and testing of the system by system personnel. To interpret the results, statistical information, system configuration data, and device capabilities must be known. This information is of little worth, however, if the performance of the system is of little concern to corporate administration. Once again, there must be a long-term plan. Without it, the determination of whether the system is performing adequately is moot.

Performance evaluation is a crucial part of the management of a data processing shop. The amounts of corporate resources invested and the organization's dependence on information processing warrant the most efficient, effective use of the system software and hardware. However, without direction or objective, this evaluation is simply an assessment of the current operation of the system. It is the corporate goals and objectives that make performance evaluation useful. In other words, performance evaluation must have a purpose rather than simply being a measurement tool. This purpose should be the refining or tuning of the system to increase its effectiveness and, perhaps secondarily, its efficiency. The distinction here is that an efficient system may perform its duties quickly, with a minimum of overhead, and still not be useful to the firm in that state. Improving the efficiency of the system may increase its effectiveness; however, this is based on what the system is supposed to do. As a result, the increase in efficiency is simply a means for improving the effectiveness of the system. For example, suppose an interactive system is experiencing 10-second response time to customer billing inquiries. This is unacceptable to management. By restructuring the database it was found that, in addition to retrieving information more quickly, more data could be stored in the system. The goal here was to make the system more effective. To do this, the system was made more efficient. Data processing managers should always weigh the costs and benefits of system change in terms of effective change.

Performance evaluation is used not only in problem determination and correction, but also as a preventive measure. It is used as a benchmark or standard against which the evaluator can judge subsequent states of the system. In so doing, changes in the system can be detected before they affect the performance of the system. This is an important tool in strategic planning. From this it can be determined when system capacity will be reached and expansion is necessary.

Performance evaluation is an information-gathering process. It provides management with data on which to base system change decisions. These decisions, as well as the overall purpose of performance evaluation, are based on organizational attitudes and long-range plans. Through this evaluation process, it is possible to construct or rebuild a system that is more effective and useful. Performance evaluation is a six-step process, summarized in Figure 6.1. First the evaluator must gather information concerning the current hardware and software inventory—in other words, what exactly the present system consists of. Next the evaluator must measure the system to determine what it is doing now. This step categorizes inputs and outputs of the system as well as the attributes of its components. Third, the evaluator combines the information gathered in the

Figure 6.1 *Steps in Performance Evaluation*

1. System Inventory:	Determine the components and capabilities of the system.
2. System Measurement:	Gather system performance data.
3. System Modeling:	Create a simulation model of the system to be used for testing alternative configurations.
4. Model Validation:	Insure the accuracy of the model.
5. Change the Model:	Alter the model to determine effect on actual system.
6. Change the System:	Alter the system based on conclusions drawn from step 5.

preceding steps into a cause-and-effect, or causal, model, in this way determining how inputs, outputs, and processes affect each other and the overall system. Next the evaluator validates the model. Without an accurate model, there is neither a realistic nor a useful view of the system. Model validation simply determines if the outputs of the actual system are approximated by those of the model. It probably will be necessary to alter the model, based on step four, so that it will more accurately represent the real situation. Fifth, the evaluator will alter the parameters of the model to observe the predicted effects on the system. Finally, based on knowledge derived from the modeling process, the evaluator will make changes to the actual system, hopefully making it more effective. In the following sections, we will discuss in detail these six steps, concluding with an example of a performance problem and its solution at Major Company.

THE EVALUATION PROCESS

System Inventory

When beginning any evaluation, it is important to remember just exactly what it is we are evaluating and the reasons why. Without a motive or direction, the performance evaluation will proceed in a hit-and-miss fashion much like a child's number guessing game. As a result, we must determine what resources we have and on which we wish to concentrate. Taking an inventory of hardware and software is not nearly as simple as it would seem. Not all data processing centers maintain a current list of available hardware and up-to-date system and application software products. The systems programming manager should be able to compile a list of current systems software. In larger shops, however, a single person does not have exclusive control over the entire system. For example, the communications specialist would be in charge of those products used within the telecommunication network, while the database administrator might be aware of the various database products in use. Taking inventory of the hardware and software can be even more difficult in a decentralized environment, for the information systems area must consider facilities that are neither operationally nor functionally under their control.

System hardware configurations are best represented by a schematic diagram called a channel configuration, as shown in Figure 6.2. From this we can see what devices comprise the system. Care should be taken here to realize that many devices within modern data processing shops are software selectable, which means that there could actually be several routes to and from a particular device depending on the programs running. The operations manager or the systems programming manager will probably have a list of these devices. Note that Figure 6.2 shows how the devices are connected to the system via channels. In Chapter 5 we discussed the physical layout of the machine room. This description of the system simply denotes how the various devices are positioned around the room. From a performance evaluation point of view, this is not very useful. We are chiefly concerned with how those devices are connected to the system rather than how they occupy floor space. This is what a channel configuration does.

Finally, we must have a list of the application programs which affect the system. In addition to needing to knowing what they do, it is necessary to know what files they access, how they interact with each other, and how often they are run. In most data processing shops, application software is in either of two states: test or production. A test system would constitute those programs that are under revision and are not yet contributing to the productive output of the organization. The production system includes programs that have been completed at some point and are being used by the organization. It is not unusual for different versions of the same program to be at the same time both production and test. In some small installations and almost all large ones, test and productions programs are run on separate systems, hence the term *test* or *production system.* This can be very useful to the performance evaluation team in that the test system can be altered without affecting the normal production programs.

The data processing manager should stress the importance of keeping current system information at hand. For effective performance evaluation to take place, it is imperative that the evaluator know just how the system is currently configured and functioning. In addition, to make changes to the system, even when not concerned with performance evaluation, this documentation would be invaluable. As previously mentioned, this can be used to determine where the system is changing. From this, we can better plan for system expansion and meet the demand for computing resources more effectively.

To summarize, the first step in performance evaluation is to gather the pertinent facts about the current status of the system. These facts include the current system software and their functions, the current configuration of hardware within the system, and the application system's functions, interactions, and files. All of this information is needed before we begin to collect system measurement data. (See Figure 6.3.)

System Measurement

This phase of performance evaluation is probably the most technically sophisticated step. It requires detailed knowledge of how the system operates and what tools are available to collect device performance and program execu-

Figure 6.2 *System Channel Configuration*

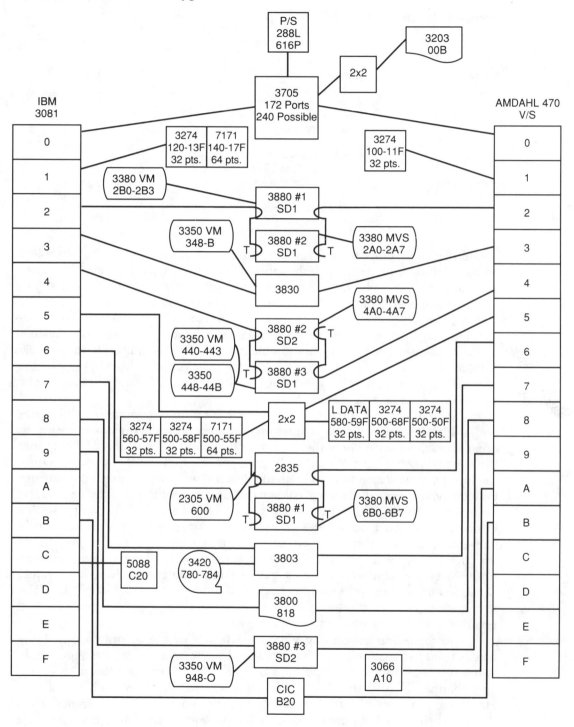

Figure 6.3 *System Inventory*

ITEM	DETERMINE
Hardware	Number of devices
	Physical characteristics
	Relationship to other devices
System software	Operating systems
	Utilities
	Compilers
	Compatibilities and restrictions
	Versions and maintenance levels
Application software	Acquired from vendors
	Internally developed
	Hardware and software dependencies

tion information. Once the information is gathered, it usually must be processed by using techniques ranging from simple descriptive statistics, such as means and variances, to multivariate analysis. Even after this is accomplished, someone with knowledge about each of the functional areas (systems, applications, and operations) must interpret these statistics. For example, suppose statistics indicate that during the execution of a certain database management system (DBMS) routine, batch job queues double in size. Whether this is an undesirable situation depends on how frequently this routine is run, the times of the day it is run, and at what priority it is executing. Only someone familiar with the specific situation can make a determination.

Generally, it is important to divide system measurement into two categories. First it is important to gather information concerning the input stream. In other words, we must know the content and amount of programs and data that the system is processing. We can collect this information simply by accumulating the input stream data and then calculate descriptive statistics about this stream. Obviously, the input stream will change during different times of the day. So it is necessary to measure the system at various times of the day. We could use this information to construct a series of test datasets on which to test the system in subsequent steps. In addition, we could actually capture a "live" input stream for later system testing. Secondly, we must measure how the system performs under a typical load. This means that we must determine how the system functions under the various input streams that we just measured. System performance is usually measured through a monitoring device or program that records how the system is functioning.

Information concerning what a particular device or program is doing comes from two main sources, hardware and software monitors (see Figure 6.4). A hardware monitor is a physical device which, when attached to a device such as a channel, records the electrical information that flows through the device. Hardware monitors are used to gather statistics concerning how frequently a device is being used. Information as to what program is actually using the device

Figure 6.4 *Measurement Tools*

MEASUREMENT TOOL	STRENGTH	WEAKNESS
Hardware Monitor	Accurately measures physical events Does not degrade system	Cannot measure logical events
Trace-driven Software Monitor	Measures resources used by specific job Can be used to measure the aggregate job stream	Consumes system resources
Sampling Software Monitor	Measures utilization level of specific system components Can also measure logical components	Consumes system resources

generally cannot be collected in this manner since it only measures the physical electrical impulses. An advantage of a hardware monitor is that the measurement process does not degrade the system. In other words, the system performs the same with or without the monitor running. Some hardware monitors are quite sophisticated digital devices themselves, with nonvolatile memory and external storage media control for data storage. They often come with software that can be loaded on the system and run on the collected data. The software will analyze this data and perhaps reformat it for subsequent processing. It is important to remember that hardware monitors are generally concerned with the physical operation of the system. They are designed to collect information associated with hardware such as voltage levels and durations. In some circumstances, they can be used to monitor fixed machine locations (addresses) and registers. At this point they approach the logical or software level of the system, but only to this point. Hardware monitors can be used, for example, to collect data concerning the position of a DASD head. From this we could collect information about accesses to certain areas of the disk, which can then be associated with specific datasets. Hardware monitors can also be used to help determine potential and actual hardware problems.

A software monitor is a system program which usually resides permanently in primary storage. Its function is to record information about specific programs, jobs, and/or devices. Since software monitors are highly dependent on the operating system, they are usually offered as components of the operating system. These monitors introduce an additional load on the system and can cause a measurement bias. However, unlike hardware monitors, they can collect more detailed information about the users of the system and can also measure logical events. Normally, they can be set up in either a sampling mode or a trace mode. Sampling indicates that the routine remains dormant much of the time, only "waking up" periodically to record system status information. This is usually called a time-driven monitor. This technique is used in the day-to-day information collection process to measure on a global scale the activities of the system. Sampling can also be used to record the activity of a specific device. For example, if a certain DASD is experiencing an unusual number of system accesses, perhaps too many system programs are stored there and should be redistributed around the system. Trace mode refers to the fact that the software monitor follows a job and/or program through the system recording its resource usage along the way. This mechanism is used to measure the characteristics of the input stream and is the primary source of job accounting data, which is used in billing the users. It can also be used when it is suspected that a certain program is causing problems within the system. Since the monitor is executed whenever specific system events occur, it is often referred to as an event-driven monitor. One can see here that the type of monitor used in dependent on the information one wishes to obtain.

Software monitors are divided into two broad groups. The first is job accounting packages, which collect information concerning the resources used by a particular job or group of jobs. As such, job accounting packages are event- or trace-driven monitors. Hence, every time a job requests services from the operating system, such as CPU time or input/output (I/O), the software monitor will record these occurrences in data records created for each separate active job. Accounting packages are very useful in measuring the input stream on a quantitative basis. In other words, from a job accounting package, we could determine the frequency and amounts of data used or produced within the system. We could not, however, determine the qualitative contents of the input stream from a job accounting package. This means we cannot discern the contents of the I/O, simply the amounts. The information gathered is also used to bill the user for computer resources used. Sometimes additional software packages are used to process further the output records of the accounting package. These programs will generate summary reports and also customer bills. Job accounting packages exist specifically to allocate costs to system users and to measure the input stream. Their output, however, can be used in performance evaluation also. IBM's System Management Facility (SMF) is an example of a trace-driven accounting package.

The other type of software monitor is a performance software monitor. Sometimes, only this group is referred to as a software monitor and the other type is simply called a job accounting package. Since there is this lack of uniform terminology, things can get a little confusing. Thus, we will try to be specific as to the meaning of the terms used. In a time-driven software monitor, sampling data is collected by the software monitor. Data concerning specific resources, such as channel or DASD utilization, is recorded to give the system programming staff a clearer picture of the activity of a device.

Sampling software monitors, such as IBM's Resource Management Facility (RMF), can measure both physical and logical devices. They function by measuring a given resource for a set number of instances at a given time interval. For example, to measure a physical device such as the CPU, the monitor may be set to sample 1,000 times in a second at each sampling event with a sampling event occurring every 30 seconds. The monitor would test to see if the CPU was in the busy or wait state. If for a specific sample it found that 850 of 1,000 times in that second the CPU was busy, then the CPU is 85% busy. The next sample would be taken 30 seconds later. Logical devices such as a specific initiator/terminator can also be measured by a software monitor. Hardware monitors are not capable of measuring logical devices. Sampling software monitors are very useful when there is some question as to the activity levels of particular devices in the system, whereas a trace-driven monitor would be used primarily for ascertaining the load on the system. Trace-driven monitors can also aid in the scheduling of preventive maintenance. For example, if a certain DASD is experiencing more than the normal number of I/O errors, which is recorded in the SMF log, this could alert system personnel to a possible faulty drive. Figures 6.5 and 6.6 show some of the types of information collected by trace driven and sampling software monitors.

It is very possible when using a software monitor to collect literally millions of pieces of data. This should not be misconstrued as being ideal. Obviously, the evaluator should have enough observations to calculate statistics accurately, but care should be taken to not compound the problem with too much information. For example, a given device may not seem to affect the system under study; then it should not be included in the evaluation. Here again, we can see just how important knowledge of the current system is. It is important to remember, however, that the software monitor introduces an additional load into the system. Also, understanding the day-to-day operations of the center is important. For example, most data processing centers exhibit different characteristics during various parts of the day. High user demand may be encountered just after noon, backups and preventive maintenance occur at three on Sunday mornings, payroll is run during second shift on the first and fifteenth of each month. Without this kind of information, the evaluator could draw erroneous conclusions concerning the operation of the system.

Hardware and particularly software monitors can collect valuable data for the performance evaluator. From this information and our experience concerning the operation of the center, we can get a clear idea of what really is occurring. However, these data must be organized into some sort of logical sequence to become useful. For example, simply knowing that during first shift the use of a certain channel is higher than other channels during that same period of time is not useful. We must organize this data so that the relationships that make a system more than a collection of devices and instructions are included with the information. To do this, we must create a model.

System Modeling

Now that we have gathered information on the configuration of the system, the input streams, and the performance of the various components, the next phase of the performance evaluation process is system modeling. System modeling, which sounds quite ominous, is actually the combination of the information gathered in the previous steps with system experience. The modeling

Figure 6.5 *Sample SMF Record Format*

THE NUMBER OF BYTES PRECEDING THIS FIELD IN BOTH DECIMAL AND HEX		NAME	LENGTH IN BYTES	FORMAT	THE OPERATING SYSTEM MODULE THAT HANDLED THE PROCESSING OF THE SPECIFIC EVENT	DESCRIPTION
0	0	SMF26FLG	1	binary	SVC83	System indicator
1	1	SMF26RTY	1	binary	internal	Record type
2	2	SMF26TME	4	binary	SVC83	Time
6	6	SMF26DTE	4	packed	SVC83	Date
10	A	SMF26SID	4	EBCDIC	JMRCPUID	System identification
14	E	SMF26JBN	8	EBCDIC	IATISJB	Job name
22	16	SMF26RST	4	binary	IATXTOD macro (Set by IATISJB)	Time, reader recognized job
26	1A	SMF26RSD	4	packed	IATXTOD macro (Set by IATISJB)	Date reader recognized job
30	1E	SMF26UIF	8	EBCDIC	JMRUSEID (Set by IATPURG)	User identification
38	26	SMF26RSV	4	binary		Reserved
42	2A	SMF26S8S	2	binary	internal	Subsystem identification
44	2C	SMF26IND	2	binary		Reserved
Descriptor Section:						
46	2E	SMF26LN1	2	binary	internal	Length of descriptor section
48	30	SMF26RV1	2	binary		Reserved
50	32	SMF26IN3	1	binary		Job information indicator
51	33	SMF26INF	1	binary		Job information indicator *BIT Meaning When Set*

(continued)

Figure 6.5 *(continued)*

THE NUMBER OF BYTES PRECEDING THIS FIELD IN BOTH DECIMAL AND HEX		NAME	LENGTH IN BYTES	FORMAT	THE OPERATING SYSTEM MODULE THAT HANDLED THE PROCESSING OF THE SPECIFIC EVENT	DESCRIPTION
					IATISJB IATIIDR IATISJB IATISJB IATISJB IATMSIN for ASP, or IATMSMS for JES3 IATPURG	0 Job priority 1 Job processed by preexec setup 2 TYPRUN–HOLD 5 Internal reader 6 ASP main or JES 3 Reader 7 Job canceled by operator
52	34	SMF26JNM	4	EBCDIC	IATISJB or IATPURG	JES3-assigned job number
56	38	SMF26JID	8	EBCDIC	IATISJB	Job identification in the form xxx0yyyy
64	40	SMF26NAM	20	EBCDIC	IATIIPR	Programmer's name
84	54	SMF26MSG	1	EBCDIC	IATISJB	Message class
85	55	SMF26CLS	1	EBCDIC	IATISJB	Job class
86	56	SMF26XPI	1	binary	IATISJB if PRTY = parameter or IATISEN	JES3 job selection priority
87	57	SMF26XPS	1	binary	IATMSIN for ASP, IATMSMS for JES3	JES3 job selection priority
88	58	SMF26RV8	4	binary		Reserved
92	5C	SMF26DEV	8	EBCDIC	IATISJB or IATNJDJ if NJP	JES3 logical input device name, or user identification
The record continues for many more fields.						

Figure 6.6 *Example of RMF Output*

```
      CPU 0 CHANNEL 01    BUSY PERCENTAGE
      0      10.0    20.0     30.0     40.0     50.0
      |————|————|————|————|————|

10:39 |**********          •         •         •         •
10:49 |*********•          •         •         •         •
10:59 |*****************   •         •         •         •
11:09 |******************  •         •         •         •
11:19 |*****************   •         •         •         •
11:29 |***********************       •         •         •
11:39 |**************      •         •         •         •
11:49 |**************************    •         •         •
11:59 |*******************•          •         •         •
12:09 |***********************       •         •         •
12:19 |**********************        •         •         •
12:29 |*****************   •         •         •         •
12:39 |*****************   •         •         •         •
12:49 |***************     •         •         •         •
12:59 |*******************•          •         •         •
13:09 |****************************  •         •         •
13:19 |********************•         •         •         •
13:29 |*******************  •         •         •         •
13:39 |************************      •         •         •
13:49 |*************************     •         •         •
13:59 |**************************    •         •         •
14:09 |*********************         •         •         •
14:19 |*************************     •         •         •
14:29 |**********************        •         •         •
14:39 |***************************   •         •         •
14:49 |**********************        •         •         •
14:59 |******************  •         •         •         •
15:09 |****************    •         •         •         •
15:19 |***********         •         •         •         •
15:29 |*****************   •         •         •         •
15:39 |************        •         •         •         •
15:49 |***********         •         •         •         •
15:59 |************        •         •         •         •
16:09 |*****************   •         •         •         •
16:19 |***************     •         •         •         •
16:29 |********  •         •         •         •         •
16:39 |***************     •         •         •         •
16:49 |**************      •         •         •         •
16:59 |******************  •         •         •         •
17:09 |********************•         •         •         •
17:19 |******************  •         •         •         •
17:29 |********************•         •         •         •
17:39 |************        •         •         •         •
17:49 |******  •           •         •         •         •
17:59 |******  •           •         •         •         •
```

Channel utilization for channel 1 on CPU 0 during primary operating hours.

process consists of three steps. First, it is necessary to define formally exactly what we are evaluating. In other words, we need to decide what *not* to model. This process of elimination, though seemingly simple, actually is the basis of modeling. Unless the extraneous parts of the system are eliminated, the model may not be accurate enough to yield useful results. The resultant model could also become too large for the modeler to conceptualize. Deciding what not to include in the model requires the experience of the systems and application programming staff. They are the ones responsible for insuring that the system functions as a whole from the application program point of view, as well as the operating system point of view. Their experiences are invaluable at this point. This step is called defining the boundaries of the system under study.

Secondly, we must identify the various characteristics or attributes of the system components, or entities. These attributes include manufacturers' hardware specifications, statistics gathered from monitors, and channel configuration information. For example, the manufacturer of a general ledger package might note that each transaction generates an average of eight execute channel programs (EXCPs) per transaction. Another example would be the determination that a particular DASD channel is accessed an average of five times more than similar channels during first shift. Appendices A and B discuss, in different ways, the hundreds of entities used in a data processing shop. Other device attributes might include access time, storage capacity, transfer rates, line speeds, printer speeds, program buffering techniques, and job queues. Channel configuration data refers to how the various hardware and some software components are related to each other. (Refer to Figure 6.2.) From all of this information, we are able to construct a view of the system as it interacts rather than on a component-by-component basis.

Finally, we must construct a causal diagram depicting the cause-and-effect relationships that exist within the model. Once again, systems experience is the key. To fix a performance problem, we must find out what the cause of the problem is. In other words, we must understand how the aforementioned interconnections affect the model entities and the model itself. This is the art of performance evaluation. Being able to sift through the data to find relationships which are causing ineffective processing is difficult for the most seasoned system professional.

There are several types of models that we could construct. First, and most simply, would be the informal model. Informal modeling consists of the assumptions, biases, and experiences of the modeler as they relate to the system to be represented. Normally, they are not mathematically or statistically based, but are a collection of valuable knowledge about how the system works. We all have informal models concerning relationships, ideas, and beliefs. Secondly, queuing models, an analytic method, views each entity within the study as a server which receives requests for and grants service to programs. While awaiting service, the programs form waiting lines (queues) until their request is acted on. Finally, simulation represents the dynamic nature of the modeled system. Simulation involves depicting the system in various stages of change and then determining how to alter the simulation to optimize the results. Most computer modeling incorporates all three types of modeling at some point. First we must have a conceptual model (informal) about how the system performs. Then we must determine where in the system resource constraints will restrain processing (queuing). Finally, we must make changes to the system and determine the effects of those changes (simulation).

Once the model is constructed, the system can be prototyped. Simulation involves using the model of the system instead of the actual system to evaluate proposed changes. For example, it would be substantially cheaper and safer to simulate the construction of a new type of bridge rather than actually build one and "wait and see what happens." In this manner, by modeling the system under evaluation, we are able to see the effects of system changes without disrupting the actual processing. At this point, we cannot assume that our model is an accurate one. Subsequently, it will be necessary to calibrate the model to insure its accurate representation of the measured system. Simulation does not necessarily incorporate the use of computer simulation techniques. Often, we are able to determine the outcome based on a specific model. In many ways, the decisions we make every day incorporate some sort of simulation. For example, we play over and over in our minds how we will make a presentation and how we might handle certain responses. Models that are too complex or span a long period of time often require computer simulation techniques. The most common of these used for modeling a computer system would be discrete event simulation. Discrete event simulation views time as very small, but distinct slices. The current state of the model is changed each time we move from one slice to another. Discrete simulation languages that could be used here would include SIMSCRIPT, GPSS, and SLAM.

The process of modeling a system is probably the most important step in performance evaluation. Without an accurate view of how the system under study acts and reacts, we cannot intelligently fix the performance problem or anticipate future problems. Simulation is simply a tool for constructing a logical model of the system. We can use simulation to make changes to a model without actually changing the system. As we will see, the construction or reconstruction of the model might occur several times until it accurately reflects the system under study. After this is accomplished, we will be able to tune the model and then, eventually, the system.

Model Validation

No matter how much time and effort go into the creation of the model, if it does not accurately portray the system under study, it is of little use to the performance evaluator. We must be able to compare the model that we have created to the actual system. In this way, we can validate the model. Using techniques ranging from statistical residual analysis to common sense, we must test the accuracy of the model. To do this, we simply ascertain that inputs to the model produce the same outputs that the original system would have produced. This implies two things. First, it implies that we are able to measure the outputs of the system. We could not easily measure user satisfaction with the system and still place that information into the model. Instead, we must understand what would make a user satisfied and then incorporate that into the model. Secondly, it is assumed that the system under study has produced those outputs against which the model is being compared. This becomes difficult when trying to model a novel situation. In these cases, the experience of the staff members becomes important. Instead of using actual system output information, the model would have to be evaluated against the ideal or expected output of the system given those sets of inputs. This can bias the view of the model, because the model was created using the opinions of these individuals. Under these circumstances, it would be better to split the staff into two groups: one for construction and the other for validation.

For example, suppose Major Company wished to employ a computer aided design (CAD) process to help reduce project development costs and times. Also assume that the existing computing resources will be used. In determining the effects of this new technology, it may be necessary to model the system including the CAD process. It is difficult to validate this model because there is no standard against which to judge. Getting the opinions of the systems staff would be useful here, but when validation comes about, the model would probably reflect just what they had expected. If for some reason the staff did not want to maintain the system, the resulting model could be biased against the process. The same process will occur if the same set of data values is used both to build and validate the model. Instead, different data should be gathered to validate the model.

The validation process is a go/no-go step. Should the model yield unsatisfactory results, the evaluator must reconstruct the model to reflect more accurately the target system. This could necessitate the construction of a completely new model or simply a refining of the old one. Under either case, the new model must be revalidated. This sequence repeats until the model is acceptable.

The validated model is the starting point of the actual performance evaluation process. It represents a changeable system. In this manner, we are able to change the various parameters within the model to study their effects. Later, we might apply these changes to the real system. However, the model must represent the system as closely as possible to allow us to make generalizations from the model to the actual system. Without this firm foundation, we could make erroneous assumptions about the effects our changes will have. This could be devastating. For example, if under a specific configuration the model predicts that the average number of EXCPs on a given channel is 20 per second, when in reality it is closer to 100 per second, our model would incorrectly reflect the true situation. It may be determined that 20 EXCPs per second is acceptable. Consequently, the proposed change may be made with the actual system performance being totally unacceptable. The change may have involved substantial expenditures for both hardware and software. The result is a very embarrassing and costly mistake.

Previously we stated that gathering performance evaluation statistics was necessary even if the system's performance was acceptable. This data should be used in both validating the model of the system and establishing target performance levels as the model is changed.

It is only after we have decided that the model is correct that we can continue with the evaluation process. Obviously, the more experience one has with a system, the quicker and more accurately the initial model creation is accomplished. Now that we have a realistic view of the system, it becomes time to evaluate that system and propose changes.

Changing the Model

At this point, we have an accurate picture of the system under study. We know how it works under various loads, its inputs, and its outputs. Our model produces approximately the same results that the actual system does. Now we can begin system tuning. The iterative process of model change allows us to see what would happen to the real system in the event we made certain changes to it. In other words, we are able to preview the reactions of the system by first performing those changes on the model. The important factor here is knowing what exactly to change. We want to tune the system to accomplish at least one of the following goals:

1. Provide better service
2. Solve a specific problem
3. Change system components
4. Predict future behavior.

By improving the efficiency of the system, we could possibly provide better service to the user community. For example, by upgrading our channel configuration to include additional block multiplexing channels, we could decrease the waiting times for DASD. This could also solve a problem if system response was not acceptable to management. Any time we change the physical or logical configuration of the system, it is imperative that we determine, as accurately as possible, the effects of those changes. It is important, at this point, to remember that simply adding components to the system is not system tuning. System tuning is accomplished only if the change or addition of hardware or software is effective and does not downgrade the performance of the system. Finally, it is necessary to estimate future needs by seeing how growth in various areas will affect the system.

The term *system* refers to the interactions and relationships between entities. We must be careful, therefore, to be sure not to make changes without sufficient thought. When changing the model, and eventually the system, we must first determine exactly what is wrong. Secondly, we must determine the cause of the problem. Third, we select the optimal change from a list of alternative solutions. Finally, we make the change in the model, and then reevaluate the model's performance. Only when we are satisfied with the outcomes should we consider making these changes to the system.

In an ideal situation, the performance evaluation team is able to detect a trend toward unacceptable performance. If possible, the system should be modified before users are adversely affected. However, in actual practice, the users may be the first to notice a problem. Hence, it is the responsibility of the evaluation group to investigate user complaints. In most cases, these complaints will be symptoms of the actual problem, but they are the best place to start. The most common complaints heard are normally associated with response time. Response time is a function of many factors (i.e., DBMS, DASD, system load, etc.).

One way of graphically representing a system's performance is a multivariate statistics tool called a Kiviat chart. Figure 6.7 shows one of these charts. This type of chart allows us to show many factors at the same time and perhaps gives us a clue as to where to begin our investigation. Other useful information would be system load statistics showing how the system was loaded and performing at the time of the complaints. Gathering all of this information and analyzing it, we can then begin to determine what is wrong with the system. For example, we might see from system load statistics that response time was longest during the execution of the weekly payroll program. This could lead us to change the program to make it more efficient or reschedule its execution during a less critical response time period.

In large computer systems, there are frequently several methods of combating a performance problem. Limiting the effects of a change should be foremost on the evaluator's mind. Of the several alternatives that are available, we should choose the one that least affects the rest of the system. Various factors, for example, could be altered to decrease response time, but of those, perhaps only one or two will not cause other problems later. For example, even though response time could be shortened, decreasing the number of simultaneous users would not seem to be a good solution. Before making any changes to the system, we must consider the consequences of our actions. Every solution could produce several effects on the overall system. The best change would be the one that

Figure 6.7 *Example Kiviat Chart*

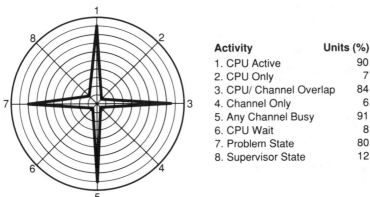

Activity	Units (%)
1. CPU Active	90
2. CPU Only	7
3. CPU/ Channel Overlap	84
4. Channel Only	6
5. Any Channel Busy	91
6. CPU Wait	8
7. Problem State	80
8. Supervisor State	12

corrects the performance problem and leaves the remaining parts of the system as they were. Simply stated, we want to change as little as possible at one time. In addition, the costs and benefits of each change have to be considered. If the system can be satisfactorily tuned simply by altering existing system components, that is a less costly option to acquiring additional hardware and software.

When we change the model, we want to be able to determine exactly what change caused the model output to change. The final step now is actually to change the model and then to consider the new output. Making large changes to the model tends to blur the cause-and-effect relationships within the model. In the event that the change had no effect on the problem, we must revert back to the original model, because it is based on how the current system works. Careful model change documentation should be maintained to trace the progress of the changes and to reduce the amount of duplication. Hopefully, we can see just how important that first model was. Without it, all of our changes would not be based on how the real system should react.

At some point in this process, one of the alternative model changes will be deemed as the best solution. This may be based on causing the least system disruption rather than creating the absolutely best environment. In either event, the model now reflects how the system should be configured. It is now time to change the system.

Changing the System

From the previous step, we determined what changes should be made to the system. The actual implementation of these changes could be as simple as changing the priority structure of system tasks or as complex as installing a new computer system. The change, regardless of its magnitude, should be adequately documented and approved before actual implementation. If the organization has a person in charge of system currency, that person should be notified well enough in advance of the actual change to allow notification of the user community. It must never be assumed that the change will go unnoticed. In a data processing environment, this is rarely the case. Now that we know what to change, we must consider when to implement that change.

Knowledge of the business cycle and the application areas themselves is useful here. The important consideration here, as before, is to implement the change at such a time as to cause the least disruption of service. Small changes can occur during periods of slack demand, usually during third shift. Large changes to the system may occur across several nights or weekends. This would require that the changes be modular in nature so they could be implemented step by step and still leave the system usable during the day. Some changes, however, cannot be made without disruption of service. In these cases, they should occur during off-peak cycles of the data processing center. For example, possibly one of the least busy periods of data processing could occur just after the printing of W-2 forms in January. At this time, sales are generally down and the accounting process has closed out the books for the preceding year. This might be a good time to implement a major change. It also might be decided to implement the changes on the test system only, then changing the production system only after the tuning process is completed on the test system. In this way we could then use a production system input stream on the test system to determine the effect of the tuning.

Once implemented, we cannot simply forget the changes and go on with business as usual. It is very important to make sure that the change fixed the problem. Even the most careful model builder using the best information could construct a model that does not represent the real system. We must monitor the changed system to determine that the problem is solved. If this is not the case, we must determine why and then construct a new model. This may also involve backing-out the changes so that the original system configuration is restored. Again, periodic system measurement is important. The changed system documentation should be updated to reflect the new implementation. After all of the work that went into the creation of the model and the determination of the solution, it would be wasteful not to document the changes in the event a similar situation occurs. Performance evaluation is a continuous process. We must be constantly measuring, modeling, and perhaps tuning to insure the effective operation of the system.

SUMMARY OF THE EVALUATION PROCESS

Performance evaluation is a systematic process of system measurement, problem determination, and correction. It uses the same problem-solving techniques used by people in everyday life. First we determine what resources we have that would affect our decision. Taking inventory here helps us determine the potential causes of our problem. Next we measure those resources to understand exactly what they are doing. The third step causes us to create a model or logical association between resources to ascertain some cause-and-effect process within the system. After assuring ourselves that the model accurately represents the actual system, we alter the model to bring the system performance to an acceptable level, avoiding or correcting performance problems. Finally, we change the system so that it matches the correctly functioning model and then remeasure the system to insure that the changes fixed the problem. Performance evaluation draws on the talents of several areas within data processing ranging from systems programming to systems analysis and design. The user community must be used as input to the process and then made aware of any changes to the system. This process can be used for hardware, software, or system performance evaluation. Performance evaluators should be knowledgeable of all of the areas within data processing along with statistical simulation techniques.

The amount of assets represented by a data processing center require that these resources be used to their maximum capabilities. Performance evaluation allows us to monitor and maintain these resources in such a manner as to take full advantage of their worth.

BENCHMARKING

When a hardware or software purchase decision is being made, management often wishes to know whether the purchased item is going to provide satisfactory results under load conditions. It is possible that several alternative solutions might present themselves for evaluation. Should this be the case, we will need to have some method of comparing these items. This form of performance evaluation is called benchmarking.

Benchmarking is used to help management make acquisition decisions. For example, if the purchase of a new accounts receivable (A/R) package is under consideration, it would be useful to know how the various packages on the market compare to each other, and perhaps to the A/R package already running on our machine. To make this comparison, we would select a representative sample of accounts receivable transactions and run them, if possible, on each of the systems, while measuring their performance using the techniques we have already discussed. The performance evaluations would then give us a basis on which to make our purchase decision. Obviously, it would be undesirable to install several software packages, particularly operating systems, just to see how well they work. In this case, we would ask the vendors for a list of other firms that are using the package. After contacting some of these installations and determining which are configured closely to ours, it is usually possible to perform the benchmark on these systems. This type of reciprocity eventually benefits both organizations. If we select the same package, then the organizations can work together and share experience and knowledge.

For both hardware and software benchmarking, it is important that all candidates be evaluated using the same criteria. Doing otherwise could bias the results. Another source of information would be hardware and software reviews found in publications such as *Datapro* and *Auerbach*. These publications, which normally are independent and accept no advertising from the manufacturers, are a good source of benchmark data. This subject is covered in greater depth in the next chapter.

DATABASE/DATA COMMUNICATIONS
PERFORMANCE EVALUATION

As a special concern, we must consider the performance evaluation of a database (DB) system and its data communications (DC) counterpart. It is, of course, possible to discuss one without the other, but here we will consider them together. The lifeblood of many large organizations is the quick and accurate access of the corporate database. Without this, the company could well be made less competitive or even put out of business. The database must be organized in such a manner as to facilitate access. In Chapter 15, we will see that there are several forms or styles of database management systems. Each of these has its own merits and liabilities. However, as a manager, you must select a DBMS based on several criteria. One of the most important criteria would be speed of access.

In addition, the database itself must be constantly monitored to assure optimal access. For example, under some database systems, the deletion of records can cause large portions of unusable space in the database. This in turn causes the search for subsequent records to be slower. The database administrator would have the job of constantly monitoring the database accesses and tuning the database to insure performance acceptability. To do this, he or she would use the performance evaluation tools discussed earlier in addition to other software monitors designed specifically for monitoring the database. The administrator must keep in contact with the user community to determine exactly how they are using the system. For example, suppose the database was created assuming that the main avenue of information retrieval would be Social Security number. However, if it appears that the users are accessing the information based on a secondary data item, department number for example, a reorganization of the database might be warranted.

However, no matter how efficiently the database is organized, if the data communications system is ineffective, overall response will be unacceptable. Most firms will have a separate telecommunications area that will be responsible for performance evaluation of the data communications system. The telecommunications manager must be a jack-of-all-trades. He or she must be knowledgeable about operating system functions, electronic communications hardware, and database organization. All of these tools are necessary to be able to diagnose telecommunications problems.

The performance of a teleprocessing system is dependent on the system load. Obviously, the more heavily used the system, the slower the response time that can be expected. We can see this problem each year when attempting to make a long-distance phone call on Mother's Day or Christmas. The telecommunications manager must determine if the slowness is correctable within corporate guidelines. This might necessitate additional, perhaps faster, data lines. A hardware solution might not be feasible, however. In this case, the manager might look to administrative or software changes that would alter user behavior during peak hours. These and other issues involving telecommunications will be addressed in depth in Chapter 16.

Because current business decisions are based so heavily on current information, the performance of the database and data communications system is probably the most noticeable arm of the computing center to the general user. Often, the adequate performance of the entire data processing group is based on this criterion. As a result, the managers in charge of these areas are constantly under pressure to keep these facilities as responsive as possible.

MAJOR COMPANY

Major Company has a separate group of performance evaluators. This group reports directly to the assistant to the vice-president of information systems. All of the members of the performance evaluation group have a strong systems programming background. The group is responsible for doing long-range capacity planning for the system and for analyzing and solving specific performance problems. Following is an analysis of one specific problem that has recently occurred at Major Company.

The online test system at Major Company has been experiencing a serious degradation of online response time over the last couple of weeks. There has been a flood of complaints about response time being as long as two minutes at some times during the regular working hours. This appears to be a serious problem since the productivity of the application development and maintenance areas has been adversely affected.

Al, from the performance evaluation area, has been requested to investigate the problem. Al first interviews some of the users. He discovers that the problem seems to occur randomly throughout the day. The response time will normally be between one and two seconds. Then, suddenly, for a period of from five minutes to over a half an hour, the response time will soar to between one and two minutes.

Al then examines the performance data that has been gathered over the past two weeks. Since this data was generated by a time-driven software monitor, it represents only random views of the system. The data shows that response time has been about one second except for two specific instances where the response time was about one minute. Further investigation of the data shows that during poor response time, almost all of the interactive tasks were in the inactive state (i.e., they were waiting for I/O before they could continue processing). When the response time was acceptable, very few tasks were in the inactive state. The only other information that Al can get from this performance data is that the system was configured the same during this entire period of time. Neither devices nor system software were changed.

At this point Al scratches his head and decides that he will have to capture a more complete picture of the system when it is responding poorly. He programs a software monitor so that on command it will capture a complete picture of the events occurring in the system. The monitor, as configured, cannot be left continually running. It simply consumes too many resources and would itself degrade the system. So, Al asks the users to report immediately when the response time degrades. Now he sits back and waits.

Two days later, a user reports that the problem is occurring. Al directs the operator to trigger the monitor. The problem lasts for about 15 minutes and then ceases. During this time, the monitor captures a complete view of the system.

On examining the data, Al finds that almost all of the tasks are in the inactive state waiting for their program to be paged into real memory (remember, in a virtual storage system, most segments of a program are not in real storage, but must be paged in when needed). The map of real memory shows that one task, a large graphics program, has over half of the real memory.

Al contacts the user and discovers that this person has been newly hired to do sophisticated graphics for the vice-president of marketing. In doing this work, this user's response time was generally slower than that person desired. One manual stated that the $V = R$ (virtual = real) memory option would speed up processing. It did, by hogging most of real memory for that one program. Removing this option brought the system back to its normal, desirable state.

SUMMARY

The investment in a corporate data processing department can often represent millions of dollars in resources. This fact, when combined with the idea that many organizations would totally cease to function without data processing support, underscores the importance of an effective system. Performance evaluation is a process of monitoring, judging, and correcting the performance of the data processing system in an attempt to obtain maximum service from the system's resources. Performance evaluation is a six-step iterative process. First we inventory the current system. Secondly we measure the current system to see how it is performing. Next we create a model to represent the system. The fourth step requires that we validate the model to make sure it accurately represents the current system. Then we change the model to reflect possible new environments (hardware and/or software) and determine the effects of these changes. Finally, we change or tune the system.

The performance evaluation process is an ongoing activity used to detect changes in the operation of the system and to correct potential or actual problems encountered. When used systematically and intelligently, performance evaluation can save the organization substantial amounts of capital and labor by the additional gains in system effectiveness and the possible increase in end-user productivity.

QUESTIONS

1. What is the purpose of performance evaluation? List the steps that should be undertaken.
2. What is the difference between system tuning and benchmarking? How are they similar?
3. In your opinion, how often should performance evaluation be performed? What factors must you consider in making your decision? Why?
4. From the standpoint of performance evaluation, why is it not a good idea to

purchase a tape drive from a new manufacturer? What would make an organization consider a new manufacturer?

5. Simulation is used in performance evaluation. Explain what simulation is and why it is often used in computer performance evaluations.

6. Why is it necessary to measure the input stream? Why is it also necessary to measure the utilization of both logical and physical devices? Can these two measurements be done independently? Why or why not?

7. The use of statistics is helpful in performance evaluation. Which descriptive statistics would be helpful? Why?

8. Why is the performance evaluation of a DB/DC different from that of the system in general?

9. What is the difference between the performance evaluation of an individual worker and the performance evaluation of a system?

10. When measuring the system, it is usually necessary to accumulate statistics during many different times of the day and different days of the week. Explain why.

11. Write a simple COBOL program that reads a blocked dataset. Measure the amounts of time used by this program. Compare this to the same COBOL program reading an unblocked dataset. Interpret your results in light of performance evaluation.

12. Sketch the Kiviat chart that would describe a system that is I/O bound and also uses the CPU heavily. What solutions would you suggest to increase the throughput of this system? Why?

CASE ANALYSIS

Case 1

A computer system is experiencing unacceptable delays in dealing with online requests. At the same time, batch turnaround is acceptable. A quick analysis of the problem shows that during these online delays the CPU is running at 99% utilization. The manager immediately decides that a new, more powerful CPU must be acquired. Discuss this decision and propose an alternative way of attacking the performance problem. Also explain why the manager's decision may not be a good one.

Case 2

Investigate how performance evaluation is done in the computer facility at your school (if you have multiple facilities, describe only one of these). Be sure to describe the tools employed to do the measurement, the frequency of evaluation, and the specific steps involved in the performance evaluation process.

Case 3

For each of the following independent circumstances, describe the probable reasons for the problem and the possible solutions to each problem.

a. One channel, which is connected to DASD, is operating well beyond what is considered normal capacity. All other channels are operating at acceptable levels.

b. The operating system is thrashing (paging too frequently).

c. Certain batch jobs are experiencing significant delays in turnaround while other batch jobs are being turned around very quickly. While the jobs use different resources, they all take about the same amount of execution time.

ADDITIONAL READINGS

ANDERSON, H. A., M. REISER, AND G. GALATI. "Tuning a Virtual Storage System," *IBM Systems Journal*, July 1975.

CANIANO, STEVEN. "All TP1s are not Created Equal," *Datamation*, August 15, 1988, p. 51.

FERRARI, DOMENICO. *Computer Systems Performance Evaluation*. Englewood Cliffs, NJ: Prentice Hall, 1978.

FLEMING, P. J., AND J. J. WALLACE. "How Not to Lie With Statistics: The Correct Way to Summarize Benchmark Results," *Communications of the ACM*, Vol. 29, No. 3, March 1986.

LEWIS, BYRON C., AND ALBERT E. CREWS. "The Evolution of Benchmarking as a Computer Performance Evaluation Technique," *MIS Quarterly*, Vol. 9, No. 1, March 1985, pp. 7–16.

LIENTZ, B. P., AND E. B. SWANSON. "Grosch's Law Revisited: CPU Power and the Cost of Computation," *Communications of the ACM*, Vol. 28, No. 2, February 1985, p. 142.

O'NEIL, PATRICK. "Revisiting DBMS Benchmarks," *Datamation*, September 15, 1989, p. 47.

SIRCAR, S., AND D. DAVE. "The Relationship Between Benchmark Tests and Microcomputer Price," *Communications of the ACM*, Vol. 29, No. 3, March 1986, p. 212.

READINGS BEFORE NEXT CHAPTER

The previous material should be adequate preparation.

7

HARDWARE ACQUISITION

After the present system has been evaluated and it has been determined that additional hardware must be acquired or existing hardware must be replaced, it is the responsibility of the information system's management to initiate the acquisition. In this chapter, we will discuss the process of acquiring hardware. Even though it is usually unwise to acquire hardware without considering software, we will avoid discussing software acquisition until Chapter 10. Many of the procedures for acquiring software are the same as those for acquiring hardware. However, as you will see later, software acquisition is a much more complex process fraught with a high degree of uncertainty. It must be stressed that software is the heart of the system and that hardware should be acquired that will support the software satisfying our needs. Too often the hardware is purchased first with no regard for available software. To simplify this chapter, we will ignore the interdependence of hardware and software and assume that additional hardware will solve the problem.

HARDWARE ACQUISITION

The hardware acquisition process can be quite interesting and informative. It is interesting to look at new products and see what the industry presently has to offer and is developing for the near future. The computer industry is so dynamic that it is almost impossible to keep track of all developments affecting the firm.

Hence, no matter how much experience one has in hardware acquisition, each acquisition of hardware will involve learning the changes that have occurred since the last acquisition. For an individual acquiring hardware for the first time, the process can appear very imposing and confusing. However, a well-organized, thorough analysis of the available equipment should lead to a good selection.

As we describe the acquisition process, we will state a series of procedures that should be followed. It must be understood that the order in which we present these procedures will not necessarily be the order that is followed in actual practice. Each situation may dictate a slightly different approach. While order of execution is not mandatory, the more of these procedures that are implemented the better chance there is of making a quality decision.

DETERMINING NEEDS

As with any decision-making process, the hardware acquisition process begins with a determination of needs. Needs come from sources either external or internal to the information system. The users of the system may have a need for new or additional hardware. In this case, the users should be interviewed to determine their needs. For example, the mechanical engineering department may want to acquire new color graphic terminals. By investigating the situation, the desired specifications can be determined. The other situation is one in which the information systems area has determined that additional hardware is necessary. Again, the specific needs will have to be determined. Hopefully, when this involves improving system performance, a good portion of this work was done during the performance evaluation and system tuning process.

For the successful implementation of the hardware, it is necessary to determine carefully the needs from both the users' and the data center's perspective. Hardware that has a direct impact on the user must actively involve that user, or there is a good chance that the selected hardware will not be satisfactory.

This needs inventory should be split into the two separate categories of mandatory and desirable attributes. Splitting attributes into the two categories of mandatory and desirable will help to specify the characteristics of the needed equipment and will also speed the evaluation process. A mandatory attribute is one that must be satisfied by the piece of equipment. This means that any vendor failing to meet that criteria will be eliminated from consideration. A desirable attribute will increase or decrease the attractiveness of the product, but is not absolutely necessary. Dividing attributes into these two categories does not preclude a specific characteristic from being included in both categories.

For example, there may be a budget limit of $50,000. This leads to a mandatory attribute of the price being $50,000 or less. In addition, price will be a desirable attribute. With no other factors considered, the vendor with the lower price will be more attractive. If there is no budget limitation, then price would only be a desirable attribute.

One of the more difficult parts of acquiring hardware is to convert the needs of the organization into the technical mandatory and desirable attributes. To a good extent this process is as much an art as it is a science. The manager must be familiar with the technical hardware attributes and be able to estimate how the various attributes will affect the entire system. Part of this process involves using the models that were created during the performance evaluation stage. This should allow the manager to experiment with different configurations. But there will be many factors that the model may not cover. The manager will have to exercise good judgment in determining these attributes.

Let us take as an example hard disk drives. The need for additional secondary storage may have initiated the request to acquire additional disk drives. There are other types of random access devices, such as drums, mass storage devices, laser disks, solid state memory, etc. The manager, through experience, knows that for this specific situation, only hard disk drives will do the required job. In addition, many of the other attributes may be determined in the same way. For example, floor space in the computer room may not be of concern, hence the footprint of the equipment may not be important. However, the cooling system in the computer room may be nearing capacity. The waste heat produced by the equipment may then be of considerable concern. These factors would not be included in the simulation model. More intangible factors, such as the reliability of the vendor and the quality of maintenance, are even more subjective.

The mandatory and desirable attributes will be different for each type of hardware and for each set of circumstances experienced by a firm. Some common necessary attributes are listed in Figure 7.1, and some desirable attributes are listed in Figure 7.2. After we discuss the evaluation process, we will describe some of the attributes for specific types of hardware.

Often the performance characteristics for a specific type of hardware are not known or the investigator is not familiar enough with the hardware to decide what factors must be considered. Naturally, in this case it would be necessary to gather preliminary information before rigidly detailing the requirements. This information can be obtained from various sources which may include professional journals, hardware evaluation services, industry user groups, and other users of this type of hardware.

Figure 7.1 *Some Possible Mandatory Attributes*

Hardware Compatibility	Software Compatibility
Purchase Price	Footprint
Speed	Capacity
Maintenance Contract	Delivery Date
Availability of Training	Waste Heat
Installation Time	Guarantees and Warranty
Operating Costs	Financing Alternatives
Documentation	Electrical Power Requirements

Figure 7.2 *Some Possible Desirable Attributes*

Field Upgradability	Purchase Price
Footprint	Waste Heat
Capacity	Speed
Maintenance Contract	Free Trial Period
Operating Costs	Electrical Power Needs
Available Training	Delivery Date
Installation Time	Associated Hardware
Available Documentation	Retention of Market Value
Cabling Constraints	Warranties and Guarantees
Available Financing	

PRELIMINARY INVESTIGATION

After the attributes have been determined, a preliminary investigation of available vendors should be conducted. This is usually done by reading trade publications designed for this purpose. These would include the *Datapro* series, *Dataworld*, and *Data Sources*. Also, common computer trade journals such as *Computerworld*, *Datamation*, and *Infosystems* should be used. Often new products are first announced in these publications, and the advertisements can also be quite informative. This process can be helpful in determining the available technology, and will also help in developing a list of potential vendors that can be sent requests for proposals.

The preliminary investigations may also include using other knowledgeable sources. These may include industry and vendor groups, managers of other data centers that have similar hardware and software configurations, and consultants knowledgeable in the area. These sources can be very helpful and usually will be able to give fresh insight into the problem to be solved.

Vendor groups are organizations of users of a specific vendor's hardware or software. Industry groups are comprised of representatives from organizations in the same industry. For example, there are computer groups for educational users, governmental agencies, and production-oriented industries. These groups can be quite helpful since there is a good chance that other members are willing to share their experiences in solving problems similar to yours.

It is not necessary to do an in-depth investigation of the performance and features of the hardware offered by the various vendors; this investigation will be done later. The purpose of this preliminary analysis is to give management a good feel for what the market has to offer and the range of possible solutions to their problem.

At this point there should be enough information to do a rough analysis of the potential costs and benefits of acquiring the specific equipment. This information will usually be organized into a report and presented to management. After analyzing this report, management will decide whether the hardware should be acquired. This often entails the development and distribution of a request for proposal (RFP). If management decides to proceed, this does not mean the equipment will be acquired. If the vendors do not present a satisfactory proposal, the acquisition will not occur.

In some instances the aforementioned feasibility assessment is not necessary. By initiating the preliminary investigation, management may have already decided that the equipment should be acquired. Of course, the larger the commitment of resources, the more closely management will want to be involved in the acquisition process.

REQUEST FOR PROPOSAL

The next step is to begin the process of selecting the appropriate hardware product. Determined by the situation, the acquisition process can be as simple as contacting one vendor and evaluating the products of just that vendor. Or the process may involve the development of a formal request for proposal (RFP). Under specific circumstances the informal process of directly contacting a single vendor may be appropriate. This is the case when the product is unique to that vendor or when the decision has been made previously to deal with a specific vendor for particular types of hardware. While the more formal procedure of issuing an RFP may be more time consuming, it will often result in a more thorough consideration of the available products. For the remainder of the discussion, we will assume that an RFP will be issued.

When the company decides to use an RFP, the development of the RFP is usually the most critical step in the entire acquisition process. The RFP is a request to all interested parties to submit formal bids to satisfy hardware needs. If the company accepts one of the submitted bids, then they will have entered into a legal contract. While the RFP itself is not a legal contract, it begins the process that results in a legal contract. Hence, great care must be taken when formulating the RFP.

The broad objectives of the RFP are to inform the vendors of what you want, when you want it, and how you will choose the best vendor. In the following section we will discuss the RFP in detail, and at the end of the chapter present an example of an RFP.

It is a good idea to prepare an RFP for most major acquisitions. In fact, some organizations are legally bound to develop and distribute RFPs in the acquisition of equipment over a specific dollar amount. These organizations include federal, state, and local governments and other publicly held institutions, including colleges and universities. The rationale behind the law is to encourage the competitive bid process in government organizations. For data center personnel, this means that the RFP and the procedures followed in the entire acquisition process must conform with the governing regulations. Failure to follow these rules may result in legal action against the organization and/or the responsible employees. In extreme cases, when proper procedures are not followed, the employees may be forced to pay for the acquisition from their own personal funds.

For less significant purchases, some firms will expedite the acquisition process by directly soliciting the vendors for bids and not issuing an RFP. This is appropriate when the market has been well researched and there are only a small number of qualified products. The major problem with this type of approach is that it appeals to some of the individuals involved, only because it "cuts the red tape" of issuing an RFP. This can lead to overuse of this approach. However, in most situations an RFP is a valuable tool in the acquisition process.

RFP FORMAT

The format of the RFP will differ from one organization to another. Often the format is dictated by the firm's procedures manual. However, the content of the document should be almost the same. Following we will discuss the contents of the RFP. The points we will discuss should be included in an RFP, but the order of presentation may differ in some cases. Figure 7.3 summarizes the various sections contained within an RFP.

The first section of the RFP should inform the vendors of the basic objectives of the document and describe the general procedures to be followed. This would include the name, address, and telephone number of the primary contact person for all inquiries regarding the RFP. In addition, the schedule of important events should be included in this section. This would include the date bids are due, when the bids will be evaluated, and the expected date of product delivery.

The next section would give a short history of the firm, a brief description of the present computer configuration of the firm, and the future expecta-

Figure 7.3 *Sections of a Request for Proposal*

SECTION	CONTENTS
1. Introduction	Reason for RFP
	Organization name
	Contact person
	Important dates
2. Organization Background	Hardware and software configuration
	History and future expectations of firm
3. Requirements	Mandatory and desirable attributes of equipment
4. The Form of Proposal	Format in which the proposal must be submitted
5. Evaluation Criteria	Methods of evaluating the submitted bids

tions of the firm. This will include a detailed list of the hardware and software of the present system. The more the vendor knows about your system, the better chance you have of obtaining a product that is best suited to your environment.

The central concern of the RFP is the attributes of the equipment to be acquired. This section must be very detailed, describing all aspects of the equipment. To simplify the evaluation of the bids that are submitted, it is best to divide the attributes of the devices into the categories of mandatory and desirable. The specific measures should be detailed in the body of the RFP, and a checklist should be included for the vendors to complete and submit with their bids. This should reduce the time it will take to evaluate bids.

The items that should be included in the attributes section of the RFP will be discussed in detail later in this chapter when we discuss individual hardware components. Of course, some of these items will depend on the specific requirements of the firm.

The checklist of attributes will usually be included in the section of the RFP entitled "The Form of the Proposal." This section directs the bidder to submit certain materials, sometimes in a specific format. Besides the checklist, other items will be included in this section. The vendor should submit all pertinent product literature with the proposal and also include a statement that certain parts of the RFP will be included in the subsequent legal contract. This section helps guarantee the completeness of the submitted bids.

The final section of the RFP details the procedures to be followed in selecting the winning submitted bid. This section can be considerably different depending on the organization developing the RFP. It may only state the series of events leading to final selection, without detailing the specific criteria to be used in the evaluation. This allows for more flexibility in the selection process. However, by law, some governmental institutions must state how the evaluation will be done. This includes disclosing the exact scoring system to be employed. This will allow each firm to determine the points earned by its bid before the bid is submitted. In addition, the full specification of selection criteria can produce a more uniform, unbiased selection process.

Care must be taken when formulating the RFP not to aim it at a specific product or vendor. By making a trivial attribute that is unique to one product or vendor a mandatory attribute, the selection of that product will be guaranteed. In this way an individual can impose a personal preference on the selection process, while retaining the appearance of objectivity.

THEORETICAL BENCHMARK

After the bidding deadline, the evaluation process begins. The first step in evaluation is to do what is called theoretical benchmarking. This entails the examination of each proposal based solely on the representations of the vendor. At this point no attempt is made to verify the vendor claims. That is done at a later time.

The theoretical benchmarking process should be divided into two separate evaluations. Each vendor's proposal must be evaluated for compliance with the mandatory attributes. If any of the mandatory attributes are not present, then the proposal is unacceptable and is eliminated from consideration. The remaining proposals that satisfy the mandatory attributes must then be evaluated based on the desirable attributes. This evaluation will determine which proposals will go on to the physical benchmarking stage.

The evaluation of mandatory attributes is usually a reasonably straightforward process. The vendor's proposal and accompanying technical literature is compared to the list of mandatory attributes. To simplify this process a checklist, could be used to organize the evaluation. As shown in Figure 7.4, the various mandatory attributes are listed down the left-hand side. The next two columns specify whether the requirements are satisfied, and the final column is for any appropriate comments. If there are any checks in the "No" column, then the proposal is eliminated from further consideration. The column for measurement value is helpful for future reference and can also be used to speed the analysis of the desirable attributes.

If no bid meets all of the mandatory attributes, then the situation must be reevaluated. The attributes must be scrutinized to be sure all the mandatory attributes are absolutely necessary. If they are, then the desired acquisition is just not possible under the present constraints.

The evaluation of desirable attributes is more complex. For most desir-

Figure 7.4 *Rating Mandatory Attributes*

ATTRIBUTE	SATISFIED? YES NO		DESCRIPTION OF ATTRIBUTE

Speed:
  Aver Seek Time < 20m
  Average Latency < 10m
  Transfer Rate > 1.5MB
Capacity:
  Each DASD > 6GB
  Total per Cntrl > 12GB
Compatibility:
  IBM 308X and 3090
  IBM VM/XA and MVS/ESA
Maintenance:
  8 hours, 5 days/week
Additional Capabilities:
  Multipathing Supported
  Cylinder Size < 2MB
  Count-Key-Data Format
Delivery & Installation:
  Delivery by 7/01/9X
  Vendor Installation			

able attributes, it is not simply whether the attribute is present, but the relative merits of its performance. For example, considering storage capacity of a disk drive, if the mandatory capacity is a minimum of 2 gigabytes, both vendor A and vendor B will meet this requirement if their drives have capacity of 2.3 and 4.5 gigabytes, respectively. However, the 4.5 gigabyte drive must be rated higher on the desirable attribute of storage since it has almost twice the capacity. It is necessary to analyze each desirable attribute in this manner and then determine the most attractive alternative.

The relative rating of desirable attributes may be accomplished by using the weighted rating scheme presented in Figure 7.5. The desirable attributes are listed in the left-hand column. Since the various attributes will not be of the

Figure 7.5 *Rating Desirable Attributes*

ATTRIBUTE	DESCRIPTION OF ATTRIBUTE	FOR INTERNAL USE		
		WEIGHT	SCORE	EXTENSION
Speed:				
Seek Time		1.0	8.0	8.0
Latency		1.0	7.0	7.0
Transfer Rate		1.0	10.0	10.0
Capacity:				
Storage per Actuator		.9	9.0	8.1
Storage per DASD String		.6	7.0	4.2
Storage per Controller		.7	9.5	6.7
Controller Cache Store		.5	10.0	5.0
Physical Attributes:				
Dimensions		.0	8.0	0.0
Weight		.0	7.0	0.0
Power Consumed		.4	9.0	3.6
Waste Heat		.4	8.0	3.2
Cabling Constraints		.0	9.0	0.0
Maintenance:				
Types of Plans		1.0	8.0	8.0
Costs		1.0	5.0	5.0
Costs:				
Controller		.8	3.0	2.4
Head of String		.8	2.0	1.6
Other DASD Units		.8	2.0	1.6
Necessary Added Software		.8	1.0	.8
Total Configuration Cost		.8	2.5	2.0
Installation		6.0	10.0	6.0
Actuators per DASD		7.0	8.0	5.6
Field Upgrades:				
Options		1.0	10.0	10.0
Costs		.8	5.0	4.0
Financing Alternatives:				
Options		.0	8.0	0.0
Costs		.0	6.0	0.0
Added Plug Compatibility		.0	8.0	0.0
Total Score				102.8

same importance, we must assign each attribute a relative weight. This weighting factor will vary from 0 (for no importance) to 1.0 (for most important). To help promote more unbiased judgments, it is best to determine these weighting factors before the proposals are received and evaluated. The relative merit of each desirable attribute should be evaluated and scored for every proposal submitted. This score should range from 0 (for not possessing the attribute) to 10 (the maximum value of the attribute). For each attribute the score should be multiplied by the weighting factor to obtain an extended score. For each bid, the extended scores for attributes are added together to obtain an overall rating of the desirable attributes.

The ratings of all of the bids that satisfied the mandatory requirements should be compared and the bids rank ordered from highest to lowest. The top candidates for further analysis can then be selected. These bids will then be evaluated further using physical benchmarking and other methods. The number of bids to be carried into the next phase will vary. In most cases, if there are a small number of bids having scores close to the top scoring bid, then these are the logical choices. The remaining bids would not be considered further. Care must be taken not to carry too many bids into the next phase, since the physical benchmarking phase can be time consuming and expensive.

PHYSICAL BENCHMARKING

The physical benchmarking phase involve testing the actual piece of hardware to validate the vendor claims made in the theoretical benchmark phase. It is necessary to obtain access to the actual equipment being evaluated. This can be accomplished in a variety of ways. The best situation is to install the equipment in your shop and test under the conditions present in your system. This is possible if the vendor will loan you the equipment for a period of time and the equipment is reasonably easy to install. An alternative is to rent the equipment during this test time. However, for some types of equipment, installation on-site is impractical. This is the case with a large CPU and with mainframe peripherals. The installation cost and time are prohibitive.

If it is not possible to do testing on-site, it is best to use another site independent of the vendor. This can be done by renting time at a service bureau or making arrangements with a firm having a similar hardware environment. The least favorable alternative is to test at the vendor's site. The vendor can control the environment and tune the system to show the equipment running at optimal performance, which may not be realistic under your circumstances.

All of the mandatory and desirable attributes should be evaluated during the physical benchmarking phase. This is where the user is able to judge the overall appropriateness of the equipment. An organized and structured series of tests is the best way of assuring a comprehensive evaluation.

The results of the physical benchmark should be tabulated using the same type of scheme discussed in the theoretical benchmarking phase. Again, a composite score will be developed and used to rank the proposals.

ADDITIONAL FACTORS

Before the final selection is made, there are other possible sources of information that can be used. Most intangible factors are difficult or impossible to measure in the theoretical or physical benchmarking phases. These include vendor service, equipment reliability, vendor stability, ease of installation, product maintainability, etc. Interviewing users of these specific products in other firms is an excellent source of additional information. The vendor should supply the firm with a customer list (the size of the installed customer base is another important issue regarding the stability of the product) for these purposes. However, since this list usually includes only satisfied customers, other users not on the list should also be contacted.

The various hardware and software rating services such as *Datapro, Dataworld,* and *Data Sources* include user satisfaction surveys for the various hardware and software products. While these surveys are general and span a large variety of situations, they involve a significant sample of the user population.

These other sources of information should be monitored during the entire evaluation process. If important information comes to light while evaluating products, this information can be used in the remainder of the evaluations. For example, the manager discovers through a current trade publication that a given vendor is filing chapter 11 bankruptcy. Since this vendor has bid on some equipment the firm is acquiring, it will be necessary to investigate the impact of this legal action on the firm's ability to deliver and support the equipment.

Also, it is important that any of this supplemental information be incorporated into the decision-making process as soon as possible. The evaluation process can be expensive, especially the physical benchmarking phase. Hence, all the available information should be evaluated before the products are selected for this phase. In our previous example, it may be determined that the bankruptcy makes the acquisition of any equipment from that firm too risky. In this case, no matter how well the equipment is rated in the theoretical and physical benchmarks, it will still be unacceptable.

Another factor that is important to some managers is the degree of equipment homogeneity of the overall system. Some managers feel that a single vendor shop (where only one vendor's equipment is used) helps assure a more compatible, upgradable, and maintainable shop. Plug compatible manufacturers (PCMs, those companies making similar equipment to the primary vendor's) usually have a lower purchase price than the main vendor, but cannot provide a full line of equipment. Because of patent and copyright laws, the equipment of the PCMs appears to function the same as the primary vendor's equipment but is not identical. There are always some subtle differences which usually are not immediately apparent. Sometimes these differences enhance the PCM's performance, other times they may cause compatibility and upgradability problems.

The most important issue in having a single vendor shop is that of maintenance. If the system fails, it may be difficult to locate the failing hardware or software component. In a multivendor shop, this leads to the problem of determining which vendor to contact for maintenance. In rare instances this can develop into a situation where each vendor blames the failure on another vendor's component. This should not occur in a single vendor environment.

A single vendor environment can produce its own problems. If care is not exercised, the firm's computing direction can be controlled by this vendor. Essentially, information system management abdicates control of hardware and software planning to the vendor. This results in the vendor deciding the role of computing in the firm. Also, future purchases by the firm can be taken for granted and some degradation in vendor attentiveness and service may result.

The vendor's financial soundness and commitment to the specific technology and product line are also very important. If the firm goes out of business or the product line is discontinued, you may end up with a white elephant which is neither maintainable nor upgradable. This would force either a costly conversion in the future or the continued use of technically obsolete equipment.

Other factors to consider include the financing arrangements and the specifics of the legal contract. Since these are such important issues, they will be discussed in separate chapters.

ACQUISITION DECISION

With the information gathered from the theoretical and physical benchmarks and the other supplemental sources of information, the selection decision must be made. The decision is usually made by management using the data and advice provided by information system technicians. The manager responsible for the acquisition of the hardware must also be allowed to make the decision of which product to acquire. Of course, at any time during the process, the decision can be made to reject all bids and not order any equipment.

If the organization is a governmental body that is regulated by either state or federal laws dealing with the procedures for processing requests for proposals, it is essential that these procedures are strictly adhered to before a final decision is made.

Whenever possible, the users should be involved in the final selection process. Satisfying the needs of the users should be the ultimate objective of the acquisition. Without their participation, this may not be accomplished.

The selection of the vendor may be very clear-cut, with one product being substantially better suited to a company's needs, or it may be quite difficult, with a number of products closely matched. In either case the decision process should not simply be a numbers game with the product scoring the highest total on the theoretical and physical benchmarks being the winner.

Subjective factors are difficult to quantify, but they must also be considered. The product with the highest perceived benefit to cost ratio should be selected. Again, the manager who must live with the consequences of this decision is the one most appropriate to determine the best choice.

ALTERNATIVE MARKETS

Instead of acquiring new equipment, there is sometimes the opportunity to obtain used equipment. For recently released products, this opportunity will not exist, but for more mature products, those that have been available for some length of time, the used market may present the best bargain.

Also, there is an advantage to buying more mature technology. It has been thoroughly tested and will usually be more reliable than products that were just recently released. Acquiring machines just off the drawing board can be a risky undertaking. They may not initially perform as advertised, and if the customer base does not develop, production may be discontinued.

Most computer equipment becomes technically obsolete well before it physically wears out. Machines that have been well maintained will have many years of remaining service and the price will be substantially lower than comparable new ones. The type and extent of maintenance performed on used equipment is a critical factor. Certain conditions must be met for the vendor or an outside third party maintenance firm to offer a maintenance contract on used equipment. If these conditions are not met, it is necessary for the machine to be reconditioned and certified before maintenance can be obtained.

The used market can be quite diverse. There are a number of sources of used equipment, including brokers specializing in the area, firms upgrading their systems, and even the vendors selling their own reconditioned machines. The primary source of information on used equipment is the computer trade publications.

DETERMINING ATTRIBUTES

In this section we discuss some of the problems of specifying and measuring the mandatory and desirable attributes involved in acquiring certain types of hardware. While these discussions are reasonably general and only involve a couple specific devices, they hopefully will give you an idea of the complexity involved in the hardware acquisition process.

Two classes of devices will be discussed: rotating rigid magnetic media (a fancy name for hard disk drives, also the most common form of direct access storage devices or DASD on mainframe systems) and mainframe central processing units. Both these devices are changing rapidly, so we will not address specific technology issues but will deal with basic attributes. In both cases we will deal with large mainframe installations. For small mini- and microcomputer situations, many of the considerations are the same but less complex. Part of the objective of the following discussion is to reinforce the idea that these acquisition decisions involve many interrelated factors.

Hard Disk Drives (DASD)

For all devices, speed and capacity are of primary concern. For a disk drive, the type of data and the way it is being accessed will influence the performance of the device. As in evaluating any good, it is best to understand how it operates. Hence, before proceeding, let's briefly review how a disk drive is accessed by the CPU.

When a program requests data from a disk, the operating system loads the appropriate channel program into a channel. The channel executes this program and requests a disk controller to fetch certain information from a specific cylinder, track, and relative position of a disk drive. The disk drive moves its read/write heads to the appropriate cylinder on the disk, rotates the disk platter to the correct position, and reads the magnetic images off of the disk, transferring them to the controller. The controller then passes this information on to the channel and central processor.

There are three speed parameters involved in fetching the data. They are, in order of longest to shortest: the time to move the read/write heads to the correct cylinder (called the seek time), the time to move the correct sector to the read/write head (called the rotational latency), and the time to move the data to the channel (called the transfer speed). Obviously, the seek and rotating latency are determined by the previous position of the read/write heads. Hence, we must talk about average times. Each of these speeds must be measured.

The capacity of a disk drive is measured in megabytes or gigabytes (millions or billions of bytes of storage). However, the organization of this data physically on the disk can be very important. For example, if fixed block architecture (FBA) is the format, then a sector is fixed at 512 bytes (or some other unit) of information that must be used as an entire block. If you store anywhere between 1 and 512 bytes of information, the entire block would be expended. The alternative scheme is called count-key-data architecture (CKD) and allows for only the data and its system identifiers to be stored, with no empty data space. Preceding the actual data will be a key to identify the data for nonsequential file processing. Some system software can use only a FBA format or only a CKD format. Obviously, this creates compatibility problems that must be considered.

The capacity of a given device can also become a negative factor. If the device stores too much data and there are not multiple paths to access this data, serious contention problems can arise. This occurs when more than one program tries to access data from the same device at the same time. Often these types of problems can only be discovered when the physical benchmark is performed.

The disk storage platters can be either removable or permanently mounted. Permanent disks are much more common because the actuator heads can be mated directly to that specific disk, allowing for closer tolerances and subsequently greater storage capacity. Additionally, a device can have multiple access heads (actuators) which allows for the simultaneous access of multiple cylinders. As mentioned previously, this is important in reducing data contention problems.

Other important factors concerning the physical properties of the disk drive include the size of the drive (usually called the footprint), the power requirements, the amount of waste heat generated by the device, and the clearance necessary to access the internal parts of the device. Each of the preceding elements may or may not be important to a specific computer center. For example, the center that is crowded should be concerned about the footprint and the necessary clearance of the device.

The controller is an integral component of a disk system. Hence, whenever disk drives are considered, it is necessary also to price and evaluate the associated controller. Controllers can significantly affect performance. They can have memory which can be used to store blocks of information to reduce the physical access to the disk drive. This is referred to as cache memory. Controllers can allow multiple data paths to the channels and devices under their control. Also, the maximum number of disk drives that can be connected to a controller can vary substantially. Drives can be grouped together in what are called strings, where one drive, the head of string, communicates with the remaining devices on the string. This means that it is best to price an entire configuration, including the controller and all devices constituting the strings connected to the controller.

All of these factors have to be taken into consideration before the RFP can be formulated. It is useful also to determine the weighting factors for each of the desirable attributes at this time. In this way, the relative importance of each attribute will be decided before the RFP is issued and well before the evaluation of the bids begins.

The RFP for these disk drives is presented in the appendix at the end of this chapter.

Central Processing Units

Probably the single most important hardware acquisition decision is the central processing unit. This unit limits and sometimes even determines the other peripheral devices and, more importantly, the types of operating systems and other software that can be used with the system. As stated earlier, the software to be acquired and its performance must be considered before the acquisition of the hardware. This is particularly true when making a decision on the appropriate CPU.

Since the CPU is such an important decision and usually a very costly decision, it is necessary to discuss some of the attributes of the system. Since this topic is so complex, we will point out some of the more important considerations and hopefully will convey the degree of difficulty in this type of decision.

When acquiring a CPU, the firm is in most cases committing to use a specific line of a vendor's product for an extended period of time. At best there may also be plug compatible manufacturers that supply compatible equipment, but these vendors will disappear if the primary vendor drops support for that specific product line. The major considerations should involve the continued existence of the product line (and obviously the vendor), the degree of future support the vendor will give this product line, the amount of growth to more powerful, compatible CPUs in the product line, and the probability the vendor will continue to upgrade the products as technology changes.

The software that runs on the system must be evaluated at the same time, with the same sort of questions being asked. The operating system is of particular importance. The loss of support for a specific operating system can force a considerable investment in converting other programs (both application and system programs) to be compatible with the new operating system. This changing of an operating system is usually accompanied by the reevaluation of the CPU and the other associated hardware.

The comparison of CPUs is not a straightforward process. The units of measure and the way programs are executed can be entirely different from one vendor to another and even between product lines for the same vendor. Following are some of the problems involved in comparing different CPUs.

Measuring both capacity and speed can be difficult and sometimes deceptive. Capacity is measured in different units of storage from one vendor to another. For example, a 4 meg machine could mean 4 million bytes of main storage where one byte consists of 8 bits of information. It may also signify 4 million words of storage where a word may consist of 64 bits of information. It appears that the machine that is measured in words and not bytes has eight times the capacity. However, a major consideration is how storage is to be used. If it is used to store mainly character data, a word addressable machine (i.e., the smallest addressable unit is a word) may considerably underutilize storage in many situations. So, not only is the capacity of the system important, but the architecture of the system is also of concern.

Measuring speed can be even more difficult. The speed of a system is commonly measured in millions of instructions per second (MIPS). This measures the number of times a specific type of instruction can be executed in a second of time. The instruction that is measured is usually a fast instruction such as a register-to-register operation. However, other features of the system including the number of instructions available (more instructions means less chaining of instructions to do specific operations, i.e., less programming), the speed of the other instructions, the average mix of instructions that the shop will be executing, and the general architecture of the CPU must be considered. For example, if we are going to be doing a lot of business data processing and not much scientific processing, the presence of packed decimal operations is important, while floating point operations are less important. Also, if the architecture uses microcode assist, then complex instructions can be executed more quickly, resulting in a significant increase in processor performance. Microcode assist is the process by which some instructions are not actually wired into hardware, but these instructions are broken into a series of commands that are executable.

The issues become even more clouded when you must consider processors that can execute instructions on multiple data items simultaneously (called vector processors) and machines that can execute multiple instructions simultaneously (called parallel processors). The concept of MIPS in these situations is meaningless.

For some of the aforementioned reasons, it may be so difficult to compare the speed of machines by measuring MIPS that this unit of measure is ignored. Some people actually refer to MIPS as meaningless indicators of processor speed. The most reliable method of comparing processing speeds is to do a physical benchmark on each of the machines using a representative load of programs. This will allow each shop to determine how the system will respond to the specific individual environment.

Other factors must be considered such as the number of channels the system can have, the maximum amount of main memory, whether the system is field upgradable (i.e., improvements can be made without having to install a whole new CPU), the maximum speed of the fastest processor in the product line, etc. An issue of growing concern is the ability of a computer system to connect to other systems. While this is both a hardware and software issue, the improper selection of CPU may limit the connectivity of the system.

We will not explore any of these preceding issues in depth. Hopefully, we have conveyed the degree of complexity it takes to evaluate CPUs. In the case of large mainframe processors, millions of dollars are at stake and the direction of the computing environment well into the future is to be determined by the selection. Thus, a thorough investigation is necessary.

MAJOR COMPANY

The performance evaluation team at Major Company has been routinely monitoring DASD utilization and has estimated that a substantial increase in total DASD storage will be necessary in nine months. This is caused by a combination of the normal growth in computer usage and the installation of a new online payroll-personnel system which is scheduled to be fully implemented in six months.

The information systems area did a preliminary investigation of the possible vendors of the hardware by consulting various industry service publications, informally discussing the options with managers at other data centers, and by talking with the various representatives from the vendors that they deal with on a regular basis. This information has allowed the data center management to develop a formal proposal that is to be included in the yearly budget presently under consideration by upper management. This proposal states the approximate costs of the equipment, the installation date, and the estimated benefits of acquiring the hardware. These benefits are expressed in the response time of the system with and without the acquisition and the possible restriction in growth of present and future application systems. This information is presented first in easily understood nontechnical terms and is then supported by detailed statistics showing the impact on the various parameters of the system. Before going to the board of directors, this proposal was reviewed and accepted by the information system steering committee.

After careful consideration, the board of directors accepted the budget with this acquisition included. The information systems area then developed a list of mandatory and desirable attributes for the new devices. Since the users will not be directly affected by the acquisition, there is little need to involve them in the process. Additionally, it is determined that DASD technology has not changed enough to force a reevaluation of the present DASD storage. Hence, only additional units will be acquired. Note at this point the importance of doing the environmental scanning that we discussed in Chapter 4. This environmental scanning gives us information about the technological advances in the DASD area.

The attributes are passed on to the purchasing department which will develop the RFP. Purchasing consults with a representative from information systems on a regular basis to ensure that the RFP is complete. At the same time, purchasing also works closely with the legal staff. The RFP that was developed is presented in the appendix at the end of this chapter.

The RFP is sent to all vendors that deal in this type of equipment. This includes vendors that Major Company has dealt with in the past and other vendors found during the preliminary investigation. For completeness, Major Company also placed an announcement in an appropriate weekly trade publication to notify any other possible bidders.

While developing the attributes for the RFP, the staff whose task it was to review the bids determined the scoring system that was used in ranking the bids. Their primary task in determining the scoring system was to decide the weight to be assigned to each desirable attribute. After the bids were received, the staff at Major Company scored each bid on both its mandatory and desirable attributes. Figure 7.6 shows how some of the bids were scored. Note that some of the bids were not evaluated on their desirable attributes since all of the mandatory attributes were not satisfied. Those bids that satisfied all the mandatory attributes were ranked by their total score on the desirable attributes. From the remaining proposals (those meeting all mandatory requirements), there are clearly three that score substantially higher than the others. Hence, Major Company did physical benchmarking only on these three products.

Since it was too expensive to install the candidate devices on Major Company's system, the physical benchmarking was done at service centers whose hardware and software configurations were similar to theirs. This benchmarking was done by the performance evaluation group using primarily a hardware monitor. Besides verifying the theoretical benchmark, the team also attempted to analyze the amount of contention for the devices and the total

Figure 7.6   *Analysis of Candidate Bids*

VENDOR	PRODUCT	MET MANDATORY ATTRIBUTES?	DESIRABLE ATTRIBUTES SCORE
A	1	Yes	102.8
A	2	Yes	83.4
B	1	No	—
C	1	Yes	105.5
D	1	Yes	67.3
E	1	No	—
E	2	No	—
F	1	Yes	99.8
G	1	Yes	44.2

access times under a series of standard benchmark tests devised by the performance evaluation group.

After the physical benchmark was completed, the acquisition team at Major Company contacted other users of these products to determine their satisfaction with the devices. This inquiry was primarily focused on determining the level of service provided by the vendor, the failure rate of the devices, and the overall performance of the systems.

The acquisition committee then met and analyzed all of the data concerning the various configurations and chose the most desirable vendor. This vendor was contacted and the legal contract negotiated to the satisfaction of both parties. After the successful contract negotiations, the other vendors were notified of the rejection of their bids.

The equipment was delivered to Major Company on 6/10/9X and installed by the vendor's personnel immediately. By 6/12/9X the system was tested by the vendor's staff and deemed operational. The systems programming staff then ran acceptance tests for two days and concluded that the system was fully operational. At this point authorization was issued to accounts payable to pay the vendor in full.

SUMMARY

The acquisition of any computer technology, be it hardware or software, could have a significant impact on other components of the system. For this reason, it is important that all acquisition decisions be made considering the impact on both the present system configuration and the limitations the decision will place on future decisions.

The first step in the acquisition of hardware is to determine the mandatory and desirable attributes of the needed equipment. These attributes and other pertinent information involved in the bidding process are then put into the request for proposal (RFP) that is sent to all prospective vendors.

Those vendors that have appropriate hardware and wish to offer it for sale will submit a formal bid. An evaluation team will examine each bid. The first step in the evaluation process is to do a theoretical benchmark. This entails comparing each of the vendor's claims with the mandatory and desirable attributes. Those products not meeting the mandatory attributes will be eliminated from consideration. The remaining bids will be compared based on the desirable attributes. This should further limit the bids going into the physical benchmarking phase.

Physical benchmarking involves testing the equipment in an environment similar to that on the actual production system. The tests will include verifying the vendor performance claims and observing the performance of the equipment under the conditions that will be encountered on the actual system.

After gathering all of the pertinent information, the manager must make the appropriate choice.

QUESTIONS

1. What should be accomplished when doing a preliminary investigation of a specific type of hardware?
2. Why does a typical commercial firm develop a request for proposal?
3. Why does a typical government agency develop an RFP?
4. Why do we classify attributes into the two categories of desirable and mandatory?
5. For each of the following attributes, describe a situation where that attribute would be a mandatory attribute (it could also be a desirable attribute).
   a. Waste heat generated
   b. Device footprint
   c. Electrical power consumption
   d. Maintenance
   e. Training
   f. Financing
6. When would it be best to acquire equipment without going through the RFP process?
7. For one of the following types of equipment (determined by your instructor), research the important attributes to be considered:
   a. Tape drives
   b. Nonimpact line printers
   c. Impact line printers
   d. Communication controllers
   e. Optical disk drives (laser disks)
8. Why do we ask the bidders to use a specific format for their bids? How can this speed the evaluation process?

9. Explain the objectives behind the theoretical benchmark phase.
10. Explain how the theoretical benchmark is done.
11. Explain the objectives behind the physical benchmark phase.
12. Explain how the physical benchmark is done.
13. What supplemental sources of information can be used to evaluate a given product?
14. Some of the decision elements in the acquisition process are subjective in nature. Explain what these factors are and why they are important.
15. After an acquisition decision is made, the performance and effectiveness of the system should be monitored. Explain why this is an important part of the acquisition process.
16. Describe in what ways each of the following groups should be involved in the acquisition process:
    a. Purchasing agents
    b. Information system specialists
    c. Lawyers
    d. Users
    e. Performance evaluators (EDP)
17. State how the RFP in the appendix to this chapter would be different if it were being issued by a government agency.

CASE ANALYSIS

Case 1

The Easy-Does-It (EDI) Company provides lawn and garden maintenance service to other companies and individuals. There are presently 35 offices located in 20 towns and cities in Arizona, New Mexico, and Texas. Easy-Does-It has decided to computerize some of its operations. Since each office is reasonably independent, it has decided that personal computers would be best suited to do these tasks. The following functions will be necessary initially:

1. Payroll
2. General ledger
3. Accounts receivable
4. Inventory control
5. Accounts payable
6. Word processing
7. Spread sheet analysis

To implement these, EDI has decided to acquire the more popular software packages such as LOTUS 1-2-3, Microsoft Word, DBASE, etc. In addition, it has been decided that to insure an acceptable growth environment, it is necessary that the PCs must have the following minimum characteristics:

1. Fully IBM/PC or PS/2 compatible running PC DOS with Microsoft windows or OS/2
2. A minimum of 640K of RAM
3. One floppy disk drive (minimum of 1MB capacity)
4. A minimum of a 20MB hard disk drive
5. Be capable of supporting both a serial and parallel printer
6. Support color, graphic displays
7. Be expandable to include possibly:
   a. a second floppy disk drive
   b. a minimum 2400 BAUD modem
   c. a plotter
   d. a mouse
   e. memory expansion to 16MB

EDI has hired you to develop a request for proposal to acquire a minimum of 50 of these systems.

REQUIRED: You are to develop an RFP for Easy-Does-It to acquire only the hardware. For you to properly develop this RFP, it will be necessary to investigate what is available in the PC market. In addition, you are to write a management letter that explains what you believe will be the best hardware solution to solve EDI's problems. This would include specific vendors and products that you recommend.

Case 2

This assignment involves developing a request for proposal and a recommendation to management on the acquisition of a new high-speed impact line printer for Major Company. Assume that the company already has a high-speed laser printer (an IBM 3800), but it needs an impact printer to handle multipart forms and special forms, especially odd-sized forms. In addition, the company insists that the impact printer must be used to produce all checks. This is to help prevent the alteration of the checks.

You are to investigate what printers are available and the characteristics of these devices. From your investigation, you should make an initial proposal and recommendation to higher management for the acquisition of the printer. Also, Major Company's policy is to invite competitive bids for all large purchases. Hence, you must develop a request for proposal to send to prospective bidders if in fact higher management decides to acquire this new equipment.

APPENDIX

REQUEST FOR PROPOSAL FOR DIRECT ACCESS STORAGE DEVICES FROM MAJOR COMPANY, INCORPORATED, RFP #9X-02347 VERSION 1.0, JAN. 15, 199X

Introduction and Reason for RFP   This request for proposal is initiated by the Major Company, Incorporated, which is incorporated in Illinois and has its headquarters in Chicago, Illinois at 1200 E. Madison Avenue. For the remainder of this document, the initiating company will be referred to as Major Co.

All correspondence, both written and oral, regarding this document or any aspect of the bidding process should be made to the following party:

Beverly Bidtaker
Purchasing Specialist
1200 E. Madison Avenue
Chicago, Illinois
60600
Phone: 312-555-3518

Any reference to this document must use the appropriate reference number. This request for proposal is RFP #9X-2347 version 1.0. If this document is revised, the version number will reflect the change. Revisions will be sent to all vendors that were originally issued this RFP and all interested parties that request revisions. All requests to have a vendor name added to this distribution list should be to Beverly Bidtaker at the preceding address.

Following are the important dates involving this request for proposal:

DATE	EVENT
1/15/9X	RFP is issued
2/07/9X	Meeting of vendors to answer questions
2/15/9X	Revised RFP issued, if necessary
2/25/9X	Last day to receive vendor bids
3/02/9X to 3/16/9X	Vendor demonstrations and physical benchmarking
3/23/9X	Final vendor selection

The meeting of the vendors will be at the data center headquarters at 1000 Liberty Bell Lane in Oakbrook, Illinois in room 107 at 2:00 P.M. on 2/07/9X. This meeting will allow the vendors to ask questions and make comments concerning the RFP. This will be the final opportunity for any changes to be made in the RFP. Any revisions to the RFP will then be incorporated into a revised document and will be distributed by 2/15/9X at the latest.

The vendor demonstrations and physical benchmarking will involve tests of the equipment in a manner agreeable to both Major Company and the vendor. These tests will be conducted by members of the data processing staff of Major Company under conditions representative of the actual production environment. Any restrictions of these tests by the vendor should be stated in the formal bid.

Organization Background   The Major Company is a diversified manufacturer and distributor of consumer goods. Its stock is traded on the New York Stock Exchange, and it is currently listed in the *Fortune* 500 as number 132. Growth of the firm has been rapid but controlled over the last 10 years. This growth pattern is expected to continue for at least the next five years.

Major Company has a large centralized data processing center located in Oakbrook, Illinois, and each division has its own decentralized computing operations which communicate with the central site. The central site has five IBM 3090 CPUs and associated compatible peripheral hardware from a variety of vendors. The MVS/ESA and VM/XA operating systems are run on these processors.

Processor growth has been at a compound annual growth rate of approximately 35%. DASD storage has been growing at a rate of about 25%. These growth rates are expected to continue for at least the next five years.

Major Company is presently converting all batch, file-oriented systems to online, database applications. This process is expected to continue over the next three years.

Equipment Requirements   The DASD and associated controller must meet certain criteria. In this proposal these criteria will be called mandatory attributes. If the bid you submit does not conform to these mandatory attributes, it will not be considered for acceptance. Other attributes which will enhance the functionality of the product will be called desirable attributes. The quality and quantity of these desirable attributes of the equipment bid will determine the winning bid.

Mandatory Attributes   The mandatory attributes are as follows:

1. Speed Parameters:
   Average seek time must be no greater than 20 microseconds.
   Average latency must be no greater than 10 microseconds.
   Transfer rate must be at least 1.5 megabytes per second.
2. Capacity:
   Minimum of 6 gigabytes (8 bits to a byte) per complete DASD string.
   Minimum of 12 gigabytes per fully configured controller.
   Controller must have a minimum of 4 megabytes of cache memory.
3. Compatibility:
   Devices must be fully plug compatible with IBM 308X and 3090 series processors.
   Devices must be fully compatible with the IBM VM/XA and MVS/ESA operating systems.

4. Maintenance:
Maintenance availability must be for a minimum of eight hours a day, five days a week with a maximum failure response time of one hour during these periods.

5. Additional Capabilities:
Controller and DASD must support multipathing; hence, controller must attach to at least two channels.
Cylinder size must not exceed 2 megabytes.
Data recording format must be count-key-data.

6. Delivery and Installation:
All units must be installed and fully operational by 7/01/9X.
Installation must be done by vendor personnel.

7. Testing and Acceptance:
The devices must be tested and deemed acceptable by the Major Company systems programming staff before the units are considered fully operational.

Desirable Attributes   Following is a list of the desirable attributes of both the controller and DASD devices. If there are additional attributes of the equipment you are bidding, these should also be included and will be considered if they are indeed deemed beneficial.

1. Speed: Any performance above mandatory minimum standards
Seek time
Latency
Transfer rate

2. Capacity: Any capacity above stated minimum standards
Storage per actuator
Storage per DASD string
Storage per fully configured controller
Cache storage in controller

3. Physical size and weight of units

4. Electrical power consumed

5. Amount of waste heat generated

6. Cabling distance constraints

7. Terms and costs of maintenance agreements

8. Cost of each individual item including:
controller unit
head of string DASD
other DASD units
necessary additional software
Total cost of fully configured controller in a ready to operate condition, including all necessary DASD and software

9. Earliest installation date of all hardware and software. This would be the date at which the storage would be fully functional on the system.

10. Number of actuators per physical DASD unit

11. Possibility of doing a field upgrade to add capacity or functionality to the units. This should include the costs involved in these upgrades.

12. Alternative financing arrangements

13. DASD device plug compatible with other vendors' controllers. This may allow us to acquire your DASD and another vendor's controller.

14. Controller plug compatible with other vendors' DASD. This would allow acquisition of your controller and another vendor's DASD
15. Vendor documentation available
16. Vendor training
17. Warranty and guarantee coverage

Form of Proposal The submitted proposal must conform to the following format. Any proposal not following this format will not be considered for acceptance. It is mandatory that the vendor complete the mandatory and desirable attributes checklist in sections 2 and 3 of the proposal and submit the checklist in exactly the format presented in this document. Following are the various sections in the proposal:

Cover Letter
A cover letter should accompany the proposal. This cover letter should be addressed to Beverly Bidtaker and should state the appropriate number of the RFP (in this case #9X-2347). The cover letter should also briefly describe the features of the product and the individual to contact in your firm regarding the proposal.

Formal Proposal
Section 1: Introduction
This section should briefly describe the proposal. This should include the model numbers and types of devices being proposed. In addition, a brief description of the bidding company should be included. This description should detail the location of the company headquarters, the number of other offices, the location of the nearest sales and service office to Major Company's computer site, a brief financial history of the firm, types of product lines supported, and history of specific product being bid. The history of the product should detail how long the product has been on the market, recent predecessor models of the product, and the installed customer base of the product.

The following materials should be included as addenda to the proposal:

1. Company financial statements for the previous two years
2. Listing of at least five customers presently using these products. This list should include the names of contact people, addresses, and telephone numbers.

Section 2: Mandatory Attributes
The mandatory attributes section must describe how the products being bid meet the mandatory attributes as set forth by this RFP. This would include completing the checklist at the end of this section. If any of the mandatory attributes are not met and your firm believes that there is justification for an exception, this must be fully explained here.

As an addendum to the proposal, all manufacturer's literature relevant to the product should be included at the end of the proposal.

Mandatory Attributes Checklist

ATTRIBUTE	*SATISFIED?* YES NO	*DESCRIPTION OF ATTRIBUTE*

Speed:
  Average Seek Time < 20m
  Average Latency < 10m
  Transfer Rate > 1.5MB
Capacity:
  Each DASD > 6GB
  Total per Cntrl > 12GB
Compatibility:
  IBM 308X and 3090
  IBM VM/XA and MVS/ESA
Maintenance:
  8 hours, 5 days/week
Additional Capabilities:
  Multipathing Supported
  Cylinder Size < 2MB
  Count-Key-Data Format
Delivery & Installation:
  Delivery by 7/01/9X
  Vendor Installation		

SECTION 3: DESIRABLE ATTRIBUTES

A description of the desirable attributes must be included in this section. This must be summarized in the checklist of desirable attributes at the end of this section. Failure to complete either the mandatory or desirable attributes checklist constitutes an incomplete proposal. Any incomplete proposal will not be considered for acceptance. Any manufacturer's literature supporting these desirable attributes should be included in an addendum to the proposal.

All pertinent information regarding each of the attributes should be explained in detail in this section. If manufacturer's literature contains these or additional facts, these documents should be referenced here. It is important that all features be fully explained in this section. The checklist should then summarize this written explanation.

To emphasize the two important areas of maintenance and financing, there should be special subsections entitled "Maintenance" and "Financing." These will describe in detail all of the aspects involved in these two areas. For maintenance, all possible maintenance arrangements, including service hours and costs, should be enumerated. For financing, all possible financing plans should be described. This should include both lease and purchase options. If the financing is totally negotiable, then some standard plans should be presented for comparison purposes.

Any features other than those included in the desirable attributes section of the RFP that your firm deems advantageous to acceptance of your product should be

Desirable Attributes Checklist

ATTRIBUTE	DESCRIPTION OF ATTRIBUTE	FOR INTERNAL USE		
		WEIGHT	SCORE	EXTENSION
Speed:				
Seek Time				
Latency				
Transfer Rate				
Capacity:				
Storage per Actuator				
Storage per DASD String				
Storage per Controller				
Controller Cache Store				
Physical Attributes:				
Dimensions				
Weight				
Power Consumed				
Waste Heat				
Cabling Constraints				
Maintenance:				
Types of Plans				
Costs				
Costs:				
Controller				
Head of String				
Other DASD Units				
Necessary Added Software				
Total Configuration Cost				
Installation				
Actuators per DASD				
Field Upgrades:				
Options				
Costs				
Financing Alternatives:				
Options				
Costs				
Added Plug Compatibility				

included in a special subsection under this section. It should be titled "Other Advantageous Features."

SECTION 4: BENCHMARKING ACTIVITIES

This section should state how the proposed system may be tested by Major Company to verify the claimed performance. This should state the possible testing dates, the test locations, the amount of test time, the configuration of the test equipment, and the technical personnel available during the tests.

SECTION 5: OTHER DETAILS

Any of the items not fully described in the other sections of the proposal should be presented in this section. This should include the schedule of both installation and testing of the equipment and the schedule of payments to be made by Major Company. Also, the extent of all warranties and guarantees should be explained.

The documentation and training to be provided with the equipment should be detailed. Any restrictions to be placed on the legal contract should also be included. If the vendor wishes to use a standard contract, that document should be included as an addendum to the proposal.

Evaluation of Proposals   Major Company reserves the right to reject any and all proposals. The lowest-cost proposal will not necessarily be accepted. A committee composed of individuals from management, the computer center, and the user community will evaluate all proposals.

The evaluation process will involve two distinct phases, the first being the comparison of all competing proposals and the second being the physical benchmarking of the more attractive products. All vendors will be notified of the committee's decision on or before 3/23/9X.

ADDITIONAL READINGS

EIN-DOR, PHILLIP, AND JACOB FELDMESSER. "Attributes of the Performance of Central Processing Units: A Relative Performance Prediction Model," *Communications of the ACM*, Vol. 30, No. 4, April 1987, p. 308.

GIFFORD, DAVID, AND ALFRED SPECTOR. "Case Study: IBM's System/360-370 Architecture," *Communications of the ACM*, Vol. 30, No. 4, April 1987, p. 291.

MAUDE, T., AND D. MAUDE. "Hardware Protection Against Software Piracy," *Communications of the ACM*, Vol. 27, No. 9, September 1984, p. 950.

McWILLIAMS, GARY. "Integrated Computing Environments," *Datamation*, May 1, 1989, p. 18.

SIRCAR, S., AND D. DAVE. "The Relationship Between Benchmark Tests and Microcomputer Price," *Communications of the ACM*, Vol. 29, No. 3, March 1986, p. 212.

SIVULA, CHRIS. "The Client-Server Perspective," *Datamation*, October 1, 1989, p. 47.

WIENER, HESH. "MIPS and Reality," *Datamation*, January, 1986, pp. 91–95.

WITHINGTON, FREDERIC G. "Five Generations of Computers," *Harvard Business Review*, July-August 1974, p. 99.

READINGS BEFORE NEXT CHAPTER

If you have not had a business law class or are not familiar with the general aspects of contract law, it would be helpful to do some reading in a beginning business law text. The sections on the fundamentals of contract law and a brief introduction to the Uniform Commercial Code (UCC) should be the focus of your readings. A good reference is *The Structure of the Legal Environment: Law, Ethics and Business*, by Bill Shaw and Art Wolfe, Kent Publishing, 1987. Chapter 5 should give you a good foundation.

8

LEGAL ISSUES

The legal implications involved in computer acquisition and software development should be of concern to the data processing professional. While it is not necessary for those involved in information systems management to be legal experts, it is important that they know where and when legal counsel should be obtained.

This chapter will address two major areas of concern. The first is a basic understanding of the process involved in the negotiation and execution of a legal contract for computer-related goods and services. The second addresses the modes of legal protection from unauthorized use of internally developed software. The major objective of these discussions will be to highlight the areas of the law that are important to a computer professional. Armed with this knowledge, legal counsel can be obtained when appropriate.

By no means can the following be construed as a highly technical legal discussion. We will assume that the reader has a reasonable knowledge of business law, especially contract law. While this knowledge is not absolutely necessary, it should be helpful.

DEFINITION OF A CONTRACT

Whenever two or more parties enter into an agreement to provide or acquire goods or services, a contract is formed. Often the contract is informal and oral. For example, you purchase some printer ribbons and paper for cash from a local retail office supply store. In this situation, a contract has been formed but there is no written agreement between the parties. However, for most business situations a contract will entail a complex legal document which may take days or weeks to negotiate.

A contract is an offer by one party to provide goods or services to a second party in exchange for some specific remuneration and then the acceptance of these terms by the second party. The contract will assign rights and duties to each of the parties involved. This means that each party may gain something (for example, you may get a piece of equipment) and each party may relinquish something (for example, you may pay money for that equipment). The major elements of a legal contract are summarized in Figure 8.1.

As stated earlier, contracts may either be oral or written. It is important that all aspects of the agreement be understood by all parties involved. This is best accomplished by the execution of a written contract. In the following discussion we will consider only written contracts.

NEED FOR A FORMAL WRITTEN CONTRACT

It is important that any complex business transaction be supported by a formal written contract. Putting all of the details in writing accomplishes some crucial things. It helps to clarify all issues so that both parties realize their rights and duties. In transactions dealing with complex technology such as computers, it is not uncommon that the individuals involved have a different interpretation of the terms of an agreement. A properly written contract should resolve these problems and also help to focus attention on important areas that may otherwise be overlooked.

Clarification of issues will hopefully help avoid conflict between the parties involved in a transaction. In the event of a dispute, the contract will also indicate the remedies available to the parties. In any case, a written contract should fully define the agreement in such a manner as to make clear the obligations of all parties. If a contract is properly constructed, the rights and duties of each party will be so well defined that the possibility of a misunderstanding is minimized. It has been said that the best contract does not just allow you to win if you go to court, but is so well written that there is never a need to go to court. The more definite the terms, the less likely the parties will disagree over the

Figure 8.1 *Major Elements of a Legal Contract*

ELEMENT	DESCRIPTION
Offer	Statement of willingness to enter into a bargain; usually expires after a specific amount of time
Acceptance	Agreeing to enter into an offered bargain
Consideration	An exchange of value, be it goods or services

interpretation of the contract. This will also reduce the chance of default and court action since the defaulting party will recognize the futility of the action.

Some lawyers claim that the best contracts are so well defined that once they are signed they can be filed away never to be looked at again. Obviously, avoiding a costly and long legal battle will benefit both parties.

COMPUTER CONTRACTS

Contracts dealing with data processing goods and services present unique problems that are not found in contracts involving other types of transactions. The nature of computing equipment is different in the sense that the function of a computer can be very difficult to define. This is partly because of the interaction of hardware and software, where neither is of much value without the other. For example, a contract to buy a fleet of trucks will be straightforward since the function of each truck is easily defined. However, a computer can be many things to many people. It could be used to perform accounting functions at one instant and then be used as a drafting and design tool moments later. By using different software on the same hardware, we can completely change the nature of the system.

Another problem in accurately specifying the legal contract dealing with computers is that the terminology of the industry is not standardized. This is primarily because the computer industry is still young and remains very dynamic. The terms used by computer professionals will often be specific to a given vendor and also in variance with the general use of a given term. This problem is compounded by the lack of computer knowledge of most legal professionals.

For example, a contract may state that a system be "up and running" by a certain date. However, if *up and running* is not defined, then it may be open to interpretation. A large computer system cannot simply be plugged into an electrical outlet and begin processing. Both the hardware and software must be tested and tuned before the system is truly ready. Imprecise definition can leave open to debate the time the system was "up and running."

It is important for a contract involving data processing equipment and services that the various technical data processing terms be fully and clearly defined. This will be primarily the function of the information system specialist. For a contract dealing with computer goods to be successfully executed, it is necessary to have a team effort involving the legal staff, the information system specialists, and the purchasing area. Each of these groups must understand their limitations and be ready to use the expertise of the others. It is a rare situation where one individual is knowledgeable in all of these areas.

THE NEGOTIATION PROCESS

The point to start planning the contents of the legal contract is when the attributes of the desired system are being developed. Hence, the RFP should be written in such a way that the terms of the final contract be explicitly stated. It is important that legal counsel be engaged during the RFP phase. This will help avoid unnecessary complications when the contract is negotiated with the vendor. It is tempting to ignore the legal details until the actual contract is negotiated. However, this usually leaves the purchaser at a distinct disadvantage. In some cases, inadequate legal planning will result in a breakdown in contract negotiations and force the rejection of all bids with the subsequent issuance of a new RFP.

If the RFP states the terms and form of the resulting contract, the vendor is then alerted to the conditions acceptable to the firm. The mandatory and desirable attributes must be clearly and precisely stated. The form of the proposal (remember this proposal is the basis of the contract) stated in the RFP must include all materials that are necessary for the resulting contract. This should include all of the factors necessary to guarantee successful performance of the contract.

The involvement of the legal staff in the RFP process should certify that governing laws are being followed and that maximum protection under the law will be afforded the resulting contract. Legal counsel should meet with the information system specialists so that all technical terms can be defined. This will also help to assure that there is an understanding among all those involved as to the intent of the RFP.

Again, as stated previously, in an organization controlled by laws dealing with the acquisition process, such as a governmental institution, it is even more important that the RFP be as precise as possible. Any imprecision in the RFP can cause problems. This can result in litigation against the issuing agency or the necessity of reissuing the RFP. For an organization governed by these types of laws, the importance of a correctly formulated RFP cannot be overstated.

For example, a government institution recently issued an RFP using specific terminology to describe the desired items. It turned out that some of these terms were only used by one vendor. The other vendors used different, more generic terminology. A resulting lawsuit claimed that the RFP was biased toward that single vendor.

Before a vendor is selected and contract negotiations begin, it is necessary to investigate whether there are any lawsuits outstanding against the vendor. If there are, each must be investigated to determine both the impact of the suit on the financial position of the vendor and on the specific product being evaluated.

In the contract negotiation process, it is important to determine which are the important issues and to resolve to stand firm on those issues. Other issues may be more negotiable. For example, a contract clause dealing with hardware and software compatibility may be considered absolutely necessary, while the location of training, be it on-site or at the vendor's location, is not as important. Figure 8.2 presents some of the more important points that should be considered during contract negotiation.

In most instances, the vendor's personnel will have substantially more

Figure 8.2   *Contract Negotiation*

Important Points:

Clearly define mandatory and desirable attributes.
Carefully construct RFP, being sure to define all technical terms.
Involve legal counsel early in RFP process.
Prioritize negotiable issues.
Examine vendor's standard contract.
Suggest changes in vendor's contract or draft new contract.
Deal directly with vendor's legal counsel, not the sales staff.
Negotiate final terms, if possible.
Sign contract if agreement is reached or eliminate bidder if terms
    are unacceptable.

---

experience in computer contract negotiation. This will be a routine task for them. On the other hand, the buyer may be involved in this type of situation infrequently. This may produce pressure for the buyer to accept a standard vendor contract instead of developing a contract unique to the situation.

For the most part, vendor contracts are designed to lend maximum protection to the vendor. Remember, their legal staff devised the instrument. This means that the guarantees and warranties will be restricted, the payment and delivery terms will benefit the vendor, and the remedies for nonperformance will be limited. Too often these contracts are accepted in an unmodified form because the vendor's salesperson states that this is "company policy." The buyer may feel pressured into acceptance because of being intimidated by the size of the vendor firm. However, the perspective should always be maintained that even though this sale may be reasonably insignificant to the vendor as a whole, it is still very important to the individual sales staff. The loss of the sale could adversely affect their sales commissions and sales quotas. Thus, reasonable changes to the standard contract should be acceptable.

No matter the situation, the contract should never be negotiated with the sales staff since these people are not legal experts. Instead, the buyer must deal with the vendor's authorized legal representative. This will make the negotiation process more direct.

The standard vendor contract should be included with the proposal submitted for evaluation. Before the vendor is contacted to begin the final contract negotiations, the legal staff should examine the document and make suggestions for alterations. This will speed the process and hopefully result in a contract that is acceptable to both parties.

The vendor contract usually has certain standard clauses which severely restrict the rights of the buyer. This is especially true when dealing with guarantees and warranties. It is probably best to reconstruct these clauses. Also, a standard contract usually will not fully document the claims of performance made by the vendor. These performance measures must be included in the final contract since oral representations made prior to the signing of the contract are nonbinding, unless they are included in the contract. Thus, statements made by the vendor's sales staff will not be enforceable unless included in the written contract.

There are three general ways of executing the contract (see Figure 8.3). The simplest method involves accepting the vendor's standard contract with a side letter which states any additional services the vendor will provide that are not covered in the standard contract. Another method is simply to negotiate separate contracts for each item acquired. The last method is probably best and includes negotiating a master contract encompassing all items to be acquired from that vendor. The master contract is particularly important in a computer acquisition since it can specify the relationships between all of the various components of the system, including hardware, software, maintenance, etc. Individual contracts cannot handle these interactions as well as the master contract. For example, the failure of a software package may lead to nonperformance of that specific contract but usually will not be related to the hardware, which is covered by a separate contract. Hence, the hardware contract is enforceable even though the software intended to run on the system does not function. This would not be a problem in a properly constructed master contract. However, because of the complexity of master contracts, they are not used as frequently as would be desirable.

CONTRACT ISSUES

In the following section we will highlight some of the areas that should be considered when a contract is constructed. For the correct legal phrasing for these various issues, there are texts that contain hundreds of different clauses that can be used to construct computer-related contracts. Most of these clauses are taken from either standard contracts or contracts that have withstood the test of litigation. Normally these clauses can be applied with only slight modification.

A contract must state the exact provisions of the agreement. The terms of performance must be presented in such a manner that both parties fully understand their duties and a determination can be made when a breach of the

Figure 8.3 *Methods of Executing the Contract*

METHOD	DESCRIPTION
Vendor Contract with Side Letter	The vendor contract can be modified by referring to a supplemental agreement.
Separate Contract	Each individual transaction involves a separate contract.
Master Contract	An umbrella agreement covers all transactions with a vendor. Supplemental agreements may also be necessary for individual transactions.

contract has occurred. This means that the performance of the terms of the contract must be measurable. In addition, the determination of a breach is of little use if the means of recourse are not clearly defined in the contract. The means of recourse for a breach are usually in two forms: rescission of the contract or liquidated damages. Rescission means that the contract is dissolved. In this case, any goods or payments must be returned to the other party. Liquidated damages assigns a specific dollar penalty to various acts of nonperformance of the terms of the contract. The amount and timing of liquidated damages must be detailed in the contract. Otherwise, it is necessary for the court to determine these monetary damages. Proving the extent of monetary damages can be quite difficult, especially in an area such as computing, which is primarily a staff function that does not have a direct measurable affect on revenues. For example, to state that delivery must be by a certain date and not set a penalty for not meeting that commitment will usually be of little value. In many cases, it would be very difficult to determine the monetary damage done to the firm by not having the system on the specific delivery date.

Care must be taken in setting liquidated damages so that they adequately compensate for the lack of performance. If the value of the computer equipment is in the hundreds of thousands of dollars, a penalty of $200 a day for late delivery makes no sense. If an immediate sale can be made to another firm using this specific equipment, it may, in fact, be financially advantageous for the vendor to incur these insignificant late charges. On the other hand, if the penalties are too extreme, then the vendor will not agree to the contract.

Any oral representations by the seller, unless incorporated into the written contract, are legally nonbinding. This is of particular importance in computer contracts. Often during vendor demonstrations or in conversations with the vendor's sales staff, statements are made about the performance of the product which are not included in either the vendor documentation or in the final contract. A common example is when the question of compatibility arises. Let's take for an example the acquisition of personal computers. A firm may be concerned about being able to run all of the software currently available on a specific brand of PC. The vendor's agents may say, "Sure our product is 100% compatible." If this is not incorporated into the contract with a precise definition of "compatibility" and specific liquidated damages for nonperformance, then it is not enforceable. For additional protection, it is also a good idea to include any vendor sales brochure or technical literature as an addendum to the contract.

If oral representations were made by the vendor that are not in the contract, the only recourse for the buyer against the vendor would be to prove that the vendor acted fraudulently. That is, the seller materially misrepresented the facts to the buyer to form the contract. Fraud is substantially more difficult to prove than breach of contract. For breach, it is only necessary to establish that certain provisions in the contract were not complied with. For fraud, it is necessary to prove that the vendor willfully intended to mislead the buyer.

Hence, if performance claims are not contained in the contract and are not honored, the chances of obtaining restitution are diminished. For example, a major computer manufacturer marketed a system based on a certain level of performance. The speed of the system was demonstrated to clients using a reduced version of the operating system since the production operating system was not as yet complete. When the system was delivered, its performance with the complete operating system was not even close to the demonstrated performance. The sales contracts did not state any performance criteria. If the level of performance had been placed in the contract, then it would have been a simple matter to establish breach of contract. However, a lengthy and very costly fraud case was decided in the favor of the purchaser, taking about six years and well after the purchasing company had already gone bankrupt.

There are various types of transactions involving computer equipment. These include the purchase of hardware and software, leasing of hardware and software, acquiring service bureau computer time, hiring data processing consultants, and any other activities associated with computing. Each of these circumstances may be governed by slightly different laws. The remaining discussion will deal primarily with the acquisition of hardware and software.

Warranties

In 49 of the 50 states, the Uniform Commercial Code (UCC) has been adopted (Louisiana has not). The Uniform Commercial Code is a basic set of laws dealing with general business transactions. Before the UCC, each state had its own unique set of laws dealing with these types of transactions. Not only was this confusing, but it tended to hinder interstate business transactions. The UCC is important since it imposes rights and duties on the parties of business transactions.

Article 2 of this code applies to transactions in goods. For computer hardware and sometimes for computer software, these laws will apply to the sale of these goods. Since such things as leasing and service transactions are not covered by the UCC, it is important that the parties understand the scope and limits of these laws. The UCC is important since it provides a unified set of rules governing the sales of goods. These laws cover most of the important aspects of a sale; including formation, breach, rescission, warranties, and liquidated damages. A sales contract must be carefully constructed keeping Article 2 of the UCC in mind.

Probably the most important aspect to the purchaser of the good is the protection afforded by this code. The most significant protection comes in the area of warranties. If the UCC applies to the transaction, then the buyer is given the warranties of merchantability and fitness for a particular purpose. Merchantability, simply stated, means that the good is saleable and of value to a user. The warranty of fitness for a particular purpose states that the buyer can employ the good for the use that it was originally intended. This later protection is of most importance in computer transactions because of the very nature of computers. While a specific system may be quite useful to one user, it may be totally inappropriate to another. This system would meet the test of merchantability, but it would not be fit for the particular purpose of the second user.

These are powerful protections that can only be removed by a direct statement in the contract to disallow them. A statement such as "all other warranties either expressed or implied are nonbinding" will not eliminate these two warranties for goods covered by the UCC. To have this implied protection, the transaction must involve the sale of goods. It does not cover transactions involving services. If there is a doubt about whether a transaction does involve goods, this issue should be resolved by stating what parts of the transaction involve goods and what part does not. For example, if we hire a consultant to design and program some software, then this could be construed as being a transaction dealing with the services rendered by the consultant. However, the contract can state that we are purchasing the system being designed. Hence, we are dealing with a good and are afforded the protection of the UCC.

Performance

The desired performance of the system, be it hardware, software, or a combination of both, should be the primary concern of the acquiring party. While it is obvious that performance parameters should be included in the contract, in most cases, this is a very difficult undertaking. Each specific situation will have its own performance measures. However, there are some guidelines that should be followed when constructing this section of a contract.

The parameters stated in the contract must be as precise as possible and should be measurable. Also, it is best that the measures be of relevance to the operation of the business, if at all possible. Assume we are purchasing a computer system to do accounts receivable processing. The contract should not state that the system operate at an "acceptable speed." This is not precise enough. Instead, state a numeric value for a measurable quantity. It would be better to measure the system in terms of a specific number of accounts receivable records that can be processed per hour instead of the number of EXCPs or MIPS of the system. These events could be measured before acquisition, in the physical benchmarking phase and then verified during acceptance testing.

Even the previous example is simplistic since there is the implication that no other jobs are running on the system and that all accounts receivable records take a uniform amount of processing. Most transactions are not this simple. The information systems area should invest substantial time in developing ways of guaranteeing the performance of a system. This will usually entail much thought and ingenuity.

Establishing Milestones

The exact schedule of events must also be included in the contract. This may be by specific date, but delivery of computer components is subject to a certain amount of variation. The latest acceptable date can be specified and certain events can be tied to the actual date of delivery. For example, installation begins two days after delivery and will take no more than three days. The important issue is to link the payments for the goods to the performance of certain milestones. Partial payment may be made before successful acceptance tests are completed. However, to retain leverage over the vendor, final payment must not be made until the system has been thoroughly tested and accepted.

A related issue deals with who will pay for delivery and installation of the goods. This must be stated in the contract. The installation, be it either hardware or software, depends primarily on the technical expertise of the acquiring firm and the level of difficulty of installing the item. In many cases, it may be to the vendor's advantage to provide installation since some, if not all, of the payment will be contingent on successful installation and testing. Hence, the quicker the hardware or software is installed, the sooner the vendor will be paid.

A comprehensive acceptance test should disclose any failing components of the system. Computer hardware suffers its highest failure rates in its first few hours of use. This is referred to as high infant mortality. Most systems will provide good service after they survive this initial shakedown period. This initial phase can be quite expensive if the purchasing firm does not anticipate it by including proper warranties and maintenance agreements in the contract. It is not uncommon for equipment to be delivered to a computer center and be left standing idle for some time because the staff was just too busy to install and test it. If the warranty period expires, this could be an expensive mistake.

Maintenance

Maintenance agreements can be either part of the original contract or a separate contract. It is best to tie the maintenance agreement directly to the equipment by placing it in the same contract. Substantial nonperformance of the maintenance agreement could then rescind the original purchase agreement.

The maintenance agreement is an important part of any computer transaction involving either hardware or software. The level of service must be explicitly stated. The number of hours a day and the number of days a week technical support will be provided and the maximum response time for service to begin are necessary. Some maintenance agreements will also guarantee a specific minimum of product availability, such as a printer being available 95% of the time based on a two-shift operation. Penalties must be associated with failures to meet these service levels.

There must also be a clear understanding of who is responsible for preventive maintenance and the frequency of this maintenance. Some vendors will provide total maintenance during the warranty period as part of the purchase of the good. If this is the case, it is necessary that this be explicitly stated in the contract. Any other conditions that must be met to validate this agreement should be stated. These usually include protection from electrical power problems, heat and humidity control, and dust control. The user must provide an acceptable operating climate for the equipment. Otherwise, the vendor may have to do extensive and costly maintenance because of the user's neglect. For example, if the user fails to protect the equipment from power surges, then the machines could be seriously damaged due to the user's lack of proper action.

It is also wise to attempt to guarantee a specific price for both maintenance and specialized supplies for the next couple of years. Vendors may not be willing to guarantee a price buy may instead guarantee a maximum percentage increase in prices for specific periods of time.

As a brief review, Figure 8.4 summarizes the important issues involved in developing a contract that help to protect the buyer.

PROTECTING NEW TECHNOLOGY

The computer field is a fast-growing and dynamic industry. The firms in the industry must continually develop new products to stay competitive. Protecting these new products from wrongful use is extremely important so that company investments in that product can be protected. It may take years of effort and millions of dollars to develop a new product. If a competitor was able simply to copy this product, then there would be little incentive for firms to research and develop new products.

Fortunately, there are laws which protect new and innovative products developed by firms. Since the inception of computers, patent laws have afforded adequate protection to advances in hardware. However, software has been an entirely different story. It has been difficult to protect adequately an investment in software. With the rapid growth of microcomputers, this has been an increasing problem. It is easy to copy the software used on most micros. Some estimates have claimed that for certain types of micro software, 50% of the copies in use are illegal copies.

We will discuss various means of legal protection available to computer technology. Since the issues involving hardware protection are well established and not substantially different from the processes outside of the computer area,

Figure 8.4 *Important Contract Issues*

Precisely state terms of performance for each party and detail damages to be assessed in case of nonperformance.

All vendor performance claims should be in writing. Oral representations are usually nonbinding.

If possible, define the transaction as a sale of goods to obtain protection under Article 2 of the UCC.

State performance criteria in terms that are easily measured and relevant to the operation of the business.

Establish milestones so that payment will be made only after successful completion of that phase.

Special consideration must be given in assuring that both preventive and corrective maintenance will be satisfactory.

we will concentrate on the means of protecting software. In addition to discussing the means of protection afforded by the court system, we will also discuss other methods of protecting the software investment.

For legal protection of software, there are three primary means: patents, copyrights, and trade secrets. Each of these methods has advantages and disadvantages. We will explore each of these methods in the following sections.

Patent

A patent is a right given to a person or group to control the manufacturer and sale of some process that an individual discovered or invented. The United States Patent Office grants and records all patents. A patent will be granted for a process, design, or device that is different from previous discoveries (referred to as being novel) and is not obvious to a person having ordinary skills in the field of the discovery. A patent is granted for a period of seven years and may be renewed once for another seven years. These rights may also be relinquished to another party.

To receive a patent, a series of steps must be performed. The discovery must be filed with the Patent Office and a patent search performed by the Patent Office. If the discovery is found to be unique, a patent will be granted. This process will be quite time consuming, usually at least one year. Most individuals will also hire a patent attorney to do a preliminary search before the item is filed with the Patent Office. This involves an additional outlay of money and time.

While the patentability of computer hardware and the processes involved in the manufacturer of computer hardware are not debatable, the issuance of patents for computer software is not as clear. In 1980, the United States Congress passed legislation making computer software subject to the patent laws. While this in itself appears to establish the patentability of software, there has not as yet been a landmark court case which has interpreted and clarified this law.

A patent is a very strong method of protecting a discovery. However, for software it is of questionable value. First, the guidelines for patentability have not been firmly established. The protection afforded by a patent is for the specific process used and not for the idea involved in the system. This may protect specific methods of coding a system, but will not protect the ideas contained in that code. Nor will it protect mathematical formula or databases. For example, the idea of using spread sheet-type computer software is not patentable, but the specific code to implement a spread sheet system may be patentable. Also, the source code to implement the system must be filed with the Patent Office and hence becomes public knowledge.

Copyright

The Copyright Act affords protection to the expression of an idea. This expression may be in the form of a sheet of paper, an electronic image, a visual image, or an audio recording. The granting of a copyright allows the holder to control the distribution and sale of any copies of the copyrighted materials. Again, as with a patent, the idea itself is not protected, only its expression. Using the spread sheet example again, the computer source and object code could be protected; also, the system documentation including user and reference manuals and all display screens and output forms could be protected by a copyright. But the actual idea of a spread sheet program is not protected.

A copyright is easily obtained. Upon creation of the work, the originator must place the copyright symbol, © or the word *Copyright,* the date of origination, and the originator's name in conspicuous places in the work. The copyright does not have to be recorded until the copyright is to be defended or transferred (however, it can be recorded at any time). A copyright is granted for the life of the author plus 50 years.

The protection afforded by a copyright is very useful in protecting the original program code, the documentation, screen formats, and output layouts. However, the copyright only protects against someone copying the material and does not protect against the development of a similar system using the same ideas but writing different programs to implement these ideas.

Trade Secret

The use of the laws governing trade secrets is the final form of legal protection we will discuss. To be a trade secret, an idea must be of value to the party trying to protect it, steps must be taken to maintain its secrecy, and the idea must be difficult for others to discover without knowledge of the secret. Probably most important is that a firm be very careful to limit the knowledge of the secret both inside and outside of the firm. This means that only employees with a true need to know should be allowed access to the secret. Note that unlike patents or copyrights, the work does not have to be novel or original. It can use a combination of existing techniques in a unique manner.

A trade secret is implemented by contract negotiation. Hence, it is by agreement between the vendor and the user of the system. The user will agree to protect the secret and restrict access to the use of the secret to only necessary parties. In most cases, there will be severe penalties for the user's failure to protect the secret.

Trade secrets are the most powerful protection of software since they do protect the idea itself. However, they restrict the marketing of the system to a great extent. Mass marketing of something expressed as a trade secret is almost impossible for obvious reasons.

The Trade Secret Act is used in another form to protect both hardware and software—by restricting past employees from using knowledge about specific products to the detriment of the firm. For example, if a team of programmers and analysts was developing a software system, an employee on that team could not join a competing firm and divulge the specific procedures used in developing that system. Again, this protection is obtained by having this stipulated in the person's employment contract when hired.

The interpretation of this part of the law can be difficult. An employee is allowed to use the general knowledge obtained in a previous job which is essential to the performance of that employee's profession. The separation of what is general knowledge and what is specific product knowledge is not easy. For many cases that have been decided in court, the pivotal factor has been the types of materials the employee has taken from the previous employer. If these materials primarily involved specific products and they have been used in the subsequent job, then the decision has been in favor of the previous employer. For example, a programmer was part of a team developing a database management system and went to work for another employer. If this programmer used the same procedures to implement a similar system for the competitor, this would violate the Trade Secrets Act. However, this programmer's general knowledge of database systems is part of the necessary knowledge for performing a job. Hence, it could be used at a competitive firm.

In summary, the strongest legal protection for software is provided by trade secrets. However, they are so restrictive that they are generally not used for mass-marketed software. Copyrights are good protection for object code and all related documentation. Copyrights will not protect against the reverse engineering of a product where a competitor can disassemble the object code and determine how the process was performed and then create a similar system. Patents still leave so many unanswered questions that at present they do not appear to be a reliable form of protection. The best method of protecting software through a patent is to imbed the software in read only memory (ROM) and sell this as hardware to be installed in a system. ROM-based software has been determined to be patentable and affords more protection. Unfortunately, this option is not viable in many situations. The methods of legally protecting software are summarized in Figure 8.5.

Protection of the code does not end simply by registering the patent or copyright but entails a continuous vigilance for any violation. All forms of infringement must be vigorously defended. If this defense is not present and violations are allowed to continue for an extended period of time, the protection afforded by copyright, patent, or the Trade Secrets Act may be lost.

Even considering the methods of protection already discussed, there are many issues left unsettled. For example, what if multiple vendors use the same user interface for their systems? That is, each vendor employs uniform com-

Figure 8.5 *Legal Protection of Software*

METHOD	PROTECTION	WEAKNESS
Patent	Right to control a novel process	Many issues involved in patenting software still unresolved
Copyright	Prevents copying of expression of an idea	Does not protect ideas or method of implementation
Trade Secret	Protects ideas and methods of implementation	Makes marketing very difficult

mands and access methods for their systems. Even though the actual systems are coded completely differently, what the user sees is identical. This type of standardization is obviously of benefit to the general computer community, but does it violate the rights of the original developer of the interface? These types of issues must be resolved by the courts or by new legislation.

OTHER PROTECTION

It is not necessary to rely strictly on legal protection. If we adopt measures that protect the software from unauthorized access and use, then we need not worry about relying on the court system to protect the product. The type of protection employed will be dependent on the circumstances. The primary objective is to make copying or misusing the software so difficult as to discourage an attempt. Of course, no system of protection is foolproof; every time a new scheme is devised, a new method of circumventing that scheme is usually also developed.

One primary form of protection is to not divulge the source code of the program. This makes interpreting the logic of the program very difficult. However, this may not be possible if the user demands source code so that the system can be tailored to that user's needs. Many vendors have been adopting object-code-only policies that forbid the distribution of source code. To solve the program tailoring problem, vendors imbed user exits in the programs enabling the user to modify the program. A user exit is simply a call to a subroutine which is initially empty. The user can fill this subroutine with code that will alter the original program or simply leave it empty.

Object code can still be disassembled and the logic more easily understood. Some vendors will not store the code in sequential order, but will instead break the code into blocks which are randomly sequenced in storage. A directory is then used to execute the code in the correct order.

Another form of protection is one that restricts the number of copies that can be made of a program. This protection is common on microcomputers. A diskette may allow no copies or a limited number of copies to be made. This approach has caused some problems since it makes the backup of the system and the transfer of the system to a hard disk more difficult. Also, programs to "crack" the copy protection scheme seem to appear almost immediately. Some copy protection schemes have been devised that rely on a critical section of the program's code residing in a ROM chip that is plugged into the system. Users, in general, have not been satisfied with this type of scheme, which seems destined to go into disuse.

For mainframe systems, the protection of software is substantially easier. Because of the high costs and the limited market, it is possible to design a package to run on only one specific processor. Before the software begins to execute, the program checks the internal processor ID, and if it is incorrect, the system will not run or in some cases the program will self-destruct. For software which is leased, vendors must be sure that the program will not run after the lease terminates. This is accomplished by having the system compare the expiration date against the current system date. The software will not run if the expiration date has passed.

Another protection that applies mainly to micro software is for the vendor to negotiate either volume purchase agreements or site licenses with large clients. A volume purchase agreement allows a fixed number of copies of the software to be made by the client at a substantially reduced price. A site license allows an unlimited number of copies to be made at a specified location (or locations) of the client for a fixed price. Both of these agreements help to reduce the incentive to copy software. In the case of a site license, it helps to remove some of the client's burden of monitoring the internal use of the software.

There are also multiple copy arrangements for mainframe software. The second and any subsequent copies of a software package will usually be given a substantial discount. For some vendors, this discount may also be dependent on the size of the processor to be used. These two concepts are usually called multiple license agreements and graduated pricing arrangements, respectively.

The various ways of protecting software are summarized in Figure 8.6. The type of physical protection employed by the vendor must be taken into consideration when doing disaster planning. For example, if a package is designed to run on only a specific processor, then arrangements must be made with that vendor to allow the program to execute on an alternate processor. Otherwise, disaster recovery could be delayed waiting for this vendor to enable the system on a different processor.

SUMMARY

A legal contract is formed whenever goods or services are acquired. When dealing with computer technology, it is particularly important to construct carefully the written contract. The legal staff, purchasing, and the information systems area must team up to assure that the contract is properly formulated.

The contract should fully define all technical terms and precisely state the responsibilities of all the involved parties. Care must be exercised in stating the performance requirements so that the resulting acquisition will indeed perform at a satisfactory level. In most cases, a solid contract is based on the quality of the work done in constructing the RFP. A well-constructed RFP will alert the vendors to the desired content of the resulting legal contract.

While the contract alone does not assure that the acquired good will satisfy the user's needs, it should give the user adequate recourse if the needs are not met.

A different area of legal concern is that of protecting a company's investment in its developed software. There are three primary methods of protection: patent, copyright, and trade secrets. These can be used in combination with physical means, such as object-code-only policies, to protect more fully a company's investment in developing marketable software.

Figure 8.6 *Other Forms of Software Protection*

METHOD	DISCUSSION
Object Code Only	No source code is provided; modifications can only be made through user exits.
Random Sequencing of Code	May slow program execution
Restricting Number of Copies	User problems include difficulty in making backup copies and using on hard disks. Utility programs exist that allow unlimited copies.
Checking Processor ID	Only practical when a moderate number of machines are involved
Timing-out System	Again, only practical when a moderate number of machines are involved
Incentive Pricing Agreements	Reduces the economic incentive of using "bootleg" copies

QUESTIONS

1. A contract is formed when there is an offer and an acceptance with consideration by both parties. What would be the normal consideration by each party
   a. when a piece of computer hardware is purchased?
   b. when computer hardware is leased?
   c. when a computer program is written by a consultant?
2. While oral contracts are enforceable, it is generally considered bad business practice to not use a written contract for major acquisitions. Why is this particularly true in transactions dealing with computers?
3. Defining technical terms in a contract is important especially in a contract dealing with computers since many terms may be ambiguous to one or both of the parties. For the following terms, describe how they may be ambiguous:
   a. Up and running
   b. Compatible
   c. Computer time
   d. User friendly
   e. Fully documented
   f. Plug compatible
4. Describe the differences between a master contract and separate contracts. Explain the advantages of a master contract.
5. Why is it important to include the vendor's sales brochures as addendum to a contract?
6. Explain the implied warranties that are granted if a transaction is a good and is covered by the Uniform Commercial Code.

7. A computer salesman claims that his device is 100% compatible with your system, but due to the expense of installation, a trial machine cannot be installed. How can a "safe" contract be written to handle this type of situation?

8. When developing the conditions involved in a maintenance agreement, what are the important points to consider?

9. In the previous chapter we emphasized the importance of the careful construction of the RFP. Describe the relationship between the RFP and the final legal contract.

10. Investigate one form of copy protection used by a vendor and describe how the protection works.

11. Why do copy protection schemes make it difficult to back up the software and also make it difficult to use the software on a hard disk?

12. Why aren't most microcomputer programs protected by identifying the specific CPU of use?

13. What problems do computer networks present when dealing with the protection of software from inappropriate use and copying?

14. A copy protection scheme that was not described in this chapter involves planting "worms" in a program. Describe how a worm works and why it can be a very dangerous approach.

15. For mainframe software assigned to run on a specific CPU, disaster recovery involving the use of a different processor can cause a problem since programs protected this way will only run under that one specific CPU. How may we handle this problem so that we assure quick disaster recovery?

16. Explain why it is important to determine if any lawsuits are outstanding against a firm from which you are contemplating acquiring goods.

CASE ANALYSIS

Case 1

For Case 1 in Chapter 7, in which you developed an RFP (Easy-Does-It Company), outline the important points that should be considered when developing the legal contract. This outline should be developed as a guideline for the attorney to follow when negotiating the final contract.

Case 2

For Case 2 in Chapter 7, in which you developed an RFP (Major Company), outline the important points that should be considered when developing the legal contract. This outline should be developed as a guideline for the attorney to follow when negotiating the final contract.

Case 3

DUNE Company has just developed a new interactive software system to track and control the irrigation of the farmland it owns. This is a revolutionary system that takes inputs from sensors in the fields and other data involving the type of crop in each field, recent weather data, past irrigation data, weather forecasts, and information involving the maturity of the crop and uses this to control the amount and frequency of irrigation in each field. DUNE has investigated the software market and has found that no other system like this exists. DUNE has hired you to develop guidelines for protecting their investment in this system so that if they market it, the chances of illegal use will be diminished. Develop a set of guidelines that will accomplish this objective.

ADDITIONAL READINGS

ADLER, PHILIP, JR., CHARLES K. PARSONS, AND SCOTT B. ZOLKE. "Employee Privacy: Legal and Research Departments and Implications for Personnel Administration," *Sloan Management Review,* Vol. 26, No. 2, Winter 1985, pp. 13–22.

BIGELOW, ROBERT P. "Legal and Security Issues Posed by Computer Utilities," *Harvard Business Review,* September-October 1967, p. 150.

BLOOMBECKER, J. J. "Malpractice in IS?" *Datamation,* October 15, 1989, p. 85.

BRADON, DICK, AND SIDNEY SEGELSTEIN. *Data Processing Contracts Structure, Contents and Negotiations,* 2nd Ed. New York: Van Nostrand-Reinhold Company.

DEVLIN, J. P., W. A. LOWELL, AND A. E. ALGER. "Self-Assessment Procedure XIV: A Self-Assessment Procedure Dealing with the Legal Issues of Computing," *Communications of the ACM,* Vol. 28, No. 5, May 1985, p. 481.

KERR, SUSAN. "Legal Laissez-Faire," *Datamation,* April 15, 1989, p. 54.

PRICE, R. LEON, AND CHARLIE JONES. "Today's Legal Environment Offers Software Protection Opportunities, Challenges," *Data Management,* April 1986, pp. 38–51.

SWARTZ, HERBERT. "Who Owns Your Custom Software?" *Computer Decisions,* February 1986, pp. 38–41.

READINGS BEFORE NEXT CHAPTER

If you are not familiar with the concepts involved in making capital budgeting decisions, it would be helpful to do some reading on how to calculate net present values and the theory behind discounted cash flows. These subjects are covered in both introductory finance texts and introductory managerial accounting texts. One source is *Introduction to Management Accounting,* by Horngren and Sundem, 7th edition, Prentice Hall. Chapters 11 and 12 deal with the concepts of capital budgeting.

9

FINANCIAL ISSUES

An important component of any business decision is the method of financing to be employed. So far, we have not considered any of the financial implications of the decisions discussed. Many questions, however, arise concerning financial issues. For example: How will we finance an acquisition? Is it better to purchase or lease a specific piece of equipment? How will this acquisition affect our financial statements? How do we bill our users for the computer services they use? These and other questions are important for both the company as a whole and the information systems area.

As with legal issues, it is not necessary for the data processing manager to be an expert in financial matters. Instead, the manager must be knowledgeable enough to understand the important issues and realize when an expert must be consulted. However, some of the financial considerations, especially in the budgeting area, are critical to the smooth operation and eventual growth of the information system. Any good manager must be able to deal with the budgeting process.

FUNDING COMPUTER ACQUISITIONS

The first issues we will discuss entail the options involved in financing computer acquisitions. The financing of computer equipment is usually different than the financing of other types of capital goods. The financing options are often limited because of the high degree of technological obsolescence associated with the industry. The physical deterioration of computer equipment is usually not related to the technological obsolescence. Many computer systems are discarded even though they have many years of useful physical life left. The reason for the disposal of the older system lies in the fact that newer equipment can deliver substantially better performance for less cost or provide functions that were previously unavailable.

The risk of technological obsolescence and the accompanying rapid and unpredictable decline in market value makes it difficult to convince a lender to accept EDP hardware as collateral for loans. For example, the market value of a CPU may decline by as much as 50% in a matter of months when a new model of processor is released. The reason for this rapid decline is not associated with any change in the performance in the older machine, but because the cost/performance ratio of the new machine is superior, making the old machine less attractive. Because it is so difficult to predict these types of events, financial institutions are generally unwilling to accept the risk and will either turn down the loan or demand a substantially higher down payment.

While the external financing of computer hardware is difficult, financing for software is almost impossible. Software developed internally usually does not have any value outside of the firm. Hence, it has no value as collateral to a financial institution. Even software purchased from outside vendors has little value as collateral since the purchase agreement involves the purchase of the right for a specific firm to use the software. Often the only way to finance software is to purchase it along with hardware and finance both under one comprehensive agreement.

Because of the restrictions placed on the sources of funding for computer purchases, the firm may be forced either to fund the system through internal funds or adopt a method other than purchase. Alternative financing methods include various forms of leasing or renting the desired products. Figure 9.1 describes some of the possible sources of funds.

Since the acquisition of computer technology involves substantial sums of money, the impact of these acquisitions must be carefully considered before the financing method is selected. Larger firms, especially corporations, are concerned about two major areas of financial impact. One is the overall outlay of cash that is involved in the transaction. This includes out-of-pocket expenditures such as the purchase amount, lease payments, interest payments, insurance, maintenance, operating expenditures, and also the income tax effects associated with the acquisition. The second area is the way in which the acquisition will affect the financial statements. In many circumstances the treatment of a transaction by the Internal Revenue Service (IRS) and the rules established by the American Institute of Certified Public Accounts (AICPA) will be different. This may result in a decision that has the lowest cash outlay to affect the financial statements adversely.

For example, using a leasing method that the AICPA considers a capital lease (i.e., lease to own) forces the firm to account for the transaction as a purchase of the good. This will increase the long-lived assets and the liabilities of

Figure 9.1   *Sources of Computer Funding*

SOURCE OF FUNDING	DESCRIPTION
External:	
Mortgage Loans	Asset is collateral, hence interest rate and/or down payment high
Unsecured Loans	Usually very high interest rates
Issue Additional Stock	Costly, usually done through very large offering
Internal:	
Use Cash Reserves	Most firms not willing to use these funds for large discretionary expenditure such as computers
Other Financing Methods:	
Lease	Involves only monthly payments without large initial expenditure; do not own asset at end of lease
Lease to Own	Alternate method of purchasing asset without large initial expenditure

the firm's balance sheet. This could make the company's current ratio, quick ratio, and percentage of debt less attractive to investors and lenders. In this situation, the IRS treats the transaction as any other lease. Hence, the tax benefits could be more attractive than actually purchasing the equipment. Figure 9.2 illustrates this situation. The company has to make the decision either to make the financial statements slightly less attractive or have a higher net cash outlay. Also, since both the IRS and AICPA rules change, the best decision at one time may not be appropriate at a later time. These decisions will usually not be made by the information system personnel, but they must realize the complexity involved in these transactions.

FINANCING OPTIONS

The options available to acquire computer equipment include purchase, rent, operating lease, and financing lease (capital lease). (See Figure 9.3.) Each of these methods has certain advantages and disadvantages.

Purchase of the item is probably the most straightforward approach. As mentioned earlier, equipment that has rapid technological obsolescence may force the firm to finance the acquisition through internal funds. In most situations, this is undesirable.

A purchase involves the immediate transfer of title. Consequently, the good belongs to the acquiring firm, making it responsible for all maintenance, insurance, and operating costs. Installation costs might also be the responsibility of the owner. If the item is purchased, all risk of technological obsolescence lies

Figure 9.2 *Impact of Operating and Financing Leases*

Equipment is acquired worth $2,000,000 with total payments of $500,000 in the first year. There will be no change in the balance sheet if this is considered an operating lease. However, as a financing lease, fixed assets increase by $2,000,000; current liabilities by $500,000; and long-term liabilities by $1,500,000.

BALANCE SHEET

	BEFORE ACQUISITION	ADDITIONS FROM FINANCING LEASE	AFTER FINANCING LEASE
Current Assets	$5,000,000		$5,000,000
Fixed Assets	200,000,000	$2,000,000	202,000,000
Total Assets	$205,000,000	$2,000,000	$207,000,000
Current Liabilities	$2,500,000	$500,000	$3,000,000
Long-term Liabilities	7,500,000	1,500,000	9,000,000
Owner's Equity	195,000,000		195,000,000
Total Liabilities	$205,000,000	$2,000,000	$207,000,000
Current Ratio	2.0		1.67
Percentage of Debt	.049		.058

with the acquiring firm. The products that best lend themselves to a purchase arrangement are those that are technologically stable. For example, CRTs and tape drives appear to have matured and will probably not change significantly over the next few years. This means that the chances of the company needing to replace them in the near future is quite slim. On the other hand, CPUs and disk drives are rapidly developing and purchase may entail a rapid decrease in market value and potential for replacement in a relatively short time.

The analysis of product stability involves a good deal of environmental scanning, as addressed in Chapter 3. Without this type of information, the quality of the financing decision may be lessened.

Renting presents a short-term method of acquisition. It is usually the most expensive method for a given period of time, but it involves the least commitment by the firm. A rental agreement is usually open ended and is on a month-to-month basis. Usually, there is only a periodic fee paid by the firm. All insurance and maintenance are the responsibility of the party providing the equipment.

Renting is desirable in some situations. A firm having a cyclical demand may rent equipment to provide additional facilities during peak periods. For example, a CPA firm may rent additional microcomputers during the four-month busy season involved in income tax processing. Renting also allows a firm to acquire technology for a short period of time to test the appropriateness of the product. If the product is acceptable, then another method of more permanent acquisition may be used to acquire the good. The risk of making a long-term commitment to inappropriate resources can be reduced by using renting.

Leasing the asset is another option. A lease allows the lessee the use of the equipment for a fixed period of time. During this time, periodic payments (usually monthly) must be made and at the end of the lease period the asset reverts back to the lessor. Some leases give the lessee the option of purchasing the asset for a fixed price at the end of the lease. This must be negotiated and included in the lease contract.

Leases come in various forms. They are designed to reach different objectives and satisfy different needs. The term of a lease can vary considerably from as short as a few months to the entire life of the asset. Some lease agreements are simply designed to provide another way of purchasing the asset. The party responsible for installation, testing, and the payment of maintenance is also negotiable. All in all, the terms of leases can be considerably different in different circumstances. Care must be taken when formulating a lease agreement that it meets the needs of both parties.

Even though leases can have many different characteristics, they are generally classified as either operating leases or financing (or capital) leases. The reasoning behind these designations is that an operating lease is primarily concerned with providing the services of the asset to the lessee, where final ownership is not an objective. A financing lease is concerned with providing an alternative method of purchasing the asset.

The American Institute of Certified Public Accountants (AICPA) has a set of guidelines that dictates when a lease must be accounted for as a financing lease. The basis of the rule is that the intent of the lease is actually an alternative method of purchasing the good. In most cases, a financing lease is one that has a bargain purchase option or has a term that is approximately the life of the asset. A bargain purchase option means that the asset can be purchased at the end of the lease term for an amount substantially below the expected market value at that time. While the AICPA rules are much more complex than this, it is unnecessary to delve into them any further here.

Knowing whether a lease is either a financing or an operating lease lies

Figure 9.3 *Financing Alternatives*

FINANCING METHOD	DESCRIPTION	WHERE APPROPRIATE
Purchase	Permanent acquisition	When acquiring stable technology
Rent	Short-term use of equipment	Cyclical demand situations Testing new equipment
Operating lease	Use of equipment for specific term	When acquiring rapidly changing technology
Financing lease	Lease equivalent to purchase	Same as purchase

in the different way these two are carried on the books of the company. An operating lease will simply have its monthly payments treated as expenses, and there will be a footnote to the financial statements describing the lease obligation. There is no recognition of an asset on the balance sheet. A financing lease will necessitate treating the transaction as a purchase on credit. Hence, the asset and corresponding liability must be entered on the books. The asset must be depreciated, and the monthly payments are recorded as principal and interest payments. Due to the large capital outlays involved in computer acquisitions, the use of financing versus operating leases can have a significant effect on the financial statements of a firm. It is important to consider carefully the terms of the leasing contract to be sure that the lease will be classified in the desired manner.

An operating lease shifts a majority of the obsolescence risk to the lessor. Of course the longer the term of the lease, the more risk the lessee will assume. Most operating leases have a fixed term and impose large penalties for early termination of the agreement. Hence, the firm is usually locked into the lease over a specific period. Maintenance and insurance are usually the responsibility of the lessor since this firm retains title and will get the item back after the lease expires. Options to purchase the asset are usually not included in an operating lease. However, they can be, as long as they are not at a "bargain" price.

Operating leases are most appropriate for acquiring equipment that is changing rapidly. In this way, newer equipment can be obtained when the lease has expired. For example, it may be best to acquire a CPU through a reasonably short operating lease since this technology is volatile. This also has the advantage of forcing the information system to keep the computer center at a state-of-the-art level. If this type of equipment was purchased, there may be a reluctance to dispose of the still functioning equipment for newer technology.

Since a financing lease is simply an alternative method of purchasing the product, this type of lease is appropriate in acquiring equipment that is a mature and stable technology. Financing leases are used when others forms of financing are not appropriate. If the firm does not have adequate internal funds or if external financing is not available or too expensive, then a financial lease should be considered. This financing option also presents some tax advantages. The tax effects must be factored into any financing decision.

For financing leases the payments for maintenance and insurance will usually be the responsibility of the lessee. This makes sense, because the asset will eventually be the property of the lessee. It will be to this firm's advantage to protect the asset.

QUANTITATIVE ANALYSIS

In the preceding discussion, we talked about the qualitative aspects of the financing decision. Of course, the quantitative aspects are also important. We must attempt to determine the financing method that will minimize the expense of the acquisition to the company. Since the cash flows occur at different points in time, we cannot simply add up these flows and choose the least-cost alternative. Instead, we must use discounted cash flow analysis to bring all of the cash flows back to present time. The present value of each financing option can then be compared and the best financing method selected.

In some firms these types of calculations will be done by the accounting or purchasing staff. However, it is not uncommon for the information systems staff to have total responsibility for the acquisition decision. This is particularly true if the firm has a decentralized philosophy. Hence, the manager must have at least a rudimentary knowledge of calculating discounted cash flows. This material is taught in finance and accounting courses and will be briefly reviewed here.

Whenever one is analyzing alternative financing schemes (commonly referred to as capital budgeting), the first step is to detail the cash flows for the duration of the useful life of the asset. Figure 9.4 gives an example problem. Figure 9.5 shows the cash flows. Note that the positive flows (inflows) are to the left and the negative flows (outflows) are to the right. Since it is not necessary to consider the revenue produced by the asset (it would be the same in both situations and would also be very difficult to estimate), the only inflows considered are those produced by saving of income taxes. Here a simplifying assumption is made that taxes are paid only once a year.

Before doing the cash flow analysis, let's discuss the characteristics of the different financing options. It is necessary to consider some important issues for each acquisition method. For example: Who has legal ownership of the asset? Who pays for maintenance and insurance? What are the tax implications?

Figure 9.4   *An Example Problem*

Purchase:	Initial Purchase Price	$2,100,000
	Monthly Maintenance Fee	15,000
	Yearly Insurance Premium	3,000
	Estimated Useful Life	5 Years
	Estimated Residual Value	100,000

DEPRECIATION SCHEDULE FOR TAX PURPOSES

YEAR	DEPRECIATION PERCENT
1	15%
2	22%
3	21%
4	21%
5	21%

Operating Lease:	Monthly Lease Payment	$90,000
	Term of Lease	3 Years

All insurance & maintenance is paid by lessor.

The cost of capital is 24% per year and the marginal tax rate is 40%.

Figure 9.5 *Cash Flow Analysis*

	PURCHASE		OPERATING LEASE	
MONTH	*INFLOWS*	*OUTFLOWS*	*INFLOWS*	*OUTFLOWS*
0		$2,118,000 (1)		$90,000 (a)
1		15,000 (2)		90,000 (a)
2		15,000 (2)		90,000 (a)
3		15,000 (2)		90,000 (a)
4		15,000 (2)		90,000 (a)
5		15,000 (2)		90,000 (a)
6		15,000 (2)		90,000 (a)
7		15,000 (2)		90,000 (a)
8		15,000 (2)		90,000 (a)
9		15,000 (2)		90,000 (a)
10		15,000 (2)		90,000 (a)
11		15,000 (2)		90,000 (a)
12	$193,200 (3)	18,000 (4)	$432,000 (b)	90,000 (a)
13		15,000 (2)		90,000 (a)
14		15,000 (2)		90,000 (a)
15		15,000 (2)		90,000 (a)
16		15,000 (2)		90,000 (a)
17		15,000 (2)		90,000 (a)
18		15,000 (2)		90,000 (a)
19		15,000 (2)		90,000 (a)
20		15,000 (2)		90,000 (a)
21		15,000 (2)		90,000 (a)
22		15,000 (2)		90,000 (a)
23		15,000 (2)		90,000 (a)
24	249,200 (5)	18,000 (4)	432,000 (b)	90,000 (a)
25		15,000 (2)		90,000 (a)
26		15,000 (2)		90,000 (a)
27		15,000 (2)		90,000 (a)
28		15,000 (2)		90,000 (a)
29		15,000 (2)		90,000 (a)
30		15,000 (2)		90,000 (a)
31		15,000 (2)		90,000 (a)
32		15,000 (2)		90,000 (a)
33		15,000 (2)		90,000 (a)
34		15,000 (2)		90,000 (a)
35		15,000 (2)		90,000 (a)
36	241,200 (6)	18,000 (4)	432,000 (b)	
37		15,000 (2)		
38		15,000 (2)		
39		15,000 (2)		
40		15,000 (2)		
41		15,000 (2)		
42		15,000 (2)		
43		15,000 (2)		
44		15,000 (2)		
45		15,000 (2)		
46		15,000 (2)		

(continued)

Figure 9.5 (*Continued*)

MONTH	PURCHASE		OPERATING LEASE	
	INFLOWS	OUTFLOWS	INFLOWS	OUTFLOWS
47		15,000 (2)		
48	241,200 (6)	18,000 (2)		
49		15,000 (2)		
50		15,000 (2)		
51		15,000 (2)		
52		15,000 (2)		
53		15,000 (2)		
54		15,000 (2)		
55		15,000 (2)		
56		15,000 (2)		
57		15,000 (2)		
58		15,000 (2)		
59		15,000 (2)		
60	341,200 (7)			

Legend:
(1) Initial cost + yearly insurance + monthly maintenance = ($2,100,000 + $3,000 + $15,000)
(2) Monthly Maintenance = $15,000
(3) Tax savings = 40% of (depreciation + insurance + maintenance) 40% × ($300,000 + $3,000 + $180,000)
(4) Yearly insurance + monthly maintenance ($3,000 + $15,000)
(5) Tax savings = 40% × ($440,000 + $3,000 + $180,000)
(6) Tax savings = 40% × ($420,000 + $3,000 + $180,000)
(7) Tax savings + residual value = (40% × ($420,000 + $3,000 + $180,000)) + $100,000

(a) Monthly lease payment = $90,000
(b) Tax savings = 40% of yearly lease payment = 40% × ($1,080,000)

The most recognizable option is to purchase the equipment. A purchase involves the legal transfer of title for the piece of equipment. That is, the purchaser owns the equipment, hence it is the purchaser's sole responsibility to pay for maintenance and insurance. Also, the purchaser would have to depreciate the value of the asset over its useful life for both tax purposes and financial accounting purposes (the method of depreciation may be different for taxes and financial statements).

An operating lease and renting are very similar in nature except for the duration of the agreement. Legally ownership remains with the lessor, and it is normal that the lessor pays all maintenance and insurance. For the tax and financial statements, the lessee can take the lease payments as a direct expense.

A financing lease is a hybrid between an operating lease and a purchase. Until the bargain purchase option is exercised, the lessor retains title; after that point the lessee owns the asset. It is customary that the lessee will pay maintenance and insurance, but that may vary by the negotiation of the parties involved. For tax purposes the lease payments by the lessee are expenses until the bargain purchase option is exercised; then the asset must be depreciated over its remaining useful life. The financial accounting treatment is to assume that the asset was purchased at the beginning of the lease, depreciate the asset over its life, and record and amortize the remaining lease payments as if they were a debt.

It is then necessary to discount these cash flows and find a net present value for each of the two alternate methods. In this situation, we use a discount factor of 2% per month (24% divided by 12 months), discount each of the flows back to the present time, and then sum all of the discounted values. The results of this process are summarized in Figure 9.6.

Note that a decision cannot as yet be made since the two alternatives have different life spans, five years and three years. The next step is to annualize the respective discounted values so that they have comparable time units (one year). As shown in Figure 9.6, this is accomplished by dividing each of the net present values by the respective annuity factor (24% for five years and 24% for three years).

A quantitative comparison can now be made concerning these two options. Since the annual net present value of purchasing is a smaller outflow (−$735,403.83 compared to −$766,609.93), this indicates that with respect to cash flow, purchase is the better alternative. However, this is only one factor that must be considered when making the acquisition decision. All of the other qualitative factors must also be considered.

OTHER FINANCING METHODS

There are other financing alternatives that have not as yet been discussed. As mentioned in Chapter 8, the acquisition of used equipment is a possibility. If this equipment is reconditioned, it will usually function as well as new equipment, but at a substantially reduced price. Hence, this may be thought of as a financing alternative. Used equipment does have certain disadvantages since it is more

---

Figure 9.6 *Net Present Values*

Total Discounted Cash Flows:
Net present value of purchase over a five-year period = −$2,018,966.21

Net present value of operating lease over a three-year period = −$1,518,886.60

Annualization of Flows:
Purchase = net present value / annuity for five years
= −$2,018,966.21 / 2.745384416 = −$735,403.83 per year

Operating lease = net present value / annuity for three years
= −$1,518,886.60 / 1.981303078 = −$766,609.93 per year

Since the discounted yearly cost of purchase is less, this is the quantitatively more attractive acquisition method.

difficult to use as collateral and may not get the favorable tax treatment of new equipment.

Third party leasing is an area of particular interest to anyone involved in computer acquisitions. Because of the pricing structure of the computer industry, there are many third party leasing firms. A third party lease includes the computer manufacturer who sells the product to the leasing firm who, in turn, leases it to the acquiring company. Most third party leases are operating leases. The reason third party leasing firms can be profitable is that the computer manufacturers will usually price their leasing arrangements significantly higher than their purchase price. This pricing policy encourages outright sales of the good which will generate cash more quickly for the vendor. The third party leasing firm is usually associated with a financial institution; hence it has access to large amounts of cash. These firms can buy a large number of the products from the vendor at a quantity discount and also take advantage of favorable tax laws. This produces the type of situation where it appears that everyone wins. The vendor sells the asset. The lessee gets the lease at a reduced price and the third party lessor makes a profit. Because of their impact, it is important not to ignore the possibility of obtaining a third party lease. Often, besides being less expensive, the lease terms are more flexible than the standard lease available from the vendor. Some large vendors have their own independent financing arm that operates in a manner similar to a third party leasing firm.

CHARGING USERS

In this section, we will examine various ways of billing users for the services of the information system. Before discussing specific billing schemes, it is necessary to discuss the general objectives of an ideal billing scheme. These objectives are summarized in Figure 9.7. One of the most important aspects of a billing system is that the user understands the bill and how it was derived. The charges must also be consistent. That is, if the same job is run a second time, the charges will be approximately the same both times.

The bill must also be predictable so that a user can accurately calculate the charges for a job using a specific amount of resources. At the same time, for obvious reasons, the charging scheme must generate the desired dollars of revenue. A billing scheme must be perceived as fair. For example, the intensive users of resources must be charged more than the casual users. Also, the scheme must be flexible so that as the environment changes, the billing scheme can reflect these changes. Finally, the changing scheme should ration scarce resources and encourage the use of resources with excess capacity. While it is difficult to design a system that satisfies all of these criteria, they should be kept in mind when a system is being designed.

The type of charging scheme used to bill computer center users is dependent on the objectives of the information system and the methods used to measure its performance. The amount of revenue generated may heavily influ-

Figure 9.7 *Objectives of Billing Schemes*

OBJECTIVE	DISCUSSION
Understandable	This is dependent on the level of sophistication of the user community.
Consistent	Best measured by running the same job at different times and under different conditions
Predictable	Allows users to estimate the cost of running particular jobs
Produces Desired Revenues	This is the basic objective of most billing schemes.
Rations Resources	Helps shift load from resources at or near capacity to those with excess capacity
Fair	Important, but very difficult to measure
Flexible	As the system changes (as it always will), we must be able to adjust the billing scheme accordingly.

ence the evaluation of the performance of an organizational unit. A department's financial performance can be measured in a variety of ways. Generally, performance is measured by classifying the specific functional entity as either an investment center, a profit center, or a cost center (see Figure 9.8). The degree of control that a manager has over an entity will dictate the appropriate performance measure. If a manager can fully determine the level of capital investment, the prices for the goods sold, and the costs of the entity, then this is an investment center and the manager will be judged on the return on investment generated by the entity. A profit center does not allow the manager to control capital investment, and performance is based on net income of the entity. In a cost center, the manager can control only costs. In this case, performance is based on costs incurred compared to a budget. In the case of both the profit and cost centers, the decisions not under the control of the manager (such as capital investment) are made by higher management, usually through an annual budgeting process.

In many companies, the information system is not a revenue-generating

Figure 9.8 *Centers of Performance Evaluation*

CENTER	DESCRIPTION
Investment	Operates as an independent entity; all decisions are made by the management of that investment center.
Profit	Responsible for setting prices, producing revenue, and controlling expenses
Cost	Only responsible for controlling expenses

activity, but an internal service function. Hence, it is treated as a cost center. Since the data processing system is very capital intensive, the amount of money allocated in the capital budget is important. The manager must be capable of dealing with both the operating and capital budgets. A major part of the budgeting process is determining the cash inflows generated by charging customers for services rendered. The specific charging scheme adopted is dependent on the methods of measuring management performance, the types of users served, and the overall goals of the organization.

For example, if the information system is an independent functional unit that services only internal users, then a pricing scheme would involve setting prices at such a level as to generate a profit but remain competitive with external data processing shops. On the other hand, a not-for-profit organization such as an educational institution may not even charge its users for computing services. In some organizations, these transfer pricing decisions are made at higher levels of the organization. Hence, data center management would not control the pricing decisions.

The charging scheme should not be taken lightly, since it is a prime vehicle for implementing some of the important goals of the organization. The cost of the services to the users will dictate the amount and frequency of use. In addition, these costs will be used to determine the cost/benefit feasibility of implementing new computerized projects.

Since many information systems are cost centers, the most common pricing scheme is based on recovering the costs of data center operations with the objective of simply breaking even. This is referred to as a charge-back system since the costs of operation are charged back to the users. There are many ways of implementing charge-back schemes. In the following, we will discuss some of these charge-back techniques.

CHARGE-BACK SYSTEMS

The basis of a charge-back system is to determine the cost of using specific resources and then to bill the customer for the proportion of the resources used. This rather easy concept can be difficult to implement. Figure 9.9 summarizes the steps in using a charge-back system and Figure 9.10 shows the formulas used to do the calculations.

First, the cost of a resource must be determined. Since costs may be shared by different devices, it is necessary to apportion these costs. For example, the cooling of the computer room applies to all of the equipment in the room. A method of allocating the cooling costs could be to use the total number of BTUs generated by each type of equipment and use this measure as the means of allocation. There are many other joint costs. The major joint costs should be allocated by some logical formula. However, it may be convenient simply to lump the minor joint costs into an overhead account and allocate it by some scheme.

Figure 9.9 *Steps in Customer Billing Using a Charge-Back System*

1. Determine cost of resource.
2. Estimate expected use.
3. Calculate cost per unit of resource.
4. Measure use of resource by customer account.
5. Calculate user bill.

After the resource costs have been calculated, the next step is to determine the use of the asset over the next budget period (the same period covered by the costs.) This expected use is the basis for a per unit cost of the resource. Dividing the cost for the budget period by the expected use gives the unit cost. The expected use can be estimated by taking historical figures and projecting the growth rate for the upcoming period.

The actual use of each resource by each user must be measured. This is accomplished by employing an event-driven software monitor as discussed in Chapter 6. These monitors are frequently called accounting software packages and accumulate statistics on the use of computer resources by each specific job. By multiplying the resources consumed by the cost per unit of resource, a total cost for the job can be determined. Monthly bills consist of simply summing all of the units of resources used for all of the jobs run under that account and then applying the per unit charge to each resource.

This type of charging system has many variations. The chance of the estimated resources exactly equaling those actually used is very small. Hence, there will be either an over- or undercharge for the resources consumed. This can be assessed to the users through some allocation process or it may be ignored, having central administration make up any difference.

The billing scheme that we have just described has some drawbacks. If the users are not very knowledgeable about computer terminology, then the bill may be confusing and be difficult to use in predicting the costs of future jobs. Some of the common individual resources billed include EXCPs, CPU time, K

Figure 9.10 *Formulas for Billing*

$C(i)$ = cost of resource i
$U(i)$ = use of resource i
$R(i)$ = per unit charge for resource i
$M(i,j)$ = use of resource i by user j
$B(j)$ = bill for user j

$R(i) = C(i)/U(i)$ for all i

$B(j) = \sum_{i} R(i) \cdot M(i,j)$ for all j

If things go right, $\sum_{i} B(j) = \sum_{i} C(i)$

Figure 9.11 *Deriving Computer Resource Units*

If we had the following bill of detail charges:

UNIT OF USE	AMOUNT USED	CHARGE PER UNIT	DOLLAR CHARGE
CPU Minutes	1.38	$10.00	$13.80
K-core Hours	7.30	.80	5.84
Lines Printed (1,000s)	4.24	.50	2.12
EXCPs (1,000s)	.891	1.00	.89
		Total Charge	$22.65

We could calculate computer resource units (CRUs) by using the following schedule:

UNIT OF USE	# OF CRUs PER UNIT	CRUs USED
CPU Minutes	10.00	13.80
K-core Hours	.80	5.84
Lines Printed (1,000s)	.50	2.12
EXCPs (1,000s)	1.00	.89
	Total CRUs	22.65

In this simplified case, each CRU would cost $1. Hence, the final bill is exactly the same.

---

byte storage minutes, etc. Many users will have no idea of the meaning of these terms. To make the bill more understandable, some centers will establish a composite measure of the resources used and will not report the detailed use of each individual resource. This composite measure is usually referred to as computer resource units (CRUs) and is simply a weighted sum of the individual resource units. Figure 9.11 shows how CRUs are derived. All charges are then based on the number of CRUs used.

Another inherent drawback of charge-back is that it does not properly ration resources. The more a resource is used, the cheaper it will be to use. The cheaper it gets, the more people will use it. Of course, the less-used resource will be relatively more expensive. This is the exact opposite effect we should employ to ration resources. As a resource nears capacity, the price of use should rise to encourage users to use alternative resources that are not at capacity. For example, if users are using disks instead of tapes, a charge-back system would decrease the price of disk usage and increase the price of tape usage. This would have more tape users convert to disk and eventually force acquisition of additional disk drives even when it would be appropriate for some files to remain on tape.

Some organizations, such as educational institutions, may want to establish a charging scheme that attempts to encourage use of the computer. One way of doing this is to use a "funny money" scheme instead of charging real money. This involves a user being given a fund of "funny money" that can only be spent on computing. All computing services are charged against that fund. No real money is spent by the user. Since the users do not generate any revenue for the center, the computer center receives its funding through an operating budget. The users are encouraged to use the system since no real money is involved. However, since the "funny money" is limited, wasteful use of the resources is discouraged. It is important, though, that the computer center monitor use so that any inappropriate activities are curtailed. A detailed bill is presented to each user so that the user knows how much of the computing resources are being used.

BUDGETING

The budgeting process is important to any administrative unit. Budgeting is a quantification of the financial objectives of a department. No matter whether the department is a cost center, profit center, or investment center, the budgeting process is an important component in the management of that area. Typically, two distinctly different budgets are developed. One is the capital budget, which details the investment needs, and the other is the operating budget, which deals with day-to-day expenses such as salaries, supplies, utilities, etc. The importance of the budgeting process is particularly true for data processing operations since often higher management does not perceive the information system as having a direct influence on the production of revenue. Instead, it is looked on as a discretionary expense. In hard times, discretionary expenses are the first to be eliminated.

The lack of proper budgeting has been a prime reason for the replacement of many a data center manager. The budget should provide adequate funds for the operation of the information system over the next fiscal period. Without these funds, schedules will not be met, services will have to be limited, and overall performance will deteriorate.

The budgeting process is as much an art as it is a science. To do budgeting, it is necessary to have a good understanding of the firm's accounting system and the ways in which activities are billed to the department. It is also necessary to have a good feel for the support the information system has within the firm. Also, being able to interpret properly both internal and external information is important. For example, judging that a recessionary period is approaching in the company's industry will dictate that large budget increases will not be acceptable and a trimming of operations may be appropriate.

The budgeting process will vary from one firm to another. However, there are some common elements that should be discussed. There are fundamentally two ways of budgeting. The first and easiest method is termed *incremental budgeting* since the previous budget is used as a base and increments are derived as percentage increases or decreases to the previous budget. Any line item from the previous period is carried into the next period with this year's increment included.

The second budgeting technique is termed *zero-based budgeting*. It involves a complete review and justification of any budget amounts. This means that nothing is continued into the next budget period unless it can be justified. Each department must rank-order its budget items and fully justify each item.

Zero-based budgeting is very time consuming and rather complex since each budget item, for each department, must be analyzed for appropriateness. This evaluation process usually involves a review team that will examine and rank-order all budget proposals. In a true zero-based budgeting process, even the essential operations of the firm must be reviewed. Critics of this type of budgeting say that the evaluation of essential operations is a waste of time since the firm cannot exist without these fundamental processes. However, zero-based budgeting is excellent in filtering out unsuccessful programs. If an incremental process is used, a project may be continued for an extended period of time, even when it is of little or no value to the firm.

In budgeting for an information system, it is best to use a combination of both the incremental and zero-based methods. For routine operations, such as running and maintaining the hardware and software, it is appropriate to use incremental budgeting. For capital acquisitions, new system development projects, and special projects, it is best to employ the zero-based method. This forces these discretionary items to be fully cost justified. A similar process is commonly used with employee compensation. An employee's base salary is carried forward with an incremental raise (usually at least a cost of living raise), and then merit increases are based on performance. Figure 9.12 highlights the two operational budgeting techniques.

No matter which budgeting methods are used, it is essential that the information system manager be involved in the process. The information system must be treated as an integral part of the business so that upper management realizes its importance. This entails a professional and business-like involvement in the budgeting process.

Figure 9.12   *Operational Budgeting Methods*

METHOD	*DESCRIPTION*	*MOST APPROPRIATE USE*
Incremental	Previous budget amounts are incremented by a given percentage.	Recurring routine operations
Zero-Based	All budget items must be justified and then reviewed. Funding levels are determined by merit of the item.	Discretionary expenditures and nonrecurring items

MAJOR COMPANY

Dealing with financial issues tends to consume substantial time of the information system management at Major Company. The budgeting process is the most time intensive of these tasks. Budgeting at Major Company is done on a yearly basis. Three to four months prior to the budget deadline, the vice-president of information systems requests detailed budgets from each of the managers reporting directly to him. These budgets are first reviewed and revised by the vice-president and his staff. From these budgets, a master budget for the information systems area is developed. This includes a capital budget for acquisition of hardware and software, an implementation plan for the development of new systems, and an operating budget. The capital and operating budgets cover the next year. The implementation plan involves projects that may span as much as five years. This implementation plan also has a schedule of the estimated impact of these new systems on both the operating and capital budgets for the next five years.

These budget documents are then distributed to the computer steering committee for discussion. The budget is presented to the steering committee with each departmental manager justifying their requests. The budget is revised based on the recommendations of the committee. This revised budget is then sent to the president of Major Company for inclusion in the overall budget. The board of directors then analyzes the total budget, makes any changes that are deemed necessary, and directs the president to implement the revised budget. This whole process takes about four months to complete.

The vice-president of information systems also gets involved in deciding the overall acquisition strategy of the information systems area. Generally, all major acquisitions of hardware are on an operating lease basis. This is done with all but the most stable technology such as terminals, which are purchased. Operating leases are used even when purchasing or financing leases have a lower net present value of expenditure. The operating leases are always short-term in nature, with no lease having a term of more than three years. There are a couple of primary reasons for this policy. First, when the lease terminates, it forces Major Company to reexamine the market and acquire the most technically current equipment. In addition, when new computer equipment is announced by a vendor, it will usually have enhanced performance over the older models but will have approximately the same cost as that equipment when it was new. By leasing, we can have approximately the same monthly payments for the newer models and get enhanced performance. This eliminates the need to make a capital budgeting decision every time new equipment comes on the market. The lease payments are simply a recurring item on the operating budget. Hence, the time-consuming justification process of making a capital budgeting decision is avoided. Higher management agrees with this logic and feels it is a good mechanism to keep the most up-to-date equipment in the computer center.

Major Company evaluates the information systems area as a profit center. The vice-president is allowed to set the prices of the services offered to the other operating units of the firm. To encourage competitive pricing, any of the other units are allowed to purchase computer services from outside of the firm if either a lower price or higher quality can be obtained from an outside source. For unique services that are not offered by an outside company or services that deal with confidential matters that cannot be allowed to be processed externally, an arbitration process is available to negotiate internal prices. The process involves an independent panel that reviews all pricing disputes within the firm.

SUMMARY

The financial decisions made by the management of an information system can be critical to its successful operation. Decisions must be made concerning the appropriate method of financing acquisitions of computer technology. Determined by the requirements of the firm, acquisition can be done by purchasing, renting, leasing (both operating and financing), and any combination of these methods. Each of these alternatives has specific advantages and disadvantages. A thorough analysis of the financing options cannot only save the firm money, but will also help in providing better service by allowing the firm to acquire the most appropriate equipment when needed.

Included in financial decision making is the task of determining the methods to be employed in charging users for services. While there are numerous approaches to billing users, the method selected must meet the objectives of both the information system area and the company as a whole.

The last area of concern involves dealing with the budget for the information system. This is a very important and, most times, a time-consuming task. However, the performance of the information system and its management will usually be based on the ability to meet or exceed the budget objectives.

QUESTIONS

1. Why is computer equipment more difficult to finance externally than other types of business equipment?

2. Why is computer software usually more difficult to finance than computer hardware?

3. The assistant to the information system manager has developed a list of hardware items the firm needs for the next year. While talking to the manager, the assistant is told that sources of external funding must be found to finance these acquisitions. The assistant finds that external funding sources are too expensive, but has examined the firm's financial statements and has found a huge amount in the retained earnings account. The assistant tells the manager the bad news about the external sources of funds, but says that the retained earnings are more than sufficient to satisfy the needs. If you were the manager, how would you reply to the assistant?

4. An external source of funding for computer acquisitions is unsecured debenture bonds. What is the problem with using this type of funding source?

5. Some organizations, such as government agencies and educational institutions, do not lease very much of their computer equipment; instead they purchase almost all of it. Can you explain why this is the case when private enterprise would normally be leasing the same equipment?

6. Some leases (especially third party leases) have a clause that forces the lessee to compensate the lessor for any losses due to changes in the federal tax laws. Why is this done and how will this affect the lessee and the lessor?

7. The third party leasing market has been described as being at the mercy of large computer manufacturers such as IBM. Why is this so?

8. Explain how changes in the tax laws can affect the financing decision. Use as an example the situation where there is a 10% investment tax credit on purchases of new assets and the lack of any investment tax credit.

9. For each of the following situations, describe the financing method that would probably be best. Be sure to explain why you chose that method.
   a. A company that sells Christmas trees decides to acquire 20 microcomputers with associated hardware and software to process the inventory and sales at each of its 10 locations.
   b. A firm that has a large mainframe laser printer decides to acquire an impact printer to process checks and multipart forms.
   c. A firm that is just starting business and does not have very much ready cash decides to acquire a minicomputer system to do all of its financial processing.

10. Some lease agreements have a "hell or high water" clause which does not allow a lessee to cancel the lease. Instead of being locked into a lease, a firm can sublease the equipment for the remainder of the lease term. What are the problems involved in subleasing?

11. A manager of a computer center has proposed the following scheme for billing the users of the system: The time from when a job is submitted to the time in which the job is finished by the system is recorded and multiplied by a billing rate to produce the charge for that job. This is commonly referred to as a wall-clock charging scheme. What are the disadvantages of a billing scheme like this?

12. Calculate the bill for a user given the following information:

MEASURE	CHARGE	USAGE
CPU Time	$50/Min	12 Seconds
EXCPs	$1/1,000	2,500
Main Storage Time	$.0005/K-core Seconds	256K for 12 Sec
Connect Time	$5/Hour	30 Minutes
Lines Printed	$.10/1000 Lines	15,000 Lines

13. For the information in the previous problem, determine a formula to calculate computer resource units (CRUs) and a price for each CRU that will produce the same charge for services as the charging scheme in the previous problem.

14. What is the difference between incremental and zero-based budgeting?

15. Many managers claim that budgeting is not as much an accounting problem as it is a political problem. Explain.

16. Describe how your school charges users for the computer services rendered. It may be helpful to divide users into the three groups of student use, faculty use, and administrative use.

17. For most not-for-profit organizations, money is budgeted for specific categories of use, and this money cannot be used for any other purpose. These uses may be such categories as computer hardware, computer software, personnel. How does this cause problems for the manager of the information system in this type of organization that a manager in a similar corporation would not have?

18. Explain what environmental scanning should be done before considering the financing options in acquiring equipment. What sources can companies look to for this information (both internal and external)? How can the company be sure that the information obtained is accurate and reliable?

19. Explain under what circumstances computer centers may be either a cost center, profit center, or investment center. Give examples of situations where each of these three situations would occur. Is it possible for a computer center to be a combination of these three? Explain your answer.

20. Why is it important that a manager understand the concepts involved in cost, profit, and investment centers?

CASE ANALYSIS

Case 1

You are to determine the best way of financing disk drives for the Yukon Minerals Company. Yukon has already decided that it will acquire IBM 3390 disk drives. IBM has quoted the following prices:

Monthly Rental	$5,105
24-Month Lease (Operating Lease)	$4,345
Purchase Price	$88,780

Monthly maintenance would by $325 a month for all three financing plans. In addition, insurance on the purchased unit would be $80 a month.

Yukon has found a third party vendor who will supply new IBM 3390 units on a capital leasing arrangement. This lease will last for three years costing $4,800 a month and has a bargain purchase option for $8,000 at the end of the lease. IBM would provide monthly maintenance for $325 a month, and insurance would have to be paid by Yukon. All of the preceding four plans provide delivery in two months.

As a final alternative, Yukon has located some used machines that can be purchased for $62,000, but they must be reconditioned, which will cost $6,500 a unit. These machines are no longer covered by an IBM maintenance contract; hence a third party maintenance company will have to provide maintenance. This will cost $420 a month. Insurance will remain the same. Because of the reconditioning, the delivery of these machines will take five months.

For all of these units, the estimated technical life is five years. Yukon's cost of capital is 18% and its marginal tax rate is 40%.

REQUIRED: You are to analyze the five possible financing plans and present a report to the vice-president of information systems. This report must show the net present value of each plan (show *all* details) and fully discuss all advantages and disadvantages of each plan. The qualitative factors must be well thought out and complete. Finally, you are to recommend a specific method of financing with full justification.

To save yourself time, use a spread sheet program to do the quantitative part of the assignment.

ADDITIONAL READINGS

ALLEN, BRANDT. "Make Information Services Pay Its Way," *Harvard Business Review,* January-February 1987, p. 57.

BENBASAT, IZAK, AND IRIS VESSEY. "Programmer and Analyst Time/Cost Estimation," *MIS Quarterly,* Vol. 4, No. 2, June 1980, pp. 31–43.

BERGERON, FRANCOIS. "Factors Influencing the Use of DP Chargeback Information," *MIS Quarterly,* Vol. 10, No. 3, September 1986, pp. 225–237.

BOHLIN, R., AND C. HOENIG. "Wringing Value from Old Systems," *Datamation,* August 15, 1989, p. 57.

KING, JOHN LESLIE, AND EDWARD L. SCHREMS. "Cost-Benefit Analysis in Information Systems Development and Operation," *Computing Surveys,* Vol. 10, No. 1, March 1978, pp. 19–34.

MANTEI, MARILYN M., AND TOBY J. TEOREY. "Cost/Benefit for Incorporating Human Factors in the Software Lifecycle," *Communications of the ACM,* Vol. 31, No. 4, April 1988, pp. 428–438.

MENDELSON, H. "Pricing Computer Services: Queueing Effects," *Communications of the ACM,* Vol. 28, No. 3, March 1985, p. 312.

RAJA, M. K. "Software Project Management and Cost Control," *Journal of Systems Management,* Vol. 36, No. 10, October 1985.

READINGS BEFORE NEXT CHAPTER

The previous material should be adequate background.

10

SOFTWARE ACQUISITION

SOFTWARE VERSUS HARDWARE ACQUISITION

The acquisition of software systems can be substantially more complex than the acquisition of hardware. There are more aspects to the software acquisition process, and the measurement of the attributes of a software system is not as straightforward as that involved in hardware acquisition. While in many respects the hardware and software acquisition processes are similar, there are enough differences that it is necessary to devote a separate chapter to their discussion. This chapter will only address those differences and will not review the procedures also used in hardware acquisition.

Determining the attributes of a software system is usually much more difficult than that of hardware. The users must be actively involved in this entire process. To develop the attributes, a feasibility study and a systems analysis are usually necessary. These can be time consuming and require the commitment of skilled staff members. Many users find it difficult to express their needs. Some are not even certain what they want, and most do not know enough about computing to understand the capabilities available to them. In certain situations, there may be a reluctance of the users to adapt to a new system; hence, they will not cooperate with the analysis team. Establishing system requirements can be a difficult task even when the users know what they want and are willing to cooperate. Modern software systems are highly integrated, serving many user groups at the same time. This leads to conflicts in the needs of the users and makes setting priorities more difficult. Compromises in the requirements must usually be made to satisfy all users; at best this is a difficult task.

Once the attributes are determined, they may not be in a form that can be easily measured. For example, the user may demand that the system is easy to use, flexible, and have a fast response time. While response time can be measured during benchmark simulations, ease of use and flexibility are qualitative in nature and may only be measurable by the user group. Hardware usually does not have these types of problems. Measurement of software is a difficult task that involves many of these subjective judgments. Even determining the capabilities and limitations of a specific system may not be accomplished until the system has been in use for a reasonable period of time. In some cases, the vendor may not even realize some restrictions until a user has encountered them. Under these circumstances, you are to a certain extent "flying blind" and must rely on the support of the vendor and the flexibility of the software system to overcome these shortcomings when they are discovered.

The decision either to make or buy software must also be made during the acquisition process. Most firms would never consider building their own hardware, but they do have their own software development teams. The decision to purchase a software system from an outside vendor or design and implement it internally can be a difficult one.

Probably the difficulties of software acquisition are caused by the nature of software. It is an intangible good that performs a service. It is difficult to specify, measure, determine costs, estimate installation time, or determine reliability. In this chapter, we will address these issues as we discuss the methods to be used in acquiring software systems.

SOFTWARE ALTERNATIVES

As just discussed, there is the possibility of designing and implementing software using the company's own internal programming staff. Actually, there is a whole spectrum of alternatives with respect to software acquisition. The decision to purchase software systems from a vendor and install them directly or to design and implement a system using internal staff are the two extreme possibilities. You can use a mixture of internal and external resources to implement a system. In addition to relying on vendors, outside consultants can be employed to supplement the internal staff.

When software is purchased from a vendor, it may not exactly meet the needs of the firm. To implement the system fully, it is necessary to change the program code. This is called tailoring the software and usually necessitates that the vendor supply program source code. This tailoring can be done by the vendor, by external consultants, or by the firm's internal staff. If no software meets the firm's needs, tailoring is the only alternative to custom design. Figure 10.1 shows some of the ways of acquiring software.

Tailoring purchased software presents some problems. Care must be

Figure 10.1   *Software Acquisition Alternatives*

ACQUISITION METHOD	INSTALLATION TIME	COST
Purchase a turnkey system from vendor	Fast	Low
Purchase system and have vendor tailor	Fast to moderate (Depending on degree of modification)	Low to moderate
Purchase System and have consultant tailor	Fast to moderate	Low to moderate
Purchase system and have internal staff tailor	Fast to moderate	Low to moderate
Consultant develops system	Slow	Expensive
Internal staff develops system	Slow	Expensive

taken to ensure that user changes to the system will not void the vendor's warranty and maintenance contract. Vendors will sometimes only offer maintenance on those programs in the system that were not altered or will only allow modifications by the vendor's personnel. An additional problem with tailoring software is that each time an updated version of the system is released by the vendor, it will be necessary to incorporate all of the changes into the new version before it can be placed into production.

If an outside consultant tailors the system, there is the problem of maintaining code not developed by your shop. This is particularly acute when the consultant has expertise that the internal staff does not have. For example, if the vendor's system is written in PL/I and your shop is strictly COBOL, it could be a major problem if a consultant modifies the code and your staff can neither update nor maintain this code.

The major advantages of purchasing a software package are that it is usually less expensive than internal design and it usually takes a shorter length of time to install the system. Of course, the more tailoring necessary, the higher the cost and the longer the installation time. It should not be misunderstood that any software system can just be dropped into place and be expected to function properly without substantial time spent in installing, configuring, and testing the new system and converting from the old system. These are necessary, but time-consuming events for any software system.

ACQUISITION STEPS

The steps in acquiring software are similar in nature to those used in hardware acquisition except that the actual execution of each individual step can be substantially different. The available options, the determination of mandatory and desirable attributes, the measurement of the competing products, and the contractual stipulations may all be substantially different in acquiring software.

As discussed earlier, the analysis of the present system and the determination of the characteristics of the new system are the first major steps of the acquisition process. Most times, the need for a new system originates with the users. The formal way of initiating the software acquisition process is through the user submitting a request for systems analysis to the information systems area (see Figure 10.2).

In the hardware acquisition case, the determination of a need for additional hardware usually comes from the performance evaluation group, an internal department of the information system area. This is also usually the case when systems software is acquired. In this regard, the acquisition of systems software is more like acquiring hardware than acquiring application software. The need for applications software is usually generated by the external user community. Because of these fundamental differences, we will address the major issues involved in acquiring system software separately from applications software.

One critical consideration in the entire acquisition process, including both hardware and software acquisition, is that, whenever possible, the available software should be considered before or at least coincident to the selection of the hardware. While it appears obvious that application software, hardware, and system software must function as an integrated whole, often the hardware decision is made with no consideration of the appropriate applications software. There have been many situations where, after the hardware has been purchased and installed, the company discovers that no applications software exists that will accomplish the desired tasks using that hardware. This forces the custom development of the software, which in some situations may not even be a feasible option.

The analysis of the system involves first doing a preliminary feasibility analysis and then a detailed systems analysis. The purpose of the feasibility study is to determine whether the acquisition is feasible under the given time schedule, budget, and other constraints. This usually involves interviewing some of the key individuals dealing with the system and investigating the possible avenues of implementation, including purchasing packages from vendors.

If the project is deemed feasible, then the detailed systems analysis is performed. This is a much more in-depth look at the desired system. All levels of personnel to be involved with the system should be contacted. This includes the users of the system, the computer operators, and both the application program development and maintenance staffs. This will be a time-consuming phase of the acquisition process. However, the ultimate success of the system is probably most dependent on the quality of the work done in this phase.

The systems analysis should produce the mandatory and desirable attributes of the system. Some of the possible attributes are shown in Figures 10.3 and 10.4. Also, during the systems analysis phase, a partial list of available

Figure 10.2 *Request for Systems Analysis*

Request for Systems Analysis
Major Company

Please fill in the applicable information:

Requesting Department: _____   Submitted by: _____

Date of Request: _____   Request Priority: _____

Describe the nature of the problem:

_____
_____
_____
_____
_____
_____

Describe the action you believe must be taken:

_____
_____
_____
_____
_____
_____

List other application areas that will be affected:

_____
_____
_____
_____

For Systems Use Only

EVENT	RESPONSIBLE PARTY	DATE RECEIVED	DATE COMPLETED	STATUS
Request Received				
Feasibility Study				
System Analysis				
System Design				
Installation				
User Acceptance				

Figure 10.3 *Some General Mandatory Attributes*

Hardware Compatibility	Software Compatibility
Documentation	Training
Type of Source Code (COBOL, PL/I, etc.)	Maintenance and Updates
Execution Speed	File and Data Limitations
Availability of Source Code	Cost
Available Functions Meet Needs of Users	Vendor Stability
Available Backup and Recovery	
Product Stability (How often does the system crash?)	

vendors should be developed with details on the costs, functions, and limitations of their packages.

With this information, the decision should be made concerning the method of obtaining the system. If the software is to be purchased from an outside vendor, then it is necessary to develop a request for proposal. In most aspects, the RFP will be the same as it was in hardware acquisition.

Even if the system is to be designed internally, it is best to develop a formal user contract. This contract will detail the requirements of the system, the responsibilities of the parties, and the timetable of events. This contract will help assure agreement on the objectives and hopefully produce realistic expectations by all concerned. From the perspective of the application development team, this contract should reduce the number and magnitude of changes in the system specifications during development. From the users' point of view, the contract sets milestones and deadlines for the completion of the system. Other aspects of managing the internal development of application systems are addressed in Chapter 13.

As described in Chapter 7, the RFP should notify vendors of the procedures to be followed to develop a bid. The RFP should consist of the introduction, organization background, the requirements, the form of the proposal, and

Figure 10.4 *Some General Desirable Attributes*

Cost	Vendor Installation
Hot Line Help Available	Execution Speed
Transaction Capacity Limits	Security Provisions
Auditability	Available Options
Available Allied Software Packages	Financing
Vendor Tailoring Available	Availability of User Exits
Modularity of Design	Installed Base
Multiple Copy Discounts	

the evaluation criteria. The mandatory and desirable attributes section will be substantially different for an RFP dealing with software. Instead of mainly addressing the physical attributes as in hardware, the less easily measured attributes of compatibility, ease of use, and flexibility are of more concern.

Additionally, the necessary level of vendor support must be included in the RFP specifications. Vendor training and documentation are very important in assuring the proper installation and operation of any software system. The vendor training can be in various forms such as at a vendor's site, presented at the user's location, via videotape, or by programmed instruction manuals. The extent and quality of the training will help determine the ultimate success of the system. The same can be said about documentation.

Usually the vendor will supply two classifications of documentation: user manuals and technical documentation. The user manuals describe the function and operation of the system in nontechnical terms. The technical documentation is aimed at the applications and systems programming staffs. The evaluation of the user manuals should be based on ease of use and understandability by the general user community, while it is most important that the technical documentation be as complete as possible.

Other areas of vendor support include the availability of a maintenance support hot line, the frequency and form of maintenance updates, the availability of new releases of the system when it is improved, and the level of assistance in installing the system. Again, these attributes are difficult to measure, but it is important that they be included in the RFP and considered when evaluating proposals.

The RFP must also state any working constraints that must be imposed on the software. This would include the operating system, the specific data access methods to be employed by the programs, the telecommunications system, the database management system, and any specialized hardware required to be used. Most situations dictate the use of the systems software already in place. It is usually too costly to install and maintain a completely different set of systems software to support an additional application system. If this unduly limits the number of candidate vendor systems, then either additional systems software will have to be acquired or the system be developed internally.

The section of the RFP dealing with the evaluation criteria should be more detailed as to the specific benchmarking tests to be performed and the desired performance measures resulting from those tests.

If an RFP is issued, the process for evaluating the competing bids is the same as in hardware acquisition. First the theoretical benchmark is performed and then the physical benchmarking is done. When dealing with application software, the physical benchmarking must involve the end-users. It is important that the physical benchmarks and vendor demonstrations are well planned. Sample data that represents all contingencies should be entered into the system. Exceptional and infrequent occurrences should be included in this sample data. These "special" occurrences usually have the highest probably of causing problems. If the vendor insists on giving a "canned" demonstration, it is best to interrupt the presentation occasionally and request the presenter to do something other than the next planned step in the procedure. This accomplishes two things. First, it tests the flexibility of the system. Since users will not be doing their functions in the same way from one transaction to the next, one must make sure the system can handle these differences. Second, it tests the presenter's knowledge of the system. This is very important, since this person will be answering your questions as to the capabilities and limitations of the system. The accuracy of these answers is dependent on the background of the person making the presentation. Remember, oral representations by the sales staff are usually not enforceable in the final written contract. Hence, unintentional erroneous or misleading answers by the sales staff can lead to false assumptions about the capability of the product.

After the physical benchmarking, an acquisition decision must be made. As in hardware acquisition, other sources of data should be sought, including other users, industry groups, and software rating services. For software acquisition, this phase of the evaluation process is more important. It is almost impossible to determine all the limitations of a large software system. Also, software systems are even more dependent on the reliability and continued existence of the vendor. The level of service provided by the vendor is best determined by talking to other users.

One thing that makes software acquisition so risky is that you are not just betting on the software product but also on the vendor. There are literally thousands of software companies, with a majority being small firms. Since the software market is so dynamic, with firms constantly entering and leaving the market, the continued financial health of the vendor must be considered. A business failure of the vendor will usually mean the loss of software maintenance support for their product. Only if a product is extremely popular will another firm continue to market it.

SYSTEMS SOFTWARE

The acquisition of systems software can be the most difficult of all the acquisition decisions. Systems software has an impact on almost all users of the system and may dictate a commitment to a specific computing direction for an extended period.

The difficulty lies in the nature of systems software. The user does not directly interact with it, instead it enhances the environment for the application programs running under it. Unlike application software, the analyst cannot directly inquire as to the user needs, since the user would not have any idea how to respond. Most users do not have a very clear understanding of system software functions.

For example, if we were to acquire a database management system (DBMS), we cannot simply go to the users and ask if a networked, hierarchical, or relational model would be more appropriate to their needs. These terms would be meaningless to them. Instead, we would have to determine the tasks being performed by the various user groups and weigh all of these needs before making a decision. For other types of systems software (for example, communications software), the task is even harder because the link between the users and the software is even more remote.

The users can very easily be lost in the shuffle when deciding on system software. Because of the complexity of the systems and their technical nature, the systems programming group may be given sole responsibility for the selection. While it is important to get input from systems programming, their criteria for evaluation may be entirely different from the user community.

Again using the DBMS example, the system programmers and even the application programmers may want to adopt a specific product because this product extends their knowledge and makes them more marketable. While the popularity of a product will have an impact on both the longevity of it and the development of allied products, the requirements of the users must be of primary consideration. If an inappropriate DBMS is acquired, it will usually take some time to realize the error. At this point, significant development will have been done with older systems converted to the DBMS and new systems implemented. To change to another DBMS could be so expensive as to make it infeasible until quite a bit later. Hence, the firm is stuck with this system.

The complexity of such a decision cannot be overstressed. In the DBMS situation there are many factors other than just the data storage model. You must be concerned about the tools associated with that DBMS: an integrated data dictionary, high-level query languages, associated screen formatters, and procedural language interfaces to just name a few. At the same time, compatibility with the other system programs is necessary. Even a DBMS satisfying all of the foregoing requirements may not be adequate because there is not a wide enough range of application systems available for purchase. If the firm cannot develop application systems internally, then this is an important issue.

OTHER CONSIDERATIONS

In software acquisition there are some points that must be considered that were not discussed in hardware acquisition. Many of these closely involve the formulation and negotiation of the legal contract.

The compatibility of the software with both the present hardware and software is essential. Establishing that the system is compatible with the existing facilities may be a difficult task. For both the system software and application software, it is difficult to confirm full compatibility. Even comprehensive physical benchmarks may fail to disclose some incompatibilities. In this area it is very important to investigate thoroughly the product with other installations already using the system.

With software, the compatibility issue should not simply be limited to the present configuration but should address any restrictions an acquisition may impose in the future. For example, if we are presently considering the acquisition of a general ledger system, we must also investigate how other related packages, such as accounts receivable and inventory control packages, will interface with the general ledger systems being considered. For many vendors' products, the acquisition of one package makes it very attractive to later acquire other related packages from that same vendor. So in the case of our general ledger system, we should make our acquisition decision based on the attractiveness of all of the integrated accounting-oriented packages the vendors have to offer. Even when the acquisition of the other related system will be in the future, the acquisition of one package may logically lock us into making all related acquisitions from the same vendor. Again, we will rely heavily on the capabilities of that vendor.

Determined by the size of the data processing facility and the expertise of the programming staff, it may be desirable to obtain the source code of a purchased system. Obviously, if the system has to be tailored to meet our needs, source code is mandatory. The availability of source code allows the acquiring company's staff to do on-site maintenance and gives the firm the opportunity to enhance the system without involving the vendor. To protect the confidentiality of their product, vendors may adopt the policy of not distributing source code. This is referred to as an object-code-only policy. For a vendor who is responsive to user needs, frequently upgrades the product, and has a well-designed, flexible product, this type of policy may not cause substantial problems for the users. Many products and vendors do not fit the preceding description, and an object-code-only policy may be unattractive enough to eliminate the product from acquisition consideration.

If object code is acceptable, it is still best that some arrangement is made to make the source code available in case of a failure of the vendor or the vendor's withdrawal of support for the product. A method which is usually acceptable to both the vendor and the user is to have an escrow agent retain the code. Then, if circumstances dictate, the code will be released to the users. The escrow agent is a independent third party who will keep the code confidential, but will release it to the users under certain contractual arrangements.

Those data processing shops that have multiple CPUs must consider the terms of the software agreement to include multiple copies of the product. Typically this would include large data processing shops and those companies with a distributed processing philosophy. For most vendors, an individual payment must be made for each CPU to run the software. Usually the vendor will give discounts for additional copies. Even if a software system is to be run on only one processor, for disaster recovery purposes it is necessary to allow the system to run on a different physical processor. The stipulation may be that upon the failure of the primary processor, another predesignated processor can run the system. It is important that this be considered before a failure occurs, for vendors can restrict the operation of their programs to specific processor serial numbers. The program will simply not run on an unauthorized processor.

Microcomputer software is a cause of additional concern when considering multiple copy arrangements. Often, because of the lack of control in dealing with the acquisition of microcomputer software, problems will arise which are not of concern in the mainframe environment. These problems include compatibility of software systems, volume discounts of multiple copies, and protection from illegal copying of software.

Compatibility problems arise if the microcomputer hardware and software acquisition process is not in some way coordinated. Individuals may determine the specific package to purchase without consideration of the existing installed base. Hence, various areas of the firm could be doing exactly the same functions, but have incompatible systems. This makes it very difficult, if not impossible, to share or consolidate data.

Another problem arises when the acquisition of software is totally decentralized. The total cost of the software may be substantially reduced if either a volume purchase agreement or a site license can be negotiated with the vendor. A volume purchase agreement allows the company to pay a reduced amount for a fixed number of copies of the software system. A site license allows the use of an unlimited number of copies of the system for a fixed dollar amount. Both of these types of arrangements necessitate centralized selection of a specific system.

The illegal copying of software is a problem of major proportions in many organizations. Since a firm must sign a license agreement which states that unauthorized copies of the software should not be made, the company is responsible for enforcing procedures which protect against unauthorized copying. Simply due to the nature of micro software, this is very difficult to accomplish.

If illegal copying is occurring, the vendor can sue the firm. Some vendors want to protect their products vigorously from unauthorized use, and lawsuits are being filed with increasing frequency. The use of site licensing can help alleviate this problem, since unlimited multiple copies can be used in the firm. However, it still cannot protect the firm from copies being used outside of the firm. Presently, the best protection is for the firm to stress to its employees the seriousness of unauthorized copying and impose stiff penalties if an employee violates these rules.

The terms of the legal contract are probably more important in software acquisition because of the intangible nature of the product and the difficulty in measuring it. It is necessary to be specific in defining the performance parameters of the system. This has to be done in terms that can be quantified and measured. An example would be to specify the number of transactions that can be processed over a specific period of time. The formulation of these terms is a difficult task but necessary to assure the proper functioning of the system.

As discussed in the legal issues chapter, a way of giving us additional contractual protection is to define the software as a good and not a service. In this way, we will be given the implied warranty protection provided by the Uniform Commercial Code. This includes the warranty of merchantability and fitness for a particular purpose. Accurately determining the quality of a software package is extremely difficult. This makes warranty protection very important.

In some cases the vendor may not offer the good for sale but may provide the right to use it by a license agreement. This could be in the form of an annual license with the option to renew each year or as a perpetual license with unlimited (in time) use. This is an important issue since it restricts rights to sell the software to another party and also may affect the implied warranties, since it will be considered a service and not a good.

Vendors will offer new software to a limited number of firms before the software has been formally announced. This is called beta testing the software. The firm doing the beta test helps the vendor thoroughly test the software in an actual production environment. Beta testing was discussed when talking about hardware acquisition, but it is an even more common occurrence when dealing with software. With software, the costs involved in beta testing can be substantial since a major software system can involve a large commitment of support personnel. However, the competitive advantages of having the system before others in the industry can also be great. The important thing is to realize the potential costs and benefits associated with beta testing.

During software acquisition, management is particularly concerned that they get no surprises. By this, we mean that all necessary hardware and software is either already present on the system or included in the price of the software. Nothing is more aggravating and embarrassing than to attempt to install a software system and find that the present computer system lacks critical components to run the software. Not only will this add to the cost of the system, but it will delay the use of the new software. If this situation entails a large additional outlay of money, it will cause even more problems.

DEALING WITH CONSULTANTS

If it is determined that purchasing a system is not feasible, then we must develop custom software to solve the problem. The use of internal staff to do this programming and design work may not be possible due to resource constraints or limited expertise. Hiring an outside consultant may then be the best way to solve the problem. However, selecting and managing a qualified consultant can be a difficult task.

The process of selecting a consultant can be a difficult one and in some ways is similar to choosing a family physician. You must rely on the individual's character, dedication, and technical expertise. These attributes are extremely difficult to measure accurately, especially in the brief period of time involved in a candidate interview. As with a physician, it may be necessary to rely heavily on professional recommendations.

A large project may entail a team of experts and hence almost necessitates dealing with a consulting firm versus an individual consultant. These situations dictate the use of a formal RFP process to select the appropriate consulting firm. There are some important points to consider when dealing with a firm versus an individual. The proposal will often state the credentials of the employees in the firm. While some of these individuals may have impressive credentials, this does not help your project if none of them are assigned to work on it. Thus, the principal employees to be assigned to the project should be designated in the contract. Because of the very formal nature of such arrangements, it is necessary to be exact when specifying all of the duties and responsibilities of the consulting firm.

Dealing with individual consultants is usually a less formal process. While it is similar to hiring a new employee, it is different in some important respects. Unlike a new employee, the consultant must have specific expertise to solve the problem at hand immediately. On-the-job training and additional education are usually not a consideration; the skills must be in place.

If the consultant is being hired for skills that present employees lack, it may be difficult even to ascertain the level of the person's expertise. Unfortunately, in the computer area it is relatively easy to learn the standard jargon and substantially more difficult to master the techniques involved in analyzing, designing, and writing large scale systems. As in choosing any professional (physician, dentist, CPA, etc.) personal recommendations are very important and should be used wherever possible. The data processing profession has certification procedures that attest to a specific level of professionalism. However, they are not as yet widely accepted, and consultants do not have to be licensed by their state to practice. Care must be taken in the selection process because even though the original assignment may be short term, the consultant's engagement may be many times longer than originally expected.

Initial selection is only one of the problems related to hiring consultants. The methods of compensation and management of the project are two additional, very closely related issues. The two basic methods of compensation are payment for the consultant's time expended (by the hour, day, etc.) or payment for the project, usually with partial payment at specific intervals. The merits of each of these methods are debatable.

Compensation for time expended does not encourage the consultant to work efficiently but gives the consultant the opportunity to do quality work with less time pressure. With this form of compensation it is not absolutely necessary to specify fully the requirements of the project at its inception. This can allow for more flexibility in modifying the system while it is being designed, but it can also lead to poor project management, where few if any completion milestones are established or enforced. Probably the biggest drawback of this type of compensation is that it may be impossible for the manager to estimate the cost of the finished project until it is very close to completion.

If payment is made for completion of various stages of the project, it is necessary to specify fully the requirements of the system before the consultant is hired. This arrangement helps the manager to have more control over the project since both time deadlines and costs will be fully specified before the project is started. The major problem with this type of payment is that it is very difficult to know exactly what the specifications are when the project begins. As a matter of fact, often the specification of the system requirements is an important part of the consultant's work. When payment is based on the completion of milestones, unless the change is very minor, there will be additional charges for changing specifications. Often this makes management reluctant to change the system during development, and hence, the system may not satisfy users when completed.

Both of the methods discussed so far have rather major drawbacks (see Figure 10.5). This leads some firms to using a compensation method which is a combination of these two alternatives. One scheme is to pay the consultant on an hourly basis but to set a limit on the total amount of compensation to be paid. This limit would be more than the expected cost of the project and would be based on reasonably complete project specifications with the possibility of some changes in these specifications during design and implementation. In this situation, we have some flexibility in design and also firm project milestones.

The final consideration in dealing with a consultant is to establish ownership of the finished system. If care is not taken when the initial contract is negotiated with the consultant, this can become a difficult issue that may end up being decided by a court. While this same issue of ownership of custom software must also be considered for all the employees of the firm, disputes most frequently occur when dealing with consultants.

The issue that must be resolved is who owns the copyright to the custom software. The Copyright Act, as revised in 1976, addresses the issue of ownership of intellectual property. If the contractual agreement is silent as to ownership, then there are two tests that the courts use to determine ownership. First is the scope of normal employment. If it is deemed that the software was developed as part of the normal duties of the individual, then the software copyright is owned by the company. However, if the software is developed outside of this normal scope, such as during the individual's free time, then ownership resides with the individual.

The second test is if a contract defines work for hire too broadly. If it is too broadly defined, for example where all intellectual work done by the indi-

Figure 10.5 *Consultant Compensation*

	ADVANTAGES	*DISADVANTAGES*
By Time Expended	Encourages quality work Allows for modifications of original specifications	Impossible to estimate project cost Does not encourage efficiency Often no project milestones exist
By Project	Details project costs Sets project milestones	Possible time pressures Difficult to modify original specifications Difficult to specify completely project at its inception

vidual even after normal working hours belongs to the firm, then the courts will probably find in favor of the individual. When dealing with a consultant, this type of contract clause will probably not be adequate even if it is not too broadly defined. The consultant can claim that the services rendered were in the form of a license to use the developed software and not a purchase of the copyright. Hence, the consultant retains the right of ownership.

The right of ownership is extremely important. Even custom software will often be marketable to other firms with only a moderate amount of change. Even if the system is not ultimately marketable to outside firms, the ownership issue becomes important if additional copies are to be distributed to other divisions in the firm. If we do not own the copyright, then additional licenses may have to be purchased.

To assure that ownership is passed to the company on completion of the project, it is necessary that a separate contract is written for each project. The contract should state that the copyright to the program (both source and object code), all documentation, and other related materials are to be transferred to the company on completion of the project. When the project is completed, it is mandatory that the company immediately records the assignment of the copyright. While the original copyright exists on creation of the work, the assignment must be recorded to be valid.

In some cases, the consultant may not be willing to sell the rights to the work to be performed. This is often the case where the same set of code can be used in multiple engagements or, as stated before, where with slight modification the system may be marketable. This is an item to be negotiated. Joint ownership of the system is one possibility. Profits on future sales can then be divided by an agreed on formula, or the firm may be given the rights to unlimited internal copies and the consultant can use the code on other engagements. If the consultant wants sole ownership of the system, then a lower level of compensation for the project is in order. All in all, both parties must decide the value of ownership. Ignoring this issue until after the work is completed can develop into a major problem.

MAJOR COMPANY

The personnel director of Major Company has submitted a Request for Systems Analysis to the applications systems development area. The request concerns the development of an integrated payroll-personnel system. The request is initially reviewed by the manager of application system development. Pat Mason, a systems analyst, is given the assignment of doing a feasibility study concerning the payroll and personnel systems. The present payroll system is an entirely batch system which in no way is linked or shares data with the present personnel system. The personnel system was originally a totally batch system. In the last couple of years, some interactive programs have been written that allow online viewing of certain data but do not allow any online updating.

With the present arrangement, there is a substantial amount of data that is duplicated in the two systems. This data redundancy has caused some major problems with data integrity. There have been an increasing number of instances in which the data for an individual on the payroll system does not agree with the same data on the personnel system. Also, due to the lack of genuine online capabilities, it is difficult to generate accurate reports on a timely basis. The final problem with the two systems is program maintenance. As changes have been made to the systems over the years, the programs have become much more complex and maintenance costs have increased substantially. At present, there are 10 requests outstanding for major changes or additions to the two systems.

The feasibility report submitted by Pat Mason recommends the acquisition of a new payroll-personnel system. It is estimated that the detailed systems analysis will take between three and five person-months to complete. In addition, if the system is internally designed, it is estimated that the system would be operational in 16 months at the earliest. If the system is acquired from a vendor, it is estimated that the operational date is six months away.

Two systems analysts, Pat Mason and Susan Torres, are assigned responsibility for doing the detailed analysis of the system. They review the existing documentation, interview both the users and applications programming staff, consult industry literature, and talk to some vendors' sales staffs. The specifications of the system including the inputs into the system, the reports, and screens to be generated and the data requirements are produced by the analysis team. The entire process takes about 10 weeks to complete.

The recommendation of the team is to acquire the software from an outside vendor. The major reasons for this recommendation include the reduction in total implementation time, the limited availability of application programmer time, and the large number of vendors having suitable products. For all of the products the team is considering for acquisition, there is a need for some tailoring of the system. This tailoring mainly involves input screens and report formats. These changes can be done by Major Company's applications development area and should not be a significant undertaking.

The systems analysis report is presented to the information system steering committee by the manager of application systems development. The steering committee concurs with the report's recommendation of outside acquisition and passes this suggestion on to the vice-president of information systems. The decision is made to acquire the payroll-personnel system from a vendor. Purchasing is asked to create an RFP in cooperation with the application systems development area. This RFP is then distributed to the appropriate vendors.

The mandatory attributes of the system are listed in Figure 10.6, and the desirable attributes are presented in Figure 10.7. Even though Major Company presently has other associated accounting systems such as accounts receivable, accounts payable, general ledger, and inventory control, they are older, file-oriented systems that are to be replaced by more up-to-date online database systems in the near future. Hence, the acquisition of the payroll-personnel sys-

Figure 10.6 *Mandatory Attributes for Payroll/Personnel System*

IBM 3090 hardware compatibility, runs under IBM MVS/ESA operating system

Payroll and personnel systems use common files (fully integrated)

Allows online data entry and query, but only prints payroll checks in batch mode

Uses full screen displays, employing either CICS or a proprietary vendor screen facility. If vendor supplied, it must be fully documented.

Accumulates yearly payroll history files, including detail and year to date figures

Handles all taxes; including federal, state, and local; does W-2's, W-4's, 941A's, FUTA, and FICA reporting

Handles at least three types of miscellaneous payroll deductions

Calculates both salary and hourly wages including overtime

Allows for electronic banking and IRS filing (via magnetic tape)

Allows for creation of custom reports

Saves entire employment history

Allows archiving of past employees

Does complete federal, state, and local employee reports, including EEO, ERISA, OSHA, FUTA, and SUTA reports

Allows for search on employee skills, attributes, education, and work experience

Records employee training and planning of future training

Source code is provided.

tem should consider the compatibility and capabilities of any vendor's related accounting systems.

From the 11 formal bids submitted by vendors, nine meet all mandatory attributes. Four bids are deemed superior to the others by the theoretical benchmark and are carried into the physical benchmarking stage. This stage includes demonstrations by each of the vendors at their sites. Prior to the installation of any of the systems, the performance evaluation group developed a comprehensive set of test data to be used to benchmark the systems. Each system is installed on Major Company's computer system and tested for a period of two weeks. The first week involves the processing of benchmarking data through the system by the performance evaluation staff. The second week involves the use of the system by representatives of the various user groups.

The evaluation staff at Major Company also contacts users of these systems in other companies. Besides telephone conversations and correspondence, the evaluation staff traveled to four different sites to observe the operation of each of the systems.

All information concerning each of the systems is evaluated and the products rank-ordered by their desirability. The vendor of the top-rated system is then contacted and contract negotiations begin. Unfortunately, this vendor is

Figure 10.7 *Desirable Attributes for Payroll/Personnel System*

Low acquisition cost, maintenance cost, and cost of updates

System uses either IDMS, IMS, or DB2 database management system

Multiple copy discounts

Produces Canadian and Mexican tax information

Is easy to install

Has large customer base

Is written in COBOL

Can process prospective job applicants, especially college recruiting

Allows for confidential processing of executive salaries

Has online audit capabilities

Vendor has other accounting packages that will integrate with system

Data compatible system is available for IBM AS400 system, HP3000, and DEC equipment

Incorporates periodic employee performance evaluation

adamant about limiting the internal distribution of source code of the system. They want source code to only reside in one central location and do not want to allow source code in any of the distributed locations. These restrictions are considered as too limiting by Major Company, and the vendor refuses to negotiate alternatives. Hence, this product is determined unsuitable and the next vendor on the list is contacted. This time there are no contractual problems, and this system is purchased. The entire evaluation process takes a total of 14 weeks.

An observation could be made at this point that the RFP should have stipulated the need for source code at all locations. The RFP did state that source was mandatory, but assumed it could be distributed to all locations. This illustrates that even a well-constructed RFP (or legal contract) will not be absolutely perfect.

The application program development area is assigned the responsibility for tailoring the system. Based on the previous systems analysis, the necessary changes were determined. The vendor programs are then modified and tested. In addition, existing data files must be converted to the format needed to run on the new system.

User training then begins. The users are given the documentation, and classes are held to demonstrate how the system functions. The system is then run parallel with the old system for three weeks. At the end of this time, the old system is dismantled and the new system is considered fully installed. For the next two months, the performance evaluation group is instructed to monitor the performance of this new system so that it can be tuned to give optimal performance. The tailoring and installation process takes a total of 10 weeks.

SUMMARY

Software and hardware acquisition must be coordinated in a manner that results in an integrated system that meets the needs of the users. Software is an important component in any computer system; however, its acquisition can be a difficult process. Determining and measuring the attributes of the software system can be much more time consuming and involve more uncertainty than a similar hardware acquisition.

There are various ways to acquire software. The firm can design its own systems or it can purchase vendor-supplied systems. If the attributes of a vendor's system closely match those of the firm, it is usually economical to purchase the software. If source code is provided, vendor systems can also be modified to meet the firm's requirements.

The steps in acquiring software are similar to those in hardware acquisition. They involve determination of attributes, developing an RFP, theoretic benchmarking, and physical benchmarking. However, the details involved in each step can be significantly different when dealing with software instead of hardware. Some of the important additional issues include source code availability, multiple copies, vendor updates, user training, documentation, and vendor warranties.

Special consideration must be given to using consultants to write or modify software. Care must be taken when selecting the consultant. Also, the method of compensation is an important issue. Lastly, the ownership of the developed programs must be agreed on before the project is undertaken.

QUESTIONS

1. Why is software acquisition usually more difficult than hardware acquisition?
2. In what ways are software and hardware acquisition similar?
3. In what ways are software and hardware acquisition different?
4. Give some examples of where the software acquisition process should come after the hardware acquisition process.
5. How can the performance of an acquired software system be linked to the payment for that system? Describe how this method of payment would be advantageous to a company.
6. Give examples of what things may have to be done when a purchased system is to be tailored.
7. How could the determination of mandatory and desirable attributes differ between when an existing system is being replaced (either manual or EDP) and when no system is present? Which would be more difficult?
8. If you were associated with a large data center that had many personnel, what tasks might you hire an outside consultant to perform?

9. If you were associated with a small data center that had few personnel, what tasks might you hire an outside consultant to perform?

10. Explain why it is desirable to get source code from a vendor when acquiring a system.

11. What is involved in the software maintenance provided by a vendor? Why can't the user provide this type of maintenance?

12. When we discuss compatibility of software, what factors must we be concerned about?

13. Explain how the physical benchmarking process will differ between hardware and software acquisition.

14. Explain how acquiring either a specific piece of hardware or software can substantially narrow the possible choice of products available to a company in the future.

15. How will the vendor's withdrawal of support for a software package affect the users of that package?

16. Why may it be desirable for the vendor to place source code for a system in escrow?

17. When working with a consultant, why is it necessary to establish the ownership of the finished product before completion of the project?

18. List the reference sources available on your campus for investigating the available application and systems programming software presently on the market.

CASE ANALYSIS

Case 1

Using reference sources at your main library and computer center library (if you have one), describe the important attributes for acquiring one of the following application software packages (your instructor will choose the specific package). Without knowing the specific circumstances, which of these attributes would most likely be mandatory?

a. Accounts payable

b. Accounts receivable

c. Inventory control

d. Fixed assets tracking

e. General ledger accounting

f. Project management

Case 2

Following is an actual case. All names and locations have been changed to protect the anonymity of the actual participants.

Mark Blue is a businessman who lives in Cloudcroft, New Mexico, a small town located in the mountains in south central New Mexico. He owns a restaurant and has decided to put his company into the space age by getting himself a computer. He decided that a specific vendor's computer would work the best because his cash registers were made by this vendor and could be hooked directly to the computer to allow point of sale entry. This would serve as the majority of his input data, and everything would be processed from this information. During the process of purchasing the computer, the people at the hardware vendor told him that they had no software to accomplish the tasks that he wanted done. They were unaware of any packages that could be purchased on the open market, but they did know of a married couple in El Paso, Texas who did programming on the vendor's machines: Joe and Carol Smith, who did business under the name of ABC Company. Mark contacted this couple, and they came to Cloudcroft to discuss Mark Blue's requirements. At this time, they showed a series of printouts that illustrated the accounting reports that could be generated. Mark Blue decided to go this route, so he entered into an agreement with the Smiths to design a system. This agreement is contained in the following two legal contracts (Documents 1 and 2). These contracts were made up by the Smiths without the help of a lawyer. They simply took a standard vendor's contract and changed it slightly to fit their needs. The system Mark wanted designed was to accomplish the tasks in schedule 1 of his letter (Document 3) to the Smiths. After many months and many more thousands of dollars, Mark did not have a system that even approached his expectations. So he sent the attached letter to the Smiths and got the reply from their lawyer as seen in Document 4.

In addition to the processing for the restaurant, Mark Blue and the Smiths agreed to develop and process payroll transactions for a local insurance agency. This was not part of the original contract, but was simply an oral agreement. This processing has been done for about four months, and the two parties equally divided the proceeds.

Your assignment is to look at the contracts and letters and to perform the following three tasks:

1. Describe what Mark Blue did wrong in obtaining the software from ABC. Be sure to include why he ended up in the position in which he found himself.
2. Speculate as to how you believe this situation would be resolved if it were taken to court. Be specific as to why this result would occur.
3. Briefly describe how Mark Blue should have handled this whole situation.

Be sure that all your work is complete, specific, and addresses all the issues that are important to this case.

Document #1

LICENSE AGREEMENT

AGREEMENT made October 5, 19X0, between ABC, CORPORATION OF El Paso, Texas, hereinafter called ABC, and *Mark Blue Restaurant, of Cloudcroft, New Mexico*, hereinafter called "Customer."

1. *License*. ABC grants and the Customer accepts, subject to the terms and conditions hereinafter set forth, nontransferable and nonexclusive licenses for the computer software products, hereinafter referred to as "Software," and associated materials, listed on Schedule A annexed to this Agreement and those which are ordered from time to time by the Customer, subject to written confirmation by ABC.

2. *Use of Programs and Optional Material*. The license granted under this Agreement authorized the customer to use the Software at only one single location, that being *Operations Office*, and in only one single central processing unit ("CPU"). If the Software will be used at more than one location or in more than one CPU, an additional license will be required for each location or CPU; provided, however, that if the designated CPU is inoperative due to malfunction, any license granted under this Agreement for such CPU shall be temporarily extended to authorize the Customer to use the Software on any other CPU until the designated CPU is returned to operation. For purposes of this Agreement "use" is defined as copying any portion of the Software, instructions, or data from storage units or media into a CPU for processing.

This Agreement and any of the licenses, programs, Software, or materials to which it applies may not be assigned, sublicensed, or otherwise transferred by the Customer without prior written consent from ABC. No right to print or copy, in whole or part, the Software is granted hereby.

3. *Charges*. The Customer shall pay the sum of $10,400.00 for the license granted hereby, one-half of which shall be paid at the time the Customer places its order and the balance shall be paid when the Software is transferred to the Customer's disk pack. In the event the Customer shall desire program modifications in the Software to meet the Customer's requirements, either before or after the transfer of the Software, the cost of any program modifications shall be billed to the Customer at such price and terms as the parties may agree.

4. *Permission to Copy Licensed Programs*. The Customer shall not copy, in whole or in part, any Software, licensed program, or associated materials which are provided by ABC under this Agreement, unless agreed to in writing by ABC.

5. *Protection and Security*. The Customer agrees not to provide or otherwise make available any Software, licensed program, or associated materials, including but not limited to flow charts, logic diagrams, and source code in any form, to any other person without prior written consent from ABC.

6. *Patent and Copyright Indemnification*. The Parties agree that ABC is sole owner of the copyright to the Software. ABC shall indemnify and hold the customer harmless with respect to any claim made against the Customer that the services and products provided hereunder by ABC infringe upon the proprietary rights of others.

7. *Discontinuance*. The Customer may terminate the Agreement and discontinue the use of any license under this Agreement by so notifying ABC in writing. Within one week after the date of the termination or discontinuance of any license under this Agreement, the Customer will certify to ABC in writing that the original and all copies, in whole or in part, in any form, including partial copies in modification, of the Software and any associated material received from ABC or made in connection with such license have been destroyed.

8. *Warranty*. ABC warrants the Software to be free of program defects for a period of sixty (60) days from the date of installation in the Customer's disk pack. Any modification of the Software made by the Customer voids this warranty. In the event program defects are discovered during the warranty period, ABC will supply corrections at no charge to the Customer. The Customer is exclusively responsible for the supervision, management and control of its use of the Software, including, but not limited to, assuring proper machine configuration, operating methods, and backup procedures.

9. *Limitation of Liability*. *THE FOREGOING WARRANTY IS IN LIEU OF ALL OTHER WARRANTIES EXPRESSED OR IMPLIED, INCLUDING, BUT NOT LIMITED TO, THE IMPLIED WARRANTIES OR MERCHANTABILITY AND FITNESS FOR A PARTICULAR PURPOSE.*
ABC liability hereunder for all damages including but not limited to liability for patent or copyright infringements, regardless of the form of action, shall not exceed the charges paid by the Customer for the particular Software involved. ABC will not in any case be liable for any lost profits, or for any claim or demand against the Customer by any other party, except a claim for patent or copyright infringement as provided herein. No action, regardless of form, arising out of the transactions under this Agreement may be brought by either party more than one year after the cause of action has accrued, except that an action for nonpayment may be brought within one year after the date of the last payment.

IN NO EVENT WILL ABC BE LIABLE FOR CONSEQUENTIAL DAMAGES EVEN IF ABC HAS BEEN ADVISED OF THE POSSIBILITY OF SUCH DAMAGES.

10. *General*.

a. The terms of this Agreement may be modified by ABC upon six months' written notice to the Customer. The Customer may terminate this Agreement or discontinue any of the licenses hereunder on the effective date of such modification upon one month's prior written notice to ABC; otherwise, such modification shall become effective.

b. The term "this Agreement" as used herein includes any future written amendments, modifications, or supplements made in accordance herewith. The terms of this Agreement will take precedence over the terms of any present or future order from the Customer for any licenses hereunder. The Customer's acceptance of future delivery of any Software from ABC is conclusive evidence of its agreement that the license for such program or optional material is governed by the terms of this Agreement.

If any of the provisions, or portions thereof, of this Agreement are invalid under any applicable statute or rule of law, they are to that extent to be deemed omitted.

THE CUSTOMER'S REMEDIES IN THIS AGREEMENT ARE EXCLUSIVE.

THE CUSTOMER ACKNOWLEDGES THAT IT HAS READ THIS AGREE-MENT, INCLUDING ALL PRINTED LANGUAGE, UNDERSTANDS IT, AND AGREES TO BE BOUND BY ITS TERMS AND FURTHER AGREES THAT IT IS THE COMPLETE AND EXCLUSIVE STATEMENT OF THE AGREEMENT BE-TWEEN THE PARTIES, WHICH SUPERSEDES ALL PROPOSALS ORAL AND WRITTEN AND ALL OTHER COMMUNICATIONS BETWEEN THE PARTIES RELATING TO THE SUBJECT MATTER OF THIS AGREEMENT.

11. *Survival.* All warranties, representations, conditions, and agreements of this Agreement shall survive the installation of the Software and the payment therefor by the Customer, and shall control the obligations of the parties for so long as the Software shall be used by the Customer.

12. *Governing Law.* This Agreement will be governed by and interpreted in accordance with the laws of the State of Texas.

IN WITNESS WHEREOF, the parties have executed this Agreement the day and the year set forth above.

BY_____
    CUSTOMER

_____
    ABC REPRESENTATIVES

SCHEDULE A

$3,000.00 payable October 5, 19X0 with the remaining balance of $6,000.00 payable on or before November 15, 19X0. The payments constitute the license payment as reflected in paragraph 3. The remaining balance of $1,400.00 due on the license agreement shall be included in the installation payment plan.

Document #2

INSTALLATION AGREEMENT

AGREEMENT made October 5, 19X0, by and between ABC, CORPORATION OF El Paso, Texas, THE STATE, hereinafter called ABC, and Mark Blue Restaurant, of Cloudcroft, New Mexico hereinafter called "Customer." The parties agree that the following terms and conditions shall govern in all cases when ABC furnishes assistance to the Customer in the installation and use of data processing products.

1. *Services.* The Agreement shall cover all assistance in the installation and use of data processing products by ABC personnel at the Customer's request, as listed on Schedule A attached hereto. The Customer's responsibilities and obligations to implement, activate, or otherwise aid in the installation of such data processing products are also set forth on Schedule A. These services may be performed at either the Customer's or ABC's premises.

2. *Charges.* The Customer agrees to pay charges for these services, including billable travel time, in accordance with ABC established rates and minimums in effect when the services are rendered, as set forth on Schedule B. Any additional services required by the Customer shall be billed to the Customer at ABC established rates, and shall be paid in addition to those amounts set forth in Schedule B. Charges will be invoiced monthly for services rendered and will be payable on receipt of invoice. There shall be added to any charges under this Agreement amounts equal to any applicable taxes however designated, levied, or based on such charges or on this Agreement or the services rendered hereunder, including state and local privilege or excise taxes based on gross revenue, and any taxes or amounts in lieu thereof paid or payable by ABC in respect of the foregoing, exclusive of taxes based on net income. The Customer will reimburse ABC for special or unusual expenses incurred at the Customer's specific request.

3. *Control and Supervision.* Customer tasks in which ABC personnel assist shall remain under the supervision, management, and control of the Customer.

4. *Rights in Data.* The ideas, concepts, know-how, or techniques relating to data processing, developed during the course of this Agreement by ABC personnel or jointly by ABC and the Customer's personnel, can be used by either party in any way it may deem appropriate. Each invention, discovery, or improvement which includes ideas, concepts, know-how, or techniques relating to data processing developed pursuant to this Agreement shall be treated as follows: (a) if made by the Customer's personnel, it shall be the property of the Customer; (b) if made by ABC personnel, it shall be the property of ABC and ABC grants to the Customer a nonexclusive, irrevocable license throughout the world; (c) if made jointly by personnel of ABC and the Customer, it shall be jointly owned without accounting. This Agreement shall not preclude ABC from developing materials which are competitive, irrespective of their similarity, to materials which might be delivered to the Customer pursuant to this Agreement.

5. *Confidentiality.* With respect to financial, statistical, and personnel data relating to the Customer's business which is confidential, is clearly designated,

and is submitted to ABC by the Customer to carry out this Agreement, ABC will instruct its personnel to keep such information confidential by using the same care and discretion that they use with similar data which ABC designates as confidential. With respect to technical data relating to the Customer's business which is confidential, and which must be submitted to ABC by the Customer for ABC to carry out its work under this Agreement, the Customer shall list such data on a confidentially supplement and supply the list to ABC. ABC will instruct its personnel to keep such information confidential by using the same care and discretion with regard to the identified technical data as they use with similar data which ABC designates as confidential. However, ABC shall not be required to keep confidential any data which is or becomes publicly available, is already in ABC possession, is independently developed by ABC outside the scope of this Agreement, or is rightfully obtained from third parties. In addition, ABC shall not be required to keep confidential any ideas, concepts, know-how, or techniques relating to data processing submitted to it or developed during the course of this Agreement by its personnel or jointly by its and the Customer's personnel.

6. *Personnel.* In recognition of the fact that ABC personnel provided to the Customer under this Agreement may perform similar services from time to time for others, this Agreement shall not prevent ABC from performing such similar services or restrict ABC from using the personnel provided to the Customer under this Agreement. ABC will make every effort consistent with sound business practices to honor the specific requests of the Customer with regard to the assignment of ABC employees; however, ABC reserves the sole right to determine the assignment of its employees.

7. *Limitation of Liability.* The Customer agrees that ABC liability hereunder for damages, regardless of the form of action, shall not exceed the total amount paid for services pursuant to this Agreement. This shall be the Customer's exclusive remedy. The Customer further agrees that ABC will not in any case be liable for any lost profits, nor for any claim or demand against the Customer by any other party. No action, regardless of form, arising out of the services under this Agreement, may be brought by either party more than one year after the cause of action has accrued, except that an action for nonpayment may be brought within one year of the date of last payment.

8. *Warranty.* ABC warrants its services for sixty (60) days from the date it completes its responsibilities under Schedule A. Any modifications, delays, or failures by the Customer to perform its obligations under Schedule A shall void this warranty. During the sixty (60) day warranty period, ABC will supply installation corrections at no charge to the Customer.

THE FOREGOING WARRANTY IS IN LIEU OF ALL OTHER WARRANTIES EXPRESSED OR IMPLIED, INCLUDING, BUT NOT LIMITED TO, THE IMPLIED WARRANTIES OR MERCHANTABILITY AND FITNESS FOR A PARTICULAR PURPOSE.

IN NO EVENT WILL ABC BE LIABLE FOR CONSEQUENTIAL DAMAGES EVEN IF ABC HAS BEEN ADVISED OF THE POSSIBILITY OF SUCH DAMAGES.

9. *General.* The terms of this Agreement may be modified or terminated by either party or by ABC upon one month's written notice to the other party. In the

event of modification, the other party may exercise its right to terminate; otherwise, such modification shall become effective.

The term "this Agreement" as used herein includes any future written amendments, modifications, or supplements made in accordance herewith.

THE CUSTOMER ACKNOWLEDGES THAT IT HAS READ THIS AGREEMENT, INCLUDING ALL PRINTED LANGUAGE, UNDERSTANDS IT, AND AGREES TO BE BOUND BY ITS TERMS AND FURTHER AGREES THAT IT IS THE COMPLETE AND EXCLUSIVE STATEMENT OF THE AGREEMENT BETWEEN THE PARTIES, WHICH SUPERSEDES ALL PROPOSALS ORAL AND WRITTEN AND ALL OTHER COMMUNICATIONS BETWEEN THE PARTIES RELATING TO THE SUBJECT MATTER OF THIS AGREEMENT

10. *Applicable Law.* This Agreement will be governed by and interpreted in accordance with the laws of the State of Texas.

IN WITNESS WHEREOF, the parties have executed this Agreement the day and the year set forth above.

BY_____
　　CUSTOMER

_____
ABC REPRESENTATIVES

SCHEDULE B

Customer agrees to pay monthly as in the schedule listed below. Interest shall be 18% per annum.
$11,0400.00 Due for installation agreement and remaining license fee
1,105.68 Total interest
_____

$12,145.68

First billing will be December 15, 19X0 with first payment due Jan. 19X1, and on the first of each month thereafter. Payments shall be $1,012.14 for twelve months.

Document #3

Mark Blue
Cloudcroft, NM
October 7, 19X1

ABC Corp.
El Paso, TX

Joe & Carol:

At the time of this letter I feel you have to comply with what I understood and with what is customary pertaining to the software I purchased from you. I must withhold all payments as described in our contract until progress and equity are made.

During our preliminary discussion—and also my discussions with the hardware vendor—it was made apparent to me that not only would the computer system supply the necessary information to replace the service I had previously been obtaining from my accountant (excluding year-end income tax service), but would also provide information pertinent to food cost control including inventory and menu costing. Myself and my wife were shown a set of restaurant printouts in your office in El Paso in August of 19X0 and were led to believe that we would be obtaining the same system capabilities. In our conversations following it was our understanding that we would be provided with the necessary training, documentation, and instruction in the use of the operating system and all of the software features and capabilities we had agreed upon when we purchased the software as related to the Mark Blue Restaurant. We also understood we would be able to do computer work for other businesses using our software, and agreed to pay ABC for any additional software modification.

In August of this year I asked for specific documentation. It was not until then that I realized it was not only necessary, but essential to the ongoing day-to-day operation and maintenance of the system as a whole. Never at any time did I receive formal documentation or any intention to do so. In our initial training sessions both myself and my wife asked if we should be writing certain information down and we were told it was not necessary. We were also persuaded not to run a parallel accounting system.

At this time I have no accurate accounting records, either manual or through the software system, for any month in 19X1 and recently had to ask my accountant to re-create our accounting records manually at an indeterminable cost. Many of the software functions that previously provided information are now inoperable because training or documentation was not provided to correct normal software maintenance and problems.

It is without question that proper training was not provided, documentation was never supplied, the software package I purchased has not performed in the way it was promised and the way I anticipated it would perform, and that my computer was used for your personal profit without my approval or notification.

At this time my accountant is manually re-creating my records and transactions for 19X1 and should be completed by November 10. I expect a complete and workable series of documented procedures that will provide me with the capability of obtaining those items listed on schedule 1 before I make any further payment. Within 10 days of the date of this letter I expect acknowledgment and a specific plan of action to remedy the problems and delays I have experienced since purchasing your software.

Sincerely,
Mark Blue

GENERAL LEDGER

1. General ledger posting
2. General ledger update and journal
3. General ledger master file maintenance
4. Company file maintenance
5. General ledger reports
   a. general ledger reports
   b. check reconcillation
   c. cash disbursements journal

ACCOUNTS PAYABLE

1. Payables posting
2. Clear invoices for payment
3. Write checks and distributions
4. Payables maintenance
5. Payables report
   a. payment extract
   b. cash requirements
   c. vendor purchases
   d. invoice reports
   e. alpha vendor

PAYROLL

1. Payroll input
2. Payroll calculations
3. Payroll maintenance
4. Payroll checks
5. Manual payroll input
6. Payroll reports
   a. payroll earning report
   b. labor cost report
   c. payroll input worksheets
   d. tip deficiency report
   e. wage review reports
   f. quarterly reports
   g. daily payroll worksheets

SALES AND INVENTORY

1. Profit sales
   a. cassette sales input
   b. manual sales input
   c. sales update
   d. sales report
   e. server reports

2. Profit inventory
   a. menu cost update
   b. menu cost report
   c. physical inventory
   d. combine company menu sales
   e. menu sales mix report
   f. inventory reports
      1) inventory status
      2) cost and usage report
      3) sales cost compilation
      4) reorder report
      5) alpha inventory listing

3. Profit file maintenance
   a. menu master
   b. inventory master file
   c. servers master file
   d. quantity conversion master file
   e. sales tables maintenance
   f. inventory transfer

Document #4

ATTORNEYS AT LAW
El Paso, Texas 99999-9999
October 18, 19X1

Mr. Mark Blue
Mark Blue Restaurant
Cloudcroft, New Mexico 88888
Re: ABC Company

Dear Mr. Blue:

Please be advised that this office represents ABC of El Paso, Texas. Your letter to that company of October 7, 19X1 has been referred to me for response. I have reviewed your letter in detail with Joe and Carol Smith of ABC, and find the points raised in that letter to be without foundation.

It should first be noted that the software which you purchased from ABC has been installed satisfactorily on numerous occasions. Every portion of the system installed for you has been documented as operational. The computer system was run parallel to your old manual system for sufficient time to insure its satisfactory operation. In addition, you have been provided with more than the standard amount of training and documentation in the use of the system. As promised, you do have the capacity of providing computer services to other businesses, and, in fact, have been doing so.

According to the records of ABC, the Smiths have spent a total of 64 days in Cloudcroft installing the system and training your personnel. Pursuant to the agreement between your firm and ABC, this time is billable at the rate of $435.00 per day, or a total of $27,840.00. The effort provided by the Smiths extended throughout the first part of September, 19X1. On many occasions when the Smiths attempted to see you, you were either unavailable or too busy to spend time with them. As late as two weeks ago Joe Smith offered to set up a meeting with you and get your system caught up. This offer did not receive any response from you.

One of the major difficulties with your system is that you have not done your processing on a regular basis. This causes the data files to fill up and become "overloaded." If the work is processed on a monthly basis, the files will automatically clean themselves out.

Regarding your allegations of ABC making personal profit from the use of your computer, I would point out that the Smiths were spending so much time in Cloudcroft that it was agreed that they would run their own processing on your machine so that they could stay current.

If you have no accurate accounting records, it is due to the fact that you apparently have not used the computer. The software is fully functional and capable of performing all of your accounting needs.

In addition to supporting your system, ABC has supported the system utilized by the insurance agency in its data processing. ABC is unable to provide further support to the insurance agency, and any further support to the insurance agency or your firm will be conditioned upon complete payment of your financial obligation to ABC in the amount of $3,036.42 and payment of the expenses incurred by ABC in helping you solicit business from the insurance agency.

Demand is therefore made for payment of the remaining balance of $3,036.42 together with payment for the expenses incurred by ABC. This must be accomplished within 10 days of the date of this letter. You should also note the requirement of the Licensing Agreement, paragraph 7, which provides that if you terminate the agreement, you must certify in writing within one week that the software, and any related modifications, has been destroyed. This will necessarily terminate data processing for the insurance agency.

ABC has been extremely patient and has completely fulfilled its obligations to your firm. Should you desire to discuss this matter with me or with Joe Smith, we will be available at your convenience.

Cordially,
the lawyer

Case 3

For Case 2 involving Mark Blue, rewrite the contracts as one contract for the purchase of that system instead of for the license of use. Content is the important consideration, so it is not necessary to use exact legal language. The contract should be constructed to lend equal protection to both parties.

ADDITIONAL READINGS

ADAM, ROBERT, AND ROBERT STANOJEV. "15 Indispensable Guidelines to Buying Software and Services," *ICP Interface—Special Edition*, 1981, pp. 66–74.

BOEHM, BARRY W. "Software Engineering Economics," *IEEE Transactions on Software Engineering*, Vol. SE-10, No. 1, January 1984.

BRYCE, TIM. "Information Systems Engineering and Computer Software Engineering: There's A Difference," *Journal of Systems Management*, July 1986, pp. 11–17.

MCCUSKER, TOM. "Project Planning Made Easy." *Datamation*, October 15, 1989, p. 49.

RIVARD, E., AND K. KAISER. "The Benefit of Quality IS," *Datamation*, January 15, 1989, p. 53.

SWARTZ, HERBERT. "Who Owns Your Custom Software?" *Computer Decisions*, February 1986, pp. 38–41.

READING BEFORE NEXT CHAPTER

The previous material should be adequate background.

11

SECURITY AND INTEGRITY

If you were to ask an information system manager to list the most critical concerns of an information system, the reply would no doubt place security high up on the list. As systems get more complex, serving a wider audience and making more information available, the problems associated with maintaining security and integrity become more difficult.

In many of the previous chapters, we discussed some aspects of security and integrity. In this chapter, we will take a closer look at the problems involved in keeping the system secure and reducing errors. When discussing these issues, we will consider not only the problems of illegal and unauthorized access and use of the computing resources, but will also investigate problems dealing with accidental loss or destruction of these computing resources. We will consider situations in which an individual, be it an outsider or an employee, willfully destroys vital company data. Also, we will discuss situations where data was destroyed accidentally or by some natural disaster. It is important to consider all of these situations, since the primary goal of the security procedures is to protect these resources. There is little difference in the final result if a new employee accidentally erased the payroll file or a disgruntled employee did it maliciously. In either case, the file is lost. Of course, the means of protecting the resource may be different in preventing willful and accidental destruction.

RISK ASSESSMENT

The first step in developing a security plan is to classify and assess the various risks to the system. The process involves the enumeration of all of the possible losses that could be experienced in the system. This is usually called investigating the exposures of the system. This inventory of possible risks is a time-consuming task, since care must be taken to be very thorough.

Along with each risk exposure, there must be a determination of the possible magnitude of the associated loss and an estimate of the probability of that loss occurring. While these two values are difficult to estimate, every effort must be made to assess these values as accurately as possible. The product of the possible dollar amount of the loss and its associated probability will give the expected dollar risk. These figures will give the firm a priority scheme by which security measures can be implemented. Some examples of loss exposure analysis are shown in Figure 11.1.

A natural question at this point is, Who does the assessment of risks? Or a more encompassing question is, Who in the firm is responsible for the security of the information system? These are not easy questions to answer, and there will be significant differences from one firm to another. Some firms will have a separate department in the information systems area that has sole responsibility for establishing system security standards. Another approach is for a section of the internal audit staff to have responsibility for information system security. Other approaches may not have one centralized area responsible for security, but each individual functional area in the information system would be responsible for the security of all matters under its control.

There are convincing arguments for each of these approaches. Having each separate area responsible for its own security is usually the least costly alternative because it does not involve a separate administrative unit. Giving the responsibility to the internal audit staff allows for a more independent, unbiased evaluation. However, centralized security under the control of the information system director encourages coordinated and comprehensive control over all

Figure 11.1 *Example of Loss Exposure Analysis*

	LOSS EXPOSURES FOR PAYROLL SYSTEM			
EXPOSURE	*TYPE OF LOSS*	*MAGNITUDE OF LOSS (PER MONTH)*	*PROBABILITY OF LOSS*	*EXPECTED LOSS*
Change of Employee Time Card	Overpayment of Employee	$4,000	.002	$80
Fictitious Employees	Payment to Persons Not on Payroll	$50,000	.005	$250
Selling List of Employees	Loss of Valuable Employees	$10,000	.05	$500
Making Employee Compensation Public	Employee Dissatisfaction	$20,000	.01	$200
Printing Duplicate Payroll Checks	Double Payment of All Paychecks	$500,000	.0001	$50

security involving computer operations. If internal audit was given oversight responsibility of the operations of this centralized security group, then there would be the additional protection of having an independent critical analysis of the security function.

No matter the type of organization, strong support of security recommendations by upper management is extremely important. Without strong management support, which includes adequate funding, proper security will be very difficult to establish and maintain. Unfortunately, many employees view security procedures as obstacles to the efficient performance of their duties. For example, controlling access to the computer room will prevent programmers from getting their own printer output, slowing up job turnaround time. Not allowing the development staff to access production data sets may be perceived as simply a bureaucratic control that interferes with rapid testing of new programs and changes to existing programs. Without strong corporate support of these policies, individuals will ignore or circumvent the security procedures.

TYPES OF EXPOSURES

When a business converts a task from manual to computerized operation, the possible number and magnitude of losses increases dramatically. This is due to the fundamental nature of computers. They can process a large number of repetitive transactions in a very short period of time, with little manual intervention. Compared to manual systems, there is a concentration of duties so that fewer individuals are involved in the processing of a transaction. While this results in the desirable reduction in labor costs, in a poorly controlled system it increases the possibility of fraud or error. Concentrating duties also concentrates the knowledge of the system, so that few within the firm understand its operation, an additional security concern. Computers also can process transactions at such a high rate that any fraud or error can quickly become large in magnitude.

When dealing with security issues, most business transactions involve certain primary functions for which we must be concerned. These include the authorization of the transaction, custody of the assets involved in the transaction, recording the transaction, and verifying the correctness of the processing of that transaction (see Figure 11.2). Most manual operations allow for a segregation of these duties to separate individuals, possibly in different departments. This is a powerful control that prevents and detects both fraud and errors. The typical data processing system will concentrate all of the duties in one department and possibly in one individual. For example, in a manual system, when goods are ordered for a firm's inventory, the warehouse foreman may initiate the order; purchasing would authorize it; accounting would record the order, the receipt of the goods, and the amount due the vendor; accounts payable would then authorize the payment of the invoice; and the cashier would write the check to pay for the goods. In a highly integrated information system, the computer may keep perpetual inventory records and automatically initiate an

Figure 11.2 *Segregation of Duties*

DUTY	DISCUSSION
Authorization of Transactions	In paying employees, this would involve signing the paychecks. Some instances may dictate multiple authorizations.
Custody of Assets	This not only involves physical custody of asset but also the ability to have the asset moved. A foreman in a warehouse may never touch the inventory but can have subordinates relocate the inventory.
Recording Transaction	This involves the records that are used to control and verify the validity of the transaction.
Verifying Correctness	This occurs after the transaction is concluded to control the operations.

order when the stock reaches a certain level. The order could be sent directly to the vendor (or even the vendor's computer) and the recording and payment of the amount due can be done entirely by the computer system. Notice the lack of human intervention in the computerized situation. Most duties are assigned to the computer programs. Without proper controls, a few changes to or errors in programs could result in substantial losses to the firm. As an example, the computer could pay invoices for which goods were not received or order goods that the firm does not need.

To discuss more easily the various security measures that should be adopted, we must divide the possible exposures into categories. First there are the physical risks to the assets. These include losses due to malicious or accidental destruction of assets. The possible sources of loss could be natural disaster, careless or inappropriate use, premeditated action by an employee or outsider, or vandalism. An example of this would be a fire that destroys some portion of the data center or an employee who accidentally drops a cup of coffee on the CPU. These exposures are summarized in Figure 11.3.

The next category is the risk of the loss or alteration of the data in the system. While this can also occur when there is a loss of physical property, there are many other risks associated with this category. For example, data sets may be either accidentally or purposefully destroyed or altered by running a utility program at an inappropriate time. This category also includes the case where the data is not lost to the company but is copied and used for another party's advantage. An example of this would be an employee making a copy of the firm's customer list and then selling it to a competitor. While the data is not lost to the firm, this could result in a substantial loss of customers to the competition. Another case would be where programs developed and owned by the firm are

Figure 11.3 *Major Categories of Exposures*

EXPOSURES	DISCUSSION
Destruction of Assets	Broad category that involves all of the physical facilities associated with computing
Loss or Alteration of Data	The most important aspect of data processing is the corporate data. Its loss could ruin the company.
Faulty Software	The category most likely to cause problems involving security and integrity
Inappropriate Use of Facilities	Difficult to detect and apprehend individuals involved in these activities

copied and sold to another firm. Another exposure in this category is that without proper controls, individuals can change the data in a file to benefit themselves. For example, an employee could remove a friend's record from the accounts receivable file, eliminating that person's debt.

Another category of exposure includes losses due to faulty software. This includes both poorly designed programs that contain errors and the unauthorized modification of software. An example of this would be the situation where a programmer places code into the payroll program to pay himself or herself an extra 10% each pay period and also to have the program self-destruct if that programmer is ever dismissed and removed from the payroll file.

The final category is any inappropriate use of the computing facilities. This would entail the wasting of resources and using the firm's computers to do work for other companies or individuals. For example, an employee may do outside consulting by programming on the firm's system and not compensate the firm for using its facilities.

CONTROL MEASURES

EDP controls are usually classified as being either general controls or application controls. General controls deal with setting policies on how personnel should perform their jobs. Application controls involve specific procedures and methods employed in the design and implementation of application programs. An example of a general control is in only allowing authorized personnel to enter the machine room. An example of an application control is checking the validity of all input fields in the fixed asset system. If any input data does not pass these validity tests, then no further processing can be done. Since these two types of controls are quite different, we will discuss them in separate sections.

GENERAL CONTROLS

General controls primarily involve establishing and enforcing policies dealing with security and integrity issues. Because there are so many individual procedures that can be classified under this category, we will discuss the basic guidelines that should be established and not deal with each possible individual policy.

General controls can be considered to fall into one of the following categories:

1. Separation of EDP functions
2. Physical controls
3. Data and program integrity
4. Access controls
5. Other controls.

Separation of EDP Functions

As we discussed earlier, in a data processing environment it is very difficult to separate the functions involved in dealing with an individual transaction. In a highly computer-dependent system, it is necessary to adopt a different approach. Instead of separating the authorization, custody, recording, and verification functions, we must attempt to limit the role of the individuals involved in the computerization of the system so that each individual has both a limited knowledge of the system and limited access to the resources involved in processing the transactions. This can be accomplished by separating the data processing duties to three distinct and separate areas. The first area is the operation of the production systems. The second area would include the development of the application systems. This would include both new development and maintenance of existing systems. The last area is the custody and access of the "live" production data. This segregation of responsibilities is the strongest control in a computerized environment. However, it is probably the hardest to enforce since the justifications of expediency and convenience are often cited as reasons for ignoring the procedures. When time pressures become extreme, these can be very convincing arguments.

Let's look a little more closely at why this separation of responsibilities is so important. The greatest exposure in an EDP system is the unauthorized changing of either production programs or data. Hence, our objective is to let only those individuals with a legitimate need to have access to either production data or programs. The best rule to attempt to follow is if a person has knowledge, do not let them have access to the production system, and if they have access to the production system, attempt to prevent them from having extensive knowledge of that system. Unfortunately, this rule is impossible to enforce strictly, but by separating operations, development, and data custody we can come close to following this rule.

The controls that should be in place deal with what, and more importantly, what not, each of these three functional areas should do. In the following sections, we will state three rules that should be followed when separating the functional areas in the information system.

System Development Should Not Be Allowed Access to "Live" Programs or Data. Those individuals involved with developing the application systems should have a thorough knowledge and understanding of the way the system is designed. Hence, a person with this knowledge could most easily perpetrate a fraud involving the modification of either the programs in the system or the data associated with the system. For this reason, those involved in development should not be allowed access to either the production programs or the production data.

This is implemented by isolating the production side of the processing from the test side. The safest way of doing this is to have a completely separate environment for production and another one for development. This would include separate hardware, software, and test data that can be used only by the development staff for constructing, testing, and maintaining the application software. The production hardware, software, and data would only be accessible by the operations staff. While completely separate environments are expensive, they provide excellent security.

If physically separate environments are not possible, then it is necessary to restrict access to the production data and programs by the development staff. This means that there must be separate source and object code libraries, data files, and some duplicate system software environments for both the production and development areas. This is accomplished by installing security software that restricts access to data sets and programs. In addition, separate test environments can be created by running duplicate copies of system software and making that environment accessible only to the development staff. These provisions will be covered in more detail when we address access controls.

Operations Personnel Should Not Have Access to Information About How Programs Are Designed or the Format in Which Data Is Stored. Probably the best form of security is to restrict sensitive information to only those with a legitimate need. The operations staff does not need to understand either the design of the system or the format of the data stored on the system. In most cases, this knowledge is critical to perpetrating a fraud. Limiting the distribution of documentation containing this type of information is the primary method of implementing this policy. This means that the run manual for a production system will only contain information that the operators must know when running the production system. This would entail run instructions on the sequence of program execution, information on what data files and devices are to be used by the system, and procedures to be followed if a problem arises.

For example, the run manual may state that when running the payroll system you need three tape drives, and the data files on disk drives 491, 495, and

681 and special forms are to be mounted on a specific type of impact printer. In addition, it would specify the order in which the programs must be run and what actions must be taken if any of the programs ABEND or generate abnormal conditions.

The run manual must not include program logic diagrams, program pseudocode, file formats, or any other documentation describing how the system was designed and implemented. In most cases, the operators will not have access to the source code, but will only be given access to the production object modules.

Do Not Allow Operations or Development Staff to Have Access to Production Data. Unauthorized changes to data files are a simple and quick way of defrauding a firm. Restricting access to data files will help reduce this risk. As stated earlier, the development staff should never be allowed access to current operational data files. The development staff has the most knowledge of the data stored in the files and hence, if so inclined, could easily change the file for their benefit. Separate test data files should be created for the testing of new systems. Often these test files are simply old versions of the production data sets.

In the case of operations personnel, the data access policy cannot be as strict. Operations staff must have access to specific data at certain times to run the production systems. However, it is not necessary for them ever to have access to all of the data files at any one time. Having a separate group responsible for the corporate data files will control this situation. In this way, if the files are on tape or mountable disk packs, then the files will be delivered to operations only when production runs are scheduled and then returned immediately after the run is completed. In addition, access to utilities that can alter or copy these files will not be allowed by operators or to those individuals that have custody of the data. If this is not feasible, then a detailed log must be kept of all uses of utility programs by these individuals.

In a batch environment, this type of data custody problem can be partially handled by having a separate library function that controls all tapes and mountable disk packs. However, in a online environment the problem is not one of physical possession, but more of the limitations placed on programs accessing the data. For many batch applications, a file is uniquely associated with either one application program or a small number of programs in one production system. In an online situation, the systems are usually highly integrated, where many programs will access the same data set. Also, the data sets will all reside on permanently mounted disk packs. Hence, the system has custody of the data set. Again, we can only control this situation by having system software restrict access to only the programs that require it. The data management group will be responsible for setting data access policy.

Physical Controls

Many physical controls were discussed at length in Chapter 5. We will only review some of those issues.

Physical controls are usually the most noticeable EDP controls, and as such are the easiest to enforce. Because of this, the absence or lack of enforcement of physical controls may be an indicator that the more important access and separation of duties controls may also be lacking. If you cannot accomplish the obvious, then you probably are not accomplishing the more subtle tasks. On the other hand, having good physical security is not sufficient. The other controls must also be in place.

One of the major physical controls is to restrict access to sensitive areas. This can be accomplished by an identification badge system in which the badge also serves as a magnetic entry key. In this way, a record can be kept by a computer of all traffic in and out of sensitive areas. Of course, security guards can also be used in highly restricted locations, but this is a more costly alternative. A careful analysis should be done to determine sensitive areas and the level of security necessary in that area.

For most organizations the security of the many personal computers distributed around the firm is a major concern. Since these items are so easily moved and are in such high demand, they are prime targets for theft. In many circumstances, it is difficult to restrict access, since, for convenience, the machines are placed in high-traffic areas. There are means of locking the machines to a table or within a cabinet designed for that purpose. These options appear to discourage theft but do not prevent it. It is important to protect these assets from being stolen, but it must be realized that there is still a reasonable chance of theft. For this reason, it is necessary to be very careful to develop and enforce standards for protecting the data stored on these machines.

The final physical control is to devise a comprehensive disaster control plan. This plan should provide alternatives for continuing the operation of the computer system no matter the circumstances. Since these issues have already been discussed in detail in Chapter 5, we will not go into any more detail.

Data and Program Integrity

The application programs owned by the firm and the data stored on the system are very valuable assets, and care must be taken to protect them. The separation of duties helps to protect both of them by restricting access and knowledge. However, other procedures must be adopted to further assure the protection of both of these.

If a data set or a series of data sets are damaged or destroyed, the firm must have the capability of restoring the lost information. Data sets can be lost or damaged in a series of ways. There may be a problem with a physical device, such as a head crash on a disk drive. An individual may mistakenly erase a given data set, thinking that it is no longer necessary or not realizing that it even resides on the given media in use. For example, many people, even expert programmers, have mistakenly reformatted an active diskette, destroying all of the existing information. Of course, data sets can also be tampered with to purposely alter or destroy the information.

The most straightforward way of recovering lost data is by establishing backup and recovery procedures. This entails the storage of duplicate copies of data to use if the original copies are destroyed. Sometimes the duplicates are a natural result of the normal processing. This is the case in batch processing using tapes, where master files are updated. This type of backup is usually referred to a grandfather-father-son backup. The son is the current master file, the father is previous master file, and the grandfather is the one previous to the father (see Figure 11.4). Hence, when we run the file updating program, the master file used as input is the father, the new updated master file is the son, and the master file used as input to the previous day's run is the grandfather. If the son is destroyed, the father along with the appropriate updates can be used to re-create it. To do convenient processing, the son must be kept in close proximity to the data center (usually in the main tape library). The father should be kept on-site but in a different location so that recovery can be done quickly. The grandfather should be stored at a completely separate facility in case there is a catastrophe that destroys the entire main complex.

Since very few systems are tape oriented, there must be other backup procedures in place. A typical scheme is to "dump" the contents of a device or a data set to tape at predetermined intervals. These backup procedures should also encompass source and object code programs, not just data files. If there is a major failure, it will be necessary to recover both the data and the programs that process that data. While backup is being run, the device or data set cannot be used or is used in read only mode; otherwise an inconsistent copy could be captured. Many installations will bring down the entire system to do backup. In this way, it is guaranteed that no data set will be altered during the backup process.

The frequency of backup is dictated by the volatility of the file (i.e., how often it changes), the ease and cost of re-creating the updates to this file, and the

Figure 11.4 *Batch Backup Procedures*

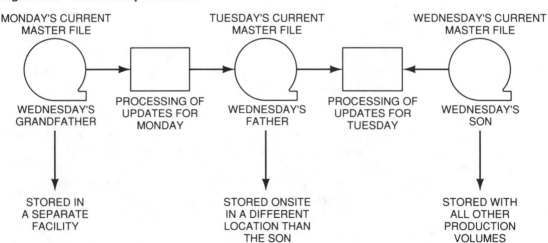

critical nature of the file. For example, a payroll data set may only be changed weekly, but when it is changed there are many updates. Hence, it should be backed up weekly. A program file may remain unchanged for months and thus no additional backup would be necessary during that time. On the other hand, a sales data set may be constantly updated and would need to be backed up much more frequently.

For critical online transaction-oriented systems, periodic backup is not adequate. The transactions are originating in a variety of locations usually in an apparently random order. It is very difficult to re-create the transaction stream if the data set is destroyed in the middle of processing. Also, if the system fails or there is an error in a program that alters the file, then there is the danger of having erroneous or inconsistent data in the file. This would be a totally unacceptable situation. Control over this type of situation is an absolute necessity in a processing environment that is highly integrated. That is, in a system where many different application programs store and process data contained in an integrated database, safeguards must be in place to prevent the actions of one program from affecting the integrity of the entire database.

It is necessary that each system create a sequential transaction log which records not only the details involved in the specific transaction, but also information that will allow for the reconstruction of the database if there is a failure. This information is usually termed *before-image* and *after-image record processing*. This involves making a copy of the data in the database before it is changed and then after it has been changed. Figure 11.5 shows this logging process.

These before and after images are used to recover the data in case of failure and to prevent data inconsistencies and errors due to application program ABENDs and component failures. These records are used to do transaction roll-forwards or roll-backs. A roll-forward involves starting at a historical point in time (such as at the last backup point) and adding all of the subsequent transactions to re-create the database at its current status. A roll-back (sometimes if this is an automatic function it is called a dynamic transaction backout) will start at the current state of the database and remove erroneous transactions until the desired point in time is reached. An example of a roll-back is when a general ledger program is recording the journal entries for a given transaction. If the debit entries are first made and before the corresponding credit entries can be made the program ABENDs, then an out-of-balance situation would exist if a roll-back was not initiated. Instead, all of the debit entries can be removed from the database, leaving it in the same state as before the general ledger program started that transaction. Figure 11.6 shows online data recovery procedures. Many commercially available database management systems create and store before and after image records and will do roll-backs automatically when a program or component failure is detected.

Another type of control is that of checkpoint restart. This is a method of providing protection from unpredictable failures during the processing of long-duration batch jobs. It involves the recording of "snapshots" of the working storage areas and the files at specific predetermined points in time. This picture

Figure 11.5 *Online Transaction Logging*

STEPS IN TRANSACTION LOGGING:

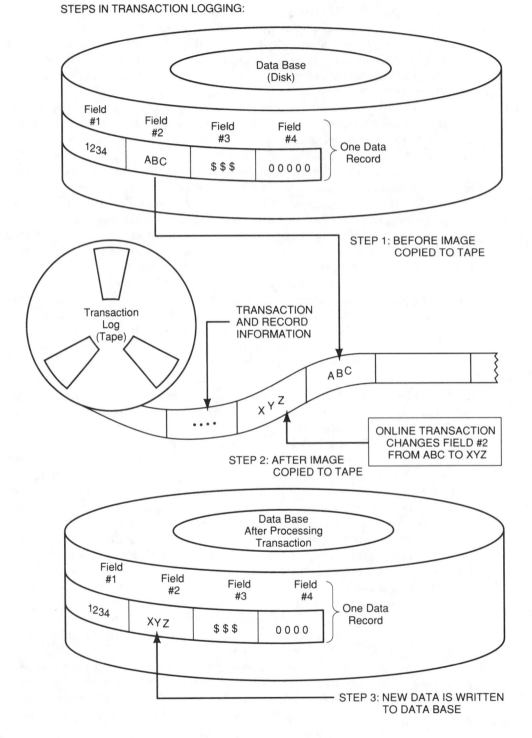

Figure 11.6 *Online Data Recovery*

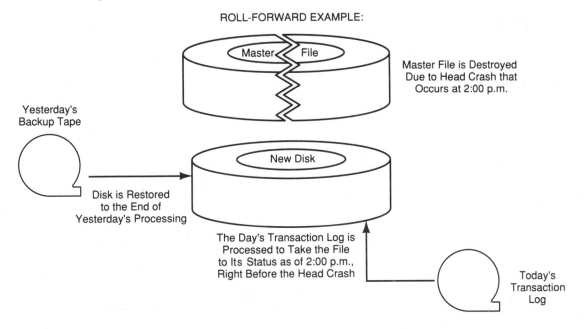

ROLL-FORWARD EXAMPLE:

Master File is Destroyed
Due to Head Crash that
Occurs at 2:00 p.m.

Yesterday's
Backup Tape

Disk is Restored
to the End of
Yesterday's Processing

The Day's Transaction Log is
Processed to Take the File
to Its Status as of 2:00 p.m.,
Right Before the Head Crash

Today's
Transaction
Log

is called a checkpoint. If a failure occurs, then the processing can be restarted at the last checkpoint and then continue to normal completion (see Figure 11.7).

For example, a large job may take 30 hours to process. It may be determined that a checkpoint be created by the program after the processing of each 100,000 records. If at the end of 26 hours of processing a magnetic tape loses its trailing reflector strip and hence runs off the reel, it is possible to fix the bad tape and begin processing at the last checkpoint. In this way, we may lose only a few minutes of processing, instead of the entire 26 hours of processing.

Access Controls

When discussing the creation of a separate test environment for application systems development, we mentioned the use of access control software to allow these individuals to only use the test system. This is one of the uses of access controls. They are a primary method of protecting the various parts of the system from being used by unauthorized individuals or to do unauthorized work. In addition to restricting access to the system, the data sets, and the programs, the access control function should also be able to record all events concerning system access. This record provides an audit trail to use in those situations where the system has been used improperly. For example, a student attempts to log on to the account of a professor to print a copy of an upcoming examination. A good access control system will not only deny the student access, but will record the time that it occurred, the location of the device the

Figure 11.7   *Checkpoint Restart*

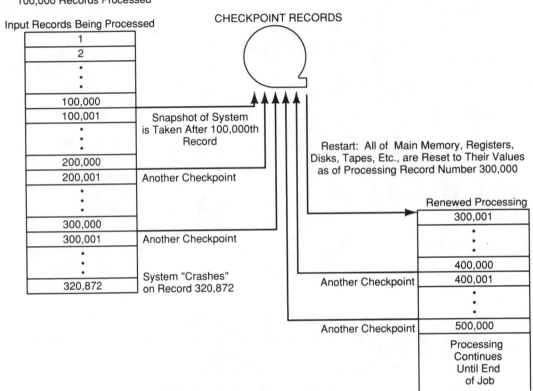

Checkpoint is Taken After Each
100,000 Records Processed

student was using, and should also notify security when this event is occurring so that the individual can be apprehended.

Access control involves restricting use of each of the following areas:

1. Logging on to the system
2. Accessing data sets
3. Accessing object code programs
4. Accessing source code programs
5. Using network and communication facilities.

Figure 11.8 presents the objectives of access control security procedures.

The most common system log-on control is by user defined passwords. If this is the case, a policy should be established so that users will frequently change their passwords and do not allow others access to their accounts. A common problem involving terminal access is that someone, such as a janitor, has access to the area holding the terminal during off hours. Use of the terminal

Figure 11.8 *Access Control Security*

OBJECTIVES OF ACCESS CONTROL

1. Uniquely identify users desiring to use the system.
2. Verify the identity of each user before allowing entry into system.
3. Determine which resources are to be protected.
4. Establish level of resource access for each user or group of users.
5. Associate level of access to resources with individual users.
6. Record all accesses to protected resources.
7. Immediately notify security of any attempted security violation.
8. Have a system that is flexible, allowing different levels of protection.
9. Have a system that allows rapid changes in status of both users and resouces.

by this person could lead to a serious security problem. To control unauthorized use of the system during nonworking hours, terminals can be disabled by the system during specific times and security personnel can be notified if an attempt is made at accessing the system. Also, in situations involving a high level of security, much more sophisticated identification methods can be employed. For example, a device could be attached to the terminal to analyze the palm print or the voice print or another unique characteristic of the individual.

Data sets must also be protected from unauthorized entry. However, there are other concerns involved. Users do not directly deal with data sets; instead programs will do the processing. There are two approaches to protecting data sets. One method is to grant the user access and thus grant all of that user's programs access. The second method is to grant access to specific application programs. In either use, the type of access allowed must be specified. This can include the ability to read only the information or to read and update or to read, update, delete, create, and add. Determined by the power of the control system, this security can control the access to the data to as low a level as a specific data item in a field.

Access control software can be in either of two forms. It can be a stand-alone software system that controls all of the data sets on the system. In this case, it is called by an operating system access method, whenever a file is to be opened. If the user or program is in the access table and is requesting functions that are allowed, then access is granted. Otherwise the access method is not allowed entry to the file, and the access method terminates with an error condition.

Another method of implementing access control is to have the security designed in a specific systems software package. For example, most database management systems have their own imbedded security. In these situations, the security of the DBMS will only cover the data sets under the control of the DBMS. To have comprehensive security, it is necessary to have both stand-alone high-level access control and control built into each of the critical systems software components.

It is very important that each layer of the security system not only restrict access to the data sets, but also records all uses. This creates an audit trail that can be used to reconstruct the events that occurred if security is broken. Remember that no matter how well designed, every security system is still subject to circumvention.

To add even more security to data set control, the stored data sets can be encrypted. For a person to use a data set, they must also be able to decrypt the data. Encrypting the file directory and the system access control tables will provide increased security from unauthorized access.

Encryption is extremely important for data that is transmitted to machines in remote locations. Both public and private communication lines can be wire-tapped. If the data is encrypted, interpretation of the message will be extremely difficult. Financial institutions that do electronic fund transfers will usually encrypt all external computer communications.

The concepts involved in restricting access to both source and object code programs are very similar; hence we treat them as one topic. The access to programs must be restricted so that the programs are not altered to perform differently than designed, also it should prevent unauthorized individuals from discovering the processing techniques involved in that system and prevent unauthorized execution of the programs. Figures 11.9 and 11.10 illustrate two commercial products used to protect source and object code, respectively.

The basis of program security is to establish separate program libraries for different purposes. There should be a set of libraries established for only production programs and a corresponding set of libraries for programs in the development and test stage. The security software would not only restrict access but record all uses and changes to each of the program files.

By restricting the development staff to accessing only the test programs, the production system can be isolated from the test system. Copies of the source code of all production programs would be on the test system for modification by the maintenance programming staff. All changes would be made only to the test copies. Testing of these modifications would be done on the test system using nonproduction data. After the program has been thoroughly tested, the manager of maintenance programming would certify the correctness of the program and then transfer the program to the production system.

Usually the operations staff will only be allowed to run the object modules and will not be allowed to access the source code. While source code must be held on the production side of the system to back up the object code, the access to this code must be tightly controlled. Allowing access to the source code would leave an easy way of making unauthorized changes. Fortunately, it is very difficult to make specific changes to object code; hence access by operators should only be granted to object code programs. Access to object code must also be restricted to prevent unauthorized executions.

With the increased use of communications between various external

Figure 11.9 *Example of Source Code Protection*

SOURCE CODE PROGRAM	MAINTE- NANCE (MODI- FICATION) LEVEL	SECURITY CODE	SOURCE LANGUAGE	TELLS HOW THE DATA SET IS USED AND ITS CURRENT STATE	DATE OF LAST MODI- FICATION	DATE ACCESSED	NO. OF BLOCKS	NO. OF STATEMENTS	LAST ACTION SINCE LISTING DONE	AVG. BYTES	% UTIL	NO. OF SUBSETS
PROG001	1	50 3	ASSEMBLER	PROD ACTV ENABL		04/12/90	11	3,926		22	96.4	
PROG002	5	999 1	JCL	TEST INAC ENABL		09/24/90	1	18		43	11.3	
PROG003	18		ANSCOBOL	T TEST ACTV DSBLD	09/04/90	09/05/90	10	2,709	STATUS	35	91.2	
PROG004	3		AUTOCODER	PROD ACTV ENABL		08/25/90	2	590		23	89.8	
PROG005	1	3	FORTRAN	PROD ACTV ENABL		01/10/90	1	322		19	88.5	
PROG006	8		RPG	N PROD ACTV ENABL		07/09/90	1	45		20	11.7	
*USER COMMENT RECORD FOR PROG006												
PROG007	1		UNSPECIFD	TEST ACTV ENABL		09/23/90	3	657	ADDED	30	78.9	
PROG008			DATA	TEST ACTV ENABL		09/23/90	1	38		76	42.9	
*USER COMMENT RECORD FOR PROG008												
PROG009		35	OBJECT	TEST ACTV ENABL	08/18/90	09/24/73	3	308	ATTACH	63	84.8	3
•SUBSET01												
•SUBSET02												
•SUBSET03												
PROG010	4	4141 2	PL/1	PROD ACTV ENABL		09/24/90	8	1,881	*	29	90.2	

The "*" indicates that a production data set has been changed.

This is only one of various reports that can be produced that gives management the status and history of each source code program.

Figure 11.10 *Example of Executable Code Protection*

ELEMENT NAME				PANEXEC ELEMENT ACTIVITY REPORT PE104					
OBJECT CODE PROGRAM	GIVES INFORMATION ON WHO HAS ACCESSED THIS PROGRAM	LAST ACCESS DATE	LAST ACCESS TIME	LAST CHANGE DATE	LAST CHANGE TIME	CHANGES MADE BY SYSTEMS PROGRAMMING	GIVES INFORMATION ABOUT EXECUTIONS OF THE PROGRAM	DATE ADDED	LAST EXECUTION
MAJORLIB	*SCOBLIB .BLDQS /EXEC 20 12	;PA 03/09/90	16.28.56	11/07/89	09.50.24	Y	10	11/18/89	03/07/90
MAJORLIB	*SCOBLIB .IKFCBL00/EXEC 9 6	;TA 03/14/90	11.30.45	01/09/90	15.20.45		6	12/14/89	02/27/90
MAJORLIB	*SCOBLIB .IKFCBL01/EXEC 14 3	;TA 02/27/90	17.49.54	02/27/90	07.44.04		3	01/10/90	02/22/90
MAJORLIB	*SCOBLIB .IKFCBL08/EXEC 4 2	;TA 02/23/90	09.22.01	02/08/90	14.22.01		2	01/24/90	02/20/90
MAJORLIB	*SCOBLIB .IKFCBL18/EXEC 7 2	;PA 03/23/90	18.22.39	03/15/90	20.22.14		1	12/20/89	03/23/90
MAJORLIB	*SCOBLIB .IKFCBL12/EXEC	;TA 03/14/90	13.23.53	03/14/90	10.23.33			03/12/90	03/14/90
MAJORLIB	*SCOBLIB .IKFCBL22/EXEC 11 8	;TA 03/14/90	14.24.32	03/14/90	14.24.32			03/14/90	00/00/00
MAJORLIB	*SCOBLIB .IKFCBL35/EXEC 22 1	;TD 03/19/90	18.04.20	03/19/90	18.04.40			01/29/90	02/06/90
MAJORLIB	*SCOBLIB .IKFCBL45/EXEC 17 9	;TA 03/12/90	10.24.48	02/14/89	15.24.48	Y	13	03/07/89	03/06/90
MAJORLIB	*SCOBLIB .IKFCBL50/EXEC 8 6	;TA 02/22/90	08.34.54	02/05/90	09.24.54			12/05/89	02/20/90
MAJORLIB	*SCOBLIB .IKFCBL51/EXEC 10 8	;TA 03/06/90	14.27.04	02/15/90	17.11.04		8	02/07/90	03/06/90
MAJORLIB	*SCOBLIB .IKFCBL6A/EXEC 25	;PD 03/21/90	16.45.10	03/21/90	22.43.10			12/05/89	03/15/90
MAJORLIB	*SCOBLIB .IKFCBL62/EXEC 9 3	;TA 03/19/90	12.51.23	01/16/90	08.29.23		3	01/30/90	03/19/90

108   INPUT RECORDS
PE191 00-00 13 ELEMENTS SELECTED

This is only one of many reports that can be generated. Data is also stored on who and when changes were made and the program executed.

devices and other computers, it is necessary to control these communications strictly. Networking and data communications are areas of concern because of the difficulty of imposing physical security on these activities. In most cases, access to communication lines cannot be easily controlled since they will be outside of the machine room and even off of the company's property.

Some of the exposures associated with data communications include the unauthorized interception of transmissions and the use of these transmission media to gain access to the system. In the first case, the party is simply listening to the "conversation" between the system components. Vital and often damaging information can be intercepted in this way. Physically shielding the wires to protect them from outside monitoring should be implemented; however, this is difficult to control. Some media are much more difficult to monitor than others. For example, fiber optic cable appears to have quite an advantage in the area of unauthorized access since it is extremely difficult to monitor. An appropriate safeguard is to encrypt the data to be transmitted. While the encryption and corresponding decryption can be expensive (it can consume substantial machine time), in many circumstances, where sensitive data is being transmitted, it is a necessity.

Another problem is the use of the communication media to gain access to the system. Log-on and other access controls can help prevent some of these abuses, but other means are also necessary. For dial-up access, the computer can have an access table of all authorized phone numbers. When a call is initiated, instead of the computer immediately recognizing the initiating terminal, it will hang up after querying the user for the number of the device and will then call that device and grant access to the system. This type of call-back system helps prevent access from unauthorized devices.

Other Controls

General controls that do not fall neatly into the previous categories will be presented here. The control that is the most powerful and by far the most important in any situation is that of hiring honest and trustworthy employees. If it were possible to measure these qualities accurately, most of the other controls previously discussed would not be necessary. However, these characteristics are not easily measured, but a conscientious attempt must be made to eliminate from consideration those individuals who are high risks.

The background of each prospective employee must be thoroughly checked. This includes verifying all past employment and interviewing the person's references. Some firms are also adopting other methods, such as lie detectors, to ascertain the trustworthiness of an individual. However, these methods are still not widely accepted, and some people even question their validity.

Another personnel consideration is that if an employee is dismissed, the computer access privileges of that individual should be immediately revoked. This can be done by disabling the user's account, and if a magnetic entry card system is employed, this card should be invalided and confiscated. All in all, this person should not be given the opportunity to alter or destroy any of the components of the system. There have been many instances where these strict measures were not taken and substantial damage was done to the system.

As discussed in Chapter 4, an excellent control is to develop and enforce data processing standards. This would include standards on programming and documentation. Having these types of standards makes auditing and verifying the proper implementation of a system much easier. Errors and unauthorized code will be easier to detect. This more easily allows rotation of programming responsibilities, eliminating the situation in which only one individual has domain over a small group of programs. There should be standards on the naming of data sets, program files, and the methods of labeling these. In this way, data sets residing in the wrong library will be obvious, and backup and recovery can be made easier.

APPLICATION CONTROLS

Application controls are those controls that are imbedded in the software of a specific application system. They are usually implemented during the programming of the system. Since these controls must be planned as the system is being designed, it is important that the internal audit staff be involved from the inception of any application development project.

Application controls can be divided into three different categories:

1. Validating input data
2. Testing the proper execution of the program
3. Other controls.

Because of the high degree of integration involved in most systems, it is mandatory that any data to be stored on the system be totally validated before it is actually written to a data set. Otherwise, the integrity of all of the data will be suspect. If one program is allowed to change the data in the file and a completely independent program uses this data, someone else's error could jeopardize the correctness of the reports generated by the second, independent program. This is not acceptable.

Following is a brief description of some of the checks that are done to assure the validity of data.

Sequence Check: Tests to see if the data is being entered in the correct order. For example, employee records are to be sorted by ascending Social Security number.

Limit Check: Tests to see if data is within the appropriate boundary values. For example, pay rates must be between $3.50 and $25.00 per hour.

Reasonableness Check: Tests to see if the data is reasonable in nature. For example, it would be unreasonable for a lower-level employee to have gross pay of more than $4,000 in a given week.

Check Digit: A digit generated by an algorithm applied to the original number. For example, the digits of a Social Security number are added together and truncated to a single digit. That is, 123-12-1234 would have a check digit of 9 (19 is the sum, truncated to 9).

Validity Check: The data field is only allowed to have certain values and is tested for the occurrence of one of these values either by comparing the field to a fixed set of values or searching a file to confirm the validity of the data. For example, the sex of an individual may be either M or F, or the Social Security number of a payroll entry is checked against the employee file to verify existence.

Echo Check: Used in online transaction-oriented systems. A data value is transmitted back to the user to verify its correctness. Sometimes this is also termed a *redundant data check*. For example, the product code of 12345 is entered into the system and the name of the product—52-inch canoe paddle—would be echoed back for verification.

To control the accurate processing of a program, there are additional application controls which can be employed. The following is a brief description of each:

Control Totals: Summation of a numeric field to verify that the batch of transactions have been completely and accurately processed. These totals are compared to the control totals generated earlier in the processing. For example, the sum of the cash receipts processed would be compared to the totals taken off of each cash register.

Hash Totals: Same idea as a control total except the field is such that its sum is of no logical consequence. For example, the Social Security numbers of all individuals in a file are totaled. If an unauthorized change is made to this field in the data set, then the hash total of the next processing will not correspond to the previous processing.

Record Counts: Simple counting of the number of records in the file that was processed. This can be compared to the trailer information contained on the data set to verify that records were neither added to nor deleted from the data file.

Internal File Labels: These are provided by the operating system. They allow the automatic implementation of the foregoing controls by imbedding them in the processing of the file. Record counts and control totals produced by the program can be compared to those in the trailer label in the file. Most firms will adopt a policy that no program can take the option of bypassing the standard label processing of the system. An example of IBM standard tape labels is shown in Figure 11.11.

These controls can be employed to detect the unauthorized alteration of production data files. Let's assume an operator erases a friend's record from the accounts receivable file. This could be immediately detected by all of these controls. This also is a good time to emphasize the importance of keeping the control procedures secret. In this case, if the operator knew of these controls, there would be little difficulty in circumventing them.

Figure 11.11 *Standard Tape Labels*

VOLUME LABEL (ALWAYS AT BEGINNING OF TAPE)

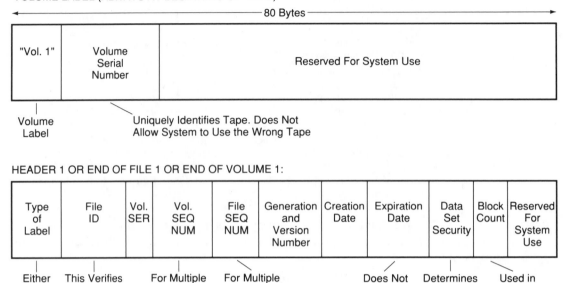

HEADER 1 OR END OF FILE 1 OR END OF VOLUME 1:

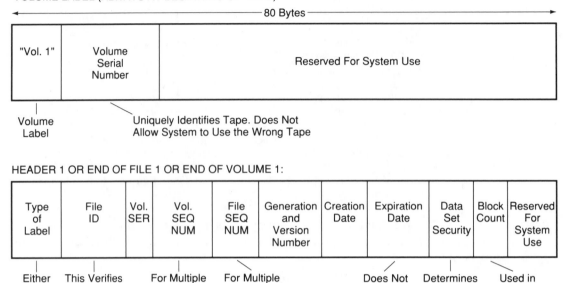

HEADER 2 OR END OF FILE 2 OR END OF VOLUME 2:

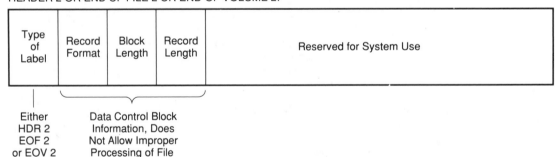

THE ROLE OF INTERNAL AUDIT

The primary oversight group in most large organizations is the internal audit function. With the increased importance of the information system, internal audit is becoming more involved in data processing matters. This increased focus on the computer is forcing the internal audit staff to become substantially more adept at dealing with computerized systems. In fact, the activities of the internal audit area have a significant influence on the smooth operation of data processing. Because of internal audit's increasing importance, we will devote some time to explaining the various activities involving the internal audit function.

There are two distinctly different groups of auditors with which a firm will deal. The group that probably has the highest degree of visibility (and usually produces the most anxiety) is the external auditors. External auditors are from an independent firm, and their primary responsibility is to render an opinion on the correctness of the financial statements of the company. They generally do not have a substantial influence on the operations of the data processing function. However, they will request specific files and reports that are produced by the information systems area and do a quick analysis of the controls in the information system area.

Internal audit, on the other hand, has a much broader function and will deal extensively with the information systems area. While internal audit will do some financial auditing, this will not be their primary role. Instead, internal audit will do both compliance and operational audits. A compliance audit determines whether an area in the firm is following the stated policies and procedures of the firm. In the computer area, this would focus on whether or not the controls were being implemented as designed.

An operational audit deals with the efficiency and effectiveness of a specific area. For example, in the information system, internal audit could analyze how projects are selected for implementation and then analyze the entire system implementation cycle. The end product of this analysis would be a comprehensive report discussing the strengths and weaknesses in the process. In addition, this report would suggest improvements. The functions in which internal audit will be involved are described in Figure 11.12.

To accomplish their mission, it is necessary for internal audit to have personnel skilled in the computer area. The auditors must be able to deal with all of the aspects of the information system. This necessitates a very broad computer background and a comprehensive knowledge of both accounting and auditing.

Figure 11.12 *Internal Audit Functions*

FUNCTION	*DESCRIPTION*
Compliance Audit	Examines internal controls and determines their adequacy
Operational Audit	Analyzes the efficiency and effectiveness of specific functional areas in the firm
Financial Audit	Not the primary function of internal audit, usually only done in assisting external auditors

The internal audit staff will be responsible for doing compliance testing on general and application controls of the information system. In addition, they should be closely involved in the development and maintenance of systems. This participation should begin during the initial analysis and design phases. In so doing, they can assure that the systems will have adequate controls designed into them and also be able to give advice on how to make the system easier to audit in the future. To provide a better idea of how internal auditors function, we will discuss some of the techniques and tools they use.

The auditor will first examine the theoretical controls (i.e., the control procedures that are documented in the standards and procedures manuals). Their adequacy does not guarantee a sound control system, for they may not be followed by the staff. Compliance tests must be conducted to evaluate whether these controls are correctly implemented. This should be done in all the areas of the information system.

Various tools are used to accomplish these tasks. To test the logic of programs, there are systems available that will analyze the source code and automatically flowchart the code. Trace-driven systems can be used to monitor the execution of a program. These systems will tabulate the number of times each section of code is executed. This allows the auditor to concentrate on the little-used or dormant sections of code that traditionally cause the most concern. In addition, comprehensive test data can easily be obtained by employing test data-generating programs.

Comprehensive testing of a production system can be accomplished by using an integrated test facility approach. This entails the incorporation of an entire series of nonexistent departments into the production system. In this way, the auditors can routinely introduce test transactions into the production system without adversely affecting the processing of the real production data. The alternative is to run test data through the system and later remove these transactions. In most cases, this second method will entail shutting down the production system during the tests. Since with an integrated test facility operations staff will not know when these tests are being conducted, a more accurate analysis of the system will be possible.

One of the most universal audit tools is called generalized audit software (see Figure 11.13). This is a series of special utility programs that allows the auditor to examine data files to confirm their correctness. They are very powerful systems that will access files in many formats and enable the auditor to perform a variety of tests to determine the validity of the data. Because of their "friendly" nature, they are easy to implement quickly and are very flexible.

MAJOR COMPANY

Security is a very important issue with Major Company. The competiveness of the industry and the cost of research and development make a high level of security a necessity. The records of the firm must be protected to maintain and enhance the position of Major Company in its industry.

Figure 11.13   *Generalized Audit Software*

COMMON FUNCTIONS FOUND IN GENERALIZED AUDIT SOFTWARE

FUNCTION	DESCRIPTION
Include/Exclude	Allows selection of specific records from a file; will usually build a new work file
Summarize	Totals amounts and count occurrences in specific fields in a file
Print	Allows for quick formatting and printing of specific fields
Mathematics	Allows arithmetic operations on multiple fields, usually to be stored in another field
Match/Merge	Allows multiple files to be merged together
Sampling	Produces a statistical sample from a specific file
Confirmation	Prints letters of confirmation which verify balances in specific fields in a record

The information system has a separate security department which reports directly to the vice-president of information systems. The security department is responsible for assuring that every other department in the information system develops and enforces adequate security procedures. While each department is responsible for its own procedures, the security area coordinates all of these procedures. Upper management has on numerous occasions supported the implementation and enforcement of control procedures. In a recent speech to the Chamber of Commerce, the president of Major Company stated that the implementation of proper control procedures is the foundation of sound management. He used as an example some of the controls implemented in the information systems area.

Some of the more important controls implemented by Major Company will be described briefly. All users of the system have a unique log-on identification number and must change their log-on password weekly. If the password is not changed, then they will be automatically denied access to their account. All confidential material is to be protected from even casual observation. This means, for example, that all output must be filed and locked when not in use, that terminals cannot be left unattended when logged onto the system, that tapes and diskettes are stored in secure locations, and that all confidential documents that are printed have the word *CONFIDENTIAL* in bold letters on each page of the document.

Access to data is determined by the data management group. A formal request must be made to access specific data. This request must detail why access is necessary, the type of access requested (read, write, etc.), the length of time for which access is necessary, and the security measures that will be employed by that individual to protect the data. There has been an increased emphasis at Major Company on more strictly limiting the access to company data. This has been a result of the increased use of microcomputers downloading data from the mainframe into their microsystems. It was found that while the security over data on the mainframe was excellent, the security over this same data stored on the micros was almost nonexistent.

Major Company has physically separate production and test environments. The system software environments of the two systems are identical. In fact, the test system is used as a backup facility to the production system in case of a major failure of that system.

Any programming change must be initiated by a request for system maintenance. This request must be approved before any modifications can be made to a program. After a system has been changed, the program maintenance supervisor must verify that all changes have been made and that the programs function correctly. At that time, the revised software is installed on the production system.

SUMMARY

As more important business functions are automated by using computers, the need for measures to insure security and integrity of the information system becomes more important. However, these security measures must be well thought out and implemented in an organized manner. Before establishing new security procedures or changing those already in place, it is necessary to evaluate the possible loss exposures. This analysis should indicate the areas of greatest concern.

While there are many procedures that can be used to assure system security and integrity, they are usually placed in the categories of either general controls or application controls. General controls establish policies and procedures that dictate how various functions should be performed. Application controls are those that are designed into the computer software. When properly designed, these controls are executed as the programs are run.

The internal audit group is an important security component in any organization. They should provide independent review of the security systems throughout the organization. Because of the increasing importance of the information system, the data processing area should involve the internal audit area in the design and implementation of controls.

No security system is perfect. In a sense, security measures are designed more to create a hindrance than an absolute barrier to those intent on defrauding the company. If someone wishes to put in sufficient time and effort, any security system can be broken. We must strive for a balance in which the controls are sufficient to discourage the dishonest, but not unduly impede operations.

QUESTIONS

1. Explain what loss exposures are and why it is important to ascertain exposures before investigating the security and integrity of a system.
2. Describe how one would go about ascertaining the probability and magnitude of a specific loss exposure. Give an example.

3. Are the magnitudes of loss exposures greater in a manual or EDP system? Why?

4. Are the probabilities of loss greater in a manual or EDP system? Why?

5. How do you calculate the expected loss of an exposure? How would you interpret this number, and how would it be used?

6. Certain industries and types of businesses have more loss exposures than others. Why is this so? Give some examples of businesses with high exposures and low exposures.

7. Why do companies segregate duties in a manual system? What duties should be segregated?

8. Give three different examples of how a programmer could perpetrate a fraud if allowed access to "live" data or programs.

9. Describe how test and production environments can be separated even though the physical computer facilities must be shared.

10. A computer operator wishes to advance in the company; hence she is taking a programming class at night. She requests that to get some practical experience, she be allowed to work part time in program maintenance and development while still holding the operator job. If you were the manager, would you allow her? Explain.

11. A tape librarian is given two weeks notice because of poor job performance. During this two-week period, he switches many of the external tape labels so that a large percentage of the library's tapes are incorrectly labeled. In this situation, is it possible for the company to correct this problem? How could have this situation been avoided?

12. Explain the differences between doing data backup in a batch versus an online environment.

13. Why would it be desirable to encrypt the system log-on password and access control tables?

14. During a routine check of the production runs made during the week, it is discovered that the program that processes customer credit ratings was run eight times instead of the normal seven times. Given some possible explanations of why this extra run was made. How could this situation be investigated in more detail?

15. It has been stated by some data center managers that the systems programming staff presents the single greatest security risk in a well-controlled data center. Explain why.

16. For each of the following situations, describe what controls may have either prevented or detected the problem.
    a. An employee runs the general ledger reporting system to print the company financial statements three days before the information is released to the public. This information allows the employee to make $10,000 by investing in the stock before the price goes up.
    b. A programmer accesses customer credit card information and sells this information to a local credit card fraud ring.

c.   An operator changes the Social Security number on a customer order so that another account is charged for the goods purchased.

d.   A programmer uses the computer system to develop software for another company.

e.   During a tour of the computer center, a visitor uses an unattended active terminal to access the system and erases a series of production programs.

17. While internal auditing deals with all aspects of the firm, it has increasing responsibility in the information systems area. Explain why.

CASE ANALYSIS

Case 1

Research a recent fraud or defalcation involving a computerized information system. Describe how this crime was perpetrated and explain why the controls that were in place did not detect or prevent the crime. Explain what controls could have been implemented to prevent this crime and how these controls would have operated in the specific situation.

Case 2

Investigate the ways in which examinations are composed, compiled, reproduced, proctored, and graded in your class. Describe what losses could occur and how they would be perpetrated. Describe the controls that are presently in place and what additional controls could be implemented. Lastly, explain how all of these aspects would change if each of the steps were computerized.

ADDITIONAL READINGS

ATKINS, WILLIAM. "Jesse James at the Terminal," *Harvard Business Review,* July-August 1985, p. 82.

BERMAN, ALAN. "Evaluating Online Computer Security," *Data Communications,* July 1983, pp. 145–152.

DAVIDSON, THOMAS, AND CLINTON WHITE. "How to Improve Network Security," *Infosytems,* June 1983, pp. 110–112.

FARHOOMAND, ALI, AND MICHAEL MURPHY. "Managing Computer Security," *Datamation,* January 1, 1989, p. 67.

FIDLOW, D. "A Comprehensive Approach to Network Security," *Data Communications,* Vol. 14, No. 4, April 1985, pp. 195–213.

KERR, SUSAN. "A Secret No More," *Datamation,* July 1, 1989, p. 53.

MAIR, WILLIAM, DONALD WOOD, AND KEAGLE DAVIS. *Computer Control and Audit,* 2nd Ed. Touche Ross and Company, 1976.

STATLAND, NORMAN. "Listen to Auditors Who Offer Low-cost Data Security Procedures," *Data Management*, May 1982; pp. 18–27.

STOLL, CLIFFORD. "Stalking the Wiley Hacker," *Communications of the ACM*, Vol. 31, No. 5, May 1988, pp. 484–497.

TATE, PAUL. "Risk: The Third Factor," *Datamation*, April 15, 1988, p. 58.

READINGS BEFORE NEXT CHAPTER

It would be advantageous to have knowledge of the application systems analysis and design cycle. If you have not already had a course dealing with this subject, there are many books that deal with systems analysis and design. One possible choice is *Information Systems: Theory and Practice,* by John Burch and Gary Grudnitski, 4th edition, John Wiley & Sons. Chapter 2 will give you a basic idea of the process.

12

MANAGING END-USER COMPUTING

INTRODUCTION

An important development affecting the structure and design of information systems is the increasing involvement of end-users in performing the traditional computing functions of designing, programming, installation, and manipulation of systems. This is termed *end-user computing (EUC)*. Users are provided with terminals, work stations, or personal computers and the appropriate software for accessing data, developing models, and performing information processing. This development, made possible by the increasing power and decreasing cost of the technology, is a significant force for change in the way information resources are organized, provided, and used within modern organizations.

End-user computing is expected to be the fastest growing area of computer use over the next few years. With the advent of microcomputers and end-user oriented software packages, the demand for access to corporate computing resources has taken on an influential role within modern organizations. Some experts project annual growth rates of 50% to 100% compared to 15% to 20% for traditional applications. This chapter provides a managerial view of the principal characteristics related to end-user computing within modern organizations. The challenge for information systems (IS) managers today is to satisfy the demands of these users while advancing a strategy for the management of end-user computing that will efficiently promote the competitive position of the organization.

EXAMPLES OF END-USER COMPUTING APPLICATIONS

Traditional computing involves users running programs primarily designed and implemented by the information system staff. The users enter data and receive a series of preprogrammed reports and results. The mode of operation can be either batch or interactive, but the alternatives available to the user are usually very limited. Additional data analysis beyond what is offered by the installed system is extremely difficult.

More advanced end-user computing involves creating an environment by which the users can exercise their imaginations and creativity to best accomplish the task at hand. Instead of having a prewritten system that performs a fixed series of tasks, the EUC environment offers a set of easy-to-use tools. The user can select any or all of these tools. The users have control over their computer environment. Often the end-users will independently store their own data and will not rely totally on the centralized database.

For an information system to be of maximum benefit to the company, it is necessary to have *both* traditional applications and the end-user environment. The traditional applications would deal with the routine operations of the firm. Some traditional applications include the receipt and entry of company orders, inventory management, production of goods, accounting applications, etc. These are all high-volume, production-oriented applications and are best designed by the professional programming staff. It certainly would not be appropriate for the accounts receivable clerks to handle data as they saw fit. Creative accounting is not an acceptable norm.

End-user tools are best employed when decision making and planning are involved. In these circumstances, it is necessary to examine data in many ways, making it very difficult to predetermine the methods to be used. For example, when doing budgeting it may be necessary to use different forecasting methods for different types of data. Multiple regression may be used to predict certain trends, while exponential smoothing may be used for others. Graphic display may be desirable in some instances but not others. For budgeting situations, the ability to change the numbers easily is also very helpful. The tools available in an EUC environment allow for this degree of flexibility, unlike a traditional environment.

CHARACTERIZATION OF USERS

In a modern organization, users of computer resources are a diverse set. There is no single, stereotypical end-user with a single, defined set of characteristics. End-user computing can be defined as the development and use of information systems by the users of the system products or by their support staff. For the director of an information system to best manage the system, it is necessary that there is an understanding of the needs of the users of the system. There exist different classifications of end-users. One possible categorization is to define four levels of users: (1) indirect end-users; (2) nonprogramming end-users; (3) information system professionals; and (4) direct end-users (see Figure 12.1).

The first three categories of users may be thought of as the traditional information system's user community. The indirect end-users are those individuals who request information from the information system staff but do not personally interact with the system. This group will include traditional managers that request the IS staff to produce custom reports and to do special programming tasks.

Nonprogramming end-users are those whose only access to computer-stored data is through software provided by others. For example, clerical workers accessing accounting databases, or travel agents requesting passenger reservations or flight information simply use the end product of the system. While most of these users will be totally reliant on the information system, they simply use it in a prespecified manner and do not really control their computing environment. It may be said that their jobs are instead controlled by the computer.

Both of the preceding groups rely on the information systems professional to do the design and programming of the system. The IS professional may be thought of as an internal user of the system while the other groups are external users. Because of the depth of expertise of the IS professional, the traditional computing tasks are best done by these people. They understand the intricacies of efficient storage and retrieval of data. For high-volume production jobs, the speed and efficiency of the system is extremely important. Also, to assure data integration of the various production systems, it is necessary to centralize or at least coordinate all development activities.

The final category of direct end-users is the new breed of users. They use the system without the intervention of the IS professional. They understand the ways to accomplish their tasks by directly using computer resources. Through end-user tools they are able to analyze data, prepare reports, and communicate results.

Figure 12.1 *End-User Categories*

CATEGORY	DESCRIPTION
Indirect End-Users	Use information generated from the IS but do not directly interact with system
Nonprogramming End-Users	Interact with system by entering data and getting results from production systems
Information System Professionals	Experts in systems analysis, design, and programming
Direct End-Users	Do their own programming and data analysis on the computer system using specially designed programming tools

The direct end-user will be involved in tasks that are programming oriented. However, the sophistication of the types of tasks they perform can be quite disparate. There are those end-user programmers who utilize both command and procedural languages directly for their own personal information needs. They develop their own applications, some of which are used by other end-users. For example, users working with specific quantitative tools and specialized applications such as actuaries, planners, financial analysts, and engineers write programs to perform specialized tasks that the IS department does not have the resources to produce in a timely fashion.

Also included in the direct end-user group are the command-level users who have a need to access data in their own ways. They perform simple inquiries often with a few simple calculations and generate unique reports for their own purposes. They understand the available database(s) and are able to specify, access, and manipulate information most often utilizing report generators. Also, they are willing to learn just enough about the database and the software to assist in the performance of their day-to-day jobs. Users working in functions such as personnel, accounting, or market research are able to maneuver through their respective databases performing ad hoc queries that aid in their decision making.

The needs of this direct user community can be as disparate as their level of sophistication. It is important to recognize this broad range of abilities and to design the information system in a manner that best services the entire user community.

FUNDAMENTAL ISSUES

Research on EUC suggests that there are at least four fundamental issues that IS managers need to address: support services, technology, data, and evaluation/planning. These four issues characterize the difficulties that are at the core of the end-user computing dilemma. Three of these issues deal with the infrastructures for technology, data, and support services that must be in place to facilitate the effective use of information systems by end-users. The last issue concerns the evaluation/justification and planning of EUC expenditures.

Support Services

The support structure for EUC concerns the ways in which the information systems area helps the users to employ the various end-user tools efficiently. If the information system manager is to understand end-user computing, it is important to know who the users are, where they are located, what they do, and what they need. End-user diversity creates a need for strongly differentiated education, training, and support for the quite different classes of users.

Before continuing our discussion, it is necessary to define the difference between education and training. Education involves an understanding of abstract theory; training involves gaining the skills necessary to accomplish a task. Under this viewpoint, training must be a key issue that IS management should address. Without adequate training, the users will not have the knowledge to use the technology to its maximum benefit.

There are several user training techniques that IS management can use to provide training programs to the end-user community—for example, (1) computer aided instruction (CAI), (2) courses, lectures, or seminars within the organization, (3) external training, (4) help systems software components, (5) interactive training manuals, (6) resident experts, and (7) tutorials (see Figure 12.2).

An alternative strategy that may reduce overall training costs is to designate an individual in each user department as a key end-user or functional support person. Each will receive intensive training, and then serve as the first source of support for the departmental trouble-shooting or problem solving. Also, they can hold classes that are smaller, less formal, and targeted at the unique needs of the department.

Key end-user or functional support personnel are sophisticated programmers supporting other end-users within their particular functional areas. These are individuals who, by virtue of their abilities in end-user programming languages, have become informal centers of systems design and programming expertise within their functional areas. They do not view themselves as programmers or data processing professionals. Rather, they are market researchers, financial analysts, and so forth, whose primary current task is providing tools and processes to get at and analyze data.

Figure 12.2   *Training Alternatives*

TRAINING METHOD	DESCRIPTION
Computer Aided Instruction	CAI involves interaction between the user and the computer so that the computer can "walk" the user through the lesson
Internal Seminars and Courses	On-site classes taught by resident experts
External Training	Many universities and private firms offer classes based on a per person fee
Help Systems Software Components	Facilities designed into systems that allow the user to have the computer give assistance on an interactive basis as needed
Interactive Training Manuals	Documentation stored on the computer that can be directly accessed
Resident Experts	Individuals intensively trained in a specific system
Tutorials	Self-study courses usually available from the vendor, these can include problems that must be solved using the computer

Figure 12.3 *Generations of Computer Languages*

GENERATION	DESCRIPTION
First Generation	Machine language–directly executable by the computer
Second Generation	Assembly language—low-level language similar to machine language but more understandable by humans, is transformed to machine language by an assembler program
Third Generation	High-level language which is procedural in format is transformed into machine language by a compiler, examples include COBOL, FORTRAN, PASCAL
Fourth Generation	High-level language which is nonprocedural, meaning that the programmer specifies what to do, not how to do it; most fourth generation languages are interpreted where source code is changed to machine code on a line-by-line interactive basis
Fifth Generation	The evolving languages that are based on natural languages such as English; the user can "talk" to the computer as one would to another person

On the other hand, information system end-user computing support personnel are most often located in a central support organization such as an information center. They are fluent in end-user languages, and, in addition to aiding end-users, also develop either application or support software. These individuals are available to the user community to answer questions, provide help, and demonstrate the capabilities of the various tools available.

Finally, there are data processing programmers who are similar to the traditional application development and maintenance programmers except that they program in end-user languages such as FOCUS, RAMIS II, EXPRESS, SQL, APL, IFPS, SAS, or SPSS to name just a few. These languages are also termed *fourth generation languages* (see Figure 12.3). This group of programmers will develop end-user applications that are beyond the technical ability of the typical user.

The basic idea of the support function is to make the user as productive as possible. Having the technology without providing the knowledge of how to best use it only results in an underutilization of the resources. Viewing the end-user as part of the information systems team helps to emphasize the important role the end-user has in a modern information system.

Technology

The technological issue includes decisions about the appropriate hardware, software, and communications equipment to best support the end-user. Care must be taken in the acquisition of new tools. In most instances, the cost to install a new product and teach the users how to use it far exceeds the initial cost of acquisition. The technology encompassed by these end-user tools is extremely broad, and there is a wealth of products available. Some of the functions that must be evaluated include office automation (OA), decision support systems (DSS), fourth generation languages, database management systems, statistical packages, and networking products, to name just a few.

Much of the hardware and software acquired for the end-user is not funded out of the information system's budget but out of the specific user's departmental budget. If the acquisition cycle was not in some way centrally controlled, there would be a proliferation of incompatible products and a tremendous amount of duplication of effort. For this reason, it is an important task of IS management to define corporate policies for acquisition of IS technology. In general, the diversity of equipment and software in use in many organizations suggests that standards are a major concern. IS management must define procedures to analyze, evaluate, and acquire hardware and software. This process should be in accordance with the general information system's architecture so as to maintain compatibility, connectivity, portability, and support for all of the products and services offered to the EUC community. Allied with the establishment of acquisition policies is the testing of hardware and software products. This is an important part of the acquisition cycle.

If the acquisitions control aspect of end-user computing is ignored, the organization will find itself with a plethora of incompatible software and hardware. This can cause duplication of effort, expensive inconsistencies among conceptually shared databases, and fragmentation of the incompatible functional units.

Data

The issues involved in properly managing data have become more complex with the rapid growth of end-user computing. The actual issues involved in data management have remained about the same. These still include questions about data standards, the accessibility of data, the sharing of data, the need for databases dealing with specific products, and security considerations. However, the number of individuals accessing and storing data has grown tremendously. This growth has made data management much more difficult. With only traditional computing, it was much easier to establish and enforce data standards. During this period, only the internal IS staff were allowed to develop and access databases.

The present end-user environment dictates that many different types of users be allowed to access and store data. The IS management must determine a policy that facilitates ease of access, but at the same time protects the data from damage and does not allow unauthorized users to access the data.

The issue of data security was discussed in the previous chapter. The remaining issues involved in data management will be addressed in depth in Chapter 15, so we will not discuss them further here.

Evaluation and Planning

The evaluation and justification of end-user computing within the organization is an important, ongoing task. Traditional cost/benefit analysis cannot always be used when trying to justify end-user computing. This is particularly true when a firm is first trying to introduce end-user tools. The start-up phase can be expensive and time consuming without initially showing great cost savings or productivity gains. Management must instead think of these start-up costs as fixed costs that will pay returns in the future.

The planning function is important since end-users need more than mere computer access. They need guidance, education, ongoing support, and state-of-the-art tools. It is the IS manager's responsibility to decide how to deliver and support these services using different approaches such as offering consulting, doing training, and helping to decide whether the applications are best run on mainframes, distributed systems, personal computers, or some combination thereof. IS management must maintain the balance between technology investments and user needs to support the products and services offered to the EUC community. Planning for the support and growth of these products and services (in accordance with the resources available within the organization) must be an important managerial task for the IS manager.

Planning also allows IS management to move more smoothly from one critical issue to another. As the end-user population grows in size and in understanding of how to use the technology successfully, IS management must be able to select and align its strategy to the relative importance of a particular issue.

STRATEGIES FOR END-USER COMPUTING

End-User Involvement

Throughout this chapter, we have pointed out the importance of user involvement in the information system. It must be remembered that, to the user, the information system is a critical component of much of the day-to-day operations of their office.

Historically, users have seen substantial portions of their budgets spent to support an information systems department that had a large backlog of requests and was not responsive to user suggestions, complaints, and inquiries. While users need regularly scheduled production systems to be run, they also need special one-time (ad hoc) reports to perform their duties.

The frustration of the end-user can be either heightened or lessened by the introduction of microcomputers and departmental distributed systems. If the proper end-user environment is not developed, then the level of frustration can actually increase. To develop this end-user environment, it is necessary to produce a well-thought-out strategic plan.

The question that must be answered is: What is the best strategy for involving the end-user in the computing process? It is probably obvious that each specific company will present a different set of circumstances. Hence, there is no single "best" way of dealing with this problem. We will discuss some different approaches that may be used when developing end-user strategies.

Strategic Alternatives

Two major issues must be addressed when examining end-user strategies. The first issue involves what specific strategy is to be implemented. The second issue determines when that strategy should be implemented. End-user computing, like any developing system, will grow through a series of stages. As the computing environment becomes more mature, it will become necessary to change the methods used as the user environment changes.

There are two extreme approaches to dealing with the end-user environment. On the one extreme, it is possible to adopt a hands-off approach in which no control is exerted over the computing done by the user. Hence, the user is free to acquire hardware and software and to design systems in any way he or she sees fit. This could be termed a *laissez-faire strategy.*

The other extreme is to dictate centralized control over all end-user decisions. In this way, all acquisitions and all system designs must be reviewed and accepted by a centralized authority. This approach could be termed the *fully centralized strategy.*

Both of these extremes have their shortcomings. The laissez-fiare approach does nothing either to encourage or promote the development and continuation of an end-user environment. As we have already discussed, because of the substantial time commitment, there is usually a good deal of inertia against users starting their own computing activities. In addition, the lack of any centralized planning can result in a proliferation of incompatible technologies.

The fully centralized approached is usually based on the premise that all computing activities must be controlled by a single organizational entity. This approach involves formal control procedures for reviewing and approving acquisitions and new projects. These procedures may necessitate full economic justification and a formal review of all activities. While this is a strong mechanism for standardization, it can have a detrimental effect on the growth of the end-user environment.

Most firms will adopt a series of strategies that are a compromise between these two extremes. These strategies will evolve as the characteristics of the end-user environment change. The way in which computing is done within a firm will change as both the technology and the sophistication of the end-users mature.

The beginning of user involvement is characterized by a lack of hardware, software, and end-user knowledge. The organization has realized that these tools exist and that they have the potential to produce impressive productivity gains. The firm is interested in implementing these tools, but has little or no experience in the area. In this phase it is important to get the technology to the users and to evaluate which ones are most effective. General management support must be given to a program to experiment with these tools and to get a base of satisfied users. The strategy at this point should not rely on cost justification or immediate productivity gains. Even standards are not as yet necessary since this may be viewed as only a feasibility study. To a certain extent, this is laissez-faire with substantial encouragement from central administration through adequate funding. Note that the scope of the activities will be limited until this phase is completed.

Once the feasibility phase is completed, management can begin to encourage widespread use of the technology. At this point, it is necessary to begin developing standards to avoid gross incompatibilities and to prevent duplication of effort. Also, support facilities should begin to be offered to the users in the form of training and help facilities. Usually this support is offered through the development of a centralized information center. We could term this the *development stage*.

Once a strong end-user environment has been established, it is desirable to have a strong infrastructure in place that supports the user. This includes a centralized function to coordinate end-user activities. In most firms this involves the strengthening of the information center. During this phase (let's term it the *growth stage*) it may be necessary for management to limit the spread of computing because of the lack of available resources. This may involve forcing users to cost-justify all expenditures.

When end-using computing reaches maturity, it should be treated like any other business function. That is, all acquisitions and new projects must be cost justified, and any existing functions are periodically reviewed. In some firms the level of sophistication of the users may be such that the function of the information center is changed substantially. Its primarily role will change from user support to evaluation of new technology and to review and establishment of hardware, software, data storage, and data access standards. End-user support will be shifted primarily to departmental key users and functional support personnel.

The aforementioned phases of end-user computing are reviewed in Figure 12.4.

INFORMATION CENTERS

To provide enhanced support to users, many firms are creating support groups called information centers (ICs). An information center is a group of programmer analysts who support end-user computing by offering suggestions related to hardware and software purchases, and by answering general inquiries related to computing. The information center has the responsibility of evaluating new software packages for possible corporate use and establishing training programs for new, in-house developed or purchased systems. It can become a very visible

Figure 12.4 *Phases of End-User Computing*

PHASE	DESCRIPTION	POSSIBLE STRATEGY
1. Feasibility	Evaluation of possible technology	Limited laissez-faire with top-management support
2. Development	Introduction of technology to the general user	Development of support facilities and technology standards
3. Growth	Proliferation of technology with goal of sophisticated users	Stricter control of resource acquisition and usage
4. Maturity	Strong base of sophisticated users	Managed like any business unit—primary support at departmental level

arm of the data processing shop and improve the morale and goodwill of all those associated with computing.

The concept of an information center was originally devised to reduce the applications backlog. This was to be accomplished by distributing many of the more elementary tasks to the users, allowing the development staff to design the complex systems. The general idea was to give the users the tools and the knowledge to do high-level computing. This involved the concepts of training the users, giving the users guidance and help in developing their own applications, and aiding the users in obtaining the right hardware and software to accomplish those objectives.

In reality, the information center has become substantially more than its original concept. In the beginning concept, the information center was to service users of the mainframe system, involving only those tools available on mainframes and in a totally centralized environment. With the rapid acceptance of micros, especially by the user community, information centers have evolved with a much broader scope. They deal with all types of computer technology including micros, minis, mainframes, and the associated software. In fact, information centers tend to lean more heavily toward the micro arena. The reason for the emphasis on micros is that they are an easy means of introducing computer technology to the uninitiated.

The concept behind an information center and the degree of success that most organizations have experienced are so strong that most firms are compelled to implement an information center. However, this decision should not be taken lightly. An information center can have a substantial impact on an organization. As discussed, it can have a broad range of benefits, but it can also affect both the staffing of the entire information system and the utilization of the computing resources.

The benefits of instituting an information center can be many. The productivity of the user community will usually increase substantially. The reasons for this productivity increase include the faster turnaround time in getting results, being able to get services not offered by the traditional information system, and having more control over the computing environment. Managers are able to make higher-quality decisions based on more current information because of the direct access they have to the data. Previously, it would have been necessary to make a formal request to have specific information gathered. The information center gives the end-user the capability to do much of this work.

In addition, an information center will increase the productivity of the information system's applications program development and maintenance staff. The main reason for this is that the information center will be able to handle most user questions, leaving the application maintenance and development staff to concentrate on their primary assignments without interruption. As users become more computer literate, they will be able to do some of the tasks that were previously done by the development staff. Probably the greatest benefit to the information system personnel is the increased understanding of the capabilities and limitations of computers by these users. This will ultimately result in the design of higher-quality systems, for the end-users will be able to contribute more to the entire analysis and design process.

On the negative side, for the information center to be a success it is necessary to place some of the most productive staff members in the center. The reason for this is that not only must these individuals have a broad technical background, they must have well-developed interpersonal skills. In some cases, staffing the information center critically weakens the maintenance and development staff. Also, as more novice users enter the system, there will be added demand on the computing resources. While this demand is warranted if the users are working efficiently, often inappropriate actions are taken by these newer users. For example, a user may do an ad hoc query to a data file that forces an exhaustive sequential search through that file. If the file is large, this simple query may consume an inordinate amount of resources. However, a similar query that is based on an inverted key may consume only a tiny fraction of the resources of the other query. Only the more sophisticated user would be able to differentiate these two cases.

Figure 12.5 summarizes the previous discussion concerning the value and possible pitfalls of implementing an information center.

Implementing the Information Center

The motivation for many ICs comes from the users themselves, particularly in instances where users feel that the IS staff is not providing adequate service. When implementing an information center, IS managers can use the IC as the center of the strategy to support and manage the end-user needs. There is no set body of rules for implementing information centers. Each organization has its own specific requirements, and each IC varies accordingly.

Figure 12.5   *Advantages and Disadvantages of Information Centers*

ADVANTAGES OF AN INFORMATION CENTER

Off-loads some of the development work into the user areas

Reduces the number of interruptions of the software application maintenance staff

Makes users more computer literate

Helps reduce the applications backlog in the development area

Allows users to get answers to questions much more quickly

DISADVANTAGES OF AN INFORMATION CENTER

Users consume tremendous amounts of computer resources

Removes some of the most highly qualified individuals from the systems development area to work in the information center

As with all functional units within an organization, clear direction is mandatory. There should be a formal statement of goals and objectives of the IC. From these goals and objectives, a formal control policy and a set of procedures can be derived. These should provide specific limits on authority of users and the IC, specifically as to how each will interact with other corporate resources. Finally, methods for continually improving EUC effectiveness and efficiency should be established. These can then be used as guidelines for future development and as a measure of the success of the current situation.

The process of starting an IC can be viewed as developing any system. Using this viewpoint, Figure 12.6 presents the basic phases of this process.

It is always necessary to analyze a problem thoroughly before attempting to solve it. This is particularly true when dealing with an information center. Almost all organizations will have some end-user computing already in place before an IC is started. Knowing the limit of this technology will establish a good starting point for the planning process.

The planning phase is obvious. This will dictate what other phases are to be implemented, the degree of implementation, and when they will be implemented. It is usually best to start the IC slowly. This will give the organization time to test ideas and time to build a competent staff.

The full implementation stage is the point in which the IC becomes accessible to the entire firm. This can be the point of greatest expenditure since the IC now has responsibility for introducing computer technology throughout the firm. Not only will the hardware and software be expensive, but the costs of training and maintenance will be substantial.

After end-user technology has become widespread, the role of the IC will begin to concentrate on helping users efficiently use the available resources

Figure 12.6 *Implementing an Information Center*

PHASE	ACTIONS
1. Inventory Present Position	Determine present hardware, software, networking expertise, and user base.
2. Develop Plan	Project what strategic steps to take in the future and how long each will last.
3. Pilot Study	Offer services to a limited number of users; during this phase different vendors and technologies can be tried before standards are adopted.
4. Full Implementation	Establish standards and begin introducing end-user computer technology throughout the firm; this phase must heavily emphasize training.
5. Maintain and Grow	This is the stable environment phase in which growth is more controlled and emphasis shifts to helping users with problems.
6. Phase in New System	There must be a point in which the firm has outgrown the need for an information center, or this function can be assumed by other areas in the organization.

and on maintaining those resources. As in any system, there comes a time when the present way of doing things becomes outmoded. The information center is no exception. Of course, most firms are not even close to reaching the end-user maturity that is involved in this final phase.

The structure of the information center will be determined by the structure of the firm and the related information system. There are some functions that are common to most information centers. They include:

1. *Management of the IC:* This includes planning, control, budgeting, evaluation, and staffing. This position should report directly to the IS manager.
2. *Training Personnel:* These individuals will work directly with the users to familiarize them with center products, software packages, procedures, or the use of any end-user technology. These people will have to be able to communicate with the users in such a way as to make complex issues understandable.
3. *Consultants:* They will work with users who need to develop a specific application or to formulate a report using the end-user tools. Also, consultants assist the user in choosing the right product or software to meet the needs of specific users. In particular, the consultants should have the ability and capability to detect problems and solve them quickly. In some cases, consultants act as a liaison to fulfill the communication gap between users and IS staff.
4. *Technical Support:* These people will maintain the equipment in the IC and are responsible for diagnosing malfunctions and making repairs. In addition, these technicians manage the operating and telecommunication system environments.
5. *Product Evaluation:* These individuals will usually have experience as training

personnel, consultants, or both. Their function is to evaluate the acceptability of new products and technologies. Based on their recommendations, new products will be added to the list of acceptable goods and old products will be dropped. In some instances, they will have to recruit users to do field tests of the goods.

Skills to assist end-users are vastly different from skills required to design and program systems within the IS organization. For example, end-user support personnel must focus on end-use, not on technology. In addition, because support personnel provide expert advice, they must not only be knowledgeable of a wide spectrum of new tools and techniques, but they must also have the desire and the skills to teach and help the EUC community.

SPECIAL END-USER ENVIRONMENTS

There are special types of systems that have been developed to support specific classes of end-users. One of these is termed *decision support systems (DSS)*. These are systems designed to aid the individual manager in making quality decisions. These types of systems are particularly helpful in dealing with problems that are ill structured—that is, problems in which it is difficult to determine the behavior of the variables involved and even difficult to determine exactly what variables are important.

Figure 12.7 shows the major components of a DSS. The manager (the user) will communicate to the system through a common user interface. This is simply a set of screens that allows the manager to use the system. There are three repositories of data: the database, the model base, and the knowledge base. The database is typically a relational database containing the corporate data. The model base is a series of skeleton programs that allow the manager to create and change system models. The knowledge base contains parameters which describe the behavior of various systems. These parameters are derived from the manager's practical experience and help define limits to problems.

An example may be helpful. A manager observes that sales have been falling recently and wants to determine why this is happening. The database of the DSS would contain all of the historical sales data, inventory data, production data, etc. In addition, the database could contain local, regional, and national economic data and forecasts. The model base contains skeleton IFPS (Interactive Financial Planning System) and SAS (Statistical Analysis System) programs (both of these products can be used in modeling) that allow the manager to create computer models of consumer demand, production schedules, shipping projections, etc. The assumptions behind each of these models can be easily changed so that many alternative patterns can be examined. The knowledge base contains information concerning the seasonality of sales, the practical limits on production capacity, the anticipated turnover of the sales force, etc. The manager can use the DSS to explore various scenarios to determine the underlying cause of the decrease in sales and then take the appropriate action.

Figure 12.7 *Decision Support Systems Components*

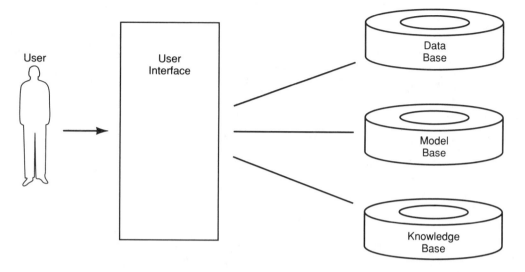

Studies have shown that DSS allows the manager to examine more thoroughly a problem and experiment with many different solutions. This tends to give the manager more confidence in the decision. But, due to the multitude of possibilities to explore, it usually does not make the decision process any quicker.

Also included in decision support systems are group decision support systems (GDSS). These systems are designed to allow a freer exchange of ideas when a group is trying to make decisions. Figure 12.8 shows how a typical GDSS may be organized. Each individual has access to a DSS, as described previously. There is a moderator (also sometimes called a chauffeur) who coordinates the sessions. Each user can send messages, screens, or register a vote. All of these activities are anonymous. In this way peer pressure and political influence can be reduced, hopefully allowing everyone to be involved in the decision-making process.

An extension and refinement of the idea behind decision support systems is that of executive information systems (EIS). These types of systems are designed for high-level management where the primary means of control had been only by exception reporting. An EIS allows the user to look at many levels of data abstraction. At the highest level, the executive may look at a corporate summary report. However, data can also be obtained by division, department, function, individual employee, or by a single transaction. In this way an executive can obtain data concerning all aspects of the organization in the degree of detail desired. In addition, an EIS has an external database which contains current information that the executive may use. This could include *The Wall Street Journal*, New York Stock Exchange quotes, leading economic indicators, etc. These sources can then be searched electronically when researching a problem.

Figure 12.8   *Group Decision Support System Configuration*

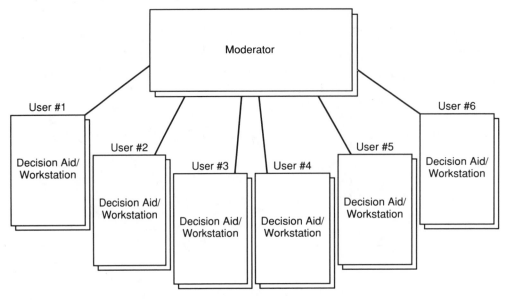

Executive information systems are usually tailor-made to fit a specific situation. They can be powerful tools when used properly. However, because of their unique nature, they can be rather expensive.

Another specialized type of end-user system is the expert system. This provides a means by which some of the knowledge of a group of experts can be stored and later used to help make decisions. The system can then be used by individuals who are not experts in the field to help solve problems.

Again, an example may be helpful. A company has a series of retail outlets. It has been determined that the inventory carrying costs at these outlets has been much too high. However, one outlet manager has continually had less than half the inventory carrying costs of any other outlet without any detrimental impact on sales. This manager is an "expert" when dealing with outlet inventory. This person can then be interviewed, and the fundamental decision rules can be determined. These rules can be imbedded in an expert system, and this system can then be distributed to all of the other outlet managers to assist them in making inventory decisions.

MAJOR COMPANY

In the area of end-usuer computing, Major Company had some problems. A few years back, there was a major applications development backlog problem. The users found that it was taking an inordinate amount of time to have even a simple computing request satisfied. In response to this, some of the user areas acquired their own independent computing resources. Since these acquisitions were made without any central coordination, there was a tremendous amount of variability between the systems owned by each department.

When the new equipment was first installed in each department, the users were very satisfied. For the few employees that were given the new technology, they were able to do more work faster. As more equipment was acquired, problems began. The initial equipment was given to employees who wanted to be introduced to the new technology. Subsequently, the additional equipment was distributed by functional area. Many of this new set of users complained that they did not have time to learn the new systems and that these systems were just too complicated. In addition, the original end-users wanted now to exchange data and programs with users in other departments and were very anxious to access data from the corporate databases on the mainframe. These capabilities were not available.

Management became concerned by the substantial expenditures going into these acquisitions and rising level of dissatisfaction. A task force was formed to investigate the problem. Fortunately, the task force members had enough insight not to limit the investigation to only the end-users, but included the entire information system. The preliminary results were disturbing. It was found that at least 15 different, incompatible systems existed in the user community. Also, on the average, 28% of all of user systems were lying idle, and a much higher percentage were grossly underutilized.

The committee concluded that there were two major causes for the problems. The first cause was the acquisition of inappropriate or outmoded hardware and software. The second cause was the total lack of any training facilities to introduce users to the new technology. The task force also cited the lack of cooperation by the information systems area. The general attitude of the IS area was that all of these end-user systems were maverick systems for which the IS area had no responsibility. Hence, IS made no attempt to help these users learn how to use the systems and would not connect these systems to the main production system.

The recommendation of the task force was that the information system be reorganized to serve its users better. Part of this reorganization included the establishment of an information center.

So as not to put an undue load on the information system area, only one department and higher management were served by the information center in its first year of operation. Hence, it was considered a pilot project that allowed the staff to implement the concept slowly. This also allowed the staffing of the information center without adversely impacting the system development and maintenance staff.

The reason for including higher management in the pilot period was to show them the productivity gains that were possible through end-user computing. It was also believed that top management support was critical to the success of the IC, and this was the best way to develop that support. During the pilot period, no controls were placed on the other user areas, but the managers in those areas were advised that within a year standards would be established. It was suggested that new technology be acquired in these areas only if absolutely necessary.

At the end of that first year, higher management concluded that the information center was an excellent way to increase general productivity throughout the firm. The information center was given sufficient staff and budget to service the entire organization. In addition, the IC was given a directive to develop acquisition and development standards for the entire organization. Any hardware or software not meeting these standards was to be phased out over the next year. While this appeared to be a costly solution to the compatibility problem, in the long run the savings in training costs alone would pay for the change.

During this growth phase, departments were encouraged to request new systems. The information center was to pay for all of these acquisitions. The only strings attached to the acquisition by a department was that the users of the new equipment had to attend the training classes involving that technology.

The character of the information center changed in the next year to that of coordinator. At this point, the funding for new systems was evaluated on its merit, and only those projects that made business sense were funded.

At present, Major Company feels its end-user computing is on track. Productivity gains have been impressive, and the users seem to be quite satisfied with their systems. There is still much room for improvement. Only a small number of users can be described as sophisticated users. Most departments do not have key users or resident experts. The IC is still concentrating on training the less experienced users in using the elementary tools.

QUESTIONS

1. What is the difference between traditional computing and end-user computing? Why is this an important difference?
2. Why would end-users wish to do some of their work without the assistance of systems analysts and application programmers?
3. Why would end-users wish to have systems analysts and application programmers assist them in doing some of their work?
4. What factors involved in a person's job dictate whether it will be advantageous to employ end-user tools?
5. In what ways would end-user training differ from the training given to the information system specialist? Explain how this would affect the types of training methods used for both groups.
6. Explain why the proper management of data is of critical importance in an end-user environment. Give some examples of how mismanagement of data can be harmful.
7. In many firms EUC was started by the user community and not by the information system organization. Explain why this happened. If it started

in the user community, should the IS function begin to adopt it? Why or why not?

8. Many users desire a laissez-faire approach to managing end-user computing. Why might this be the case? Is this a good approach?

9. List the five generations of programming languages and give examples of each.

10. When starting an information center, why might it be desirable to limit the scope of the center to a small part of the user community during the initial start-up phase? How would you select the part of the user community to be serviced first?

11. Many employees are afraid of change, especially changes in their jobs that involve computerization. Why is this so? Explain how introducing end-user tools may affect an individual in an office environment.

12. What types of standards should be established when dealing with end-user computing? Explain why each standard is important.

ADDITIONAL READINGS

ALAVI, M., R. R. NELSON, AND I. R. WEISS. "Strategies for End-User Computing: An Integrative Framework," *Journal of Management Information Systems*, 1987–1988.

ALAVI, MARYAM, AND IRA R. WEISS. "Managing the Risks Associated with End-User Computing," *Journal of Management Information Systems*, Vol. 2, No. 3, Winter 1985–86, pp. 5–20.

CARR, HOUSTON, H. "Information Centers: The IBM Model vs. Practice," *MIS Quarterly*, Vol. 11, No. 3, September 1987, pp. 325–338.

HAMMOND, L. W. "Management Considerations for an Information Center (IC)," *IBM Systems Journal*, Vol. 21, No. 2, 1982, pp. 131–161.

HUFF, SID L., MALCOLM C. MUNRO, AND BARBARA H. MARTIN. "Growth Stages of End User Computing," *Communications of the ACM*, Vol. 31, No. 5, May 1988, pp. 542–551.

NELSON, R. R., AND P. H. CHENEY. "Training End Users: An Exploratory Study," *MIS Quarterly*, Vol. 11, No. 4, December 1987, pp. 547–559.

RIVARD, SUZANNE, AND SID L. HUFF. "Factors of Success for End User Computing," *Communications of the ACM*, Vol. 31, No. 5, May 1988, pp. 562–561.

WHITE, C. E., AND D. P. CHRISTY. "The Information Center Concept: A Normative Model and a Study of Six Installations," *MIS Quarterly*, Vol. 11, No. 4, December 1987, pp. 451–458.

READINGS BEFORE NEXT CHAPTER

The previous material should be adequate preparation.

13

MANAGING APPLICATION PROGRAMMING

INTRODUCTION

The development and maintenance of applications software is one of the more difficult tasks faced by data processing management. This difficulty arises because the design and creation of such systems represents the management and control of artistic talent in an advanced technological medium. Data processing managers encounter problems guiding and nurturing the creative energies of their system development staffs. In addition, most programs are written and maintained for functional areas other than data processing. Consequently, the manager is controlling a project that is funded by, or needed by, someone else. The result is that the manager is faced with the dilemma of directing a creative process to meet deadlines and budget constraints.

The unrealistic or overoptimistic estimation of a software development project's completion time and cost has been a serious problem for most data processing operations. Missed deadlines and budget overruns cause much friction between the user community and the information systems area. Add to this the high likelihood of poor communication of the necessary attributes of the desired system between the users and the development team, and problems become even more severe.

The task is not finished when the development project is completed. System maintenance is just as vital a component to successful system performance as was the initial design that formed the system. In fact, studies have shown that many large organizations spend from 50% to 90% of their annual programming budgets on the maintenance of existing programs. Stated simply, a poorly designed system can become more expensive the longer it is used. However, after completion of a system project, many programmer/analysts want to move on to new assignments. The job of maintaining the system then falls on the shoulders of another group whose task is to shepherd another's creation, rather than create their own. This often is viewed as onerous duty and is relegated to those with little seniority. As could be expected, morale in the maintenance programming department can become quite low. Consequently, the successful management of the application development effort must be concerned with the creation of well-structured, maintainable code.

To make matters worse end-users are demanding more and more information from existing and new systems. This is creating a backlog of requests for application system investigation. Studies have shown that the average number of lines of code written per day by a programmer over the life of a project is 8 to 12. This figure seems astonishingly low because it includes time spent in development meetings, user interviews, and, hopefully, documentation. While there have been dramatic developments in the efficiency of hardware systems, similar advances have not occurred in application software development productivity. Hence, the backlog of requests continues to grow, often at an increasing rate. This is a problem that information system management must come to grips with before data processing will reach its true potential in most firms.

In this chapter, we will look into the problem of application programming management. We will discuss the area of new program development and see what tools and techniques are available for new system development. Next, we will look at the problem of maintenance programming and discuss how certain problems in this area can be handled. As always, we will conclude with an example tying these concepts together in Major Company.

SYSTEM DEVELOPMENT

In this section, we will address the issues involved in managing the development process. These include estimating the time and cost of the development project, evaluating the performance of the individuals involved in development, methods of guaranteeing user involvement, ways of assuring quality control, and other related issues. It is assumed that the reader has at least a familiarity with the steps involved in system analysis and design.

Information systems exhibit a life cycle much like that of a new product or a living organism (see Figure 13.1). Application system development is just one phase within this cycle. This life cycle is important to the data processing manager because it provides a framework around which resources can be allocated and budgets estimated. For example, a major system that has been in use for quite some time might need to be replaced soon, necessitating the allocation of resources for the project. For these reasons, managers should chart the life cycles of each of the major systems under development or in use.

Figure 13.1   *The System Life Cycle*

PHASE	DISCUSSION
Problem Recognition	The need for a new system is recognized, usually by the user area.
System Development	Systems analysis, design, and programming are done.
System Installation	The new system is installed and run on a test basis and then put into production.
System Operation	This is a mature system. It is run in production mode, and necessary maintenance is performed to keep it operational.
Obsolescence	It is no longer feasible to continue to operate the system, and it must be replaced.

The first phase is associated with the recognition of a need or problem. For example, a cursory analysis of the accounts receivable function indicates that the average age of an account balance is 10 weeks. Compared to other companies in the industry, this collection period is unnecessarily long. Because of the high volume of orders processed weekly and the antiquated nature of the software system, aggressive balance collection is hampered, thus tying up a portion of the firm's capital. The operations involved in accounts receivable must be analyzed to determine if there is a reasonable solution to the collection delay. This phase normally is not under the control of the information systems department, but is usually initiated in the user area. The user, after some investigation, submits a formal request for analysis to initiate development of a new system to the director of information systems. An example of this type of request was shown in Figure 10.2 in Chapter 10.

The second phase is system development. The system development life cycle, discussed in greater detail later, encompasses the set of procedures used to analyze, design, and develop an information system. Entire courses are devoted to systems analysis and design, and indeed most management information system curricula are focused on this phase.

The next phase is system installation. This important step is often discussed as the final step in system development and represents the point when a system actually comes into use. System installation is a phase of great visibility for the information systems department and should be approached cautiously.

Phase four represents system operation. In this phase, the developed system is in routine use and changes to the system comprise system maintenance. Maintenance programming can be a very costly activity and symbolizes a point of great savings to the organization if it can be managed properly.

Finally, a system becomes obsolete. When changes in procedure or technology make maintaining a system too expensive or unnecessary, the system falls into disuse and may be replaced by a new system. There is a point in time in which the continued maintenance of a system is no longer cost-effective. However, the pressures on the development staff caused by the applications backlog may be such that a system is kept well past its useful life. This is a self-destructive situation that consumes increasing resources to maintain obsolete systems, reducing the staff available for new development. These old systems, if well designed and maintained, can provide fertile learning grounds for new system development and should be stored for future examination. It is possible that portions of the old system could be extracted for later inclusion in new systems.

The systems life cycle has five very distinct phases when viewed over time. Keeping in mind that information systems are created to meet a need, it makes sense that, unless the organization is operating in a very static environment, the use of the system is going to change. This life cycle represents a method of anticipating these changes and managing resources to meet these conditions.

THE SYSTEM DEVELOPMENT LIFE CYCLE

The development of an application software system, which is the second phase in the system life cycle, can be partitioned into four distinct phases.

1. Understand the Problem
   a. Feasibility Analysis
   b. Requirements Definition
2. Formulate the Solution
   a. Preliminary Design
   b. Detailed Design
3. Build the Solution
   a. Construction and Verification
   b. Integration and Validation
4. Install the Solution
   a. Installation and User Acceptance
   b. Maintenance and Support

We will use the system development life cycle to point to areas where management attention is necessary. Remember that management can halt the development of the new system at any point. They have the final authority to start and stop a project, and its success is ultimately their responsibility. Just as a team of analysts and end-users investigates and designs the proposed system, and a team of programmers develops and tests the system, a team of managers must manage the overall system development. This management team is composed of end-users, data processing managers, and usually a representative from the internal audit staff. This team has the responsibility of planning, organizing, directing, controlling, and evaluating the information system.

DETERMINING FEASIBILITY

When a user makes a request to the applications programming department for the creation of a new system, the staff will form an initial team to identify and document the request in such a manner as to quantify its feasibility. The initial team is charged with the duty of collecting information about the proposed system to determine whether it is feasible to create and use this system. Not all requests can or should be satisfied.

During the feasibility study, it is necessary to examine the various approaches to solving the problem. This involves knowing about the technical, economic, legal, operational, and schedule environments. This relates to environmental scanning, which was discussed when addressing strategic issues. It is very important that feasibility issues are resolved before extensive analysis and design work is invested on the problem. Too often, the benefits of the system are overestimated. This results in a general dissatisfaction by upper management when anticipated cost savings or revenue increases do not materialize. The first step in the analysis phase is to conceptualize the problem accurately. Many projects have gone to completion, much to the users' dissatisfaction, without having the development team clearly understand the nature of the problem. This will involve much time and effort and requires substantial cooperation between the end-user area and the investigative team.

The feasibility study gives us the basis for deciding to develop a new system. The time and effort spent here will reap returns later in the project. Now let's look at the different areas of feasibility.

Technological feasibility is concerned with whether the proposed system can be created using current technology, hardware, or software. Under certain circumstances, it may be determined that being an innovator in a new area may be worth the costs and risks. This usually occurs when management discerns that a competitive advantage could be gained from the new system or that this system could be sold to other companies.

Economic feasibility is a clear concept. The team must determine whether the new system will be worth the investment of necessary resources. The determination of costs and benefits is important here; however, the specific cost estimates for detailed analysis are often not immediately available at this point. Some attempt must be made to derive a realistic estimate of the costs and the benefits. There are, however, some situations where cost-benefit analysis is unnecessary. If the development of the system is prompted to be in compliance with the laws or regulations in a jurisdiction, the organization may reap no benefits at all (other than staying out of jail and/or not paying fines).

Businesses become more regulated during certain political climates than others. Because of this, it is necessary to consider the legal ramifications of the design and development of certain types of information systems. Legal feasibility may be affected by legislation such as the Fair Credit Reporting Act of 1971, the Right to Financial Privacy Act of 1978, and the Electronic Funds Transfer Act of 1978. It is expected that the Information Age will see increased legislation affecting the use of computers in day-to-day business. Many large firms routinely retain the services of lawyers to investigate the consequences of proposed systems.

Operational feasibility helps determine whether the proposed system will function properly within the current structure of the organization and the information system. The new system may recommend the restructuring of a department within the organization. Additional personnel may need to be hired, or perhaps employees might be displaced from their current positions. This is often the most difficult aspect of feasibility to evaluate.

Finally, schedule feasibility is used to determine when the proposed system might be ready for implementation. With the growing backlog of requests for new systems, the information systems department may not be able to begin work on this system for some time, which may be cause for the consideration of other alternatives, such as the hiring of a consultant or reorganization of priorities of other projects. Of course, there is the possibility of purchasing the system from a vendor. At this point, there usually is not enough information available to decide whether to build or buy. However, the feasibility of acquiring the system from a vendor should be investigated. The types of feasibility are summarized in Figure 13.2.

If a project is deemed to be feasible, then an expanded analysis team must be selected. The constitution of this team will often determine the success of the project. The investigative team is normally composed of three groups. The first group comes from end-user management. It is important that the requesting department be involved with the development of the system from the beginning. Systems analysts and information systems department management form the second group. Finally, an independent representative of the organization's general management, usually a member of the internal audit staff, should be included to facilitate communication among and between the investigative team and management and to help assure the quality and auditability of the system.

The requirements definition phase embodies a more detailed study of the system. This includes specification of user interfaces, delineation of system

Figure 13.2 *Types of Feasibility*

FEASIBILITY	DISCUSSION
Technical	Examination of available hardware and software
Economic	Determination of costs and benefits of proposed system
Legal	Evaluation of coexisting and proposed legislation to determine impact on proposed system
Operational	Examination of present system to determine if this new system can be supported
Schedule	Analysis of deadlines to determine if system can be completed within acceptable time limits

functions, and data flow requirements for the system. Management reassesses the costs and benefits of the project and designs a strategic "plan of attack" for the subsequent phases. This strategic plan is a long-range plan for the development, implementation, and maintenance of the system. One common component of this plan may be a Gantt or PERT/CPM chart detailing the stages in the development process. This plan should also include detailed estimates of all the necessary resources, including personnel, computer resources, and all expenditures.

This will usually be the point where the decision must be made to purchase the system from a vendor or develop it internally. Too often there is the temptation to design and implement the system internally without considering the acquisition option. Unfortunately many times the development process is begun and after the expenditures of considerable effort, it is decided that the best alternative is to acquire an existing product. Not only is this a waste of resources, but it almost always involves time and budget overruns.

ESTIMATING RESOURCES

One of the most difficult tasks for the manager of a development project is to estimate the resources needed to complete the project (see Figure 13.3). This entails estimates of the length of time, the number of employees, and the cost for each of the development phases. The major difficulty lies in the relative uniqueness of most application systems. In addition, the true requirements of a system may not be completely known until well into the development process.

However, often an estimate of these resources must be made during the feasibility phase. The managers of user departments will want cost and time estimates before committing to a project. Also, if consultants are involved, it will be necessary to negotiate compensation, usually based on these estimates.

For many projects, the estimation process is an iterative one. Rough estimates are first made during the feasibility study and then refined through

Figure 13.3   *Necessary Project Estimates*

ESTIMATE	DESCRIPTION
Budget	Evaluate all costs involved in the project, including personnel, hardware, and software. This must be done for each phase of the project.
Personnel	Estimate the employees needed in each stage of the development. The necessary employee skills must be described for each stage.
Schedule	Determine the length of time for each event involved in the development of the system. This would include the scheduling of personnel.

the analysis and design phases. Most managers find estimation of costs, manpower, and completion schedules are complicated by many different factors. Figure 13.4 shows some of the factors that must be considered.

One of the key elements in developing sound estimates is to have access to historical data on previous projects. This means that it is necessary to measure and record the actual performance compared to the estimated performance at various milestones for each project. The more complete this information is, the more valuable it will be in estimating future project costs and schedules.

Much theoretical work has been done on software project estimation. While formulas and algorithms have been derived from this work, most managers still reply on using personal experience as the basis for project estimates. By referring to historical information and considering each of the various factors involved in a project, an informed judgment can be made.

In most situations the project manager will have to estimate both project time and resources. Typically, time estimation falls into two groups. First, requirement estimation provides an estimate of how much time will be required to complete the project. For example, a manager might estimate that a project will take 16 person-months, plus or minus 3 person-months to complete. The second

Figure 13.4 *Factors Affecting Software Estimation*

FACTOR	DESCRIPTION
Personnel Skill Levels	The technical ability of the employees can have a significant influence on project cost and completion time.
Application Complexity	Obviously, projects with more complex logic and data structures will require more effort.
Project Size	The cost and duration of a project may not be a linear function of project size. Very large projects may take substantially more resources.
User Cooperation	Helpful users can increase the productivity of all concerned.
Available Technology	Having the right development tools can greatly affect productivity.
Previous Similar Experience	Valuable lessons are learned by working on similar projects.
Required System Reliability	Errors in some systems may simply be an annoyance, while in others an error could be life threatening. More effort must be expended with an increased need for reliability.
Time Deadlines	Extreme time pressures can cause gross inefficiencies.

Figure 13.5   *Project Completion Estimates*

		COST	TIME
1.	Understand the Problem	3%	10%
2.	Formulate the Solution	18%	25%
3.	Build the Solution	40%	35%
4.	Implement the Solution	39%	30%

type is constraint estimation. Constraint estimation involves the estimation of project completion based on a constraint external to the development of the system. An example of constraint estimation would be the deadline imposed by a new piece of legislation or the release date for a new product. Constraint estimation is very stressful because the project completion date is not controlled by the development staff but by some external agency.

One way of estimating the total project time and resources is to extrapolate from the time and money spent on the initial phases of development. For example, similar projects in the firm have shown that the preliminary analysis and feasibility study make up approximately 3% of total project expenditures and 10% of total project time. The estimates for each stage are shown in Figure 13.5. Using these estimates, it is possible to estimate total project cost and time.

Using the data in Figure 13.5, if it took one person-month to understand the problem at an estimated cost of $3,000 then the entire project is expected to take 10 person-months at an approximate cost of $100,000. It should be noted that these figures are estimates for building a new system rather than purchasing one. Since this will vary from firm to firm, it is important that the company tracks these statistics and investigates the reasons for significant deviations from the expected values.

At this point, the team will recommend whether the new system is feasible, and whether any more resources should be devoted to its investigation. They may request that a more detailed study be made of the problem or recommend postponing the development, perhaps indefinitely.

MONITORING PROGRESS

Before discussing the next step in the development process, it is important to talk about the control aspects of a project. As we just stated, it is difficult to estimate the time and resources needed to complete a system. Delays and cost overruns can at least be foreseen if the project is properly monitored during its development cycle. To do this, there must be a formal set of review procedures established for all projects.

The use of structured analysis and design techniques is an excellent mechanism by which to control a development project. While we describe the analysis and design process as a series of distinct steps, in reality many of these steps can overlap and be poorly defined. A structured analysis and design approach assures that one step is completed and reviewed before the next step is authorized. The more formal the review process, the more control there will be over the project. A formal review will usually entail a structured walkthrough. This is where the completed work of the specific project phase is presented for peer review. The details of the process are explained and any problems are resolved before proceeding to the next phase.

Structured methods and walkthroughs are powerful tools for managing development projects. They give a definitive beginning and end to each phase of the process. This allows for better determination of development progress. Also, the sharp boundaries between phases makes it easier to measure the time and money spent on each phase. Hopefully, this information can then be used to predict more accurately the resources needed in future projects.

SYSTEM DESIGN

The preliminary design phase includes the specification of the function and information flow for each of the possible solutions for the problem. Management evaluates each alternative and selects the most feasible. It is possible that management may decide that none of the alternatives is feasible and the necessity or scope of the entire project should be reevaluated. Management must also develop a plan for transition from the existing system to the new one. At this point, a development team is formed.

The purpose of the development team is to create a system and prepare it for installation. The team is normally directed by a senior systems analyst. Sometimes, this person was involved with the feasibility study as well. This project leader and a team of systems analysts, with information gathered from the previous phases, will design specifications that will guide the programmers in the creation of program modules. The lead analyst is responsible for insuring module integration and allocating project resources.

When the system is to be acquired, a team must be assembled to evaluate the available systems and possibly do tailoring of the acquired system. The tailoring of a system is very similar to the development of a new system, except with a narrower scope. Hence, it is necessary to do the same type of planning. Even when the acquired system is to be installed as delivered from the vendor, there is still substantial installation work to be done. This would include selecting available options, configuring the system properly, converting existing data files, comprehensively testing the system, and training the users. These all take a good deal of time and planning to implement successfully.

When developing a new system, the analysts will create a detailed flow diagram or module flowchart that will aid in estimating the number of programmers needed to complete the project. Often, the relationships that exist between various modules suggest how many individuals make up the rest of the team. The end-user must not be forgotten at this point and should occupy a key position in the development team to make suggestions and clarify design points. The programmers and analysts refine the selected preliminary design, specifying algorithms, data definitions, module interfaces, and initial testing schemes. Management develops plans for resource allocation (e.g., CPUs, DASD), system verification, and testing. These performance standards will be used in subsequent phases. Again, they will be used in monitoring costs and benefits to judge the project's progress.

PROTOTYPING

One way of assuring that the users' needs are met is to develop a prototype system. This entails doing a "quick and dirty" development of the eventual system. In most cases, the prototype will not be totally functional, but it will include all of the major components of the desired system. In this way, the users will be able to see what they will be getting. If the user is not satisfied, then changes can be made to the prototype until the users' needs are met.

Prototypes can be quickly developed using special high-level programming tools such as relational database systems and fourth generation languages. While these tools are efficient with respect to programming time, they are extremely resource intensive during execution. This inefficiency usually prevents using the prototype system in a large-scale, high-volume production environment.

A problem with prototyping is that user expectations concerning the completion date of the production system become unrealistic. Seeing the prototype developed after a brief period of time leads the user to expect the finished product in the near future. Unfortunately, the production system entails much more time and effort.

Sometimes these user expectations force management to adopt the prototype of a large-scale production system. Even with some enhancements, this can lead to major problems when response time and transaction processing rates reach unacceptable levels. This could also degrade overall system performance and adversely affect other unrelated application systems. Figure 13.6 highlights the advantages and disadvantages of using prototyping when developing applications.

DEVELOPMENT TOOLS

There are a number of software tools that can be used to aid application system analysts and programmers in the more rapid and accurate development of new systems. These tools will either enhance a third generation programming environment or can be used instead of third generation code. However, care must

Figure 13.6   *Prototyping*

ADVANTAGES OF PROTOTYPING

Allows user to see the system operate before full-scale project is even undertaken

Lets project team learn by doing test development before actual production system

For smaller systems, the prototype may be used as the production system

Allows for rapid system development in an emergency situation

DISADVANTAGES OF PROTOTYPING

Creates undue pressure to implement prototype as production system

Gives users unrealistic expectations of project complexity

Causes some duplication of programming effort

be taken when selecting these systems. Many of them are not as mature and worry free as the vendor may imply. Also, the tools one selects will define the development environment well into the future.

Let's look at some of the different types of tools that may be of interest. First there are the products that help one to better utilize third generation languages. These include precompilers, reformaters, program analyzers, data modeling and structuring tools, and screen formatters. A precompiler allows the programmer to write in a special shorthand and to have the precompiler automatically insert certain preprogrammed reusable sections of code and data. This is particularly helpful in verbose languages such as COBOL. Using COBOL as an example, the precompiler will take the original shorthand code and convert it into the appropriate COBOL source statements. These can then be compiled in the usual manner.

A reformatter takes nonstructured source code and rewrites it in structured format. A tool of this type is useful in organizations that have many older systems that are poorly documented, need a lot of maintenance, and are not structured. These are the systems that are very expensive to maintain. Without a reformatter, the only alternative is to reprogram the system completely.

Program analyzers can help to debug new programs and to document old programs. They usually involve a system that outlines the logic of a program and also determines sections of code that may cause problems.

Data modeling and structuring tools help the analyst and programmer to develop the various data relationships within a system. Using COBOL as an example again, these tools could develop the input formats for a given data file or database and create the corresponding DATA DIVISION for the COBOL program. Of course the same thing can be done for output reports and files. Screen formatters are actually specialized data modeling tools that allow for quick and easy design of online screens. Instead of the programmer having to define the data definitions and attributes of the screen, with the formatter the programmer simply "paints" the screen using a series of simple commands. Not only is this simpler, but it allows the programmer to see how the screen will look as it is developed.

The most comprehensive tools for system development are what are termed *computer aided software engineering (CASE)* tools. These are complete systems that theoretically allow for cradle to grave development of a system. That is, the system will allow for the development of the original design concepts, expand these into detailed specifications, and then produce high-level code for that system. Notice that we said "theoretically" since most of these tools are not quite as powerful as one would wish. However, they are rapidly improving and will have a major influence on future systems development.

Ideally, a CASE environment starts with the high-level design of a system. This general design will usually describe how programs and files relate. From this, more specific data and program structures can be expressed. The next step would be to develop screen and report formats. Of course, these would be directly linked to the data files and the program logic. For example, a screen may state that a certain data field must have specific characteristics (numeric, nine digits long) and be matched with other items in a particular file (the Social Security number in the customer file) before it is considered valid data. It would be necessary to specify in the program logic what to do if the data is valid or if it is invalid. The CASE system would then convert all of these specifications into a functioning system.

It can be seen that a system of this type can have a tremendous affect on productivity. An additional benefit is that it is a self-documenting system. Simply by its nature it creates a more efficient maintenance environment. Instead of the maintenance programmer changing the source code (and usually not updating the written documentation), only the design specifications would be changed. The new source code would then be derived from these new specifications. The documentation is automatically changed since the CASE specifications are the documentation.

QUALITY CONTROL

Quality control is an important aspect of system development. Because the creation of a system can involve a substantial amount of resources, it makes sense that the system be well constructed. Quality control is often divided into two areas. First, if all of the programs created follow the same standards, they would be more easily debugged and maintained. Programming standards include consistent variable naming conventions, field descriptions, module construction, input testing, and documentation. Many organizations employ a module "template" that programmers use to begin each project and also have standard routines and data definitions that can be copied into the programs.

Secondly, the information systems staff should critique each piece of code, checking for potential problems and adherence to standards. As discussed earlier, this is called a structured walkthrough and it involves presentations by the development team to both the users and other programmers and analysts at predetermined milestones in the project (usually at the end of each phase). Often, this structured walkthrough will point out the programmer's or analyst's assumptions and avoid errors later. The next stage will not be started until the previous step of the project passes this review process. No code, no matter how straightforward it may appear, should bypass these reviews.

Constructing the system involves programming and testing the modules and creating the necessary documentation for each module. Management must analyze the performance of the modules against the planned performance standards developed in the previous phase. The structure of the code, adherence to programming standards, and inclusion of internal documentation will influence the overall quality of the system and its future maintainability. Management must also develop plans for validating the system before it goes into production.

Not only is it necessary to be able to judge the progress of the project development effort, it is also necessary to measure programmer productivity. Performance evaluation of the analysis and programming team is necessary to reward good performance and is also helpful in determining future assignments. Every project appears to be unique. However, there is often a great deal of similarity between various parts of projects. One of the more frequently used measures of programmer productivity is historical information. For example, if, in the past, a programmer normally took 10 days to complete a module of a certain size and difficulty, then that fact could be used in measuring the performance of a programmer constructing a similarly dimensioned module. Obviously, this is a subjective measure, depending heavily on the experience of the evaluator. Again, note the importance of accurate time and resource estimates.

A commonly used and less subjective measure is the amount of code written per day. Unfortunately, this method of evaluation can have its problems. First, there must be a very precise definition of lines of code. Does this include imbedded comment statements? Are we measuring original source code or the source code after expansion due to COPY statements? Do we have different standards for different source languages? Even if terms are precisely defined, this measure can be easily manipulated by the programmer to enhance the evaluation. Usually, this manipulation will be to the detriment of program performance. If this measure is used, it should be evaluated over the long term, rather than on a day-by-day basis. Of course, the development environment will have a strong impact on individual performance. An environment with many development tools available to the analyst and programmer should be a more efficient environment. Whatever the criterion, the programmer should be made aware of how he or she is being evaluated.

The next step of integration and validation testing involves putting the various modules together and determining whether they work correctly together. This is often accomplished by using copies of "live" data to determine the adequacy of checks and controls. Management compares these results to the validation plan developed previously and then estimates an implementation schedule. The user group is alerted for the upcoming acceptance testing and training.

A failure to test a system comprehensively can be a costly one. For many, the testing process is viewed as a mundane task. For this reason, the testing may not be as thorough as it should be. If the errors are not detected during testing, they will be found during either implementation or when the system is in operation. If the problem is a major one, it can result in a very embarrassing situation.

IMPLEMENTATION

The implementation of a new system can wreak havoc on existing system functions. In fact, if the new system is comprehensive, currently operational systems may be in jeopardy during the test. To guard against this, many shops have a development system and a production system. All development, testing, and conversion occurs in the test environment. It is only when the new system has been granted production status that it is moved over to the production environment.

There are three methods of converting from an existing system to the new system. These are summarized in Figure 13.7. The simplest and most risky is the direct conversion. This involves the discontinuance of the old system and immediate use of the new system. This method is normally used when the new system is not really replacing an existing system or both systems cannot logically operate simultaneously.

The second approach to conversion is modular conversion. Modular conversion involves the replacement of old system modules with new modules. In this manner, conversion is accomplished on a module-by-module basis rather than as a replacement of an entire system. This method requires that both systems have compatible modules that can be integrated in a piecemeal manner.

Figure 13.7 *Conversion Methods*

METHOD	DISCUSSION
Direct Conversion	New system is implemented and previous system is immediately disabled.
Modular Conversion	Old system is slowly replaced on a module-by-module basis.
Parallel Conversion	Both systems are run simultaneously, and the results are compared. Old system is removed only after correctness has been verified for some period of time.

Modular conversion is a popular method when the new system has been developed using prototyping.

Finally, the most conservative method of conversion is parallel conversion. Parallel conversion involves the operations of both systems simultaneously with comparisons of results occurring for verification. This method is a natural outgrowth of the test/production environment.

Whichever method of conversion is used, it is important to remember that the point when data is the most vulnerable is during system conversion. Accurate backups of all programs and data should be accomplished and safely stored before any conversion takes place.

SYSTEM MAINTENANCE

When the new system goes into production, its maintenance and continued support become the responsibility of the program maintenance department. Any changes that the end-user desires after the system is accepted are made by the maintenance group. Initially, organizations viewed this group as performing a needed, but not very demanding, task. Consequently, individuals hired as maintenance programmers typically were new employees with little experience who desired to move up into the ranks of application programmers. Unfortunately, this attitude is still common in data processing organizations today.

With the increasing costs of program maintenance, many organizations are beginning to understand the importance of good maintenance support. In these companies, a maintenance programmer represents a prominent position because it is the maintenance programming staff that conducts the structured walkthroughs of application code for quality control. The outcome of this is that they will not accept any program that they cannot easily understand and maintain. In this type of situation, no system will be placed into production until the maintenance group has accepted it. This guarantees that the system is properly structured, tested, and documented.

With the increasing importance of computer support to the end-user and the increased integration of application systems, change management has become another important facet of program maintenance. Programmers can no longer arbitrarily change procedures, file structures, or program segments without adequately understanding the consequences of their actions. The end result is that when a change to an existing system is anticipated, change management must be consulted and the impact of the change assessed. Those individuals affected by the proposed change must be contacted and approve the alteration. Much of the responsibility of change management also falls on the shoulders of the data administration group. Consequently, program maintenance and data administration must work closely together. These individuals must also be advised when a new system is being developed. In addition to approving the code and data structures used in the new system, they may also alert users and other programmers to potential impacts. As can be seen, change management is a vital component of a data processing organization and should be supported in a like manner.

The maintenance of an existing system will often involve formal releases and versions of a system. This means that changes, enhancements, and new functions will be incorporated in batches. In this way, all of the aforementioned steps can be followed before the new version of the system is ready for the users. No matter whether there are formal versions, it is very important to establish a set of procedures for version control. Without control, changes can cause many problems. This is particularly true in a very large system.

When a system is composed of thousands of modules and macros with many individuals working on the code, changes made by one individual can be overwritten or lost when a second individual simultaneously makes changes. This situation is best managed using "library" software in which a check-out procedure allows only one person at a time to change a module or macro. The part remains locked until the change is completed.

Proper change control dictates that all changes to a module be documented within the module. This allows for any errant changes to be quickly diagnosed. In addition, there should be a system of ownership, so that each module has an owner. The owner is then responsible for monitoring all changes to that module, whether made by the owner or another individual.

EFFECT OF END-USER INVOLVEMENT

As discussed in the previous chapter, the end-user community is becoming more involved with the information system. The question is: How does this involvement affect the system development and maintenance process?

For the most part, the increased involvement by users is a very positive force within an organization. The users become much more computer literate. They begin to better understand the opportunities and the limitations presented by computerization of a function. A more informed user community is generally more cooperative when developing the specifications for a new system.

If an information center has been established within a firm, then there will be fewer interruptions of the development and maintenance staffs. The users will seek help from the information center staff in solving a majority of their problems. Also, the simpler development tasks will be done by the users. The development staff can then concentrate on the major development projects.

The biggest drawback of an information center from the point of view of the development and maintenance areas is that it will require some of the best employees to staff it. Considering all factors, increased involvement by the users should be beneficial to the organization as a whole.

MAJOR COMPANY

Proper management of application development projects has been a serious problem at Major Company. Studies have shown that on average there have been schedule delays of 30% and cost overruns of about 50%. In the extreme, some projects have taken over twice the estimated time and have had costs 400% greater than the original estimate.

Top management has sent a directive to the information systems area that this problem must be resolved. The vice-president of information systems formed a task force to investigate the problem. This group found that product quality and user satisfaction with the final system were quite high, but that the bad estimates were primarily a function of inexperienced managers and overly optimistic estimates. In some cases, the projects would not have been initially undertaken if the schedule and budget had been accurately estimated.

To solve this problem, the applications development area must negotiate a project contract with the primary user department of that system. This contract establishes commitments for both the completion time and cost for each phase of the project. If at any stage the time is 10% higher than the estimate or the cost is more than 20% over budget, an emergency meeting must be held between representatives of the user area, the lead analyst of the development project, and the manager of applications development. At this meeting, all schedule discrepancies must be justified and, if necessary, a revised estimate must be negotiated. A major component of a lead analyst performance evaluation will be based on being able to deliver a system on time and on budget.

To assist the project managers in making accurate estimates, Major Company has developed a computerized expert system to store and analyze the development data. Unfortunately, the development of this system was also late and over budget. It looks as if they still have some learning to do.

Another approach to solving some of the software problems involves the acquisition of new technology to aid in the development of systems. Major Company has been investigating CASE oriented tools. They believe that these tools can both speed the development process and provide more uniformity to the process. Some of these tools have been used as pilot projects in developing a couple of small systems. Because of the substantial cost of these tools and their impact on the entire development process, Major Company is being careful before committing to a specific set of products.

QUESTIONS

1. List the advantages and disadvantages of each of the conversion methods discussed in this chapter. Can you think of any advantages or disadvantages that were not mentioned?

2. What information should appear on a project tracking sheet? Why?

3. List the steps and objectives of each of the system development phases. Do you think the estimates in Figure 13.5 are accurate? What problems can you foresee that would alter the percentages?

4. What is prototyping? Can it be used for very large programming projects?

If a prototype is constantly being updated, when is it no longer a prototype?

5. How is maintenance programming accomplished in your school's data processing shop? What are the rewards of being a maintenance programmer there?

6. Many programmers think that the change management department simply gets in their way. Why do you think this is? Can you suggest a solution to this problem?

7. Some individuals speculate that user satisfaction is not strongly correlated with user involvement in information system design. Do you think this is true? Why or why not?

8. It is necessary to have strict change control for both source and object code. Explain why and give at least one example for each type of code (source and object) of how a system can be backleveled when these controls are not exercised.

9. List the responsibilities of management for each phase of the system life cycle.

CASE ANALYSIS

Analyze the steps you take when doing a class programming assignment. Equate these steps to the stages in the application development cycle. How are they the same? How are they different?

Also describe how you estimate the time it will take to complete the assignment. How do you measure your efficiency in completing the assignment? Can you compare your efficiency to that of your classmates?

ADDITIONAL READINGS

Brown, Patrick. "Managing Software Development," *Datamation*, April 15, 1985, pp. 133–136.

Case, Albert, and John Manley. "Fourth Generation Languages Offer Pros and Cons," *Data Management*, March 1986, pp. 10–11.

Conte, S. D., H. E. Dunsmore, and V. Y. Shen. *Software Engineering Metrics and Models*. Benjamin/ Cummings, 1986.

Kearney, J. K., R. L. Sedlmeyer, W. B. Thompson, M. A. Gray, and M. A. Adler. "Software Complexity Measurement," *Communications of the ACM*, Vol. 29, No. 11, November 1986, p. 1044.

Kemerer, Chris F. "An Empirical Validation of Software Cost Estimation Models," *Communications of the ACM*, Vol. 30, No. 5, May 1987, p. 416.

Loh, Marcus, and Ryan Nelson. "Reaping CASE Harvests," *Datamation*, July 1989, p. 31.

MOAD, JEFF. "Contracting with Integrators," *Datamation*, May 15, 1989, p. 18.

YOURDON, EDWARD. *Managing the System Life Cycle*, 2nd Ed. Yourdon Press, 1988.

READINGS BEFORE NEXT CHAPTER

The preceding material should be adequate preparation.

14

MANAGING SYSTEMS PROGRAMMING

SYSTEMS PROGRAMMING

Management of the system programming function may be one of the most critical factors to smooth day-to-day operation of the centralized computer system. In fact, many information system managers feel the systems programming area is one that warrants considerable concern. One reason for this is that the system programmer's job necessitates access to the most sensitive information in the computer system. In essence, the system programmers need the keys to the kingdom in order for them to accomplish their jobs. This concentration of power within a small group of individuals can be a cause for concern. An additional concern with respect to system programming is that the job demands extensive technical competence. Because of these requirements, it is difficult and the expensive to attract, train, and then retain system program professionals.

Before one can manage a sophisticated function such as system programming, it is necessary to have a basic understanding of the responsibilities of the area. The following will describe the responsibilities of the system programming function.

The systems programming staff plays a very important role in keeping a large computer center operating smoothly and efficiently. This is one of the most technical, if not the most technical, positions in the center. The role of the systems programmer is probably the least understood of any in the computer center. Many people not having any contact with systems programming do not have the slightest idea of their function. Even many individuals that have frequent contact with them do not fully understand the responsibilities of the area.

One of the problems stems from the name, systems programming. This conjures up the image of extensive writing of computer code. In most cases this is not so. Actually, a systems programmer may seldom write a program in the normal sense of the term. Instead of describing more of what systems programmers do not do, let's explore their responsibilities.

The systems programming staff is responsible for the continued efficient running of systems software—that is, the software that enhances the functions of the hardware, but is not primarily designed to solve problems for the end-user. Operating systems, compilers, utilities, and database management systems are examples of systems software. These can be contrasted with general ledger, payroll, inventory control, and financial planning programs which are end-user oriented and are the responsibility of the applications programming staff.

While the systems programmers' primary duty involves the system software, this does not preclude them from getting involved in both hardware and applications programming. To increase efficiency or solve a specific problem, it may be necessary to analyze or reconfigure both the hardware and application programs. For example, there may be a system failure during normal processing. If the problem cannot be diagnosed and solved by the operator, a systems programmer would be asked to examine the situation. Since the modern computer environment is so complex, the systems programmer may have to look at the hardware, systems software, and the application programs that were executing when the failure occurred. Often, the cause of the problem can be determined and corrected only after an extensive analysis.

DETAILED RESPONSIBILITIES

In the previous section we broadly defined the responsibilities of the systems programmer. Let's now take a more detailed look at these responsibilities.

The primary duties involve the functions summarized in Figure 14.1. We will now examine each of the areas in more detail.

Figure 14.1 *Systems Programming Responsibilities*

RESPONSIBILITY	FREQUENCY OF IMPLEMENTATION
Evaluate and Reconfigure System	Evaluate periodically and reconfigure when necessary
Corrective Maintenance	Upon system failure
Preventive Maintenance	On a periodic schedule
Software Installation	Upon acquisition of new software and when necessary for new releases and versions
Tailoring Software	Upon installation of new software and sometimes with new versions or releases
Evaluate New Software and Hardware	Upon request

SYSTEM EVALUATION AND CONFIGURATION

We have already discussed this area in depth in Chapter 6. These tasks are usually done by either the systems programming staff or a separate special performance measurement and evaluation area. In either case, a systems programming background is necessary since these individuals have the best understanding of the complex interrelationships between system software and hardware.

The major responsibilities include measuring the performance of the system, determining the causes of degraded performance, and subsequently reconfiguring the system to improve performance. As mentioned previously, this process may also lead to the proposal to acquire additional hardware or systems software. Since we covered this subject in Chapter 7, we will not discuss this in any more detail.

PROBLEM CORRECTION

Occasionally there will be a failure of a system component which is either difficult to pinpoint or not possible to correct without the intervention of the systems programming staff. The failure may involve an application program, system software, or system hardware. Before we describe the actions taken by systems programming, we will look at examples of possible failures that would involve the systems staff.

1. An applications programmer writing COBOL programs has attempted to use the virtual storage access method (VSAM) on a data set residing on three separate disk drives. This is the first time this has been attempted at this installation. The program fails even though all the correct procedures have been followed.
2. A new system program product has just been installed, and now programs which ran successfully before, abnormally end.

3. A memory board in a printer fails, but is not detected by the operators. This problem causes an error condition in the operating system which causes a failure of the spooler program.

In each of the preceding cases the systems programming staff must be involved to diagnose and hopefully resolve the problem. In the first case, the applications programmer has followed correct procedures, but the program still does not run. The most probable cause is a problem with the systems software. In the second case, the new product has altered the environment in such a way that certain programs now fail that previously ran. Again, this is a systems software problem. In the last case, this appears to be a systems software failure; hence the systems programming staff is involved. They should be able to discover the hardware failure and initiate action to replace the failed component.

In any corrective maintenance situation, similar procedures are followed. Figure 14.2 shows the typical steps involved in doing corrective maintenance. First, the problem is fully documented. This would include obtaining program listings, memory dumps, console logs, and any other pertinent information. The next step is for the systems programmer to attempt to duplicate the conditions that caused the failure. If these conditions can be duplicated, then additional diagnostic information can be gathered. This may include the specific error messages, the contents of all pertinent registers and control blocks, and the sequence of events leading to the failure.

All this diagnostic information can then be used by the systems programmer to determine the cause of the problem. In many instances, the process ends at this point, since the problem has been resolved. If the cause of the problem appears to be in part of the vendor-supplied system software or the systems programmer cannot resolve the problem, then it is necessary to contact the vendor's software support center. This center is a service provided by the vendor, and a monthly maintenance fee must be paid by the user for this type of support.

The actual operation of the support center will vary for different vendors; however, the procedures are usually quite similar. The systems programmer will usually call a central location and supply the dispatcher with the company's account number and a brief description of the problem. At this point, the call will be routed to the appropriate person for examination. This person will

Figure 14.2 *Corrective Maintenance Procedures*

Step 1:	Fully document problem.
Step 2:	Attempt to duplicate failure conditions.
Step 3:	Isolate cause of problem.
Step 4:	Resolve problem, if possible.
Step 5:	If problem unresolved, contact appropriate vendor.
Step 6:	Apply vendor's fix to problem.
Step 7:	Document all changes.

Figure 14.3 *Typical Organization of a Major Vendor's Software Support Center*

All customers enter the system here.

1st level specialists, usually differentiated by operating system or major product line. Searches vendor's data base to determine if this particular problem has occurred before. If the problem is new, it is sent to the appropriate 2nd level specialist.

2nd level specialists, experts on specific sub-systems. Examines problem and writes fixes to correct problem if possible, otherwise contacts appropriate field representative to visit customer's site.

Field representatives, most experienced personnel. Usually has broad experience in all aspects of an operating system. Solves problems at customer's site.

Central Problem Routing Dispatcher

Specialists for System X

Specialists for System Y

... Etc.

Specialist for Sub-system 1 of Operating System X

Specialist for Sub-system 2 of Operating System X

... Etc.

Field Rep. 1

Field Rep. 2

... Etc.

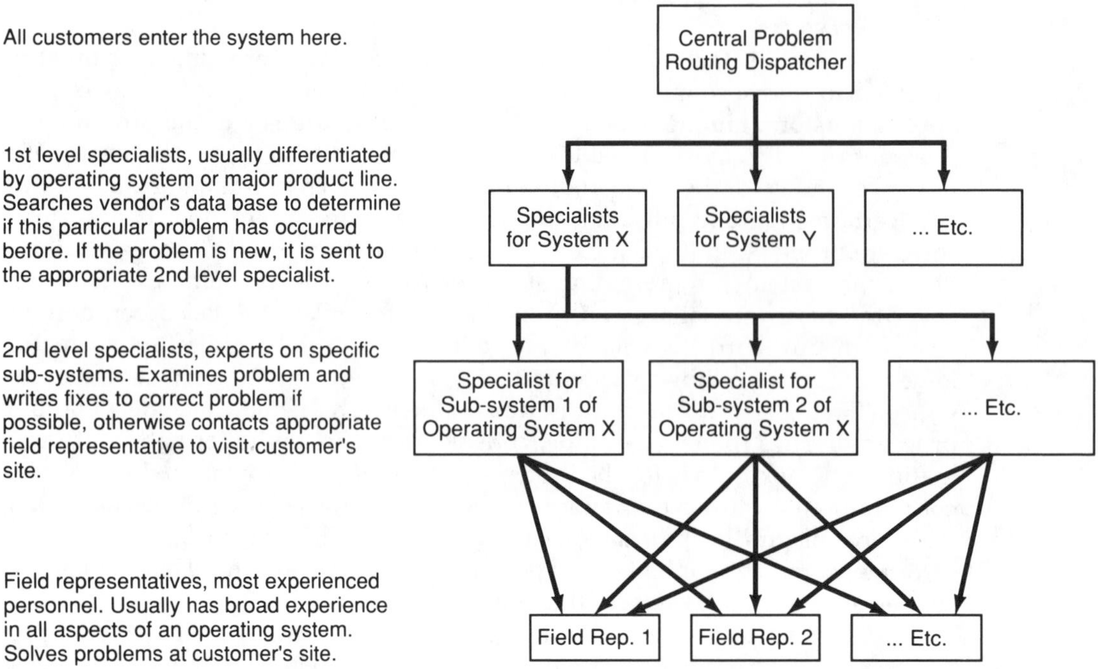

ask for the full details of the problem and will examine an online database to discover if this problem had occurred at any other customer sites. If it had occurred at other locations, then the problem has already been solved and the "fix" necessary to correct the problem can be sent to the customer immediately. It is then the customer's (the systems programmer's) responsibility to apply the fix to the appropriate systems software. Figure 14.3 illustrates the function of a typical software support center.

Some vendors will also allow authorized users to log onto their problem databases. This can speed the diagnostic process and help reduce the time needed to solve the problem.

If no other customer has experienced this problem, the vendor will issue a work order for a systems maintenance programmer to investigate the problem. The customer will be asked to supply all documentation concerning the problem and will also be asked the severity of the problem. If the problem is very serious, such as not being able to run the entire system, the vendor will attempt to solve the problem immediately. Otherwise, the solution may take longer.

The vendor will investigate the problem at its own site. This is done by using the documentation supplied by the customer's systems programmer and, in some cases, through accessing the customer's system directly via a communications link. If the problem cannot be resolved in this manner, then the vendor will send a systems software specialist to the customer site to resolve the problem.

The systems program fix can take several forms. If the error in a given systems module is severe, then the whole module will be replaced. Otherwise, only part of the code in the module will be replaced. If the code to be replaced is longer than the new code, then the new code will simply overlay the old. If the new code is longer, then this code will be placed in the empty space at the end of the module. Instructions transferring control to this new code are then imbedded in the module. The application of fixes is usually done by a specially designed systems maintenance program supplied by the vendor. Figure 14.4 illustrates how software fixes can be applied. Each type of software can have its own way of applying fixes.

PREVENTIVE MAINTENANCE

To help prevent system software failures, it is necessary to do preventive maintenance. The vendor will send the customer fixes that solve all recent system software problems. The problems are usually discovered by the users of the systems, as discussed in the previous section. The vendor will distribute preventive maintenance fixes on a periodic basis (usually monthly). The customer's systems programming staff will apply these fixes on a scheduled basis. Most installations will not have a large enough systems programming staff to apply preventive maintenance on a monthly basis. Hence, they may accumulate the fixes and only apply them periodically (such as every three months).

However, it is important that preventive maintenance be done frequently enough so as not to void the software maintenance agreement. The vendor will insist that no system be at a preventive maintenance level older than a certain period of time (for example, one year). This reduces the number of different systems with which the vendor must contend.

Preventive maintenance can be a time-consuming and tedious job for the systems programming staff. The vendor will send the fixes (usually on a magnetic tape or cartridge) for all problems dealing with a specific version of an operating system, including all program products that will run under that system. This may entail hundreds of different program patches. The systems programmer must first determine which of these pertain to their system. For example, there may be a patch for the linkage editor to correct a problem that occurs when a PL/I program calls a COBOL subroutine. If this shop does not use PL/I, then this fix should not be applied.

An additional problem arises because some fixes are dependent on each other. Some fixes cannot be applied until other fixes are applied (precedent fix). Some fixes cannot be applied if other fixes have been applied (mutually exclusive fix). Some fixes must be applied at the same time as other fixes (coincident fix).

If all this sounds rather complicated, it can be. However, the systems

Figure 14.4 *How Software Fixes Are Applied*

CASE 1: A MAJOR CHANGE IS NECESSARY

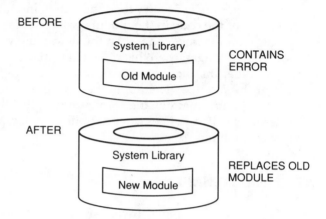

CASE 2: A MAJOR CHANGE IS NOT NECESSARY

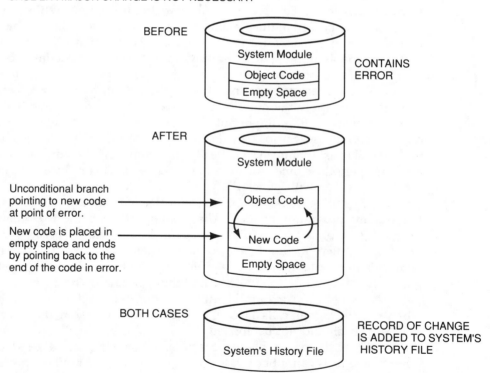

Figure 14.5 *Some IBM Software Maintenance Terminology*

Program Temporary Fix (PTF): The patch supplied by IBM to remedy the problem. This must be applied by the systems programmers.

Authorized Program Analysis Report (APAR): This has two meanings. First, it is the request by the user to have a problem resolved. In addition, it refers to a patch similar to a PTF, but usually not quite as complex, that fixes the specific problem.

Program Update Tape (PUT): A magnetic tape containing all of the fixes applicable to a given operating system for a specific period of time (usually a month).

Personal Service Representative (PSR): Software maintenance field representative who will visit customer site if a software problem cannot be located and solved by other means.

Support Center: Organization that is responsible for maintaining all large IBM systems software.

Systems Modification Program (SMP): A software program written by IBM to apply all software maintenance to the system (MVS operating system).

Installation Productivity Option (IPO): Interactive product that assists the systems programmer in installing an operating system.

programmer's job is made easier by the vendor-supplied system maintenance program. This program keeps track of all of the fixes applied to the system (through the use of history files) and checks for precedent, mutually exclusive, and coincident relationships before a fix is allowed to be applied to the system. To assist the reader, Figure 14.5 presents same IBM software maintenance terminology and Figure 14.6 gives an example of a software fix.

Figure 14.6 *Example of a Software Fix*

Version/Environment: (Z099) Program ID: (MAJ1234)
Predecessor PTFs: (UZ11112, UZ21111)

Predecessor PTFs and APARs. These must be applied before applying this PTF.

Supercedes: (UZ060558, UZ020361, UZ031387, AZ091859, AZ112862, AZ040672)

These PTFs and APARs have been superceded and need not be applied if this PTF is applied. The U prefix stands for a PTF and an A prefix stands for an APAR.

Problems Addressed: These are the problems the users encountered and that are fixed by this PTF.
OZ082380 – (MAJ1111) KEYWORD CHANGE IS NOT REFLECTED IN REPORT A10 OR IN MESSAGE MAJ7537E
OZ080139 – (MAJ1112) DYNAMIC MEMORY ALLOCATION OVERWRITES CACHE WITHOUT REQUESTING OPERATOR APPROVAL
OZ102340 – (MAJ1113) TAPE LABELS NOT CORRECTLY WRITTEN WHEN NONSTANDARD LABELS ARE SPECIFIED

APARS fixed: OZ082380, OZ080139, OZ102340

Modules fixed: 06/05/91
        MAJ1111
        MAJ1112
        MAJ1113

SOFTWARE INSTALLATION

The systems programmer is also responsible for installing new software on the system. This entails copying the program modules into the appropriate system libraries, applying precedent fixes to associated system software products, applying the necessary fixes to bring this product to the same fix level as the rest of the system, and testing the system to guarantee a smooth transition when the new product is put into operation.

This also includes the more difficult task of installing and testing vendor software which is not yet available to the general user community. After a vendor has designed and internally tested a software package (this is usually called the alpha test), this package is then given a last comprehensive test prior to commercial release (called the beta test). This test is usually done by a customer who has a special need for this package. The systems programmer will install the package and document all problems encountered while using the system and make suggestions on how to improve the software. While this process can entail much work for the firm, it can also be beneficial by allowing the firm to use the software before its release, usually for a substantially lower price.

It is also necessary to install new versions and releases of products already installed. The vendor will issue a new version of an existing product if a substantial number of fixes have been made to the product. The program is rewritten by the vendor with all of the known problems corrected and other rather minor changes made. This gives the customer clean code without the patches of the old version. A new release is issued by the vendor when significant enhancements have been made to the product. Figure 14.7 shows an example of IBM's release and version numbering conventions.

New versions and releases are installed in a manner similar to the installation of a new product, except that the old system will remain the production system until the new system has been thoroughly tested. When testing is complete, the new test libraries containing the new program modules will be copied into the production libraries. At this point, the new release is the production system.

So far, we have only addressed the installation of individual products. A much more complex situation occurs when an entire operating system is to be

Figure 14.7 *Example of IBM's Numbering Conventions*

DFSMS/VM Rel 2.3 Put Level 9106
> This is the second release of the software product. This includes the original release and one major enhancement to the system.
> This is version 3 of the second release. This means that changes were made to the second release three times (versions always start with 0, hence the first version was Rel 2.0).
> This information is dependent on the preventive maintenance done by the customer. In this case, all fixes involving this product on or before June of 1991 have been applied.

installed. This operation is commonly referred to as a SYSGEN (system genera-tion). This involves configuring the operating system to the specific demands of your environment. This includes defining all peripheral devices, telling the oper-ating system where specific system libraries will reside, deciding where the various modules of the operating system will be placed in main memory, and deciding which compilers and other systems products are going to reside under the operating system.

This can be a time-consuming task. Proper planning and preparation can reduce the SYSGEN time. However, problems can still be encountered no matter how extensive the planning. In many situations, the system must be stopped for an extended period of time. For this reason, the new operating system should be installed as a test system while the old system is used as the production system until the new system has been extensively tested. If this procedure is followed, users can continue their processing even though the installation of the new operating system may take a few days.

In this way, most users will not even be aware of the change in operating system versions after the new system is operational. For this reason, even a reasonably sophisticated user may not understand how complex the process is and may become intolerant when problems are encountered.

The SYSGEN can be done in several ways; some heavily involving the systems programming staff and others needing little or no systems program-ming support (see Figure 14.8). The most labor-intensive and time-consuming method of GENing a system is for the systems programmer to determine where each of the systems modules will reside and copy these modules to the appropri-ate libraries using standard utilities. This is an extremely time-consuming pro-cedure since the amount of space necessary for each library must be calculated by hand. However, this allows for the most efficient use of the machine re-sources by organizing the operating system to meet the specific demands of this site.

Figure 14.8 *Procedures in Doing a SYSGEN*

Receive all system tapes and fixes from vendor.
Back up present system disks.
Install starter system (single user OS used to GEN main system).
Configure operating system as desired, i.e., nucleus size, buffer areas, link
    pack area, etc.
Load operating system into system libraries.
Determine program products to be installed.
Load program products into system libraries.
Apply appropriate fixes.
Thoroughly test new system.
If successful, begin using as production system.
If unsuccessful, back up new system and restore old system until problems
    can be resolved.*

*Some operating systems (such as IBM's VM) allow "guest" operating systems to run simultaneously. This eliminates the need to bring down the old system to bring up the new one.

Probably the most widely used method of GENing a system is by employing a vendor-supplied productivity program which does all storage space calculations and automatically loads the modules into the appropriate libraries. All the systems programmer has to do is answer an extensive series of online questions. The program then processes the answers to do the SYSGEN.

An increasingly popular method of doing a SYSGEN is to obtain a pre-GENed system from the vendor. This reduces the need for a sophisticated (and usually expensive) systems programming staff. Many small firms are selecting this avenue to reduce costs.

To get a pre-GENed system, the customer must tell the vendor exactly what peripherals and software products its system has. The vendor will then do a complete SYSGEN at its central location, copy the libraries to tape, and the customer simply has to copy these tapes to disks as they would when doing a disk recovery from a backup tape. The major problem with a pre-GENed system is that it is very difficult to reconfigure the system once it is installed.

TAILORING SYSTEMS SOFTWARE

Another important function of systems programming is to modify the vendor-supplied software to do tasks that are unique to the specific installation. For example, a security system designed to protect against unauthorized access of data sets may not be able to discriminate between certain classes of users. This function may be necessary at our installation. Hence, the program must be modified to handle different types of users. This would be the systems programmer's responsibility.

There are two ways to make these modifications. The first way involves reprogramming parts of the vendor's system program. If this is to be done, the vendor must supply the customer with source code, and some of the vendor's code will be rewritten to incorporate the necessary modifications. This altered code will then be assembled and loaded into the appropriate systems libraries.

This approach has some rather serious drawbacks. Changing the vendor's code may cause problems with the vendor's warranty and maintenance contract. At worst, it may make the vendor's warranty null and void. It is also possible that the vendor will charge a fee in addition to the monthly maintenance charge if the vendor has to resolve problems caused by a user modification. Also, each time a new version or release is installed, the program must be changed to incorporate these modifications. This can be a significant load on the systems programming staff.

Changing the vendor's code was previously the most frequent way of incorporating user modifications; however, most vendors are adopting an object-code-only policy. This means that no source code is supplied with the systems product. Instead, the vendor supplies a series of user exits (sometimes called "hooks") in its system programs. User exits are branches from the main program to a series of external subroutines. A user exit is placed in the program wherever the vendor believes a customer may want to modify the function of the program. When the program is first delivered to the customer, these user exits are null (empty). Hence, they do not affect the functioning of the program. If the user so desires, additional code can be placed in these subroutines to incorporate the desired modifications. When a new release or version is installed, the vendor will retain the same user exit points in the system program. The subroutine from the old release will still be operational even though the vendor's program may have changed substantially. Figure 14.9 summarizes the advantages and disadvantages of changing the vendor code and creating user exits.

A major problem occurs with user exits when the customer desires to modify the program at a point where the vendor does not have an exit. This prevents the user from making any modification. This problem and the fact that the vendor's logic is hidden in object code has caused many large users to resist vendors' attempts at implementing object-code-only policies.

EVALUATE SYSTEMS SOFTWARE AND HARDWARE

Because of systems programmers knowledge of the complexities of the computing environment, they are usually involved in the evaluation of new hardware and systems software. Their involvement could encompass the entire acquisition process. However, the heaviest involvement will usually be during the physical benchmarking stage. This process would include designing the benchmarking tests, running the actual benchmarks, and then interpreting the results as discussed in Chapter 7.

Systems programmers must also be aware of new products that may be applicable to their system. Any product that could increase the efficiency of the system or that could reduce costs should be brought to the attention of higher

Figure 14.9 *Methods of Tailoring Systems Software*

METHOD	ADVANTAGES	DISADVANTAGES
Change Vendor Code	Can accomplish exactly what you want	Requires vendor source code Usually must be rewritten for each installation of a new release or version of system Requires substantial system programmer intervention
Create User Exits	Quicker and easier to implement Usually little or no systems programmer maintenance after initial implementation	Heavily dependent on vendor putting user exits at the "right" place in code Not as flexible as changing the source code Vendor's logic is not disclosed

management. In most cases, the systems programmers will have the most fre-quent contact with the various vendors' technical personnel; hence the systems programmers will become aware of new products or enhancements of existing products before most others in data processing.

The systems programmers' actual evaluation of products should only begin when the acquiring area has requested their participation. The final selec-tion of the product and the management of the acquisition process must be under the control of the acquiring area. The systems programming area will determine the technical merit of the products under consideration and advise the acquiring area.

NEED FOR SYSTEMS PROGRAMMERS

In most firms using multiple large mainframe processors, the need for experi-enced systems programmers is acute. As these shops become more complex, the systems programming tasks continue to increase. The extensive amount of train-ing time for these specialists has caused a substantial unmet demand in this area.

Not all firms using computers need to have a full-time systems program-ming staff. Smaller firms using only mini- and microcomputers usually either will not have systems programmers or will have a very small staff. This is mainly possible because of the substantially smaller size of operating systems and other associated systems software.

The cost savings allowed by reducing the systems programming staff can be substantial. Because of this, firms are attempting to find ways to reduce their dependence on systems programmers. One method would be to adopt a policy of absolutely no modifications to the vendor-supplied software. Another method would be to use pre-GENed operating systems. While the expertise of a systems programmer may still be needed in these instances, this function could be performed by a part-time outside consultant. For some firms, the cost of systems programmers is a significant factor in going to a system of distributed minis and micros.

Some data center managers feel a little uncomfortable over the con-centration of responsibility in the systems programming area. In many shops, the continued smooth operation of the system is substantially dependent on the systems programming staff. In a smaller installation, this may mean the suc-cessful operation can be very heavily influenced by one or two individuals. The internal audit staff will also be concerned about systems programming having almost unlimited access to all of the system resources. In fact, systems program-mers may be the only individuals allowed to access the test, development, and production systems. This makes it very important that these employees be ex-tremely trustworthy and loyal.

Despite some of the cost-cutting measures being adopted and other problems, the demand for systems programmers will remain quite strong over the next few years. This means that staffing of the system programming function may remain the concern of the information system manager.

MAJOR COMPANY

In order to illustrate some of the points of the chapter we will describe how Rick, one of the system programmers at Major Company, performs his job. First, we will briefly describe Rick and give you a brief look at his personality and background. Rick has been employed by Major Company for the last three years. He has a bachelor's degree from State University with a major in computer science. After graduation, he accepted a position with Major Company as a system programmer trainee. Rick underwent extensive training on-site and at vendor-offered training seminars. A large majority of his first year was spent in training. The few tasks he was assigned during this time were either quite trivial or were under the direct supervision of a more experienced staff person.

After about two years on the job, Rick had become a very valuable asset to the firm. At this point, he was given substantial responsibility for the maintenance and installation of a major software subsystem.

Rick is now proficient with the various system software components and has a good feel for maintenance and tuning of the system. The major tools he uses include the massive amount of documentation supplied by the vendor, his knowledge of assembly language (including his ability to read storage dumps), a wide variety of vendor-supplied utility programs, and his extensive knowledge of both the hardware and the software.

Rick's personality has been described as introverted. In the beginning, many unsophisticated users believed that he was totally incapable of speaking English because of all the technical jargon he used. However, the more he has worked with users, the better his communication skills have become. He still has difficulty explaining a situation to a nontechnical user without using a heavy dose of jargon, but he has improved greatly over the last year.

A typical day for Rick might involve a variety of tasks. Each day will be different, and his job cannot be described as routine. For example, at any one time he may be working on the installation of a new systems software product, deciding what new fixes should be applied to the system and scheduling their application, and investigating new product releases by the vendor. He will always be on call to help solve systems software problems. Since system failures can occur at any time, Rick may get a call at night or early in the morning. In addition, when a major product is being installed, it is best done when it would cause the least disruption. Hence, Rick can put in a lot of late night and weekend hours.

Major Company has a large computer installation with extensive systems software and employs a large programming staff. Rick is primarily responsible for only one subsystem under a specific operating system (JES3 under MVS/ESA). Because Major Company wants their employees to grow professionally, Rick will be assigned to a different subsystem next year (IMS/DB and IMS/DC). He has been learning about this system and is scheduled to go to a couple of vendor-offered classes. He is excited about this additional experience and feels this will broaden his background.

Overall, Rick is satisfied with his job. Sometimes the long hours can be aggravating, but he is being challenged and really enjoys working with complex systems. Over the past year Rick has had over a half-dozen offers to work for other firms at a substantial increase in pay. At present, he wants to stay at Major Company; however, the additional money is tempting.

SUMMARY

In a large information system, the systems programming staff plays a key role. Their primary responsibility involves keeping the systems software running efficiently. Systems programmers' detailed responsibilities include the following:

1. They should measure and evaluate the present system configuration. If necessary, the system must be reconfigured to improve performance.
2. They must diagnose and correct problems involving the systems software. This may include contacting the vendor to help solve the problem. If the cause of the failure lies in the vendor's systems software, then the systems programmer must apply vendor-supplied fixes to the software to correct the problem.
3. They must do preventive maintenance by periodically applying vendor-supplied fixes to the systems software. This should reduce the number and severity of systems software-related problems.
4. They must install and test both new systems software and new releases and versions of existing systems software. This would include the major task of installing new versions of the operating system.
5. If the vendor-supplied systems software does not accomplish all the tasks the customer desires, then the systems programmers will have to modify the vendor's code. This can be done either by changing the vendor's source code or by writing user exits which are added to the vendor's object code.
6. The systems programming staff is usually involved in the evaluation of both software and hardware. They are usually called on to evaluate alternative products.

The increased complexity of large mainframe systems makes systems programming a highly technical field. The training time and the lack of qualified applicants makes this a field that is present in high demand.

QUESTIONS

1. Briefly describe the function of a systems programmer in a typical large computer center.
2. Some systems programmers will design and write compilers and operating

systems; however, we do not talk about these functions in this chapter. Explain why.

3. Explain the difference between preventive and corrective software maintenance. How are the two similar?

4. Explain what a systems software fix is and how it is applied.

5. Explain how systems software fixes can be dependent on each other and how the systems programmer must compensate for this.

6. If your application program failed and you wanted a systems programmer to examine your problem, describe what documentation you would gather to submit to the system programmer to have the problem resolved.

7. Why do vendors issue new releases and versions of systems programs?

8. What is a SYSGEN? Briefly describe how a SYSGEN is done.

9. Why does a customer sometimes have to modify a vendor's systems software? Explain how modifications can be done.

10. Describe a user modification to a vendor's systems software that has been implemented at your installation.

11. Examine the employment pages of a major metropolitan newspaper or a national weekly computer publication and list the systems programming positions. Be sure to note the types of experience desired, the vendors involved, and the benefits offered.

ADDITIONAL READINGS

ANDERSON, D. A. "Operating Systems," *IEEE Computer*, June 1981, pp. 69–82.

DENNING, PETER J. "Operating Systems Principles and Undergraduate Computer Science Curricula," *Data Base*, Vol. 4, No. 2, Summer 1972, pp. 5–10.

JANSSENS, M. D., J. K. ANNOT, AND A. J. VAN DE GOOR. "Adapting UNIX for a Multiprocessor Environment," *Communications of the ACM*, Vol. 29, No. 9, September 1986, p. 895.

MOAD, JEFF. "The Allure of UNIX," *Datamation*, September 15, 1989, p. 20.

MOAD, JEFF. "Can Unisys Juggle Open Systems, Too?" *Datamation*, September 1, 1988, p. 50.

RUSSELL, CHANNING H., AND PAMELA J. WATERMAN. "Variations on UNIX for Parallel-Processing Computers," *Communications of the ACM*, Vol. 30, No. 12, December 1987, pp. 1048–1055.

STAMPS, DAVID. "Beta Site Politics," *Datamation*, April 1, 1986, pp. 62–77.

READINGS BEFORE NEXT CHAPTER

The previous material should be adequate background.

15

DATA MANAGEMENT

VALUE OF DATA

The data that is stored on the computerized information system can be of tremendous value to the organization. The value, however, is not simply determined by what information is stored on the system, but also by how it is stored. The type of storage device, the format of the stored data, and the types of access available to that data can have a significant influence on the ultimate value of the stored data. Simply storing more data will not necessarily always be of value. For example, if the same information is stored multiple times in different locations and is conflicting, then this can have a significant negative influence on the value of this data to the firm.

Because data can originate from many sources and be stored in various locations in different formats, the task of data administration is a very important but difficult one. Most information systems will have a separate department dedicated to the task of data management. The mission of this area is to coordinate the storage and retrieval of computerized information and attempt to maximize its value to the firm.

For most firms, the role of data management is still evolving. As computerized systems become more complex, the importance of a strong, well-focused data management policy is becoming more evident. Many future productivity gains will hinge on coordinating the integration of the computerization of diverse business functions which demand proper data management. In this chapter, we will address some of the issues involved in data administration.

DATA MANAGEMENT FUNCTIONS

The functions of the data management area are very much dependent on the degree of centralization of the information system in the firm. The most complex task of data management is to establish policies that allow for maximum integration of the firm's data. The more decentralized the information system, the more important the task of data integration becomes. In an absolutely decentralized firm, that is, one in which all components are truly investment centers, there may be no data integration or system coordination at all. In fact, in this type of environment there may not even be a data management group. Instead, most of these functions would be performed by the system programming staff.

Another function of the data management area would be to devise guidelines for data access. These guidelines should establish a policy on who should be allowed to access data and the type of access to be allowed. Without these guidelines, there would either be no control over the data or decisions would have to be made on a case-by-case basis.

Establishing policies that protect the corporate data is another function commonly performed by the data management area. This would include working closely with the security group in establishing backup and recovery policies and in implementing methods to protect the data from unauthorized access or alteration.

The data management area must also monitor the performance of the various physical storage media. This involves measuring the utilization of the space on the devices, measuring the access times for specific applications, and reconfiguring these devices when appropriate.

The day-to-day management of the corporate databases is probably the function that consumes the most resources in data management. This area is so important that it usually is headed by an individual with the title of database manager or database administrator. In fact, in many organizations instead of calling the broad area data management, it will be called database management. However, there really is an important distinction between the two. Database management deals with the technical issues involving the storage and retrieval of data in the complex environment of a database management system. Data management deals with higher-level policy issues involving all corporate data and not just the data that is stored in database systems. Figure 15.1 summarizes the aforementioned data management functions.

In the following sections we will discuss each of these functions.

Data Integration

Data integration is one of the monumental tasks in the information system. It involves trying to coordinate and satisfy the data requirements of all areas of the firm. The objective is to store data so that it can be used by many related applications. This means that each application will not have its own unique data files. Also, in an integrated system, the data items will be stored

Figure 15.1   *Data Management Functions*

FUNCTION	DESCRIPTION
Data Integration	Allows multiple users to access data in various ways with a minimum of data redundancy
Establish Data Access Policies	Determines who should be allowed to read, write, create, etc. various data items
Data Security	Protects data from unauthorized access or alteration
Physical Media Management	Monitors performance of physical storage devices (DASD, tape, etc.) and reconfigures when needed
Database Management	Coordinates the usage of the database management system

uniquely or with very little redundancy. The more times the same data item is stored in different records, the more chance that inconsistencies may develop, resulting in a loss of data integrity.

An example may help to illustrate the point. The production area of a firm will have data concerning the employees in that department. This would include data on the jobs worked on by the employee, the hours worked, the type of skills that employee possesses, etc. The payroll department will also have data on these same individuals; however, much of this data would be different than that held by the production department. Data on the wage rate, salary history, tax data, employee benefits, etc., would be included. In addition, the personnel department will store other information concerning these employees. In a file-oriented (nonintegrated) system, each of these areas would have data stored in their own files. Much of the basic information, such as employee name, address, phone, etc., would be repeated in each separate file. Hence, a change could be made to the address in one file, but not to the others. This would lead to a loss of data integrity.

If the manager of the production department was making a promotion decision, it would be helpful to have the salary history of an employee. This would be difficult in a system lacking integration, since this data would be contained in the payroll system. Also, the manager, to do future recruiting, may want to get information on the colleges certain outstanding employees attended. This is data concerning personnel records, which would be difficult to obtain if the system was not designed to accommodate such an inquiry.

Each time a new system is proposed or an existing system is to be redesigned, a decision must be made as to how to best store and access the data. It is first necessary to classify the system as to whether it will be an independent, stand-alone system or whether its data must be integrated with that of other corporate functions.

If the data is unique to that application and other users will have no need to access it, then this is an independent application. For example, research and development may wish to have a system to store, access, and analyze the data generated by various experiments. No other department in the firm will use this information. Hence, the methods employed in storing and retrieving the data will be totally dictated by the needs of the users in research and development. Since this data is specific to one department, that department can determine who can access the data and the level of security to be applied to the data.

If the data must be shared, then it should not be "owned" by only one department. Instead, it must be treated as a corporate resource. This means that the needs of various departments must be assessed before the data storage and retrieval methods can be determined. This coordination will usually be the responsibility of the data management group.

Of course, the opposite extreme, in which all the data of the firm is placed in one massive integrated database, can also lead to serious problems. Here, the coordination and organization of the data becomes such a huge task that it overwhelms the data management and application program development areas. There has to be a trade-off between costs and benefits of data integration. Most firms will create separate databases for various subsystems, such as a production database, a marketing and distribution database, a payroll/personnel database, etc. The appropriate method is one of professional judgment and is usually dependent on the characteristics of the specific firm.

Again, the way in which a system is first implemented, especially the methods and types of devices used to store data, can have a significant influence on the usefulness of that data. This can extend well into the future since it is usually very time consuming and expensive to reconfigure the data. A major change in data storage will usually entail changes to all programs that access that data.

There may be some special situations in which integrated systems are not developed, even though the data should be shared by multiple users. Lack of sufficient time is usually the reason for developing a stand-alone system. It does take more analysis and design effort to develop integrated systems, but this extra effort will pay big returns in the ultimate usability of the data.

The primary users of a system may pressure the development team not to consider the other users' needs. Their main concern is usually to get an operational system as quickly as possible. This pressure should be resisted. Otherwise, the firm will eventually have a patchwork of independent, file-oriented applications.

DATABASE MANAGEMENT SYSTEMS

Developing an integrated system will involve the use of special software tools. Most important is a database management system (DBMS). This is the heart of an integrated system. It allows for storing very complex data relationships. Additionally, it will have a series of related tools that build a sophisticated

development and user environment. This includes report writers, fourth generation query languages, program development tools, and system utilities.

Because of the pivotal role of the DBMS in the application development
process, the selection of a DBMS is an important decision. There are three basic
database models associated with commercial DBMSs. These are the hierarchical,
networked, and relational models. Figure 15.2 summarizes the attributes of each
of these models.

The selection process should involve all areas of the information system.
The needs of the entire user community must be investigated, including a projection of future needs. The application development and maintenance staff and
systems programming must also be consulted. Since the DBMS acquisition process involves such a comprehensive analysis, we really cannot cover all of the
aspects in enough depth in this limited space. However, Figure 15.3 does summarize some of the important factors involved in a DBMS acquisition decision.

DATA NORMALIZATION

Simply having the data management tools, such as a DBMS and sophisticated
query languages, does not necessarily mean that data integration has been
achieved. The manner in which the data are stored and the way in which they
relate to each other will dictate the ultimate usefulness of these advanced tools.

Figure 15.2 *DBMS Models*

MODEL	DESCRIPTION	ATTRIBUTES
Hierarchical	Logical Tree Structure	Restricts data relations to trees
		Must store redundant data to represent other data structures
		Efficient with respect to physical storage
		Very fast in execution
		Relatively difficult to program
		Entails substantial systems programming commitment
Networked	Logical Network Structure	No restriction on data relationships
		Very powerful in representing data relationships
		Fast in execution
		Difficult to program production systems
		Most systems have high-level query tools
		Entails substantial systems programming commitment
Relational	Series of Tables	No restriction in data relationships
		Has limited data redundancy
		Easy to program
		End-user friendly
		Can be very resource intensive in execution
		Does not entail as much systems programmer intervention

Figure 15.3 *DBMS Acquisition Factors*

Types of possible data relationships
Amount of data to be stored
Primary processing mode: batch or online
Skill level of employees
Level of end-user involvement
Number of simultaneous users
Source languages to be used
Type of processing: production or ad hoc queries
Available hardware and software resources
Available systems programming staff
Desired response time

The use of database management systems allows for the normalization of the data on the system. The concept of data normalization is complex, and a detailed discussion is beyond the scope of this text. Much time is usually spent on these concepts in a database management course. However, we will attempt to describe briefly some of the concepts behind normalization.

Simply stated, the normalization process attempts to divide data into its logically constituent parts. Probably the easiest way of explaining this is by way of an example. Assume that we wish to store information about an employee. The straightforward approach would be to have a single record hold information for each employee. This record format is shown in Figure 15.4.

Notice that the first five fields deal with characteristics of the employee. The next two fields are concerned with the department, and the following five fields detail the educational background of the employee. With this configuration, each employee in a given department will have the same departmental data. Obviously, this produces a waste of storage and a high risk of having data inconsistency. Also, if one wished simply to list all of the departments and their attributes, it would be necessary to search this employee file exhaustively. If an additional file of departments was also created, this would just cause more data redundancy.

Other problems are caused by the part of the file holding information on universities. If an individual leaves the firm and he or she is the only graduate in

Figure 15.4 *Employee Information File*

Employee I.D.	Employee Address	Employee Phone	Employee Age	Employee Name	Department Location
Department Head	Degree	University	University Address	University Phone	University Location

EMPLOYEE #1
EMPLOYEE #2
EMPLOYEE #3
EMPLOYEE #4
EMPLOYEE #5

Figure 15.5 *Employee Database*

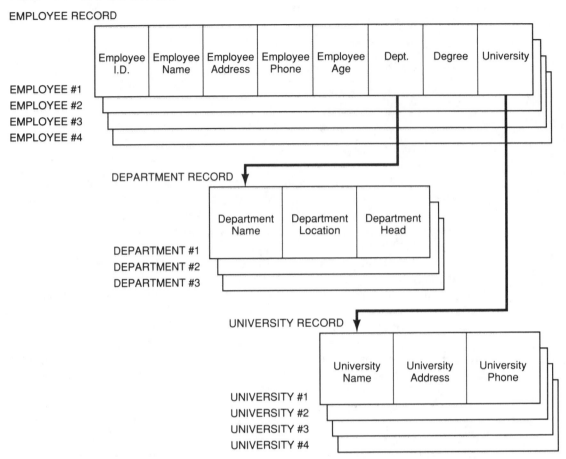

the company from that university, the information on that university is then lost. If someone in personnel wishes information on that university, they will not be able to get it from this file.

Figure 15.5 shows how the data can be stored in a DBMS. Notice that the problems discussed with respect to the file-oriented system are solved under this format. It would be a simple task to list and maintain data on departments and universities, with substantially reduced data redundancy.

This has been a very simplistic example. Hopefully, it should make it clear why data normalization and the entire data design process is so important.

DATABASE ADMINISTRATION

The database administrator (DBA) is responsible for managing the use of the database management system. This includes establishing policies and standards, monitoring the performance of the DBMS, and coordinating the diverse needs of the users. The DBA will usually report directly to the data manager. But the database administration staff will work very closely with the application system development and maintenance areas. The addition or modification of data in the DBMS must be cleared through the data administration group. Obviously, this is one of the ways of assuring proper data integration.

The standards and procedures developed and enforced by the DBA are primarily designed to guarantee consistent usage and to establish minimum performance targets. This would include the specification of the types of access methods available to certain groups of application programs. It could also include a limit on the average or maximum number of I/Os generated by calls to the DBMS. Another possible limiting parameter is the number of records allowed in a given database. These limitations are designed to prevent the degradation of service provided by the DBMS. A DBMS is such a powerful tool that, in an uncontrolled environment, a substantial commitment of computer resources can be made with little effort on the part of the application programmer. Without these limits, one user could very easily adversely affect all of the other users.

Other standards would include naming and documentation requirements for all data to be stored on the DBMS. If the DBMS has the capability, then a data dictionary can be useful in enforcing these standards. Most data dictionaries will define each of the records and their data elements in the system and will relate these to the application programs in which they are used.

Monitoring the performance of the DBMS is of particular importance in an online processing environment. This is usually accomplished by using a monitor system that is imbedded in the DBMS. This monitor will typically supply an online display of the tasks that are executing with their performance statistics.

The DBA is also responsible for tuning the DBMS when performance is not acceptable. After a problem is detected, the next step is to locate what program or part of the DBMS is causing the problem. Due to the complex nature of a DBMS, this may involve substantial effort. After the problem has been located, then some action must be taken to correct it. Some of the actions that can be taken to tune a DBMS are listed in Figure 15.6.

Figure 15.6 *Some Ways of Tuning a DBMS*

METHOD	DESCRIPTION
Develop additional access paths.	This involves creating new alternate keys that allow for different ways of entering and searching the DBMS.
Reorganize DBMS.	This changes the physical storage configuration of the DBMS without altering the logical views of the data.
Request changes to application programs.	If inefficient methods are being employed in a specific program, this is the only solution.
Restrict privileges of certain users.	This is a drastic, but sometimes necessary, action when some users are abusing their access privileges.

DETERMINING ACCESS PRIVILEGES

Deciding who gets access to specific data and the type of access granted can be a politically volatile process. To prevent friction, many firms will establish a data authority committee which is responsible for establishing guidelines for granting authority. This group is often a subcommittee of the computer steering committee or at least reports to the computer steering committee. Like the steering committee, its membership is comprised of representatives of various user areas.

The importance of data access lies in the fact that the extent of access to data may be used to define decision-making authority within an organization. Functionally, the exact opposite should be true; that is, decision-making authority defines data access. However, being able to control the data may allow the individual the opportunity to take certain actions. For example, assume the vice-president of marketing was allowed access to research and development data involving new products. By leaking new product information to prospective buyers, the release date of the new product may be affected by raising customer expectations. In most companies, this could cause friction between engineering, production, and marketing.

While the access policies are established by the data authority committee, the data management group must enforce them. For the DBMS, the DBA will be able to grant or revoke access privileges through mechanisms designed into the DBMS. Essentially, this involves each user being given a specific, sometimes unique, view of data in the database. For file-oriented data, the access control software discussed in Chapter 11 will restrict access to the data. For both situations, it is important that internal audit and the security group are involved in the process.

For decentralized organizations, each functional area may be granted domain over the data most closely associated with that area. In this way, the functional area would then be responsible for extending access rights to other users. The more integrated the environment, the more difficult it is to implement this type of distributed data policy. Additionally, decentralization of data authority can make data security a much more difficult task.

DATA SECURITY AND INTEGRITY

As in the case of granting data authority, establishing data security, backup, and recovery policies usually lies outside the realm of the data management group. However, implementing these policies can be the responsibility of data management. For file-oriented data, this entails developing schedules for periodically backing up specific data sets. This is commonly based on some measure of the file's activity. It is also desirable to do a complete backup of the physical media (usually disk drives) on a scheduled basis. In this way, a complete media failure (such as a head crash) could be quickly resolved simply by restoring that device using its backup. Otherwise, each file would have to be restored individually, a time-consuming task.

In a DBMS, many of the backup and recovery functions are designed into the system. Hence, as discussed in Chapter 11, dynamic roll-backs and roll-forwards can be easily done. Many security capabilities are also built into a DBMS. Since we have already discussed how access can be granted in a DBMS, we will not pursue the subject further.

Retention of files is an issue yet to be addressed. For backup copies, it is usually necessary to keep only three or four generations of the files. For some files, especially those containing financial and personnel data, there are laws which dictate the retention period. The Internal Revenue Service, Equal Employment Opportunity Act, state governments, and many other official bodies require that specific data be retained for some minimum length of time, usually measured in years. For this type of long-term storage, special high-density magnetic tape can be used. This also appears to be an excellent application for write once read many (WORM) optical disks. For added protection, there are firms that will store archival data in a secure location. Underground salt caverns seem to have the most stable environment for this type of storage.

DATA SET AND DEVICE MANAGEMENT

Industry figures show that the online storage capacity of many large data processing installations is growing at a compound rate of almost 40%. The management of tape and DASD storage is presently an expensive and time-consuming task. With this rapid growth rate, proper management becomes an increasing problem.

Most large shops will have thousands of individual data sets in addition to the data stored in databases. These data sets could be source code programs, object modules, load modules, libraries, catalogs, test data, or production data. Some of these data sets could be frequently accessed and updated, while others may be dormant for months at a time. Determining the device on which to store these data sets, when to relocate them to a different device, or when to reorganize a storage device is the responsibility of the data management group.

The first task is to monitor the utilization of the physical devices and the data sets stored on them. This would entail measuring the number of I/O requests to a given device, the amount of contention for that device (i.e., wait time), the amount of storage fragmentation (i.e., too many extents on separate cylinders), the activity of individual data sets, and the amount of free space on each device.

The statistics gathered during the monitoring process may indicate that either preventive or corrective action should be taken. Some of the possible actions that can be taken are listed in Figure 15.7. Traditionally, most of these actions have been done manually by the data management or system programming staff. However, the sheer volume of data in most information systems

Figure 15.7   *Possible Actions to Improve Storage Performance*

ACTION	DESCRIPTION
Move inactive data sets from disk to tape.	This will free up valuable disk space for the more active data sets.
Relocate disk data sets.	This can relieve congestion on specific devices.
Reorganize a disk pack.	This will eliminate fragmentation where data sets are scattered throughout the disk. It will also make the free space contiguous.
Compress certain data sets.	Some data sets (such as partitioned data sets) will have imbedded dead space that can be compressed out to save storage.
Archive or erase unused data sets.	Some data sets are no longer of value and should be eliminated to free up valuable space.
Scratch unauthorized data sets.	If installation naming and cataloging procedures are not followed, then these data sets must be eliminated from the system.

makes manual data set and device management too expensive. An alternative is to use software especially designed to do this maintenance. This saves money and also helps guarantee that established data policies are being followed.

Some vendors have adopted the philosophy of systems-managed storage. This entails the concept of allowing the operating system to make most of the tactical decisions concerning storage management. Using systems-managed storage facilities, it is no longer necessary for the user to specify where a data set will reside. Instead, the system will determine the type of media (tape, disk, etc.), the location on the media, the amount of storage allocated, the frequency of backup, how long the data should be retained, and other important decisions.

Under systems-managed storage, the data management group will develop the desired attributes for each of the various classes of data in the system. For example, one class may be data which is very active, critical to the company and also volatile. This data may be stored on a disk drive with rapid access speed and may be continually backed up. On the other hand, data that is infrequently used may be stored on cartridge tape.

All the user then has to do is designate the appropriate data class. The system will store the data based on its classification. The system can also help to monitor data set activity, reduce media fragmentation, and recover and consolidate free space. The rapidly growing demand for increased storage facilities makes systems-managed storage an economic necessity for most large installations.

MAJOR COMPANY

As can be seen in the organization chart for Major Company's information system (Figure 3.12 in Chapter 3), there is a separate data management department. Actually, this department has just recently been established. Three years ago, a consultant was hired to investigate the application systems development and maintenance situation. This person found that even though Major Company had a DBMS and many sophisticated tools associated with the DBMS, many of the development efforts were being done in a vacuum. The system analysts and programmers were dealing only with a single functional area. The data being stored in the DBMS was not integrated with data from other applications in the company. In some cases, the data in the DBMS was being stored simply as a file.

The result of this type of development was that a large majority of the changes requested by users involved almost a complete redesign of both the associated data elements and the application programs in the system. What initially appeared to be minor requests quickly developed into major redesign projects. At the time the consultant studied the problem, the applications maintenance backlog was staggering.

In the consultant's final report, the establishment of a data management department was strongly recommended. In addition, it was suggested that all system analysts and eventually all programmers be sent to classes dealing with data normalization and data integration. Both of these proposals were implemented.

Presently, all requests for system development are reviewed for impact on other applications. If it is determined that this project will need to be coordinated with other functional areas, then the scope of the development is widened to include these areas. During the structured walkthrough of both the systems analysis phase and the design phase, a specialist on data integration from the data management area must review and accept the data design components before the project can go on to the next phase. The word has gotten around that if you do not do it right the first time, you will work on it until it is done right.

This year a follow-up study was done to investigate the effectiveness of these changes. It was found that approximately 20% of all new development projects involve no new data. The data is already on the system in an acceptable format. This substantially reduces the development time of these projects. However, it was found that projects that do need to store additional data now take an added 10% of time to complete. The biggest change has been on the program maintenance side. It is taking about 50% of the time to complete maintenance requests. The maintenance programmers believe this figure is still too high because there are many older, poorly designed systems that have not as yet been redesigned employing the new methods.

All in all, the changes have been very successful. Management is now embarking on a training program for the user community. This will be a watered down version of the data normalization and integration series that the analysts and programmers attended. Hopefully, this will help to eliminate the users' reluctance to consider the needs of other functional areas. Maybe this will even help to reduce the proliferation of redundant, and often obsolete, data files scattered throughout the firm. A majority of these are stored on stand-alone micros, where only the owner knows they exist.

SUMMARY

The proper management of the data resources can be very beneficial to an organization. This will allow for the more efficient use of the computer resources and will, more importantly, allow users to access the information stored on the system more easily and efficiently.

Data management involves establishing policies for the storage and access of data. This includes coordinating the data needs of all of the departments in the firm so that data can be shared and data redundancy can be kept to a minimum.

A database management system (DBMS) is a key component in developing integrated systems. It allows for a variety of storage and retrieval options. Selecting a DBMS is a difficult decision that will have a long-term impact on the system development environment. The database administrator will be responsible for the coordination of the DBMS and for enforcing policies on the use of the DBMS.

The data management group has responsibilities in implementing data access, data security, and data integrity policies. In most firms, the policies will be developed by someone other than the data management group. Special cases and anything not covered by the established policy will have to be referred back to the initiating group.

Data management must also monitor the activity and measure the performance of data-related operations. If problems appear, then action must be taken to correct the situation. The possible actions include reconfiguring the data, relocating data sets, and changing the access methods used by the application program.

Data management has been the neglected child of the information system. Unfortunately, many firms have left the design and configuration of the stored data up to individuals concerned only about single function application systems. In this information age, the true value of data must be realized and nurtured so as to provide maximum benefits.

QUESTIONS

1. Describe and briefly explain the functions of the data management group.
2. Why can data redundancy lead to a lack of data integrity?
3. Explain the difference between a database management system and file-oriented processing.
4. Describe what data integration involves. Why is it important to consider data integration when designing the storage and retrieval of data?
5. What is meant by data normalization? How is it related to data integration?
6. What are the responsibilities of a database administrator?

7. What is the difference between a data manager and a database administrator?

8. What is the reason for doing data set and data device management? Describe some of the problems that can occur and the possible actions that can be taken to solve these problems.

9. A programmer decides to archive disk data sets to another disk drive instead of to a tape. Why is this not acceptable? How can the data management group prevent or detect this type of action?

10. Explain how information about classes and the students taking those classes will interact with information concerning professors. Are there any other interactions between students and professors? Give examples where appropriate.

11. Different users of a DBMS can be given different views of the data stored in the DBMS. Why is this done? How is this done?

12. If you were assigned the job of hiring a data manager, what attributes and qualifications would you be looking for in this individual? Explain your answer.

13. If you were assigned the job of hiring a database administrator, what attributes and qualifications would you be looking for in this individual? Explain your answer.

14. There is a saying that "information is power." Explain this statement in terms of granting users access to data.

15. Some systems will allow the DBA not only to grant access to data to an individual user, but also to grant a user the ability to grant access to that same data to other users. Under what circumstances would it be appropriate for the DBA to use this power, and in which circumstances would it be inappropriate?

16. In reference to disk fragmentation:
    a. Explain what it means to have a data set fragmented on a disk.
    b. Explain how fragmentation of free space on a disk can cause problems.
    c. How can you eliminate both data set and free space fragmentation?

17. The payroll department wishes to obtain a computerized payroll system. The manager of the department has taken a few computer courses and insists that to run the weekly payroll, a batch-oriented system using a sequential tape file should be implemented. A representative from the data management area strongly disagrees. Who is right? Explain and defend your answer.

18. The head of the marketing department has just been denied write access to the inventory files by the data management group. The marketing department head had asked for permission from the inventory manager to read, write, and update this data. The permission was granted by the inventory manager. His statement was, "If marketing can't figure out what we have, then they can't sell it and there's no reason for us to store it." The head of marketing claims that this is the inventory control area's data, and they

should be able to dictate what can be done with it. Fully discuss this situation and explain which is the correct position.

CASE ANALYSIS

Case 1

Investigate the main database management system used on your campus (there may be more than one system). Describe each of the following characteristics involving the DBMS:

1. Type of data model (i.e., networked, relational, etc.)
2. Associated development tools
3. Associated user tools
4. Levels of security available
5. Types of backup and recovery available
6. Source language interfaces
7. Types of processing allowed (i.e., batch, line by line interactive or full screen interactive)

In addition, analyze at least one application system that is implemented under this DBMS and describe how the data is stored and how this system integrates with other application systems.

It will probably be necessary to do some of your investigation using a reference service such as *DataPro* and also by interviewing one of the lead system analysts in the application development or maintenance area.

Case 2

Research at least two data set and data device management software packages that run under the IBM MVS operating system. Describe what functions they provide and how they operate. Be sure to compare and contrast the two systems. Which would you recommend? Why?

ADDITIONAL READINGS

APPLETON, DANIEL. "Information Asset Management," *Datamation*, February 1, 1986, pp. 71–76.

DOLK, DANIEL R., AND ROBERT A. KIRSCH, II. "A Relational Information Resource Dictionary System," *Communications of the ACM*, Vol. 30, No. 1, January 1987, p. 48.

FISHER, MARSHA. "Digging Out with Image Technology," *Datamation*, April 15, 1989, p. 18.

LEDERER, ALBERT L., AND AUBREY L. MENDELOW. "Information Resource Planning: Overcoming Difficulties in Identifying Top Management's Objectives," *MIS Quarterly,* Vol. 11, No. 3, September 1987, pp. 389–399.

SHAH, ARVIND. "Data Administration: It's Crucial," *Datamation*, January 1984, pp. 187–192.

VERITY, JOHN. "Taming the DASD Monster," *Datamation*, December 1, 1986, pp. 77–80.

READINGS BEFORE NEXT CHAPTER

The preceding material should be adequate preparation.

16

MANAGEMENT OF DATA COMMUNICATIONS

INTRODUCTION

With the increased use of distributed microprocessor technology, it is not surprising that telecommunications (TCOM) has risen from a relatively minor managerial concern to one of the top 10 problems faced by data processing managers. Telecommunications is an area that focuses on the acquisition, transmission, delivery, and management of electronic signals over some distance. The electronic signal can be voice, video, and/or data and can originate from or be delivered to telephones, computers, VDTs, and other devices.

Because telecommunication (TCOM) technology is in its infancy and continually evolving, the management of these systems is even younger still. It is not at all clear as to what the long-term implications of TCOM will be for an organization or what elements of the system must bear the closest scrutiny. Data processing managers understand the general importance of the field, if not the specifics.

The purpose of this chapter is to acquaint you with some of the terminology, elements, and potential control points of telecommunications. In many organizations, TCOM is used synonymously with data communications. When this is the case, voice transmission concerns are not part of the responsibilities of the communications specialist or the data processing manager. However, in this chapter, we will consider all forms of telecommunications.

The objectives of network management include satisfaction of system users and cost-effective service. User satisfaction is a function of reliable system performance, adequate system availability, and information dissemination. Cost-effectiveness is created by adequate system planning, modular design and expansion, and sound systems analysis and design methods.

BRIEF HISTORY OF TELECOMMUNICATIONS

Figure 16.1 presents a summary of some of the important events in communications. At first glance, it appears that the industry is not as young as previously mentioned. However, at closer inspection, we can see that the timeline is divided into pre- and post-computer revolution (circa 1946). Precomputer communications are mostly concerned with the postal service and manual point-to-point communication between telegraph or telephone units, while postcomputer communications are oriented toward the transmission of data as well as voice.

Some of the events listed in Figure 16.1 are worth discussion. SABRE (Semiautomatic Business Research Environment) was an online, real-time airline

Figure 16.1 *Important Events in Communications*

1639: First government postal service
1800: Railroads
1835: Telegraph
1844: First telegraph line
1850: Western Union founded
1860: Pony Express began
1861: Demise of Pony Express
1861: High-speed teletype
1866: Transatlantic cable laid
1876: Bell telephone introduced
1877: Bell telephone company formed
1880: American Bell
1882: Western Electric purchased
1885: American Telephone and Telegraph formed
1890: Marconi invents the radio
1891: First PBX
1915: First transatlantic phone call
1921: Mobile phones used in police cars
1934: FCC formed
1946: ENIAC, the first usable digital computer
1947: The transistor
1952: Area codes introduced
1954: The transceiver
1956: AT&T prohibited from engaging in non-common-
        carrier services
1959: Integrated circuits
1962: First communications satellite launched
1962: SABRE network
1968: Carterfone decision
1969: MCI gains microwave use
1971: Value Added Networks
1974: IBM's SNA
1984: AT&T divestiture
1988: AT&T writes off analog systems

reservation system developed by American Airlines and IBM in 1962. Twelve hundred terminals were connected to the system performing queries and updating data. Today, the evolution of SABRE is attached to 19,000 terminals and has given American Airlines a significant competitive weapon.

Probably more interesting than the technical developments in the industry are the legal issues that have arisen. In 1956, a federal court prohibited AT&T and its companies from engaging in business other than communications. This caused quite a controversy concerning the supply of data processing and transmission services. In 1968, Thomas Carter sued AT&T for the right to attach his mobile radio service to the local phone lines. The Federal Communications Commission (FCC) ruled in his favor, producing the Carterfone Decision, setting the precedent that companies other than AT&T could use the telephone system. A year later, the FCC granted Microwave Communications, Inc. (MCI) the right to use microwaves for transmission. The private use of telecommunication satellites also began around this time. In 1971, another FCC decision allowed other vendors to resell telephone service. In this manner, a company could lease AT&T telephone lines, add additional communication services, and sell the entire package to consumers. This concept is called a Value Added Network (VAN).

Probably the most significant event in recent telecommunications history has been the divestiture of AT&T. As of 1984, AT&T no longer had total control of both the telecommunication lines and telecommunication equipment. This decision was an attempt to insure that the world's largest TCOM company, which was anxious to enter the computer market, could not specify what equipment would attach to their network. The stakes were enormous: Almost every home and business has telephone access. If AT&T could market a computer that would simply plug into the telephone network, they would have end-to-end control over distributed data processing throughout the United States and more—a situation that the FCC viewed as harmful to fair competition. Contrary to the views of local telephone subscribers, the purpose of the divestiture was to "detach" AT&T from local service (i.e., the computer ports in our homes and offices). This allowed AT&T to sell computers and computer services that potentially could attach to the Bell system. The result of the divestiture was that, essentially, many companies could provide telecommunication and computer services.

Business and personal uses of TCOM are readily evident. Consumers can make withdrawals, deposits, and account inquiries at automatic teller machines (ATM) throughout their community. Many organizations use electronic mail (E-mail) to circulate memos and keep records and voice mail (V-mail) to provide freedom from time boundaries. The Iran-Contra investigation of 1987 produced several such memos as evidence. Data that was once placed on magnetic tape and shipped through the mail can now be transmitted over data lines at substantial savings in cost and time. It is possible to plan and pay for a world cruise from your home. Many periodicals, such as *USA Today*, are published from a single source in many remote locations around the world. Faculty and students at over 300 universities across the world can communicate with each other through an international network called BITNET. Cable television systems are also examples of the application of telecommunication technology, some transmitting data and voice signals, as well as the video/audio signal of the television channels.

The widespread use of telecommunications has had effects on our society. We routinely expect to see live video of important events happening around the world, and even in outer space. Our satellites relay pictures of hurricanes, cold fronts, landing strips, troop movements, and animal migrations. All of this has made our world seem smaller and changed the emphasis that we place on certain events. For example, *Live Aid* was a live, world-wide benefit concert that raised money for the world's hungry. Without telecommunications, the concert could not have been broadcast around the world and the pictures of the starving peoples would have had a limited audience. Wall Street also has been affected. Concern was raised recently about the trading of large blocks of stocks by computers at remote sites, causing wide swings in volume traded and prices.

Our telephone systems are becoming increasingly complex. The simple public branch exchanges (PBX) of the mid-1900s have been replaced with automated exchanges (PABX) and computerized exchanges (CBX). These intelligent devices route incoming calls throughout the organization, queuing them at appropriate telephones, placing them on hold, and playing music for the caller. With some systems, the caller can route his or her call to other departments by instructing the CBX. Outgoing calls are distributed to the various line trunks to minimize collisions (no outbound lines available) and maximize line usage. Detailed accounting reports can be generated from data gathered by these devices. Our home phones are also becoming more sophisticated. When having a phone installed, the customer has the option of call forwarding, call waiting, three-way calling, and speed dialing—all features provided by computer-controlled branch exchanges.

As we have seen, telecommunications is quite pervasive in our lives. It is no wonder that managers feel that one of the most important areas confronting them in the coming years will be related to the transmission of voice, video, and data across short and long distances. In the next sections, we will cover some of the terminology and methods used in telecommunications.

TRANSMISSION MEDIA CHARACTERISTICS

Data is transmitted from one point to another through a medium. Common media include twisted wire pairs, coaxial cable, optical fiber, microwave, and satellite. These media can be compared by costs, transmission speeds, and common applications. Figure 16.2 summarizes these characteristics.

Transmission speeds are measured in different units. Bits per second (bps) refers to the number of data bits transmitted through a media per second. This is also sometimes called the bit rate. The effective bit rate is the number of useful bits transmitted per second. For example, some systems use a parity bit to

Figure 16.2 *Transmission Media Characteristics*

MEDIA	COST	SPEED	USES
Twisted Pair	.16–$1.00/ft	Up to 281 Mbps	Cheap, short-haul transmission, low data rate, telephone network
Coaxial Cable	.65–$4.00/ft	Up to 400 Mbps	High data rates, multiple bands, LANs
Optical Fiber	$2.00–$7.00/ft	Up to 1 Gbps	Very high data rates and long distance point-to-point transmission
Microwave	n/a	Up to 45 Mbps	Long distance "line of sight" transmission, high data rate, multiple bands
Satellite	Up to $500/hr	Up to 50 Mbps	Very long distance, multiple bands

help detect transmission errors. This additional bit is not "useful" in the same sense as the original eight data bits were. The baud rate refers to the number of times a transmission media can change states during a second. By using different modulation techniques, the bit rate can be several times larger than the baud rate.

The bandwidth of a media refers to the difference between the maximum and minimum signal frequencies that can be transmitted, and is measured in cycles per second (Hz). A narrow band is less than 3,000 Hz, a wide band greater than 3,000 Hz. Voice band, the average frequency of the human voice, is 3,300 Hz to 300 Hz for a bandwidth of 3,000 Hz. To transmit several signals along a single media, the original signal frequency must be altered (modulated). FM (frequency modulation) and AM (amplitude modulation) radio signals each use a different modulation technique to alter the voices of musicians and DJs.

Most buildings are routinely wired with twisted pair for telephone service. This type of wiring cannot transmit at the high data rate shown in Figure 16.2. A typical speed of these unconditioned lines is around 56 Kbps, which works fine for voice traffic. Consequently, large amounts of data cannot be transmitted using most existing wiring. However, smaller amounts of data (memos, short reports, electronic mail, etc.) can be easily transmitted. In fact, using voice-over-data modems, voice and data can be transmitted over the same lines at the same time, greatly increasing the effectiveness of existing wiring.

Coaxial cable (coax) presents an attractive alternative. Because of the wide bandwidth, voice, video, and data signals can all be simultaneously transmitted. Coax is slightly more difficult to handle and attach than the extremely pliable twisted pair. However, a single cable can be used for a variety of applications including closed circuit television, digital data transmission, and telephone traffic.

Optical fiber can transmit at a high data rate with very low error rates. Because of the difficulty of adding and deleting stations, fiber optics is most commonly used in static environments. Consequently, fiber optics are suited for the interconnection of local networks and long distance point-to-point communication.

Microwave and satellite transmission are not used for transmission within a building, but are very popular for communications between distributed locations. Microwave relay stations can be seen in metropolitan downtown areas and in the middle of an oil field. Microwave transmission is not "secure" in that signals are radiated and can be intercepted. Satellite earth stations can be seen popping up around office buildings across the country. Several companies provide transponders (sending/receiving units on satellites) and rent time on their satellites.

Choosing the correct media can be difficult. Figure 16.3 lists some of the variables that should be considered.

The availability of a transmission media is concerned with whether it is ready to be used when needed. Expandability and maintenance refer to the ability to add, delete, or update nodes and lines in the network. Coaxial cable and satellite usage is relatively easy to expand while fiber optics are very difficult. Some media are more susceptible to signal distortion than others. Error detection deals with this distortion and is discussed in greater detail later in this chapter. As previously mentioned, microwave transmission is a broadcast media and can provide poor security when used by itself. Data encryption techniques can help overcome this shortcoming. Coaxial cable is also relatively easy to tap and poses security problems. The distance that a signal is to travel is another consideration. Shorter distances can be covered by twisted pair or coax while longer distances are typically covered by fiber optics, microwave, or satellite. Some applications require specific media. For example, when installing a PABX, managers may have no choice as to what types of lines may be connected. Twisted pair may be the only option. Finally, local standards imposed by fire codes, local management directives, etc. may require that only certain media be used in specific situations. For example, a fire code may insist that all wiring that is to be installed in ceilings or walls be placed in metal conduit or be Teflon-coated cable.

As can be seen, the decision as to what media to select is not at all a straightforward one. In fact, quite often the selection is out of the hands of the manager and is dictated by the equipment or data rates required. However, an eye must always be kept on the future since the technology is changing so rapidly. This means that the flexibility of media should be of primary concern.

Figure 16.3 *Variables Affecting Media Choice*

Cost	Speed
Capacity	Availability
Expendability	Maintenance
Error Rates	Security
Distance	Application
Local Standards	Sources of Interference

PROTOCOLS

The physical connection between devices in a network is the simplest element in the structure. The formatting of the message and subsequent routing to the appropriate destination is the job of the network protocol. They are the rules that control the conversation between sender and receiver. Figure 16.4 contains a list of requirements for an effective protocol.

In a telephone conversation, to be effective, both parties must not transmit at the same time. A protocol exists between the callers which dictates when the parties should talk and when they should listen. The protocol must also be able to detect when an error occurs and attempt to correct it. Data transparency is concerned with making the data appear to the receiver exactly as it was sent. For example, many protocols divide long messages into shorter messages called packets or frames. These packets are sent individually and help increase the efficiency of the network. The message must be put back together before presentation to the receiver. A network is simply a collection of physically or logically connected devices. Consequently, those devices must be manipulated for the smooth operation of the network.

Protocols used in large systems are divided into three types. Asynchronous protocols do not require that the devices be synchronized when transmitting. In other words, the sender can transmit at any time and the receiver must be ready to accept data. Many dumb terminals are asynchronous. Character synchronous protocols require that the sender and receiver be synchronized. The beginning and end of each message is delineated by a specific character in the character set. If the user wishes to use one of these characters within the original message, trouble could arise. Bit synchronous protocols rely on a specific bit pattern to delineate messages, rather than a character.

Those associated with small local networks are grouped based on how they access the transmission media. The two most popular protocols are Carrier Sense Multiple Access with Collision Detection (CSMA/CD, which is embodied in Ethernet) and token passing. CSMA/CD protocols specify how each device in a network must "listen" to the media while it is transmitting. If another device is currently using the media, the sender must wait. A collision occurs when two or more stations begin transmitting simultaneously. Token passing protocols gain access to the network by transmitting a set of bits (a token) around the network. To send data, a station must wait until the token is passed to it. While the token is "in use," no other station may transmit.

There are a great number of different protocols. One can imagine the difficulty in attempting to interconnect systems of differing hardware, operating

Figure 16.4   *Protocol Requirements*

Orderly Exchange of Data	Error Detection
Error Correction	Data Transparency
Device Control	

systems, and protocols. As has happened frequently in the data processing industry, standards have been developed to aid this.

REFERENCE MODELS AND STANDARDS

There are two types of standards found in the data processing industry. The formal standard is created by a committee of interested parties and often is vendor neutral. A de facto standard has arisen because of repeated product usage in the work place and the reluctance of users to abandon it. SDLC is such a standard. IBM developed SDLC in the early 1970s to implement SNA. Wouldn't it be nice to have a single standard around which to build systems?

However, because there is no clear standard, a manager could, potentially, make the wrong decision. Many managers use this point either to defer the decision until a standard is created, or choose a protocol by not choosing one (e.g., let the vendor decide). The International Standards Organization (ISO) determined that the creation of a standard protocol was, obviously, necessary but could not be easily implemented given the de facto standards already in place. Consequently, they created a reference model called the ISO Open Systems Interconnection Model, or OSI.

The OSI model has become a very important mechanism for comparing and creating communications networks. The model is called a layered model, a concept taken from operating systems design. Figure 16.5 depicts this model.

The physical layer transmits the bit stream over the physical medium. The data link layer provides for reliable transfer of data across the physical link. It handles error control and sends the frames of data. The network layer segments the messages, addresses the frames, and handles confirmations. The transport layer provides transparent communication between end-users. It is responsible for making sure that the frames are presented in the correct order and that all have arrived before presentation. The session layer provides a control structure for interfacing the application programs to the network. From a communication manager's point of view, this represents the end of his or her domain. The presentation layer marks the boundary of the application program-

Figure 16.5 *Open Systems Interconnection Model*

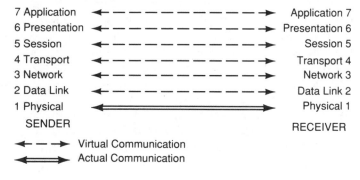

mer. Its responsibilities include the formulation of correct syntax for presentation to the session layer. The application layer is actually the application program. This includes the operating system as well as the executing tasks.

The segmentation of responsibilities provides ease of access and maintenance of network units. It is interesting to note that none of the aforementioned protocols adheres strictly to the reference model. The CCITT standards committee is also developing a version of the OSI. These models are aimed at large networks. Smaller local networks also have standards. Specifically, the Institute of Electrical and Electronics Engineers (IEEE) created IEEE 802 as standards for two types of local area networks (CSMA/CD and token passing).

The bulk of the data communication manager's time is spent debugging problems. The process of detecting network failures, diagnosing symptoms, and correcting problems can be frustrating. Fortunately, some of these tasks can be performed by the network itself.

ERROR DETECTION AND CORRECTION

The efficient detection of errors is a complicated process. For example, the letter *A* in EBCDIC is represented as 1100 0001 while the letter *C* is represented as 1100 0011. During data entry, the grade of *A* was entered, but because an air conditioner turned on at approximately the same instant causing a shift in the electromagnetic field around the motor, was transmitted as a *C* (i.e., the second bit was turned on). It is interesting to know why this happened, but not enough so to experiment with a report card. Both the *A* and the *C* are legal characters so neither would appear to be wrong to the human eye. We must rely on the hardware to detect such errors.

There are many error detection schemes, some very simple (parity checking), some very complex (polynomial error checking). Although we will not discuss in detail the mechanisms of these methods, we will discuss their abilities.

All transmission media are subject to signal distortion. While noise is caused by the movement of electrons and is proportional to the temperature of the medium. Over telephone lines, we can hear static or hissing. Impulse noise is caused by electronic equipment starting up or lightning strikes. It sounds like a "click" over the telephone. Crosstalk occurs when signals from one channel interfere with those of another. This is often evident in long distance phone calls where we can almost understand someone else talking "on our line." Signal attenuation is the weakening of a signal as a result of distance. An electronic signal encounters resistance in the medium as it moves toward its destination resulting in a decrease in signal strength.

Parity checking, discussed earlier in this text, is the simplest form of error checking and is also known as vertical redundancy check. The likelihood of detecting a burst error (i.e., a single error with multiple bit changes) is approximately 50%. Longitudinal redundancy checking (LRC) is the checking of a group of characters in parallel rather than serially as in parity checking. By adding LRC to VRC we have a greater probability of catching burst errors. The cyclic redundancy check, also known as a polynomial error check, is a complex routine that can detect over 99.998% of all burst errors over 16 bits long. To implement any of these mechanisms in software would be prohibitive and expensive to run. Consequently, they are placed in firmware for faster execution.

Error correcting codes are not nearly as sophisticated. In fact, most systems implement error correction by asking the sender to retransmit the message. Fortunately, this too is handled by the hardware and does not cause too many problems for the user.

Error prevention is a positive step in this process. By leasing conditioned lines from the telephone company, less distortion is encountered. Also, by transmitting at a lower rate, the probability of an error lasting long enough to destroy the message is decreased. By shielding lines and equipment, crosstalk and impulse noise are reduced. The use of repeaters on a line combats the effects of attenuation in the line and increases the range of the network. Finally, new equipment tends to be less noisy and better shielded than older equipment. Physical switches are replaced by digital switches and fewer moving parts are encountered.

There are times when a TCOM manager or technician needs to inspect a data line to view the quality of transmission first hand. Line monitors and breakout boxes can be used to diagnose problems on the communication line or interface. These devices allow for the trapping and sending of bit patterns, and monitoring line and circuit status in real time. Many network operating systems provide these services through software at graphic terminals as well.

THE TELEPHONE COMPANY AND CATV

Most of our discussions so far have focused on digital data transmission. This normally, but not necessarily, does not include voice traffic. Each telephone has two or more wires that attach it to the telephone company's nearest end office. The connection between the end office and the telephone is called a local loop. The end office is connected to a toll office by way of a connecting trunk. Toll offices are connected to each other by way of intermediate switching offices. To increase local phone system efficiency, many organizations purchased private branch exchanges (PBX). A PBX is an on-site facility which connects the telephones within the site to the public telephone system. The first PBXs were manual switchboards seen in old movies. In the 1920s these were replaced by private automatic branch exchanges (PABX), which were electromechanical devices which allowed for unassisted line connections. Computerized branch exchanges (CBX) used digital technology to digitize voice (by way of a COder/DECoder—CODEC) and then use digital switches to route the bit stream to the proper line. Today, CBXs provide for the use of digital phones with integrated voice/data capabilities and intelligent extension switching. The term *PBX* is still popular even when referring to these more sophisticated devices.

Long distance service has become quite complex after the divestiture. Many companies are vying for business, each offering a wide variety of services. Managing a telephone system can be a difficult undertaking. Figure 16.6 is a list of the steps for controlling telephone costs.

Much of the information needed in Figure 16.6 can be collected by a PBX. Because the telephone is such a common feature in the modern office, small changes in the system could reap substantial rewards or incur the wrath of every user in the organization. When selecting a long distance service, the manager should note the frequency of calls, the time of day that the service would be used, the cities covered by the service, the billing increments used, and the level of service provided.

Many large organizations are now setting up their own voice networks using microwave and leased lines. These systems can decrease the costs and improve the quality of voice/data communication over heavily traveled routes. The unused bandwidth can be sold to other organizations to decrease the costs further.

The cable television industry has greatly affected telecommunications. So-called superstations like WTBS-Atlanta and WGN-Chicago are seen in homes across the U.S. Community Antennae Television (CATV) was first developed to provide television services to small communities that were too far away from the television signal repeaters for adequate individual signal reception. CATV uses coaxial cable that originates from a central office and, with the use of repeaters, transmits many channels to subscribers. Originally, the transmission was only simplex (i.e., one direction) and limited to the television programs. However, recently, not only are the programs being transmitted, but also digital data. To combat cable fraud, cable companies have increased the intelligence of their systems so that the computer in the home office communicates with the control unit attached to the subscriber's set, verifying that the service has been paid for. It should not be surprising to know that this same technology could be used for digital data communication between other computers as well. It appears that not

Figure 16.6   *Steps for Controlling Telephone Costs*

Step 1:
  Inspect basic service, line charges, connect charges, rentals
    for all local calls, long distance calls, operator assisted calls, informa-
    tion calls, other charges and credits
Step 2:
  Identify calling patterns (time of day, day of week, day of month, loca-
    tions called, inbound traffic)
Step 3:
  Develop alternatives to inbound and outbound calls pinpointed in 1
    and 2
Step 4:
  Review service levels

only do we have a computer port in our homes represented by the telephone jack, we have another attached to our television sets.

VALUE ADDED NETWORKS

Value Added Networks (VAN) allow vendors to purchase multiple circuits from AT&T and resell the service with added features to subscribers. Examples of VANs include Arpanet—a research application of the department of defense, Tymnet—a commercial network from McDonnell Douglas, and Telenet—a terminal access network from GTE. VANs provide packetized data handling, network optimization, error handling, speed conversion, protocol conversion, store and forward, contention routing, and broadcast capabilities. Businesses and individuals use VANs to carry on correspondence, share data and programs, and to attach to remote systems. VANs are not necessarily public domain. Private networks are very popular and are used to speed correspondence between distributed sites.

LOCAL AREA NETWORKS

A Local Area Network (LAN) is a network of terminals, personal computers, hosts, and other devices (file servers, printers, etc.) that are closely located and, typically, wholly owned and operated by an organization. These networks have very high data rates (up to 100 Mbps) and cover relatively small distances (up to 25 kilometers). Because of the limited area and the absence of switching devices, very low error rates are usually the case. A typical LAN would connect several personal computers in a department to the organization mainframe or the department minicomputer. A high-quality laser printer could be attached to the system and shared among many users. Figure 16.7 shows the advantages of local area networks.

LANs can be divided into broadband and baseband networks. Broadband networks are expensive and can be difficult to manage. However, the advantages of broadband transmission include the fact that many signals can be

Figure 16.7 *Advantages of Local Area Networks*

Centralized Control
Enhances Terminal Utilization
Resource Sharing
Intermachine Communication
Incremental Expansion
Attachment to Large Computers
Broadcast Abilities
Reduced Wiring
Office Automation

modulated and shipped over a single media. As a result, a local area network could be used for voice, video, and data transmission allowing all devices to work simultaneously. Baseband networks provide only one channel for transmission; all of the devices on the network must contend for use of the media. Baseband networks are more easily managed because they lack the ability to send multiple signals simultaneously.

Local area networks are normally composed of coaxial cable, networked devices, and network controllers. Networked devices could be personal computers or other intelligent devices with controller cards supplying network access. Like LANs can be attached to one another by way of a bridge, while different LANs use gateways. It is not unusual for multiple LANs to be attached, with gateways or bridges to a backbone, baseband LAN. Figure 16.8 shows this configuration. A gateway is a network node that connects two different networks while a bridge connects two similar networks.

From a management perspective, there is relatively little difference be-

Figure 16.8 *Interconnection of LANs*

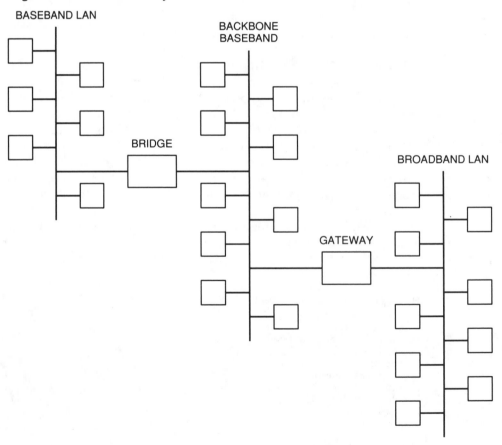

tween CSMA/CD and token passing protocols. Both allow for the interconnection and sharing of devices. In fact, when simply looking at the networks, it is not evident what protocol is being used. There does not seem to be a clear winner in the LAN market. Perhaps the biggest difference is the fact that most, but not all, implementations of CSMA/CD are baseland while most token passing networks are broadband. A great deal of research is needed in the area of LAN before clear-cut solutions exist.

DATA COMMUNICATION PLANNING

The telecommunications department is a collection of individuals who are charged with the maintenance and management of an organization's telecommunications resources. Figure 16.9 shows a typical TCOM department.

The analysis and design of telecommunications systems occurs exactly as it does for computerized business systems. Feasibility studies are undertaken and followed by analysis, design, development, and implementation. Probably the largest difference between software systems and TCOM systems lies in the fact that TCOM is a very hardware intensive field. Consequently, the abilities of the devices used play a more significant role here.

TCOM systems planning begins with the recognition that a communications problem exists. A preliminary investigation is undertaken to better understand the problem and determine whether further investigation is warranted. The manager of telecommunications appoints project directors and task forces to investigate the problem and present a summary of the preliminary study. The purpose of this study is to define the benefits sought by a new system. Specific questions concerning requirements of the system are investigated. A more detailed investigative study can be used to look at the performance of the proposed system weighed against selected alternatives.

Because of the hardware orientation of telecommunications, this preliminary study is often overlooked. It is sometimes very easy to talk to a vendor and

Figure 16.9 *Typical TCOM Organization*

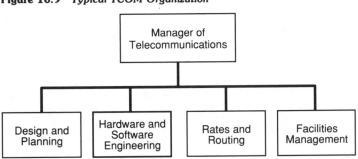

send in a purchase order. A thorough preliminary study should be accomplished to be sure that the correct problem is being solved.

DATA COMMUNICATION ANALYSIS

The analysis of the existing system can shed some light on the problems being experienced. Audits of records and documents can produce some useful insights into the current situation. Some audits investigate queue lengths. These audits determine the causes and effects of transactions delayed by the communications system.

The analysis of costs is another important aspect. The costs of purchasing, installing, and operating the existing system should be thoroughly documented for management to make realistic comparisons. An inventory of current hardware, software, and personnel related to the telecommunications problem under scrutiny should be included.

Traffic analysis assesses the traffic through the network. The volumes, kinds, and times of transactions are important. An important variable here is response time. Response time is the delay experienced between making a network request and the receipt of an answer to the request. Peak periods as well as normal operating conditions should be analyzed. Throughput is a measure of the amount of information that is moved through the system. Here it is necessary to determine how much useful information relative to total information is passed through the network. Throughput is a function of effective bit rates. The error rate of the system must be recorded. Logs of errors should be maintained with information such as time of day, date, line used, transaction mix, response time, and line load. This information is used to determine whether a new system is required or if simply the upgrading of line service is warranted. The mean time between failures (MTBF) for telecommunication equipment is also useful here. Figure 16.10 presents lists of useful network statistics that should be gathered at various times of the day.

A very important element of the systems analysis is user feedback. Very often, users discern a problem in a system before management does. Consequently, a user's insight might be very useful. The user might be able to tell you

Figure 16.10 *Useful Network Statistics*

Response Times	Queue Lengths
Transaction Mix	Routing
Error Rates	Buffer Usage
Line Load	Processing Time
Circuit Utilization	

that system response time is terrible just before lunch. This information is very valuable and should not be overlooked.

Systems analysis can also help in the design of transactions. It may be necessary to join or split transactions to improve network performance. Longer transactions can accomplish more, but may tie up the network for longer periods of time.

COMMUNICATION SYSTEM DESIGN

The proposed system need not be installed before ascertaining its affects. Simulation models can be effectively used to "get a feel" for the new system and anticipate its behavior. This is an important tool for the evaluation of specific TCOM alternatives. Figure 16.11 lists the major items that should be considered when designing a new system.

A totally secure system is one that performs no I/O. This type of system is also useless. Consequently, a trade-off occurs between system usefulness and security. The ease of access that we build into a system may come back to haunt us in the form of computer hackers or computer crime. A clear definition of system accessibility and vulnerability should be constructed before a single device is installed or program written, and included in the design specifications for the new system.

The design of a TCOM system also includes the specification of device and system interconnection. Bridges and gateways are important considerations to a network solution and should not be left to be added later. Protocol converters may be needed to provide handshaking between different devices. For example, to attach ASCII terminals to IBM systems that expect block mode 3178 devices requires the use of a protocol converter that will make the ASCII bit stream appear to the mainframe to be a 3178.

System software is another important aspect of the design of a TCOM system. The ISO reference model provides for operating system interface in layers 6 and 7. These are the points where the operating system controls the devices that are members of the network. Telecommunications access methods

Figure 16.11 *Network Design Considerations*

Hardware Required
Software Required
Communication Circuits (lines)
Personnel Required
Accounting Procedures Needed
Overall System Costs (including installation, mainte-
    nance, operations, major capital expenditures)
Benchmarks
Security
Documentation

---

that are associated with an operating system relieve programmers from the tedium of compensating for device specific attributes of terminals and other devices and provide uniform connection, disconnection, and data transfer between the devices and application programs. IBM's VTAM and TCAM are examples of this type of access method.

COMMUNICATIONS IMPLEMENTATION AND EVALUATION

The installation of communication systems occurs much as it would with data processing systems. A major difference, however, is the pilot installation. The installation of hundreds of terminals all at once would be a very time-consuming and expensive task. In addition, in the event that some part of the system design misspecified the requirements, the results could be catastrophic. Consequently, pilot installations occur to test out the solution as a last safeguard for adequate system performance. After acceptance, the rest of the conversion occurs at an orderly pace, in much the same manner as the pilot installation progressed.

After the system is installed, it should be periodically inspected to determine its effectiveness. The statistics listed in Figure 16.10 should be reevaluated. This might suggest that some system tuning is needed. Because these systems do not act in a vacuum, changes could occur that impair performance.

COMMUNICATION APPLICATIONS

Distributed data processing is becoming very popular. With the advent of departmental computers, the desire to interconnect many different machines is growing. Distributed data processing provides computer access on multiple processors that interact regularly by passing data. Inquiries into remote databases are supported as is the execution of programs on remote processors. Figure 16.12 lists the advantages and disadvantages of distributed data processing.

OFFICE AUTOMATION

Office automation (OA) is the integration of technology and management practices to increase the productivity and effectiveness of the office professional. This mainly involves enhancing the ability of the organization to develop, process, and analyze both formal and informal information. The proper implementation and management of the office automation resources can reduce operating costs, improve efficiency, and lead to higher-quality decision making.

The functions usually included in office automation are word processing, electronic mail, automated document filing and retrieval, desktop publish-

Figure 16.12 *Analysis of Distributed Processing*

Advantages

    Gives managers at remote sites more control over their data processing requirements

    Data processing capacity more nearly matches users' needs

    Reduces load on central facility

    Reduces the risk of significant central system failure

Disadvantages

    Conflict arises over differences between local and organizational needs and standards

    Duplication of effort

    Incompatible systems

    Increased security risk

    Dilution of programmer expertise

ing, and decision support functions. It is the manager's job to determine the correct mix of these technologies and to assure that they are employed to the firm's maximum advantage. This includes the coordination of the acquisition and installation of these resources so that the hardware and software are compatible.

This coordination is a difficult, but important function. The lack of compatibility can lead to many problems. For example, if each department was allowed to select its own word processing hardware and software, it may be very difficult or impossible to exchange documents between the various systems. Also, in this situation, it may be difficult to get these systems to communicate to a common host system.

The developing technologies in office automation must also be periodically scanned to determine future directions. For example, significant productivity gains may be possible in the near future as both voice recognition and document scanning technologies mature. Determining the appropriate cost and performance thresholds for these products is the responsibility of the office automation coordinator. Committing to this technology too early could be a costly mistake. However, delaying too long could give competitive firms an advantage.

Most firms will implement office automation in stages. This allows for a more orderly transition. Figure 16.13 lists some possible stages in the office automation process.

INTELLIGENT BUILDINGS

Office buildings that are constructed so as to bypass the local phone company by operating private intra- and interbuilding communications are called intelligent buildings. Some of the features include long distance service, shared CBX, com-

Figure 16.13 *Possible Stages of Office Automation*

STAGE	PRIMARY OBJECTIVE	EXAMPLES
1	Improve secretarial productivity	Stand-alone, noncommunicating word processors
2	Improve communications	Communicating word processors, electronic mail, and teleconferencing, multi-function terminals for word and data processing
3	Improve the support of planning and decision making	Decision support systems based on departmental and personal computers

plete lines of intelligent telephone instruments, video teleconferencing, electronic mail, local area networks, voice mail, modem sharing, terminal-to-mainframe wiring, and automated environmental control. An advantage of such a building is that the tenants, who alone might not be able to afford such technologies, can share the costs. These buildings are typically wired with broadband coaxial cable allowing a wide variety of services.

The intelligent building concept allows a great deal of expandability. Tenants can add features as their needs grow. The increased usage of departmental computing normally would require substantial rewiring of an office space. However, an intelligent building already has much of the communication channel already in place. Connection to other sites is provided by microwave or satellite transmission, or dedicated local lines.

MANAGERIAL IMPLICATIONS OF TELECOMMUNICATIONS

Because telecommunications affects many aspects of the organization, planning is essential for successful selection, installation, management, and utilization of the system. This must occur at many levels within the organization. At the operational level, managers must plan for the expansion and use of the system. For example, if the marketing department is planning to introduce a new product, they might wish to include a product support hot line to answer questions and record complaints or suggestions. The 800 service requires that trunks and data lines be in place and operational before the campaign begins. The design of a new building must include inputs from the communications department as to the types and placement of lines, wiring closets, jacks, PBX, and other equipment. Policies and procedures must be established concerning the use of these assets. Tactical managers set, accept, or reject standards that affect the compatibility and obsolescence of the telecommunications resource. Flitting from one technology to another, one standard to another, will be costly, unproductive, and ultimately disastrous. Strategic planning is required to put these assets in productive use as competitive weapons, marrying the technology to the strategy. In this section, we will discuss some of the key areas for managers of communications. Without exception, effective planning is at the heart of each of these issues.

Telecommunication systems are the most vulnerable part of a data processing operation. This is partly because there are so many organizations taking part in the transmission and because of the potentially long distances involved. The manager must contend with the hardware vendors, system software vendors, application software vendors, local telephone company, and long distance company. Each of these may subcontract part of their operations to yet another vendor. Consequently, when something goes wrong, there is often a good deal of finger pointing, and diagnosis can take quite a while. Fortunately for the majority of the "simple" errors, correction can often be applied quickly. Communications systems, no matter how well isolated, can be affected by a variety of factors outside of any of the forementioned. The construction of a building may interfere with microwave or satellite transmission. Relocation of an electric substation or rerouting traffic along a nearby street may increase the error rate on some communication lines. Within the building, the installation of fluorescent lighting may cause an increase in spurious errors.

The installation of a local area network is also fraught with problems. Microcomputers that once provided quick response time can be slowed by a poorly designed LAN. Local area networks are local only in the geographic sense. They can cross departmental boundaries providing interdepartmental access to data or hardware or software that was intended for intradepartmental use. The responsibility of LAN operation must be made clear from the beginning. In a typical organization, the protection (or lack thereof) of the microcomputing resources is the responsibility of the individual user. However, when the LAN is installed, the responsibility for file server protection must be explicitly stated. Users give up some of the control of their systems once the LAN is installed because they must acquire equipment and software that is network compatible. Finally, just as the distinction between minicomputers and microcomputers is getting fuzzier, so are the differences between local and wide area networks. LANs can be connected to modems, to departmental systems, to T-1 digital lines, to satellite earth stations, and to microwave transponders. As we will see, connectivity is another very important managerial issue.

Voice systems are equally susceptible to external interferences. However, because of the relatively slow speed of the traffic, the users are not aware of the problems. Voice systems are more sensitive to network load. The selection of a long distance carrier should be predicated on the abundance and quality of available long distance circuits. The attended and unattended "switchboards" must operate flawlessly and quickly. Operationally, users of voice systems are less tolerant of poor network performance than their data counterparts. We have grown accustomed to the transmission quality provided by predivestiture AT&T. We have also grown accustomed to the do-it-yourself phone installation that we do in our homes. Consequently, the installation of a new telephone in an office is expected to occur quickly. For the manager of a voice system, there are very few positive reinforcements concerning a job well done.

Policies and procedures must also be established for the procurement, implementation, and use of communication technology. Compatibility and expendability are the two most important characteristics of a communication system. Managers must be able to forecast the future and build on the present. Selection and adherence to a communication system standard is essential. This does not mean that we must use a single vendor for hardware and software. In fact, an important characteristic of systems is their connectivity. Vendors advertise systems as being able to connect to a wide variety of other devices, including their own. For example, Wang advertises its products as being able to connect to DEC, HP, and IBM systems. Connectivity is different, however, from compatibility. Compatibility refers to the ability of hardware or software to be used with or on another piece of hardware or software. For example, communication software might require Hayes compatible modems to operate correctly. Connectivity or intervendor connectivity is, ideally, the seamless connection between devices of different manufacture allowing the user the luxury of not knowing (or needing to know) what device or network they are using. Vendor connectivity is becoming less of an issue. In the past, it was not unusual to purchase a device from a vendor that could not communicate with other devices from that same vendor. The important aspect of connection is the cleanliness of the seam.

There are several forms or degrees of connectivity. The most basic and simplest type is hardware compatibility. Actual and de facto standards exist for a variety of hardware interfaces. In addition, the plug compatible manufacturers have created a large number of de facto standards by supporting connections between their devices and those of the major vendors. Software connectivity is provided, in varying degrees, by operating systems, communication software, and application systems. Standard operating systems provide a level of interconnection by providing a common operating system interface to application environments and the underlying hardware. Communication software and standards are the most commonly thought of types of connectivity vehicles. Finally, the applications themselves provide some connection between devices. At the data level, encryption, storage formats, and data structures provide a means of sharing information between different devices. The regulatory agencies "create" connectivity by specifying, among other things, media usage, transmission frequencies, and competitive market issues. As can be seen, there are many methods of achieving connectivity. It can be achieved by specifying the use of RS-232-C as the hardware interface. It can be achieved by storing and transmitting

ASCII data. Alternately, it could be implemented by using the UNIX operating system. It could be attained by using protocols and transmission procedures that implement the ISO OSI reference model. By combining these options, the manager can determine the level of seamless interconnection desired. The easiest solution is to implement a single vendor environment, but this is no longer a realistic solution.

By successfully attacking the question of connectivity, the issue of obsolescence can be addressed. If managers stay the course by making sure that the equipment and software they are installing can easily communicate with existing systems, the threat of purchasing a system that will become quickly obsolete is lessened. This is not to say that by having a seamless, connectivity-oriented system the worries of obsolescence will go away. The point here is that the newly acquired system will communicate with the rest of the equipment and be useful for a longer period of time. The question then becomes where to start. If existing equipment is neither compatible nor provides connectivity, then the decision is clear, although painful. When the usefulness of the old system is ending, it must be replaced with one that provides the desired growth path, compatibility features, and connectivity options. No matter how tempting, the manager must bite the bullet and make the change. However, if the existing equipment is compatible with other equipment in the market, the manager must decide on the degree of seamlessness desired. It may be determined that another product will provide the flexibility, and the change is required again. The product evaluation occurs much as it was discussed in Chapter 7. The big difference here is that after looking at the objective measures (throughput, bandwidth, bit rates, etc.), the subjective measures (degree of connectivity or seamlessness, compatibility, growability, etc.) are even more important.

A network should be "growable." The design of a network should include enough capacity to handle easily a doubling of transmission over a three-year period. This does not mean that we must have an extra hundred terminals in storage, but that the existing wiring should have enough excess or unused bandwidth to facilitate this expected increase in demand. The most conservative decision made by communications managers is to put off the decision. The next most conservative is to build a network that is compatible with a wide variety of devices and software with enough capacity to handle an immediate doubling of demand. This can be accomplished in several ways. One method used is to install bundles of wiring with more wires than necessary. When the cost of wire is low, this reduces the labor cost of eventually running more wire. Another solution is to install wire with more bandwidth than is required. Finally, the network can be "overdesigned." An overdesigned network experiences almost no trunk or capacity shortages, even during peak loads. This might be accomplished by overusing fiber optics in a LAN or using more terminal servers than necessary or having extra trunks for outside lines. There is, of course, a break-even point where the excess capacity exceeds the cost of installing more capacity later. History shows us that demand for network services rarely shrinks and often grows much faster than anticipated. Consequently, a manager that is prepared to meet this growth will have fewer headaches in the future.

Network users also have a responsibility. Users must be instructed as to the limits and capabilities of their networks. It should not be assumed that employees know what WATS lines are and how they work. Users should understand the use of a computer cluster and how the network responds to different instructions and database queries. They must be taught about moving and altering networked equipment. All of this information should reside in a network policy and procedures manual. If the data processing manager has responsibility for several forms of communication, each should be specifically, accurately, and explicitly covered. The manual should be kept current and be required reading for anyone who will use a networked device.

Finally, senior executives must be taught the importance, the abilities, and the consequences of using telecommunications as a competitive weapon. A well-designed telecommunications system can break time and geography boundaries, perhaps opening new markets for products and services. If consumers are persuaded to buy a product or service, the communications network can provide an effective barrier against losing that customer. Consequently, it is very easy (and exciting) to look at the examples of American Airlines and their SABRE system or at the American Hospital Supply Corporation and decide that using a communication system to cut costs, to increase market share, and to put up barriers to market entry is the way to go. However, senior executives do not see the hard work and expense that went into the SABRE system, for example, for over a decade. Nor do they readily see the litigation that followed as a result. Telecommunications provides an interesting conduit for the transport of information within and between organizations. It requires the same executive support as the introduction of a new product line or the opening of a new factory. A telecommunications project is a long-term investment. It must have commitment from the top down. Consequently, the DP manager must play educator and teach these very busy people about how a telecommunications system works and what it can and cannot do. The advantages, such as freer flow of information, should be pointed out as well as the disadvantages, such as outside hackers breaking into the system. One way of doing this is through the use of case studies and examples from the trade journals. Show upper management how their peers are using telecommunications. Show the successes and the failures. Support for communications projects will be more genuine and long lasting if upper management understands the long- and short-term implications of their decisions.

For a telecommunications system to be successful, it must be supported from the bottom of the organization to the top. It must be reliable, growable, and be easy and flexible to use. Users at all levels of the organization must understand that using the communication system does not end at their fingertips or at their ears, but simply begins there. The use of networks is becoming a pervasive part of our lives. We go to parties or meetings to "network." Our checking accounts have little float left in them. Credit cards are accepted throughout much of the world. The act of computers or humans easily conversing over great distances is accepted as matter of fact and with little surprise. It is important, then, that we manage this resource with the same fervor that we heap upon inventories and accounting systems. Good short- and long-range planning for telecommunications systems is essential.

MAJOR COMPANY

Major Company has adopted a policy of encouraging the interconnection of most computer systems. This means that all buildings are wired so that additional devices can be easily and economically connected to the building's network. In addition, all networks are linked together by bridges and gateways.

There is a separate telecommunications department. The director of the TCOM area reports directly to the vice-president of information systems. The TCOM director has responsibility for the coordination of data, voice, and video communication.

To assure continued compatibility of systems, the TCOM area restricts the hardware and software that can be acquired. This policy is implemented by having the TCOM department develop a list of acceptable items. A user department can acquire any of the items on this list, without prior TCOM permission. For a user to acquire any product not on this list, special permission must be obtained from the TCOM area.

Hence, Major Company has firm-wide compatibility of all office automation products, spreadsheet programs, etc. In addition, hardware compatibility allows the various terminals, micros, and other work stations to access information from the minis and mainframes attached in the network. Additionally, firm-wide standards for all types of documents are enforced by a series of document templates that are available to all users. For example, all internal memos will be constructed using the same template. Not only does this make them easier to read, it also forces certain information to be included in each memo.

SUMMARY

The area of telecommunications management is quite new. It presents a new set of challenges to the data processing manager. TCOM is at the leading edge of technology and has been recognized as an important concern of top managers. It is undoubtedly the most visible aspect of data processing. Consequently, it requires much attention and dedication.

QUESTIONS

1. Rank the list of events in Figure 16.1 in order of importance. Defend your rankings.

2. What are the similarities and differences between systems analysis and design of telecommunications systems and data processing systems?

3. Identify all of the components necessary for a telecommunications network to operate. Include hardware and software.

4. List 10 important issues with which a manager of telecommunications should be concerned.

5. What publications should a manager of telecommunications subscribe to? Why?

6. Using the information gained in this text, design a 10-story intelligent building. It should be able to communicate with other buildings with microwave and satellite. Services provided include long distance access, CBX, voice mail, teleconferencing, local area networks, and terminal-to-mainframe connections.

7. Select a long distance service firm in your area. What characteristics did you look for? Why did you select this particular service?

8. What questions should you ask users concerning the adequacy of telephone service?

9. Compare and contrast the communications media discussed in this chapter. Which is best? Why?

10. What are the implications of the AT&T divestiture for the computer industry? Why do you think that AT&T has not captured more of the data processing market?

11. Discuss how telecommunications has affected (a) marketing strategies (b) banking (c) commuting.

12. Explain the disadvantages and advantages of distributed data processing. Do you think the advantages outweigh the disadvantages? Why or why not?

ADDITIONAL READINGS

CLEMONS, E. K., AND F. W. MCFARLAN. "Telecom: Hook up or Lose Out," *Harvard Business Review,* July–August 1986, p. 91.

HILTZ, S. R., AND M. TUROFF. "Structuring Computer-Mediated Communication Systems to Avoid Information Overload," *Communications of the ACM,* Vol. 28, No. 7, July 1985, p. 680.

NOTKIN, DAVID, ANDREW P. BLACK, EDWARD D. LAZOWSKA, HENRY M. LEVY, JAN SANISLO, AND JOHN ZAHORJAN. "Interconnecting Heterogeneous Computer Systems," *Communications of the ACM,* Vol. 31, No. 3, March 1988, pp. 258–273.

QUARTERMAN, J. S., AND J. C. HOSKINS. "Notable Computer Networks," *Communications of the ACM,* Vol. 29, No. 10, October 1986, p. 932.

SASSONE, P., AND A. SCHWARTZ. "Cost-Justifying OA," *Datamation*, February 15, 1986, pp. 83–88.

STALLINGS, W. "Master Plan for LANs," *Datamation*, November 15, 1986, pp. 91–92.

"Telecom and MIS: Managing the Merger," *Datamation*, October 15, 1985, pp. 119–124.

REVIEW OF MACHINE OPERATIONS: A BIRD'S EYE VIEW

INTRODUCTION

To effectively manage in a computerized environment, it is necessary to have at least a basic understanding of the operation of the computer system. Without this basic knowledge, the manager runs the risk of making decisions based on inadequate or misleading information. Also, there is the associated risk of losing the respect of the technical staff under your control. Computer professionals are usually not very tolerant of superiors lacking these basic skills. This can lead to very serious personnel problems and substantial tension between management and staff.

This appendix discusses the functions of the major components of a mainframe system and the relationships between these components. Since we will be looking at the functions of the individual components of the system and not the sequence of events occurring in the execution of a job, we call this the bird's eye view of the system. In Appendix B, we will look at the system based on the execution of a computer job; we call this the worm's eye view. In both appendices, we will discuss IBM mainframe terminology and architecture, with specific examples from that class of computers. If you feel that you have sufficient knowledge in this area, you may skip these appendices. However, they may serve as a good review.

While a computer system is composed of many different components, we generally classify these components into either of two categories: hardware or software. Hardware can be most easily described as physically tangible items;

those that you can touch and hold. Software is intangible and is simply a set of instructions that directs the system to perform certain tasks. Neither hardware nor software is of any functional value without the other. This fact alone can cause substantial confusion. The same hardware performs an unbelievable variety of tasks by simply changing the software.

In the following, we first describe the functions of most of the major hardware components. Then we will describe some of the system software components. System software, as opposed to application software, is the set of programs that allows the computer system to function in a coordinated, easy-to-use fashion. Application software, which is not discussed in this appendix, processes information to accomplish a specific goal. An operating system is an example of system software, while a payroll program is an example of application software.

Throughout the next two appendices, we will discuss only what we think are the high points. Anything even approaching a detailed and complete explanation of a large-scale system would take books and not chapters. We encourage you to examine each of the areas we discuss in more detail. Because of their high degree of complexity, computers can be fascinating and absorbing.

Before we proceed, we must make a disclaimer. Since we are only discussing the basics of a system, there will be situations where what we state is not true in all cases. Don't worry. In attempting to explain these complex situations, we would only confuse the reader. Once you understand these basic system functions, you can explore the more complex situations. For the present time, let's act like these cases don't exist.

HARDWARE

First let's take a view of the major hardware components of the system. Figure A.1 shows a typical hardware configuration. The "brain" of the system is the central processing unit (CPU). It processes the program instructions and implements the logical operations of the system. The CPU cannot directly communicate with the outside environment. Instead, the CPU relies on other devices to do this communication. When the CPU wishes to send or receive messages, it first "talks" to a specialized computer called the data channel. This in turn signals the system's needs to another special computer called the controller. The controller directs the function of the peripheral devices under it control. These peripheral devices include user terminals, tape storage devices, disk storage devices, printers, and many other devices. This is a very simplified view of a system. We will now look at each of these components in more detail.

The central processing unit consists of four major components: the control unit, the arithmetic logic unit (ALU), primary memory, and general purpose registers (GPRs). See Figure A.2. The control unit fetches program instructions and data from memory and prepares the instructions for execution. The instruction is then executed by the ALU, which performs the actual arithmetic and

Figure A.1   *Major Hardware Components*

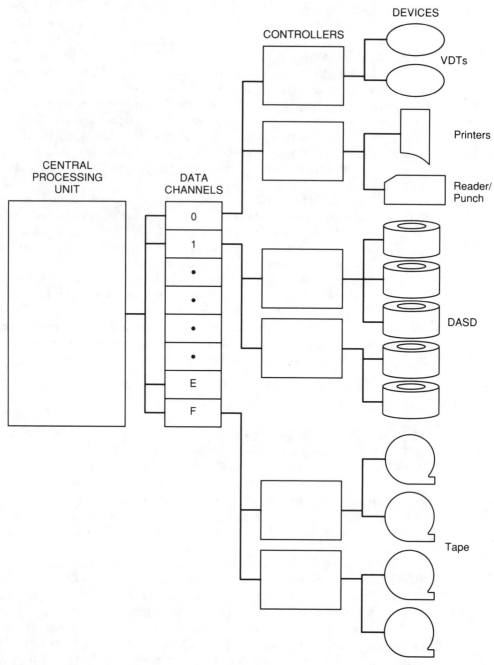

Figure A.2 *Central Processing Unit Components*

CENTRAL PROCESSING UNIT COMPONENTS

Control Unit								Logic Unit								General Purpose Registers
0	1	2	3	4	5	6	7	8	9	A	B	C	D	E	F	

Primary Storage

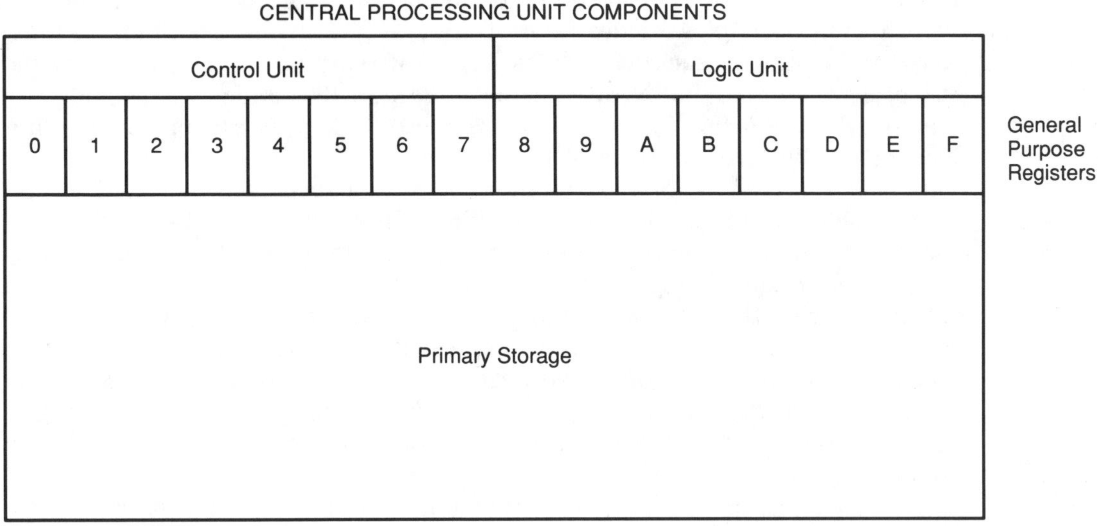

Boolean logic on the data. The ALU works under the direction of the control unit. The speed of a CPU is generally measured in millions of instructions per second (MIPS). However, because of the major differences in architecture between various systems, MIPS may not be a reliable measure by which to compare the performance of diverse systems.

Primary memory, or sometimes called primary storage, is that area of the computer where both the program instructions and data items are stored during execution. It is only through primary storage that the ALU can operate on the data. Data that is collected at some external location must be moved to primary storage before execution can begin. General purpose registers are specialized memory areas.

Computer memory is composed of row upon row of integrated circuits. Data is represented in these circuits as a series of electrical charges. A high charge represents the number one in the binary numbering system, while a low charge is a zero. Each zero or one is a bit (binary digit). We can represent numbers, characters, or program instructions in memory through different patterns of bits.

Primary storage is organized into groups of bits for ease of access and increased system speed. A group of eight bits is called a byte. A byte represents the smallest addressable unit of storage in the system. This means that each byte in the system will have its own unique address. If the address of byte N is 10723, then the address of byte N + 1 would be 10724. The lowest address is 0 and the highest address is machine dependent.

Variable names are used in computer programs to refer to data values that are changed as processing takes place. Suppose the variable NAME currently refers to the value MAJOR COMPANY, which is stored at location 1000. In other words, the "M" is in location 1000 and the "A" is in 1001 and so forth. The word MAJOR occupies 5 bytes from M through R. It can be seen that we must know the length of each variable as well as its starting location to access the value. If we assume that NAME begins at location 1004 and is 9 bytes long, we would get R COMPANY. And if we assumed the length is 3 and the starting location is 1001, we would get AJO.

If you wished to read the information in a specific bit, you would first have to obtain the byte containing that bit and then process that bit. For convenience, a byte can be thought of as one character of information. Bytes can then be grouped together to form additional units of storage. Four bytes (32 bits) is called a word; while two and eight bytes form half-words and double-words respectively. Other vendors may use different word sizes, and some vendors will use a word as the lowest addressable unit. Word length of a computer system will dictate to a certain extent the speed of the processor, sophistication of its instruction set, the maximum memory size and the accuracy of the computing.

Since computers can store large amounts of data, we have other measures of storage. For example, a kilobyte (usually expressed as 1K) represents 1,024 bytes of data. Computer memory in large systems can contain millions or even billions of bytes (megabytes or gigabytes).

To summarize, primary memory is that portion of the CPU where variables (data) and instructions (programs) reside during execution. The smallest addressable unit of storage is the byte, which is made up of eight bits. Each byte is stored in a unique address location.

Special characters, letters, and numbers are represented as bytes. For example, the character A might be represented as 1100 0001, and the character 1 is represented as 1111 0001. The set of rules that governs the mapping of "people readable" characters into "computer readable" bit patterns is known as a translation table. Most IBM CPUs use the EBCDIC (Extended Binary Coded Decimal Interchange Code) table, whereas others use ASCII (American Standard Code for Information Interchange).

The CPU uses 16 specialized 32-bit devices known as general purpose registers (GPR) as temporary storage areas for intermediate calculation results and addresses of needed storage locations. We will talk more specifically about the use of general purpose registers and other registers later.

CHANNELS

On mainframe computers, the CPU communicates with the outside world through devices known as I/O channels, which are actually small special purpose computers. Connected to the channel, through varying grades of shielded cable, are different I/O devices. A series of impact printers or a couple of strings of disk drives could be connected to a single channel. The number of devices that can be attached to a single channel is usually based on the type of channel. A byte multiplexor channel is used to connect slow-speed equipment, such as card readers/punches, impact printers, and operator consoles. Block multiplexor channels connect faster devices such as disk and tape drives. Block multiplexor channels are able to handle large amounts of data very quickly. Most large computers have 16 or more channels, some capable of 4.5 megabytes per second or higher data transfers.

You can see how important a channel is in a computer system. Without a channel, the CPU would have to interact with any external media. Because of the extreme difference in speeds between the CPU and I/O devices, having channels allows the CPU to continue processing while I/O operations are in process. Channel failure can cripple a system, as can channel imbalance. For example, if too many frequently used datasets are placed on the same disk, that disk and the channel that controls it could become tied up causing other processing tasks to slow down. System programmers must constantly monitor channel utilization to keep bottlenecks at a minimum.

To aid in this effort, some vendors allow for virtual channels. With virtual channels, devices can be accessed from multiple channels. In this way, programs can access data sets through one of several different routes, known as paths, reducing channel contention.

The purpose of a channel is to off-load the I/O function from the CPU. The CPU, which operates in the nanosecond range (a nanosecond is one billionth of a second) is much faster than the fastest external device, which operates in the millisecond range (a millisecond is one thousandth of a second.) If the CPU was responsible for performing I/O, it could spend a million times longer waiting for data to be read from secondary storage than it would take to manipulate that data later. It is the job of the channel, then, to accept instructions from the CPU regarding data transfer, issue the proper instructions to the I/O devices, and wait for the results. The CPU can perform other duties while waiting for the I/O results. When the device has transferred its data to the channel, the channel notifies the CPU that the requested data has been retrieved.

PERIPHERALS

A CPU can have dozens of different types of devices, or peripherals, attached to it. The peripherals might include I/O devices such as printers, plotters, terminals, or secondary storage units such as magnetic disk and tape. In most cases, each of these devices is attached, directly or indirectly, to a controller. The device controller is responsible for monitoring and controlling the device, at the direction of the channel. A disk controller, for example, moves the read/write mechanism to the proper location on the specific disk, ascertains the device's operational status, and causes the data to be read from or written to the disk. Just as several controllers can be attached to a single channel, several devices can be attached to the same controller. Figure A.3 shows a typical computer equipment channel configuration.

To many users, the most frequently used I/O device is the visual display terminal (VDT), also commonly known as a CRT (Cathode Ray Tube.) A VDT is a television-like device on which character data is displayed. Graphics terminals allow the display of graphical pictures as well as text. In addition, both terminal types can display in color. Most terminals have typewriter keyboards for input. A CPU interacts with VDTs through a controller (called a communications controller or front end processor) and a channel just as it does with other devices. We talk of a communication controller's VDT capacity in terms of ports. Most large systems can handle thousands of ports. This rather high number should not be surprising. A human comprehends and responds to terminal I/O in a matter of seconds, while the CPU reads billions of times faster. Thus, the computer can handle many terminals at once, usually giving each user the illusion of exclusive use.

Communication controllers are complex computers in their own right. They do many functions that would otherwise have to be done by the central processor. For example, the communications controller will do error checking to see if a message is properly received. If an error is found, the terminal is asked by the controller to retransmit the message. The CPU would not be involved until the correct message is received. Complex communications software is loaded and executed in the communications controller. Besides error detection, this software does message switching, line polling, and many other tasks that relieve the load on the CPU.

In most situations, a large percentage of the available terminals will be inactive at any given time. Inactive terminals still have to be physically connected to the communications controller. This leads to an inefficient use of the relatively expensive ports. Instead, we can use other devices that connect to the ports and allow various terminals to access the same port at different times. One of these devices is called a port selector. A port selector allows a limited number of ports to be dynamically allocated (shared) among a larger number of terminals. Another, more sophisticated alternative is to use networking. This will be discussed later in the appendix.

Hardwired terminals are connected directly with the port selector or communications controller. Dial-up telephone lines are also able to provide terminal hookups to the computer. Lines, which are designed to carry analog (voice) signals, are normal voice grade telephone lines. Digital signals generated by computer equipment must be converted into analog signals before transmission and then back again into digital signals. This requires the use of a modem (MOdulator DEModulator).

Most IBM systems were designed to interact with intelligent terminals. An intelligent terminal contains an internal processor that can be programmed to perform specific duties, such as data editing, thus relieving the CPU from additional tasks. Intelligent terminals are more expensive than dumb terminals,

Figure A.3 *Sample Channel Configuration*

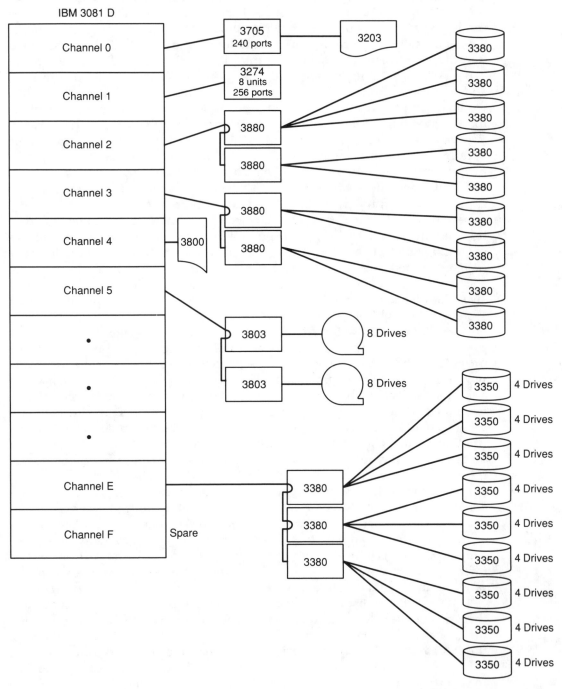

which have no internal processing logic. To connect these dumb terminals to an IBM system, the terminal must be made to appear as an intelligent terminal. This can be done by using devices known as protocol converters or by using special emulation software. Signals going to the terminal from the CPU are converted into the proper control sequences (protocols) for the terminal, and vice versa.

A special function terminal, the operator's console, is used to control and interact with the operating system. Without this I/O device, the system would be unmanageable. The operator's console, or consoles, does not compete for the attention of the computer in the same way that other terminals do. Requests are immediately responded to. Very powerful system functions can be performed from the operator's console, including system start and stop, I/O device control, and user job management.

Printers are another type of I/O device. Whereas a CRT provides "soft copy" output, a printer displays "hard copy" output which may be kept and reviewed later. Printers are classified by many characteristics. The first would be the quantity (character, line, page) printed in a single print operation. Thus we could compare fast and slow printers. A fast printer may be measured in pages or lines printed per minute, and a slow printer can be compared at lines or characters printed per minute. Generally, the faster the printer, the more expensive it is. Character printers are most often used with mini- and microcomputer systems, although this does not have to be the case. Printers can also be compared in terms of how the characters are placed on the page. Impact devices print the characters by striking the paper or ribbon. Nonimpact printers burn the image onto the paper, spray ink on the page forming the characters, or fix ink powder to the paper xerographically. These types of printers are normally faster and more expensive than impact printers. Finally, printers can be classified as letter quality and draft quality printers. Letter quality printers print characters at a high enough quality as to look typewritten or photo typeset. Draft quality printing creates characters that are not wholly or correctly formed or are of insufficient quality to be used in certain situations. For equivalent speeds, letter quality printers are usually more expensive than draft quality.

It can be seen that the type of printing quality is not necessarily associated with the grade of paper used. A fast letter quality printer, a laser printer for example, can be used to print program listings on standard printer paper as well as the stockholders' report on water-mark bond. In addition, many nonimpact printers can efficiently create and include graphics with the text as well as intermix character sets in a single line. While some impact printers can also produce graphics and different print fonts, they are usually unacceptably slow.

A printer must be attached to a controller. Several printers, because of their slower speeds, can be directed by a single controller, which determines a printer's status and controls the actual printing and other activities. Because of the mechanical nature of the devices, maintenance costs can be quite high.

A class of I/O devices known as secondary storage is used to store data for later use. In many cases the data files, called data sets, can be transferred from one machine to another giving some device interdependence for the data.

Tape drives record data as a series of magnetized spots on a half inch wide piece of mylar plastic coated with a magnetic oxide. As the tape crosses the read/write heads, data is recorded vertically, usually in 9-bit patterns (eight EBCDIC data bits plus one parity bit). A typical reel of tape is about 2,400 feet long and costs around $15. Data can be recorded on the tape in various densities. Common densities include 6,250, 1,600, and 800 bytes per inch (bpi). Transfer speeds of 40,000 bytes per second can be reached when using tape. Obviously, the tape is a sequential medium and the data contained on it must be processed likewise.

A newer form of tape storage involves cartridge tapes, which hold about twice the data that a 2,400-foot reel-to-reel tape will hold. The cartridge system has some major advantages over reel-to-reel. It has a faster transfer rate, the cartridges take up substantially less storage space and, most importantly, the error rate of the system is considerably less than the reel-to-reel system.

Data placed on tape is usually recorded in groups of records, different than those processed by the CPU. For example, if a general ledger package writes 120 byte records to tape, the data may be grouped into blocks of records containing 1,320 bytes (i.e., 11 records per block). The records as they appear to the application program are called logical records, and those actually transferred to and from the drive are called physical records or blocks. All of the records in a data set do not have to be the same length. It can be more efficient to use variable length records and blocks. For example, a program that keeps track of checked out library books would use variable length records because each person checks out a different number of books. To implement this, a 4-byte header is added to the beginning of each record to tell the system the length of that record. Each block also has a 4-byte length descriptor. A file's record is either fixed, fixed blocked, variable, variable blocked, or undefined. See Figure A.4. We differentiate between logical records and blocks because of the physical nature of the tape drive. Between each physical record written, a blank area is inserted. This gap, called an interblock gap, is usually 6/10 of an inch and is used for timing of the

Figure A.4 *Record Types*

TYPE	DESCRIPTION
Fixed	All records the same length
	Only one record per block
Fixed Blocked	All records the same length
	Each block contains N (an integer) number of records
Variable	Records of different sizes
	Only one record per block
Variable Blocked	Records of different sizes
	Multiple records per block
Undefined	Totally unrestricted

start/stop motion of the drive. When logical record lengths are small and there is only one logical record per block, then most of the file will be interblock gap. See Figure A.5.

Several data sets can reside on a single reel of tape. Each file is preceded by a header label which contains the name of the file, the number of physical records in the file, and all of the file format characteristics. These characteristics are jointly referred to as a data control block (DCB) and include logical record length, block size, and record format. Trailer labels follow each file and denote the end of the file. Each reel of tape is called a volume and has a volume header and trailer label. The volume header labels are used to allow the system to check that the proper tape has been mounted. Because a single file can span volumes, the volume trailer label indicates which volume follows the currently mounted tape. See Figure A.6.

The advantages of using tape is its low cost, transportability, and high storage capacity. Data is routinely stored on tape and mailed to other data processing locations. Magnetic tape is also used for backing up important data sets. The reel can be locked away at an offsite location in case of destruction of

Figure A.5   *Blocking of Records*

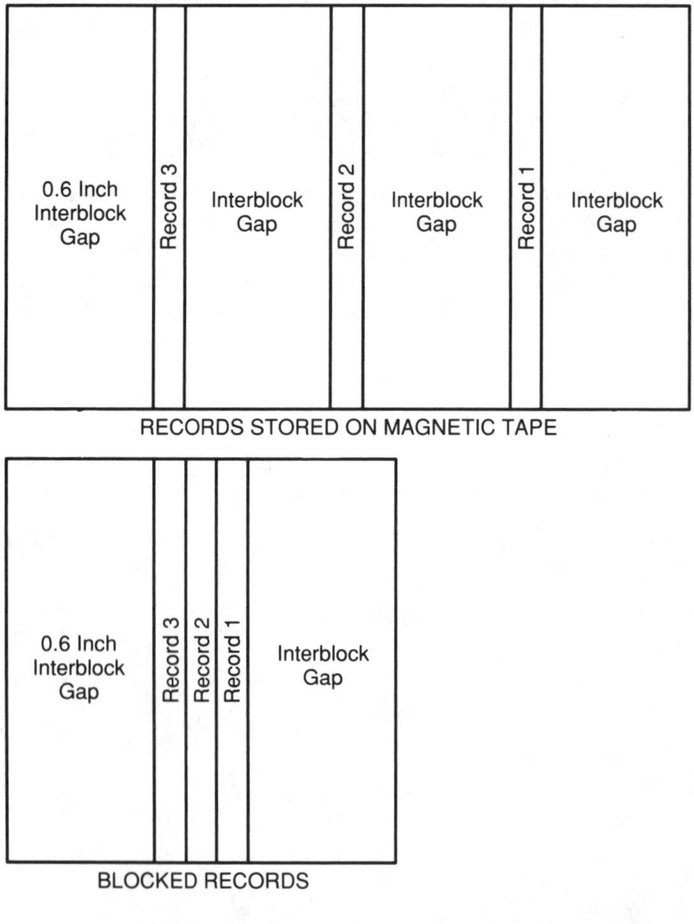

RECORDS STORED ON MAGNETIC TAPE

BLOCKED RECORDS

Figure A.6 *Tape Labels*

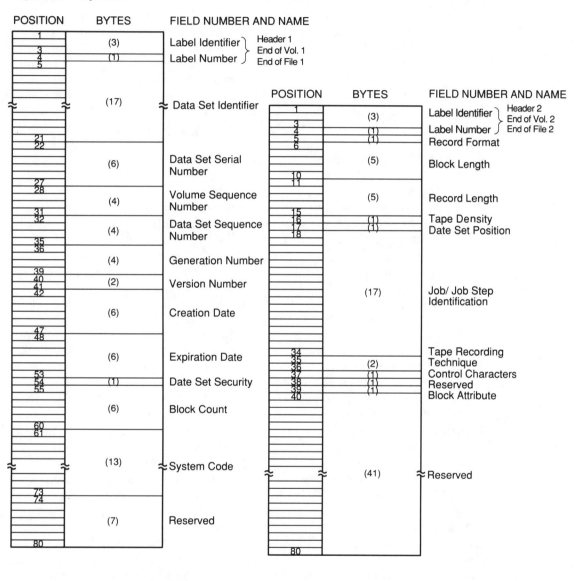

the original. Several tape drives are normally connected to a single controller in a string, which is attached to a block multiplexor channel. Tape drives require a substantial amount of maintenance because of their mechanical nature and the speed at which data is written and read. The read/write heads must be cleaned frequently, just like those of an audiocassette player. The drive motors must perform within specific tolerances to make sure that the tapes are not damaged. Many drives use vacuum columns to help maintain the proper tape tension.

The use of tape drives has personnel management implications, also. Industry has yet to develop a fully automated tape system. Tape librarians, console operators, and system programming personnel are all affected by the use of tapes. The advent of cartridge tape systems that have an autoload capability may soon relieve some of this burden. In addition, because a great amount of data can be stored per volume, the tapes should be stored in a safe location and managed as the corporate resource they are.

Another type of secondary storage is the direct access storage device (DASD). DASDs allow the fast random retrieval of data. In this fashion, we are able to process record 27 without regard to records 1 through 26. Disk storage is by far the most common form of DASD, although drums are also direct access devices.

Data is placed on volumes called disks. These disks can be removable or nonremovable referring to the fact that they can or cannot be mounted during normal processing. Removable disk packs normally hold much less data than nonremovable ones, to compensate for the slightly different ways they are mounted each time. A disk attached to a large mainframe may hold multiple gigabytes of data.

A disk pack is composed of around 15 metal oxide coated platters which spin around in the drive as a unit (approximately 120 mph). Removable packs include a protective dust cover and mounting assembly. Each volume is divided up into manageable sections for data set storage. Unlike a phonograph record, each platter is composed of a set of concentric circles called tracks (around 500). We record data on both sides of the platter. When lining up all of these tracks on all of the platters, we create a logical grouping of data called a cylinder. A cylinder consists of all of the tracks that can be accessed by a single positioning of the read/write heads. See Figure A.7. The number of bytes stored per track is device dependent. Disks with larger diameters can hold more data than smaller ones. It should be made clear that the same amount of data can be stored on the inside most track as can be stored on the outside most track. This apparent inconsistency allows the disk to spin at a uniform speed and for data to be written and read in the same fashion all over the pack. The extra space is taken up as the interblock gap size is increased as we move toward the outer rim of the platter.

The disk drive head is the mechanical device which reads from and writes the data to the disk pack. The read/write heads float just above (or below) the surface of the platter on the cushion of air generated by the spinning disk. The heads are attached to an access mechanism or actuator which moves the

Figure A.7 *Disk Configuration*

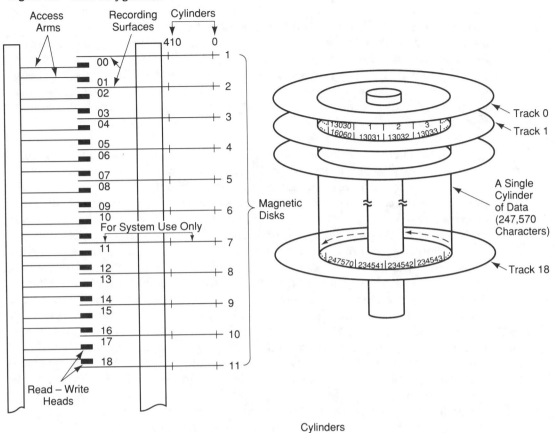

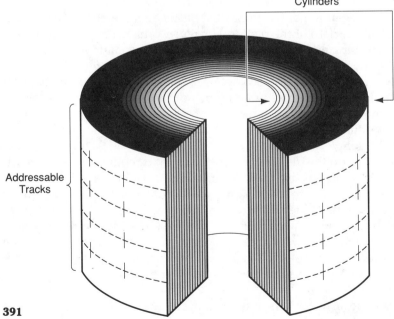

Cylinders

Addressable
Tracks

391

heads into and out of the spindle, positioning them, as a unit, over the proper track and cylinder. Each surface has its own read/write head. Only one set of heads is reading or writing at a time per actuator.

Some disk drives provide multiple independent actuators per disk pack. In this manner, we can access data via multiple paths, at the same time. Obviously, this does not increase the capacity of the disk, but decreases the contention for the drive. Should one actuator malfunction, the data can still be retrieved through the others.

DASD controllers are complex. A single controller can direct up to 16 different DASD or actuators. More advanced controllers allow dynamic path selection, which facilitates data access as previously mentioned, and also contain cache storage that allows for intermediate storage of data. Data transfer speeds in excess of 4.5 megabytes per second can be achieved, and in the near future these transfer rates should increase dramatically due to changing technology.

Direct access implies instantaneous access, but this is not so. Several things must happen before data is transferred to the channel. First, the access mechanism must be positioned over the appropriate cylinder. This is seek time and can take from zero to 30 milliseconds. Second, the proper track within the cylinder must be selected. Head selection is an electronic function and is usually not included in DASD I/O measurements. Finally, the correct record must rotate beneath (or above) the head. Rotational delay can take from zero to 20 milliseconds. It should be evident how important timing can be when using DASD. Fortunately, system software and intelligent hardware keep the programmer from worrying about it. As a manager, though, one should always be on the watch for new technology that will shorten these delays.

Each track contains an index point and a home address. The index point marks the physical beginning of the track. It should be remembered that a track is a thin circle on the surface of the platter. However, unlike a true circle, a track has a physical beginning and ending. The home address contains five pieces of information: first, the physical address of the track (it is a 2-byte field that is used by the controller to make sure the access mechanism is correctly positioned); second, a 1-byte flag that indicates whether or not the track is operative; third, the cylinder number (2 bytes) to which the track belongs; fourth, the head number (track) within the cylinder, also 2 bytes; finally, a cyclic check pair of bytes for error checking. See Figure A.8.

Data is placed on the disk on one of two formats: count-data and count-key-data. Count-data formats are used when the data will always be retrieved sequentially. The count area contains, among other information, the length of the data written (a 2-byte field) and record number (a 1-byte field). The count-key-data format is used when we want to retrieve data randomly. Its format is the same as the count-key except that the key area contains the value of the highest logical record key per block. The key is not taken out of the record, but is duplicated. It is through the use of the count-key-data format that online data retrieval occurs.

Another type of DASD includes drum storage systems. A drum is a

Figure A.8 Disk Data Format

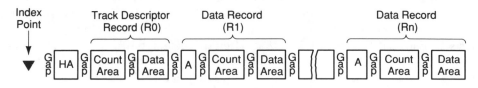

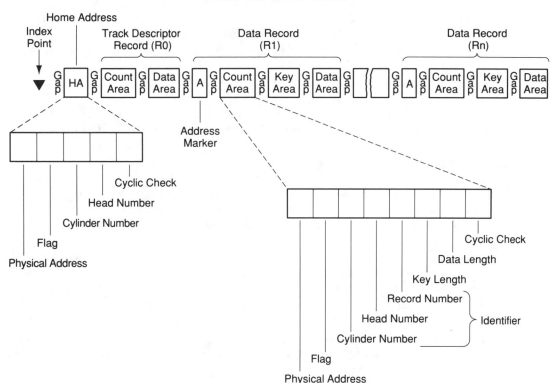

rotating cylinder or disk pack that has a read/write head positioned over every track, thus removing seek time from the DASD access time problem, reducing it almost entirely to rotational delay. Drums are used for very high activity files where response time is critical.

A record is written to disk, whether count-data or count-key-data format, at a specific address. It is retrieved later by this same address. We call the addressing method cylinder head addressing. By first locating the cylinder number, and then the correct track (or head) within the cylinder, and finally the target record number or key on that track, we are able to recall the stored data record. In this fashion, we can scatter records all over the disk. The concept of discontinuous data sets allows us to use the DASD more effectively and reduces the amount of unused space caused by fragmentation. If a data set had to reside on contiguous tracks and cylinders, then smaller fragments of disk space would become "wasted" space. Our only restriction, however, is that we cannot split tracks among data sets. In other words, a data set entirely "owns" all of its tracks. It should be remembered that when discussing hardware, we are talking about the physical organization of our data and not how it logically appears in our programs. As such, when discussing records and record numbers, we are actually referring to physical records (blocks).

To keep track of the location of data sets (no pun intended), a system file is maintained on the DASD. The volume table of contents or VTOC contains a data control block (DCB) that describes the attributes of the data set and also contains address information about each file on the volume. In addition, it contains a list of all of the available space. When a file is created, erased, or extended, that fact must be made known, through system software, to the VTOC.

Another type of DASD storage format is known as fixed block architecture or FBA. Under this approach, each track of the disk is divided up into 512-byte, fixed length, sequentially numbered blocks or sectors. Addressing is accomplished through the specification of correct cylinder, head, and sector. FBA, types of which are popular on mini- and microcomputers, reduces the amount of information necessary to use DASD. Because the programmer no longer writes variable length blocks of data with variable length interblock gaps, and because addressing problems of spanned tracks or cylinders is not a concern, FBA can be a useful format.

DASD management can be a very time-consuming activity. Backup must occur with regularity, as should preventative maintenance. Constant monitoring of channel utilization and data set usage will allow systems programmers to better balance the DASD controllers, strings of DASD, and their paths. For example, a single path to a heavily used database file will cause problems, as will having several high-activity files on the same channel or controller. It is usually DASD I/O that will slow a system down, causing degraded terminal I/O and poor job performance. Because a single disk can contain so much data, this resource must be managed as effectively as the data center itself.

SYSTEM SOFTWARE

The hardware is of no use without systems software to direct it. The single most important piece of system software is the operating system. The operating system (OS) in a computer is simply a program that allows the computer to control itself. Without an OS, large amounts of human intervention would be required to execute even the simplest tasks. For example, only one job would be in memory at a time and the machine operator would have to load that job into the system and then actually start the execution. If the program abnormally ended (ABENDed), the machine would stop (hopefully) and the operator would record the appropriate abend code (also hopefully) and the programmer then could debug the program. When no job is in memory executing, the CPU is idle.

There are many varieties of operating systems. To employ more efficiently the valuable system resources, larger systems use multiprogramming operating systems. This means that several programs can be loaded into memory at the same time and the processing of these programs is interleaved. Virtual storage operating systems manage memory in such a way as to make computer memory seem unlimited. We will talk more about this later. Timesharing operating systems allow multiple interactive users to share the computer's time.

The operating system is a very large and complicated series of programs that are designed to interact directly with system hardware. Its purpose is to manage the computing process in the areas of job, task, device, data, information, and communication management. The OS also provides services to the users of the system in the form of utility programs and data access methods.

Job management concerns the selection of user activities that the OS chooses to perform. A job is a sequence of one or more units of work that will accomplish a purpose. For example, Major Company sends out bills twice a month. The generation of these bills occurs in three steps. First, new accounts receivables are added to the A/R register. Then all payments received are credited to the proper accounts. Finally, the bills are printed. All three of these steps comprise the accounts billing job.

Job management is responsible for scheduling the various jobs to be executed and allocating resource to these jobs. As mentioned, several jobs can be in memory at a single time, although only one is ever executing at a given moment. Each of these jobs is competing for a series of resources and as such must be prioritized. When there is no more room for additional jobs, a job waiting line or queue must be maintained. Jobs with common characteristics are grouped together in specific job classes. For example, all jobs which require less than 512K of memory, use no tape drives, and will print less than 10,000 lines of output might be placed in class A. All of the jobs within the class A queue would then be ordered by priority and then by first-come-first-served basis for equal priorities. Each job class also has its own dispatching priority. It is the function of the job scheduler, then, to make sure the proper jobs are ready to execute at a given time. A program called an initiator/terminator is responsible for actually starting and stopping the job. Each class is assigned to a specific initiator. It is at this point that the job, broken down into its component steps, becomes a series of tasks for the computer to perform.

The operation of a multiprogrammed operating system requires special handling of I/O. Since the execution of programs is interleaved, it is necessary to "stage" some of the input and output on disk storage. This both maintains the integrity of the data and speeds the I/O operations. For example, during execution many programs may request the same printer to output lines of data. If the lines were printed in this manner, the output would be an incomprehensible jumble. Instead, the output of each program is accumulated separately and printed only at the completion of the job. A specialized I/O handler called a spooler is included in the operating system to "stage" the I/O of slower devices and to facilitate the "simultaneous" use of these devices. The spooling program intercepts all programs requests for input from card readers and output to line printers and card punches and routes them to DASD. When a program needs to read or write, the data comes from or goes to a very fast device. In this fashion, even though an installation may have only one printer, several jobs can be writing to the printer at once. The term SPOOL is an acronym for Simultaneous Peripheral Operation On Line.

Task management is responsible for the allocation of the processor for all of the executing tasks. Prioritized tasks within memory make requests (compete) for time and space. In a multiprogrammed environment, each task receives a fixed amount of time in which to perform its function. For example, if there are 10 tasks in memory and each is allocated one-tenth of a second to execute, one full second of CPU will be taken before the first task gets to resume execution. This method of time sharing among tasks is called time slicing. The tasks continue to compete in a round-robin fashion for CPU time until a task completes or exceeds its maximum allocation. The order of execution of tasks is controlled by the processor management part of the task manager.

Memory, like time slots, is partitioned by priority to tasks. Quite often, a single task can spawn a series of other tasks. Each of these must have memory allocated to it. Task management, then, responds by granting more memory to the task.

Because the optimal use of main memory is so important, entire operating systems have been rewritten to make them better memory managers. The result of this evolution is virtual memory. A virtual storage (VS) operating system, such as IBM's Multiple Virtual Storage (MVS), makes each task think it has more memory than is physically available to it. Under a VS system, memory is divided up into 2K or 4K byte segments called page frames. The task, then, is split up into 2K or 4K byte pieces called pages. Only those pages that are presently being used or have been recently used are in memory. The rest are placed on high-speed DASD until they are needed later. The process of moving pages back and forth to DASD is called paging. To determine which pages should be in memory or on DASD requires task management to employ sophisticated paging algorithms. This greatly complicates task management, which must maintain tables of which pages and page frames belong to which task, which pages need to be written to disk before new pages can be swapped in, which pages can simply be overlaid with other pages because they have not been changed, and when to page at all. These functions are controlled by part of the task manager called memory management.

Although being able to run a program that requires more memory than is available is useful, it also complicates the job of the system manager. Paging rates must constantly be monitored to make sure that the system is not spending too much of its time paging. We say that a system is thrashing when it is primarily paging in and out pages and is not executing user tasks. CPU utilization can reach 100% while thrashing and perform not one single user instruction.

Task management, sometimes called supervisor services, also performs those duties which are too risky or complicated for the user task to perform. For example, if two separate tasks want to share memory or pass data, the supervisor must coordinate the process and maintain security. After all, it would not do to have everyone's program changing the data areas of others' tasks. Machine instructions are classified in two groups: supervisor state and problem state. Problem state instructions modify memory according to the task's purpose. Supervisor state instructions manipulate devices such as printers or terminals, allocate or deallocate memory, and control the manipulation of instruction and address registers. Supervisor state instructions are directly processed by task management. Problem programs can only indirectly use supervisor state instructions by requesting supervisor services from the operating system.

Task management and the task communicate through the use of interrupts. Just as the term implies, an interrupt disturbs task management. The supervisor can then choose to ignore the interrupt or respond to it. There are several types of interrupts. A page fault is an interrupt that instructs the supervisor to bring in a page that is paged out. An I/O interrupt is particularly useful. When a task requests data from secondary storage, that task can do no more processing until it receives that data. As a result, another task receives control of the processor while the previous task waits for data. When the desired record has been transferred to a buffer, an I/O complete interrupt is sent to the supervisor. Task management will then interpret the interrupt and restart the previously executing task and stop the processing of the other. External interrupts, those originating from a peripheral, are rarely ignored by the supervisor. An external interrupt, which might come from the operators console, carries a very high priority. There are many more interrupt including power-fail interrupts, timer interrupts, privileged operations interrupts, and supervisor call interrupts. All of these communicate with the supervisor, which then handles or ignores them as it is programmed.

The data management portion of the operating system controls the creation, cataloging, and deletion of data sets. Most large operating systems maintain a structured list of the data sets that are available on the system. This catalog is simply a set of pointers that lead from the catalog entry to the volume table of contents (VTOC) and eventually to the physical location of the file. This provides central control over the access of all files in the system.

Probably a more important function of data management is the access method. An access method is a program, invoked by the operating system, that performs I/O. Without a common set of access methods, most user programs would create incompatible data set formats. In addition, every program written would have to include its own set of I/O functions. This would amount to reinventing the wheel. Access methods allow us to access data sequentially, indexed, or random, or some combination of these. An access method should provide high-performance data storage and retrieval, ease of use, data set security, and a wide range of applicability. It is, of course, the access method that writes the data on the DASD in either count-data or count-key-data formats and fills in the physical record with logical records and control information.

Tied very closely to job management is device management. Device management is in charge of the allocation, deallocation, manipulation, and status monitoring of all of the peripherals directly attached to the system. In reality, device management is simply a table that maps device name and type to its physical address in the system. Through device management, an operator can vary a printer offline (i.e., disable it) while a new print train is installed or reallocate a newly repaired disk drive. Sometimes included in device management is line control. This entails monitoring the status of data lines over which communications between the CPU and a peripheral or peripheral cluster travel. In this manner, the communication line is viewed as a device separate from the device at the end.

Information management is in charge of the collection of system and job performance data. Through this data we can bill individual users for the computer resources they used. In addition, the performance data can be used to tune the system to make it work more efficiently and effectively. For example, we could gather statistics on the number of page faults certain jobs create. By analyzing this, we could determine that a different method of program segmentation might improve program productivity.

Job accounting packages and other software monitors gather the job accounting and system performance information as part of the information management function of the operating system. Quite often, other duties are placed in information management. Log-on security and user profiles are sometimes included here. This portion of the OS acts as the system's gatekeeper. It keeps track of who is logged on and for how long, who has what capability while logged on, and how many total users can be logged on at a single time. User accounts can be authorized or deauthorized from this module. The information management function is the most frequently changed portion of the operating system. System programmers can install organization specified routines to handle special situations by altering the vendor-supplied code.

As can be seen, the operating system in a large computer environment is an extremely complex set of interrelated programs. See Figure A.9. Without each of the modules, the use of the system would be limited and cumbersome. As a manager, it should be obvious that finding and keeping qualified systems personnel should be a high-priority item. A haphazard, lackadaisical attitude toward the operating system only invites trouble. Probably more so than any other type of programmer, the systems programmer is unnoticed until the operating system hangs up and then this person becomes too popular. Finally, a DP manager must always keep abreast of new developments in operating systems. It is not unusual for several new versions of an OS to come out during a single year. Hopefully, these changes will not affect the application programming effort

Figure A.9 *Operating System Functions*

OS FUNCTION	DESCRIPTION
Job Management	Schedules jobs to be executed
Task Management	Controls processor and memory allocation
Device Management	Allocates devices to tasks
Data Management	Provides access methods and controls data sets
Information Management	Accumulates job accounting and system performance statistics
Communication Management	Facilitates distributed processing

too much. In any event, the manager must be aware of what operating system versions are running on the system.

Operating systems are normally accompanied by a package of utility programs that allow the programmer to manipulate data sets, devices, and programs. An example of a utility would be a program that would read a tape file and print it. Without a utility to perform this function, a programmer would have to write one. Other packages that are usually purchased with the operating system include language translators (i.e., COBOL, FORTRAN, and other compilers), linkage editors and loaders (to be discussed later), sorting programs, and specialized access methods.

JOB PROCESSING

Let's return now to the actual processing of a job. A job is normally thought of in terms of batch processing, although this is not necessarily the case. One needs to remember that a job is a set of tasks that the system must undertake to achieve some goal. As a result, a school's online registration system could be viewed as a job or set of tasks that is recurring rather than ending at a certain point, since it is always ready to accept input. Batch jobs are normally defined and submitted to the system, usually via an internal card reader (a CRT that sends a file to job management in card image format) with a special control language. The job control language (JCL) communicates the needs of the batch job to the operating system.

Job management invokes a reader/interpreter program that reads the JCL, analyzes it, and places the job in the appropriate job queue based on job class and priority. The initiator/terminator, another job management subfunction, selects individual programs and performs the initial duties necessary to start the program. This normally includes device and memory allocation, which are managed by other OS routines. When the program terminates, the memory and devices are deallocated for subsequent use. If output was generated, the output writer (spooler) is given control of the output spool files.

It is important to note that the initiator/terminator operates only on machine executable programs. A COBOL program as it is written by a programmer is not machine executable. It must first be translated into a format that the CPU can execute. This is the compile step in a three-step process that readies a program for execution. In this case, the COBOL program is called source module or source code. We say that source code is "people readable." The COBOL compiler is a machine executable program that is loaded and started by the initiator/terminator. It uses as input the source module, and produces an object module which is a machine executable program that usually will need several utility subprograms linked or attached to it before it can run successfully. This is the purpose of the linkage editor program. The linkage editor takes as input all of the object modules and external references that are necessary for a program to run. It combines all of these into a single unit, a load module, and places it out in a library data set for later execution. Another important duty of the linkage editor is address assignment. The compiler assumes that the COBOL program should start at address zero. This is so that the program can be relocated later to any available area of memory. The addresses are manipulated using an addressing scheme known as base-displacement addressing. Base-displacement addressing uses the general purpose registers (GPRs) as bases or starting points and adds a displacement or offset to this to calculate the actual address. For example, suppose the variable NAME is referenced by base register 6 with a displacement of 100 bytes. To calculate the actual address, we would take the value stored in register 6 by the linkage editor, say 50000, and add to it 100 making the first byte of the variable NAME start in actual address 50100. Should location 50000 be occupied by another program before subsequent execution, simply changing the value in register 6 to, say 20000, would relocate the program to another area of memory.

The use of the GPR is essential to the execution of a program. It must be remembered, though, that each program in a multiprogrammed OS requires the use of these registers. Thus, when execution of a program is suspended for some reason, such as an I/O interrupt, the value stored in the registers must be saved before another program can begin or resume execution. When the pending interrupt is satisfied, let's say an I/O completion interrupt, again the registers must be saved, the previous values restored, and execution of the first program is resumed. The operating system itself also uses these registers. It is the duty of task management to save and restore the general purpose registers as needed.

The load module is now a machine executable program that can be loaded and started by the initiator/terminator. Because the load module can be stored in a library, it can be used over and over again with no need for additional compilation or linkage editing. The process of changing source code into a load module is often collectively called a CLG (compile-link-and-go).

The execution of a single machine instruction is a stepwise process just as the execution of the entire job is. The instruction cycle is the process in which instructions are fetched from primary storage to the control unit in the CPU and then executed by the ALU.

The first step is to fetch the next instruction to be executed. A special register, the program status word (PSW), is used for this purpose. The program status word, among other duties, contains the address of the next instruction to be executed. In other words, it points to the machine language instruction that will be fetched after the currently executing instruction is finished. Should a program abnormally end (ABEND), the PSW would be left pointing to the instruction just after the abending instruction. The updating of the PSW is a supervisor state activity. An instruction that causes a nonsequential instruction to be executed, such as a GOTO, results in a branch interrupt, in which case the supervisor must recalculate the PSW based on the destination of the branch.

Once the instruction has been fetched, it must be interpreted. This is done by decomposing the machine instruction. In IBM mainframes there are seven instruction formats ranging from 16 to 48 bits long. There are over 200 different machine instructions. The type of execution needed (addition, subtraction, data movement, etc.) is determined by the first byte, the operation (op) code. The instruction also includes either the data itself, the general purpose registers to be used, or the memory location needed for the execution. The third step entails the control unit selecting the appropriate electronic circuitry to perform the operation.

Next, the data is brought in from primary storage and placed in the ALU. The operations specified by the op code are executed and, finally, the result is stored back in primary storage. When comparing CPU speeds, we sometimes refer to how many millions of instructions per second (MIPS) can be executed. It should be remembered that all data and instructions are treated the same in memory, as a series of binary digits grouped into bytes. The distinction between data and instructions in memory is based on the structure imposed by the language compiler.

DATA COMMUNICATIONS

The final area to be covered in this appendix is that of data communications. Data communications or telecommunications is concerned with moving information from point to point. It is then possible to enter data on a terminal in San Francisco, process that data in Houston, and send the results to New York. Teleprocessing, data processing at a distance, is without a doubt one of the most important matters for data processing managers to consider.

Early trends in teleprocessing amounted to the submission of batch jobs at remote, off-site locations. In this manner, a remote job entry station (RJE) could be placed in branch banks and communicate with the centralized computer at the main office. As the costs of hardware came down, the concept of distributed data processing became popular. Each off-site location now had its own processing capability. Data, then, could be passed from one machine to another as was necessary. Finally, as distributed processing became more prolific, DP managers began to notice that not all processors are busy all of the time.

In addition, an optical character reader or laser printer, for example, would be desirable devices to share among sites. The moving of information processing from site to site to take advantage of certain peripherals or excess CPU capacity facilitated the development of networks.

A communications network is composed of six parts. We have already discussed the CPU, front end processor, and terminals. In addition, the communication lines, associated connecting hardware, and control software make up the rest of the network. Communication lines can be compared in several categories. First, we could compare analog lines to digital lines. As we discussed with modems, telephone lines, which carry the bulk of network data, are in analog format where the computer requires digital signals. Secondly, we can compare the speed of transmission of the lines. To compare the speed of a line, we use a measure known as baud rate. Baud, which is a measure of the transmission media capacity, refers to the number of times per second that a line can change state and is often misdefined as bits per second (BPS), which is a measure of information transmittal speed. Finally, we characterize lines in terms of the direction of transmission. Simplex lines transmit in only a single direction. Half-duplex lines transmit in both directions, but only one way at a time, while full duplex lines transmit both directions at the same time.

The associated connecting hardware entails devices that allow the communication lines to be linked to the computer on one end and system peripherals on the other end. These include modems, concentrators, multiplexors, gateways, repeaters, amplifiers, etc.

The communication control program (CCP) manages the flow of data across transmission lines. This program formats data so that it can be used on other systems by their CCPs. The format used is called a protocol. Data that is sent through a network is packaged in such a way that the receiving system knows that device sent the data and what the destination is supposed to do with it. Two systems that do not use a common protocol cannot easily communicate. IBM synchronous protocols, Bisynchronous and Synchronous Data Link Control (SDLC), are used even in non-IBM environments and are becoming standards themselves. IBM collected several protocols and access methods and combined them into its System Network Architecture (SNA).

The devices in a network can be arranged in several different topologies. The star network uses a central CPU to handle the switching of messages from one user to another. Note that should the central system go down, the entire network becomes isolated. The ring topology makes each member in the network a data passer. It may be undesirable to have so many nodes handle the data, perhaps for security reasons. A desirable topology minimizes the effect of the loss of a network component and still reduces the number of data handlers. Bus topologies can distribute network control equally among nodes. Stations can be easily added or dropped without affecting the network. See Figure A.10.

A local area network (LAN), as opposed to the wide area networks we have been discussing, are normally confined to much smaller areas (up to approximately 10 kilometers). LANs normally connect microprocessor-based work

Figure A.10 *Network Topologies*

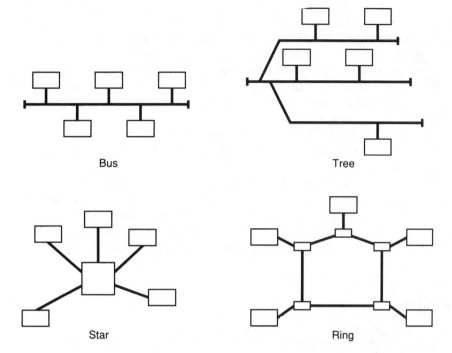

Bus

Tree

Star

Ring

Hybrid

stations and can be divided into two groups, baseband and broadband. Baseband systems, the most common, use coaxial cable to connect nodes in either a ring or bus topology. Ethernet is a popular baseband system. Many baseband systems use a protocol, called Carrier Sense Multiple Access/Collision Detect (CSMA/CD), to avoid and resolve collisions, in which multiple nodes try to communicate simultaneously. This passive protocol listens to the transmission line to see if it is being used. If not, it sends the appropriate packet. Work stations do not handle messages sent to other nodes, only those sent to their specific address.

Broadband networks can carry voice, video, and data simultaneously. Quite often, broadband and baseband networks are combined to take advantage of both.

As a manager, the growing demand for more data processing and instantaneous access to the corporate data resources will require you to consider networking more seriously. Network specialists are in high demand, and the need is growing. The most important item to remember is expandability. Make sure that any networking decisions include room for growth and innovation.

SUMMARY

The computing environment is an extremely complex and rapidly changing place. It is equipped with devices that were unheard of even five years ago and staffed with extremely creative and dynamic personnel. It is important that the manager of such a site be well acquainted with all of the aspects of the center. The hardware which is the most visible form of data processing must be viewed as a cohesive whole. The management of the hardware as simply a black box can be disastrous. As a result, it is very important that you understand the operation of each component and its interaction with the rest of the system.

The software that keeps the system running and productive is even more complicated than the hardware. With a poor foundation in systems and applications software, the purchase of additional hardware or software could be of little benefit.

Finally, it is important that the future of teleprocessing be kept in mind in all decisions. This very important issue will gain more and more attention as time goes on. It is extremely important that planning for such developments be done well in advance of need.

Although we viewed the system as individual components in this appendix, it is vital that we remember that it is a system that must work effectively and efficiently toward a goal as a whole. It is the responsibility of management to assemble, maintain, and modify the system to meet the growing corporate information needs. The data processing manager must know how the system works before this can be accomplished.

QUESTIONS

1. Define the following terms:
   a. Hardware
   b. Systems software
   c. Applications software
   d. Operating system
   e. Compiler
   f. I/O interrupt
   g. CPU
   h. Channel
   i. Controller
2. Describe how an application program will find and fetch specific data that is stored on a disk drive on the system.
3. Describe each of the management functions of an operating system.
4. Why are multiple logical records of data stored in a single physical record (called a block) on both disks and tapes?
5. When a call is made to the operating system by an application program (this is termed a *supervisor call* or *SVC*), why does the operating system first save all of the contents of the general purpose registers before it does any processing?
6. When would it be appropriate to use magnetic tape to store data? When would it be appropriate to use disk storage?
7. Why do all large computer systems have multiprogramming operating systems?
8. Why must an information system manager have some technical knowledge of the computer systems he or she manages? What problems may arise if this knowledge is lacking?
9. If a given form of technology, let's say disk storage devices, is rapidly changing, how may this affect the decisions made concerning this technology?
10. In almost all instances, the hardware available to a firm is more advanced and can perform some functions that the systems software has not as get been fully developed to take advantage of. Can you explain why this is the case?

CASE ANALYSIS

Investigate the characteristics of the computer system you use to do your student processing. Describe in detail each of the major components in the system, including the CPU, peripherals, and system software.

ADDITIONAL READINGS

BASHE, C., W. BUCHOLTZ, G. HAWKINS, J. INGRAM, AND N. ROCHESTER. "The Architecture of IBM's Early Computers," *IBM Journal of Research and Development*, September 1981, pp. 363–375.

BHANDARKAR, D., AND S. ROTHMAN. "The VAX-11, DEC's 32-Bit Version of the PDP-11," *Datamation*, February 1979, pp. 151–159.

CONNORS, W., J. FLORKOWSKI, AND S. PATTON. "The IBM 3033: An Inside Look," *Datamation*, May 1979, pp. 198–218.

CORMIER, R., R. DUGAN, AND R. GUYETTE. "System/370 Extended Architecture: The Channel Subsystem," *IBM Journal of Research and Development*, May 1983, pp. 206–218.

STALLINGS, W. *Computer Organization and Architecture: Principles of Structure and Function.* New York: Macmillan, 1987.

STALLINGS, W. "Local Networks," *Computing Surveys*, March 1984, pp. 3–42.

REVIEW OF MACHINE OPERATIONS: A WORM'S EYE VIEW

INTRODUCTION

In Appendix A, we studied the individual components of the computer system independently of each other. This bird's eye view enabled us to see the function of the hardware and software, but did not show us how these units form a useful, whole system. For example, in studying the disk drive, we did not look at how that drive was allocated to a specific job, but only discussed how it functioned mechanically. In this appendix, we approach the data processing environment not as a collection of units, but as a system of these units and their relationships to each other. We do this by taking the worm's eye view through the system. In this manner, we will follow the execution of a sample job through the system.

WHY WORM'S EYE?

The data processing manager must be able to see the big picture of the computing center. As such, the manager must be aware of the various relationships that exist between system components. This information can affect purchase decisions as well as project scheduling and system configuration. We can see that the manager must be able not only to understand the operation of each system component, but to use the relationships between these units in center management.

It is important to remember at this point that data processing is very dependent on the concept of the system. A working definition of a system might be a grouping of interrelated parts that operate together for a common purpose. This definition could apply to people as well as mechanical devices and software systems. In addition, a system is often composed of many subsystems, which in themselves could be viewed as systems. For the data processing manager, the concept of the system must affect the management function. Very few decisions made today, especially in a highly technological field, are made in isolation. Many factors must be taken into account before the decision maker has enough information on which to make a rational decision. The understanding of how a system fits together is extremely important.

In this appendix we will discuss job control languages, the purpose and execution of the initiator/terminator program, system recognition of the job, job queues, and the printing of output. All of these items comprise the system of job submission and execution.

JOB CONTROL LANGUAGES

Job control languages (JCL) are specialized and often cryptic programming languages designed specifically for the manipulation of jobs and the system resources necessary for execution. JCL is used to communicate the resource needs of the job to the operating system. It is used to identify users to the system, inform the system of processing requirements, detail the various I/O devices needed, and instruct the system of what to do under exceptional circumstances. A typical job might consist of a job header statement, one or more program execution instructions, and the data definition statements for each program. Figure B.1 presents a sample IBM OS JCL job.

A job header, called a JOB card, contains accounting information for the job. In other words, it identifies which department will be responsible for paying for the use of the system. In addition to accounting information, the job card also uniquely identifies the job to the system. It also specifies the amounts and dispositions of resources, such as job time and output destinations. In Figure B.1, we can see that the job ARSYS can use a maximum of 30 seconds of CPU time.

An execute program statement, called an EXEC card, is used to cause the execution of a program to begin. Each EXEC card represents one step or logical division of the job. The job in Figure B.1 contains three steps and consequently performs the execution of three programs (FILEFIX, ARPGM, and ARCHIVE).

Associated with each step is, usually, one or more JCL statements that define various data sets or files that the program requires. We say that this is the mapping of logical file names to actual or physical data set names. These data sets can exist in the form of DASD, tape, printed, or punched output. In interactive environments, terminal output can also be specified. These data definition statements are called DD cards. We can see that the program ARPGM requires

Figure B.1 *Sample IBM OS JCL*

```
//ARSYS    JOB (0737,,2),'MAJOR COMPANY'
/*JOBPARM    TIME=30
//STEP1    EXEC PGM=FILEFIX
//INPUT    DD DSN=ARDATA.UPDATES, DISP=OLD
//OUTPUT   DD DSN=&&NEWFMT,
//    DISP=(NEW,PASS,DELETE),UNIT=SYSDA,
//    SPACE=(CYL,(10,1)),
//    DCB=(LRECL=512,BLKSIZE=10244,RECFM=VB)
//SYSPRINT    DD SYSOUT=A

//STEP2    EXEC PGM=ARPGM,COND=(0,NE,STEP1)
//UPDATES    DD DSN=&&NEWFMT,DISP=(OLD,DELETE)
//MASTER    DD DSN=ARDATA.MASTER,DISP=OLD
//SYSPRINT    DD SYSOUT=A
//PARMS    DD *
030987041087
256
0011982310675
/*

//STEP3    EXEC PGM=ARCHIVE
//ORIGINAL    DD DSN=ARDATA,MASTER.DISP=OLD
//BACKUP    DD DSN=ARBACKUP(+1),
//    UNIT=TAPE,VOL=SER=1072
//    DISP=(NEW,KEEP,DELETE),
//    LABEL=(,,,ARPASS),DCB=(LRECL=121,
//    BLKSIZE=121000,RECFM=FB)
```

the use of four data sets. The first two DDs associated with the ARPGM step specify DASD files while the third is a printer file definition. The fourth DD indicates that data will be included with the job itself rather than on a specific device.

Again, it is important to remember the purpose of JCL. When we instruct the operating system to execute a program, or a series of programs, it is necessary to specify the system resources that our program requires. Should we include these specifications within the program itself, the program could quickly become outdated and require frequent revisions. With JCL, the addition of a new type of DASD to the system does not necessitate the rewriting of the program, which uses files which could now be placed on this DASD.

The use of JCL is a very fundamental concept in batch data processing. In addition, interactive processing, particularly in a networked environment, also requires the mapping of logical files to physical locations, resource allocation, and user identification to the system. To the operating system, the interactive program must vie for limited resources just as batch programs do. Although the JCL used in an interactive environment will appear different and does not control a job as such, it performs the same types of tasks as batch JCL.

It is through JCL accounting information that data processing centers are able to determine the resources consumed by each user, calculate charges, and subsequently bill system users for data processing activity. In addition, much useful system performance information can be gathered as the job executes, possibly facilitating system measurement and tuning. As can be seen, the concept of the job and its control through JCL can be very useful to the management of the computing center. Too often, it is viewed as a necessary evil to those unfamiliar with it, but this should not be the case.

JOB EXECUTION

The process of executing a job requires the assistance of several operating system programs. These routines interpret the JCL to determine job requirements, schedule the job for execution, allocate resources to each job step, and finally load the program into memory for execution. When the program finishes executing, the primary storage allocated to it must be relinquished and the output produced must be printed. While the program runs, it may require the assistance of additional operating system programs. In the next few sections, we will discuss the various operating system components of job submission and execution. We then concern ourselves with some of the many operating system routines that our programs must use and how they communicate with each other.

READER/INTERPRETER PROGRAM

The reader/interpreter program is an operating system program that is responsible for reading and then interpreting the JCL. JCL has a very exact set of syntax rules. The violation of these rules results in the cancelation of the job, and causes a JCL error listing to be produced and sent to the job's originator. Successful interpretation of the JCL will cause the interpreter program to place a coded version of the JCL in a spool file for subsequent execution. Any data that is submitted along with the job is placed in its own spool file. The kinds and quantities of resources needed to run the job are noted in a table that will later be used to schedule the job for execution.

SCHEDULER

The scheduler is another operating system program that determines which job will execute next. The scheduling table entry made by the reader is used to determine the class of the job. Remember, the class of the job is determined by the resources requested in the JCL. These resources include the estimated execution time, lines of output, types of input and output devices, the requested memory, etc. Each job class has an assigned priority. Those jobs with higher priorities get scheduled for execution before others of the same class. All job classes and their assigned priorities are system programmer defined. From a system management standpoint, much thought must be given to the creation of job classes. By allowing more efficient jobs to execute first, the performance of the system can be increased. Figure B.2 shows a typical set of job classes and their scheduling priorities.

INITIATOR/TERMINATOR PROGRAM

The allocation of computing resources to particular jobs is performed by programs called initiator/terminators. An initiator has the responsibility for determining whether existing resources are available for the job. Although the initiator does not actually load the job into memory, it does make that request to another piece of software called the loader.

A system may have dozens of initiators, each responsible for the resource allocation of different classes of jobs. For example, an interactive system such as CICS might have its own initiator, while a batch job requiring over a minute of CPU time might have another. A job might have several uses of an initiator. Each execution of a job step requires the assistance of the initiator. Likewise, the ending of each job step requires the services of the terminator program. The terminator program cleans up after the execution of the program step. It handles the disposition of the spooled program output and the deallocation of main memory from the program. Upon program completion, the terminator provides the operating system's output writer with the printer/punch spool files created during execution for output.

Figure B.2 *Example of Job Classes*

CLASS	MAXIMUM MOUNTABLE DISK PACKS	MINIMUM TAPE DRIVES	CPU TIME (MINUTES) >	BUT < =	OUTPUT RECORDS
A	0	0	0	10	<=20,000
B	0	1	0	10	<=20,000
C	0	2	0	10	<=20,000
F	1	0	0	10	<=20,000
G	1	1	0	10	<=20,000
H	1	2	0	10	<=20,000
K	1	2	10	30	<=100,000
L	1	2	30	60	<=100,000
Z	—	4	0	—	—

LOADER

The loader program is responsible for loading the program into memory. Most programs employ the concept of base-displacement addressing, which refers to how the program instructions and variables are accessed by the system. Using this method, a program may be loaded into any available portion of storage, rather than have to wait for a specific memory range to free up. Once this is done, the program is referred to as a task. This distinction is made because all programs in memory, including the scheduler and initiator/terminators, are viewed as subprograms of the operating system program. It is even more important to remember that all of these share the same physical CPU, including general purpose registers and primary storage.

ACCESS METHODS

Most programs need to read or write data from or to external I/O devices. To do this, a set of system routines called access methods are used to transfer the data. The choice of an access method depends on the type of processing the application program requires. The simplest form used is the sequential access method, sometimes called SAM. SAM can be used for I/O between a wide variety of devices including printers, DASD, and tape. As its name implies, SAM is used for strictly sequential transfers of data. More sophisticated access methods allow for the placement and retrieval of data from DASD based on the value of a specific record field or key. Examples of this include the indexed sequential access method (ISAM) and IBM's Virtual Storage Access Method (VSAM). Access methods are also needed in interactive environments for terminal communication, such as telecommunication access methods. Access methods are normally memory resident; hence for efficiency purposes they will never be paged out of real memory.

An efficient method of conserving secondary storage space uses the concept of packing or blocking groups of logical records into larger physical records, which are subsequently written out to the media. This blocking of records requires special handling considerations by the application program and the access method. The access method, normally called a queued access method (such as queued sequential access method or QSAM), must gather the various logical records to be written in a buffer area. When the buffer becomes full, the block of records is then written. Conversely, blocked records read from disk or tape must be unblocked in the buffer area by the access method, which then passes the appropriate logical record to the program. When the buffer is empty, a new block must be fetched from secondary storage. Figure B.3 shows the transfer of a physical record from DASD to the buffer area for a COBOL program. Figure B.4 shows the transfer of a logical record to the application program from the buffer area.

Figure B.3 *Example of Blocked Data*

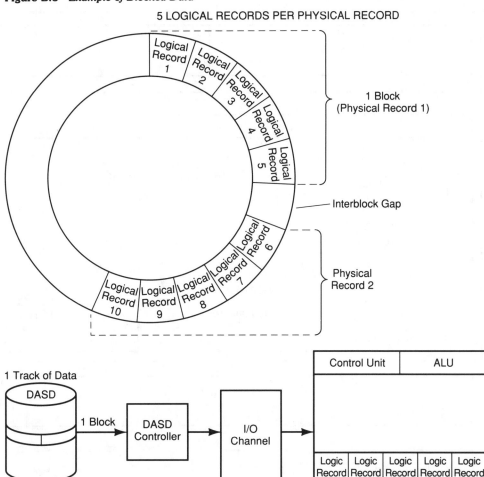

5 LOGICAL RECORDS PER PHYSICAL RECORD

As a manager, the choice of the appropriate access method should be based on the data processing requirements. For example, an order entry system might collect data based on a unique product code. In this case, an access method with random retrieval capabilities, such as VSAM, should be used. However, a paycheck printing program would print using a sequential method. It should be noted that a data set written with one access method can be subsequently accessed by another method. Likewise, a single application program can make use of several access methods simultaneously. The choice of blocking records is dependent on the types of storage media used and the amounts of buffer storage available to the program. Many of the more common access methods are available in queued and nonqueued versions.

Figure B.4 *Unblocking of Data*

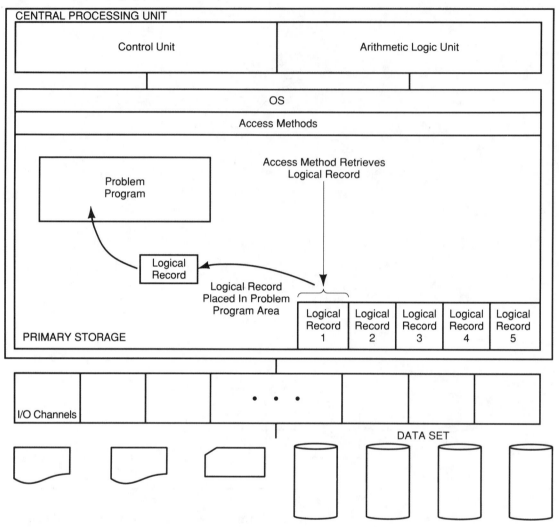

OUTPUT WRITERS

In a multiprogrammed environment, individual programs which produce printed or punched output (SYSOUT) must be handled differently than those written to faster devices. For each SYSOUT, the system creates a spool file, which is simply a DASD file to which the printed or punched records are sent instead of the actual physical device. A system routine called an output writer is used then to move the file to the appropriate device when that device becomes available. As a result, several programs can actually be executing, each writing to the same line printer. Spool files are printed when the job terminates. Thus the terminator program must communicate with the appropriate output writer for the files to be dispatched.

INTERRUPTS AND THE DISPATCHER

We must remember that all of the programs mentioned thus far, initiator/terminator, loader, access methods, output writers, reader/interpreter, scheduler, and the application programs themselves all execute as tasks or subprograms running under the main supervisor program. As can also be seen, the interaction between each of these tasks can be quite complicated. Most modern computers use interrupts to facilitate communication between tasks and the supervisor. An interrupt, as the name implies, causes the interrupting task to halt temporarily while the supervisor executes. At the time of interrupt, the values of the general purpose registers as well as the address of the interrupting instruction are saved for later use. An interrupted task is said to be nondispatchable, i.e., no longer eligible for execution. After the supervisor completes its processing, the saved registers are restored and the program is marked as being dispatchable. The dispatcher is that component of the supervisor which determines which of the dispatchable tasks can use the CPU based on the dispatch priority. It should be mentioned here that there are many types of interrupts. The two most common interrupts are supervisor calls (SVC) and I/O.

An SVC occurs when an application program requests the supervisor to perform a task such as read a certain record from DASD. At this point, the operating system access method will determine if a physical read operation is necessary. If the records are blocked, it may be possible simply to remove a record from the buffer area. If a physical read is necessary, the operating system will build a program for the channel. This channel program is formed from the data contained in the data control block (DCB) that describes that data set. An execute channel program instruction (EXCP) is then issued to the channel, and the channel accesses the data. An I/O interrupt occurs when the requested record has been made available to the supervisor (and consequently the application program). To better understand these interrupts, consider the following example.

Figure B.5 shows the contents of main memory prior to an interrupt occurring. As can be seen, seven programs currently occupy memory (CICS, Initiator 2, IEHPROGM, IKFCBL00, PAYROLL, Initiator 6, and Output Writer 2). The PAYROLL program is currently using the processor (i.e., it is the problem program). After processing for a period of time, it requires data which are stored on a DASD. These data could be stored as the result of spool file creation or as an ordinary dataset. PAYROLL issues a read request for the data. Ideally, this request would actually be made to the appropriate access method, which would load the channel program and then issue the EXCP command to the channel. However, to simplify this example, no access method is assumed. In a later complete example, we will consider the entire process. When the SVC is issued,

Figure B.5 *Logical Map of Main Memory*

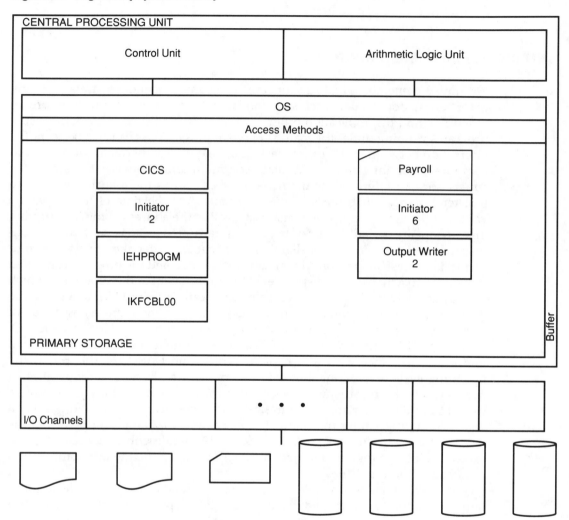

the PAYROLL program is placed in the WAIT (nondispatchable) state. Figure B.6 shows the system after the SVC. Note that Initiator 2 now has control of the CPU. After the DASD read is completed, the channel issues an I/O interrupt to alert the supervisor of this fact. The PAYROLL program is now marked as being dispatchable and must wait its turn to gain control of the processor again.

From a manager's point of view, we can see that it is very important that programs should cause as few interrupts as possible, keeping control of the processor as long as possible to complete their duties. This can be accomplished by decreasing the number of times the supervisor is called upon to perform I/O. Blocking of data and efficient use of access methods are very helpful here. Also,

Figure B.6 *Revised Map of Main Memory*

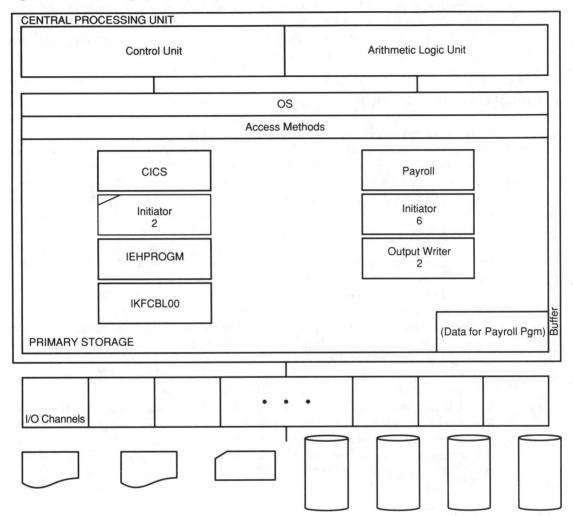

some types of application program instructions which cause the flow of control to behave in some nonsequential manner (GOTOs, for example) cause the program to wait while the supervisor resets instruction pointers or while an additional page of program code is paged into real storage. Hence, minimizing the number of these instructions will allow the program to run more efficiently.

The worm's eye view of the scheduling and execution of jobs can be very beneficial knowledge for the DP manager. One must not only be aware of the functions of the various hardware devices, but must also understand the relationships these have with each other. We have just considered some of the critical operating system routines and procedures used to allocate these resources among the many jobs within the system. The importance of the supervisor program cannot be overstated. Multiprogrammed environments could not exist without it. From the time the job enters the system to the moment the last SYSOUT record is printed or punched, one of the supervisor routines or the supervisor itself is facilitating its execution.

COMPILE-LINK-AND-GO PROCEDURES

Thus far we have discussed the logical organization of system procedures necessary for the execution of a program. We have assumed, although not explicitly stated, that these programs are in machine executable form. However, programs rarely start out that way. Probably the most common event that takes place within academic data processing is that of program creation (or revision) and submission. Several steps are necessary for a COBOL program, for example, to become ready to execute. These steps are normally referred to as compile-link-and-go procedures or CLGs. A CLG changes the application program from its "people readable" form (source code) into a form that the machine can not only read, but also execute (object code).

The COMPILE step is responsible for taking the COBOL or FORTRAN program, sometimes referred to as the source module, and translating it into a machine readable (binary) form, called an object module. The program which does this is known as a compiler. The object module is then processed by another program, called the linkage editor (or linker-loader), which makes available to the application program any subprograms (such as access methods or mathematical routines) required and prepares the resulting load module for use by the loader in the LINK step. This module is called a load module. Finally, the load module is loaded into memory and executed as the GO step. Every time the source module is altered, even slightly, these steps must be followed to execute the program. Figure B.7 shows the relationships between the modules and the steps that create and use them.

COMPILE STEP

A compiler is a system program that translates source code into object code. Every high-level programming language has its own compiler. Compilers, unlike the high-level languages themselves, are machine specific load modules. Compiler input normally comes from two sources. First, the source module itself acts as an input data set to the compiler program. Secondly, the compiler usually can copy records from external files into the source module. These external files are often called COPY libraries. Copy libraries are useful in helping to standardize program data structures and variable naming conventions. In addition, they allow portions of program logic to be shared among application programs. This is a relatively simple, but effective DP management tool. Compiler output

Figure B.7 *Relationships Between Modules*

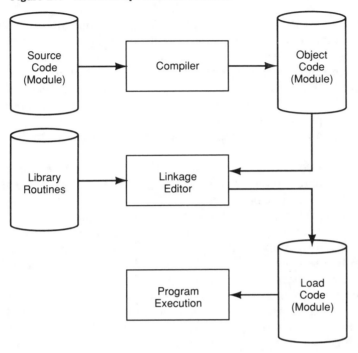

also normally is of two forms. As already mentioned, the object module is the machine readable version of the source module. This is not to say, however, that there is a one-to-one correspondence between each source record and each object record. This most definitely is not the case. The purpose of high-level programming languages is to allow the user to use a few statements to do many things. The compiler translates these statements into their many corresponding machine language counterparts. This phenomenon is known as the instruction explosion.

The source listing is the second major output from the compiler. This usually contains a formatted printing of the source module and perhaps some summary statistics concerning the number of bytes or statements used. The compiler is the enforcer of language syntax; consequently, the source listing might also contain a syntax error message section.

To execute the compiler program, the user must issue the appropriate JCL statement that will cause the compiler program to be loaded into memory and the necessary resources to be allocated to the task. The compiler program is treated by the supervisor just as any other application program. It uses SVC interrupts and requires the services of access methods and initiator/terminators. Output writers are used to handle the printing of the generated SYSOUT files.

LINK STEP

The linkage editor is responsible for combining into a single module many object modules that were separately compiled. This is often known as resolving external references. An external reference is a reference to a program (or sub-program/subroutine) which was not part of the original program. In this manner, a large and consequently unwieldy program can be broken (segmented) into smaller, more manageable components and then linked back together at a later time. A team of programmers can thus be given parts of an assignment and, using common copy libraries, create programs that will eventually be joined together into a working whole.

The input to the linkage editor is the object module produced by a compiler. Also, a library of other object modules to be linked together along with system modules is used as input to the editor. The main form of linkage editor output is a single, relocatable load module. The term *relocatable* refers to the fact that the program can be loaded anywhere in memory by the loader. Often, a cross-reference listing of external references is also printed on a SYSOUT spool file. This can be useful to make sure that all of the proper (current and applicable) object modules have been combined into the load module. An important fact concerning the use of linkage editors is that the resulting load module can be stored on an external storage device for later loading and executing. This is not the case for the compile-and-go procedures discussed later.

The linkage editor program must be loaded into main memory, just as the compiler was. It requires the same services from the supervisor as any program does. It must be dispatched, and if it causes any interrupts, it must be placed in wait status and then redispatched. Any SYSOUT must be handled by the appropriate output writer.

GO STEP

The go step is, finally, the execution of the application program. It is normally not until this time that the program could be executed by the system. If, however, there had been no external references to be linked by the linkage editor, the object module could have been executed. For the program to be executed, an initiator must allocate the necessary resources to the program, a loader must load the program into available storage, and the output writers must handle the SYSOUT records. Seeing this, we note that the system treats the application program in precisely the same way it treated the compiler and linkage editor before it.

As previously mentioned, the linkage editor creates a relocatable load module that can subsequently be saved on disk or tape and later used and reused. This reduces the number of needless compiles and link-edits to execute a program. When a DP shop purchases a program from an external source, that program may be an object or load module, rather than source code. Because object and load modules are so difficult for a programmer to alter or even understand, the vendor can protect its investment of time and effort by not giving the user the source code. When the group is purchased in load module form, it is assumed to be entirely self-supporting and needs no other modules (external references) to function properly. Object modules, however, frequently require the services of a linkage editor to become usable. This allows the buyer to upgrade the program as time dictates, adding or deleting those necessary modules.

COMPILE AND GO

For those smaller programs which require neither segmentation nor external references, a two-step procedure is used rather than the compile-link-and-go. The compile-and-go procedure simply compiles the source module into object code, which is then immediately executed. Quite often, the ability to save the object module is not available in this procedure, presumably because it is assumed that the small program will not be executed frequently. Should this be the case, the storage of the object module for subsequent execution would not be necessary. If needed, the source module could be recompiled and executed. The compile-and-go technique is often used in introductory programming classes where the usefulness of the programs is short-lived and no link-editing of subprograms is required.

COMPLETE EXAMPLE

As can be seen, the process of creating, submitting, and eventually executing a job can be quite complicated. To summarize this, we will follow the compilation, linking, and execution of a batch COBOL program. It is not necessary that for this example you know the function of each JCL or COBOL statement. However, you must know the individual functions of the supervisor and the necessary operations of the respective programs.

Figure B.8 contains the IBM OS JCL job stream that will be considered for this example. We will discuss the JCL only in such a manner as to make its functions clear. For further reference concerning JCL, you must consult a JCL text appropriate for your installation.

The job listed in Figure B.8 is a COBOL CLG. The program will simply read a blocked data set and print out the records in a different format. The program employs a subprogram, which is not listed here, that will reformat the student's name. Line 01 is the JOB card from which the system will gather information to aid in computer usage billing. This job contains three steps: COMPILE (Line 02), LINKEDIT (Line 54), and GO (Line 63). Figure B.9 shows the contents of main memory, before this job is executed.

When this job is submitted, the reader/interpreter collects the JCL and

```
01  //EXAMPLE JOB DEPT42,'D. ADAMS',MSGLEVEL=(1,1)
02  //COMPILE EXEC PGM=IKFCBL00,
03  //    PARM='APOST,SUPMAP,LIB,LANGLVL(1),NOADV',REGION=128K
04  //SYSPRINT DD   SYSOUT=A
05  //SYSPUNCH DD   SYSOUT=B
06  //SYSUT1   DD   UNIT=SYSDA,SPACE=(CYL,(4,1))
07  //SYSUT2   DD   UNIT=SYSDA,SPACE=(CYL,(4,1))
08  //SYSUT3   DD   UNIT=SYSDA,SPACE=(CYL,(4,1))
09  //SYSUT4   DD   UNIT=SYSDA,SPACE=(CYL,(4,1))
10  //SYSLIB   DD   DSN=WYL.ON.E23.BCS.COPYLIB,DISP=SHR
11  //SYSLIN   DD   DSN=&&LOADSET,DISP=(MOD,PASS),UNIT=SYSDA,
12  //           SPACE=(CYL,(1,1)),DCB=(LRECL=80,BLKSIZE=3200,RECFM=FBS)
13  //SYSIN   DD   *
14         IDENTIFICATION DIVISION.
15         PROGRAM-ID. EXAMPLE.
16         ENVIRONMENT DIVISION.
17         CONFIGURATION SECTION.
18         INPUT-OUTPUT SECTION.
19         FILE-CONTROL.
20             SELECT INPUT-FILE ASSIGN TO UT-S-INPUT.
21             SELECT PRINT-FILE ASSIGN TO UT-S-OUTPUT.
22         DATA DIVISION.
23         FILE SECTION.
24         FD INPUT-FILE
25             BLOCK CONTAINS 5 RECORDS
26             LABEL RECORDS ARE STANDARD.
27         01 INPUT-RECORD COPY STUREC.

28         FD PRINT-FILE
29             LABEL RECORDS ARE STANDARD.
30         01 OUTPUT-RECORD          PICTURE IS X(133).
31         WORKING-STORAGE SECTION.
32         77 WS-END-OF-FILE        PICTURE IS XXX VALUE 'NO'.

33         01 PR-PRINT-DATA COPY STDFORM.

34         PROCEDURE DIVISION.
35             OPEN INPUT INPUT-FILE, OUTPUT PRINT-FILE.
36             READ INPUT-FILE AT END MOVE 'YES' TO WS-END-OF-FILE.
37             PERFORM 020-PROCESS-INPUT THRU 020-PROCESS-INPUT-EXIT
38                 UNTIL WS-END-OF-FILE = 'YES'.
39             CLOSE INPUT-FILE, PRINT-FILE.
40             STOP RUN.

41         020-PROCESS-INPUT.
42             CALL 'FORMAT' USING IN-STUDENT-NAME.
43             MOVE IN-STUDENT-NAME   TO PR-PRINT-NAME.
44             MOVE IN-STUDENT-AGE    TO PR-PRINT-AGE.
45             MOVE IN-STUDENT-MAJOR   TO PR-PRINT-MAJOR.
46             MOVE IN-STUDENT-PHONE   TO PR-PRINT-PHONE.
47             MOVE IN-STUDENT-ADDRESS TO PR-PRINT-ADDRESS.

48             WRITE OUTPUT-RECORD FROM PR-PRINT-DATA.
49             READ INPUT-FILE,
50                 AT END MOVE 'YES' TO WS-END-OF-FILE.
51         020-PROCESS-INPUT-EXIT.
52             EXIT.
53  /*
54  //LINKEDIT EXEC PGM=IEWL,PARM='SIZE=(195888.065536),LET',
```

```
55  //    REGION=256K,COND=(5,LT,COMPILE)
56  //SYSLIN    DD   DSN=&&LOADSET,DISP=(OLD,DELETE)
57  //SYSLMOD   DD   DSN=&&GODATA(RUN),DISP=(NEW,PASS),UNIT=SYSDA,
58  //         SPACE=(CYL,(1,1,1))
59  //SYSLIB    DD   DSN=SYS1.COBLIB,DISP=SHR
60  //         DD   DSN=WYL.ON.E23.BCS.OBJLIB,DISP=SHR
61  //SYSUT1    DD   UNIT=(SYSDA,SEP=(SYSLIN,SYSLMOD)),SPACE=(CYL,(1,1))
62  //SYSPRINT DD   SYSOUT=A
63  //GO       EXEC PGM=*.LINKEDIT.SYSLMOD,
64  //         COND=((5,LT,COMPILE),(5,LT,LINKEDIT))
65  //STEPLIB   DD   DSN=SYS1.COBLIB,DISP=SHR
66  //SYSOUT    DD   SYSOUT=A
67  //OUTPUT    DD   SYSOUT=A
68  //INPUT    DD   DSN=WYL.ON.E23.BCSDATA,DISP=SHR
69  //
```

Figure B.9 *Main Memory—Before Execution*

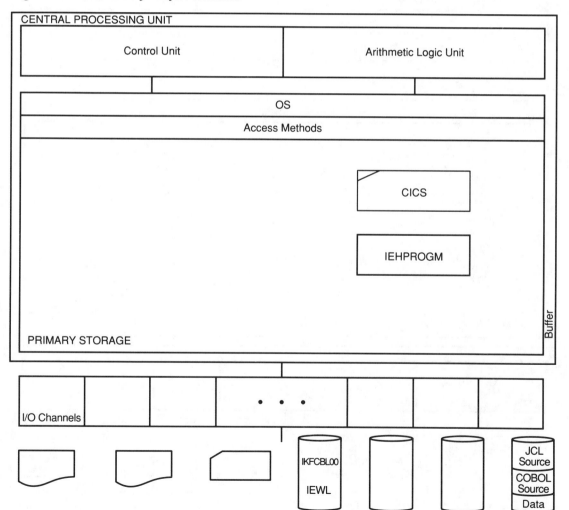

then interprets it. Hopefully, Figure B.8 contains no syntax errors. Should this not be the case, the job will not be executed and it will be returned to the user. The JCL is decoded by the interpreter and placed in a spool file to await scheduling. Any data submitted along with the job is placed in separate spool files. For Figure B.8, this data would be lines 14 through 52, the COBOL source module. Figure B.10 shows the changes in the system which arose from the reading and interpretation of the JCL.

The EXAMPLE job will be scheduled for execution based on the table in Figure B.2. From this we can see that this job will be classified as a class A job. Initiator 3, shown here in Figure B.11, has been loaded and will allocate the necessary resources to the COMPILE step for this job. Remember that the ini-

Figure B.10 *Main Memory—After JCL Interpretation*

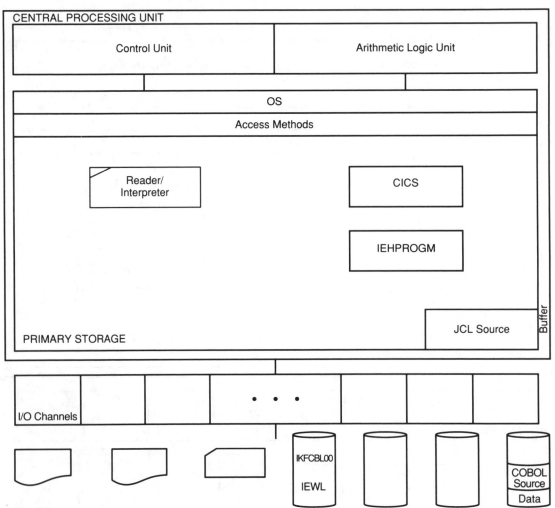

Figure B.11 *Main Memory—After Initiator Is Landed*

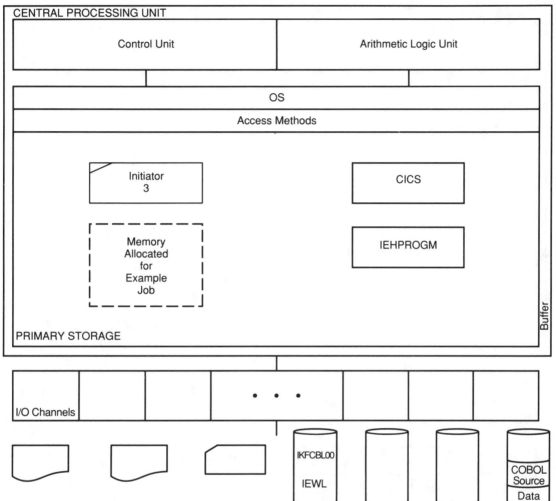

tiator does not actually load the COBOL compiler here, but simply allocates the required resources to that program. From the JCL, we can see that the COMPILE step requires two SYSOUT datasets (called SYSPRINT and SYSPUNCH; lines 04 and 05). It also needs DASD files. The SYSLIB card (line 10) specifies the data set that contains the COPY library. Looking through the COBOL program, we can see that lines 27 and 33 require copy records. The SYSLIN card (line 11) specifies the output data set for the compiler, the object module.

After resource allocation, the initiator requests that the loader load the COBOL compiler (called IKFCBL00; line 02) into memory. Figure B.12 shows the system while the loader is in the problem program state. All other programs are waiting. Figure B.13 shows main memory after the compiler has been loaded.

Figure B.12 *Main Memory—During Compiler Load*

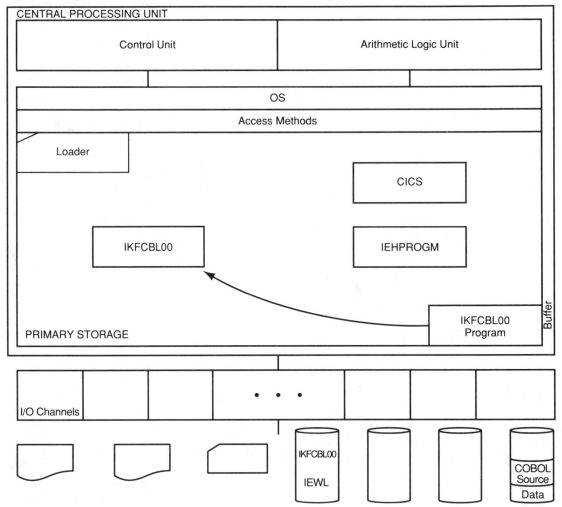

Notice, however, that at this point the loader is still using the CPU; hence the execution of the compiler has not occurred yet. When the compiler begins execution, it reads the spool file data set which contains the COBOL program source code. It also reads the copy library, inserting the copy records into their proper places. The compiler requires the services of an access method to read these data sets. As a result, Figure B.14 shows how the access method transfers data from storage, to the buffer area, and then eventually to the problem program. Should the buffer be empty, IKFCBL00 is placed in the wait state until the data is retrieved from external storage. We can see from Figure B.15 that the CICS program is in the problem state while COBOL source records are retrieved from the spool files. If the buffer is not empty, then the record is passed to the compiler and execution continues without the need to relinquish the processor.

As the compiler executes, it writes SYSOUT records to a spool file, which can also be seen in Figure B.16. An access method is also required to write object module records to SYSLIN. When the compiler completes executing, control of the processor passes to the terminator, which is then loaded into memory (Figure B.17). The terminator determines whether an output writer should be loaded to handle any SYSOUT files created. In this case, an output writer is not required because the job has not been completed, only the first step.

For the second step of the job, LINKEDIT (line 54), another initiator is

Figure B.13 *Main Memory—After Compiler Is Loaded*

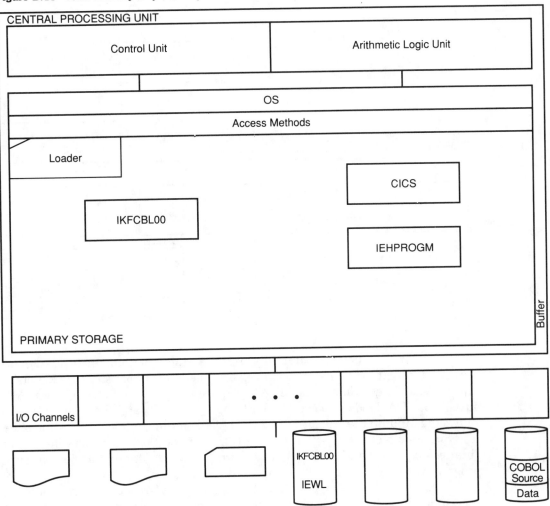

Figure B.14   *Main Memory—Before Data Transfer*

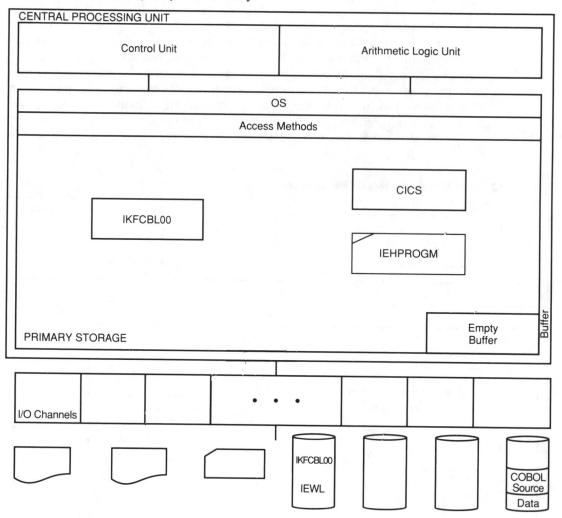

required. For this step, initiator 4 is used. A different initiator is used here because different amounts of resources are needed for this step (256K versus 128K). The linkage editor, called IEWL, requires only one SYSOUT file (line 62), but several DASD files (SYSLIN, SYSLMOD, SYSLIB, and SYSUT1). Line 56 shows the input to the linkage editor, the object module, while line 57 shows the resulting load module. The SYSLIB card (lines 59 and 60) references the object libraries for the standard COBOL subprograms and for the FORMAT sub-program referenced in line 42 of the COBOL program.

Once the initiator has allocated the required resources, the loader is used to load the linkage editor. Figure B.18 shows the contents of main storage after IEWL has been loaded. The linkage editor will require the services of an access method to read and write files. The access method can also be seen in Figure B.18. Notice that the same access method used by the compiler is used here. This does not necessarily have to be the case, but is more often than not.

After the linkage editor has completed, the terminator is loaded to relinquish the resources. Because the job has still not completed, the SYSOUT files are not yet printed. Figure B.19 shows the contents of memory after the linkage editor has completed. Notice that even though the terminator is shown here, the problem program is IEHPROGM. Even initiator/terminators must wait their turns.

Figure B.15 *Main Memory—After Data Transfer*

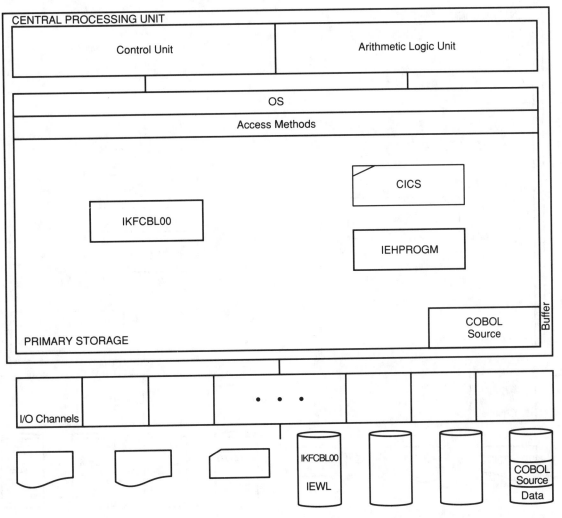

Finally, initiator 3 is loaded to begin the execution of the load module produced by the linkage editor. The GO step (line 63) requires two SYSOUT files and two DASD files. The INPUT card (line 68) refers to a blocked data set which is used as input to the COBOL program. This file is referenced in the COBOL source at lines 20, and 24 through 27. Notice particularly line 25, which describes the data set as containing physical records that are composed of five logical records.

After the loader has loaded memory with the program, execution may begin as soon as the dispatcher selects it for processor control. After execution begins, the first read (line 36) immediately causes the access method to request

Figure B.16 *Main Memory—During Compiler Execution*

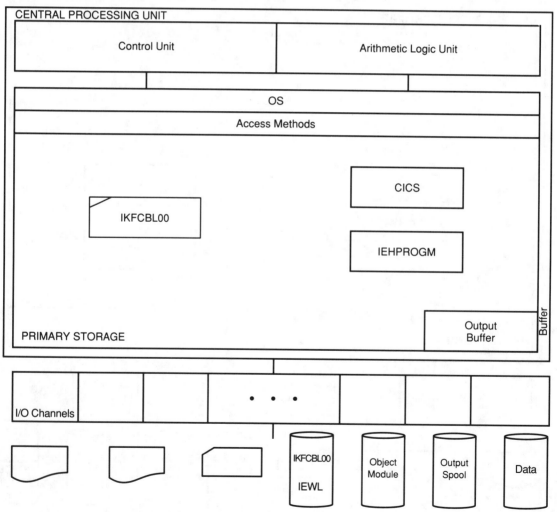

Figure B.17 *Main Memory—After Terminator Is Loaded*

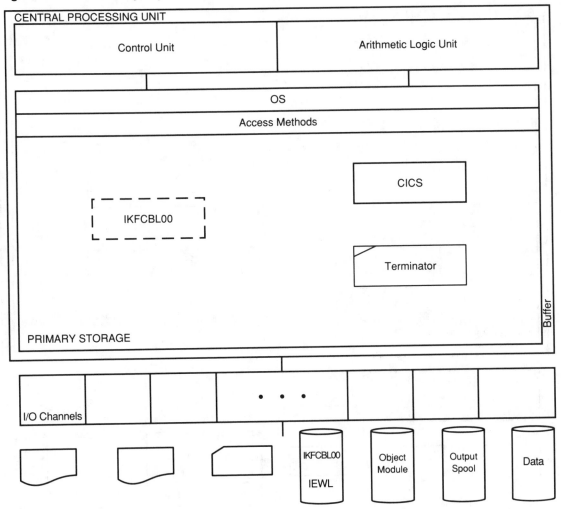

that the I/O supervisor transfer a physical record from DASD to buffer memory. This causes the program to be placed in the WAIT state while another program, IEHPROGM, controls the processor (Figure B.20). Notice that the access method formed a request for the I/O supervisor, which then passed the request to the proper communications channel. The channel then manipulates the proper DASD controller, which positions the read/write heads over the appropriate location on the DASD and begins to transfer the record. Once the record has been read, the channel signals the I/O supervisor that the requested record has been retrieved. The supervisor then marks the COBOL program as being dispatchable so that, when its turn comes around, it may use the processor. Figure

Figure B.18 *Main Memory—After Linkage Editor Is Loaded*

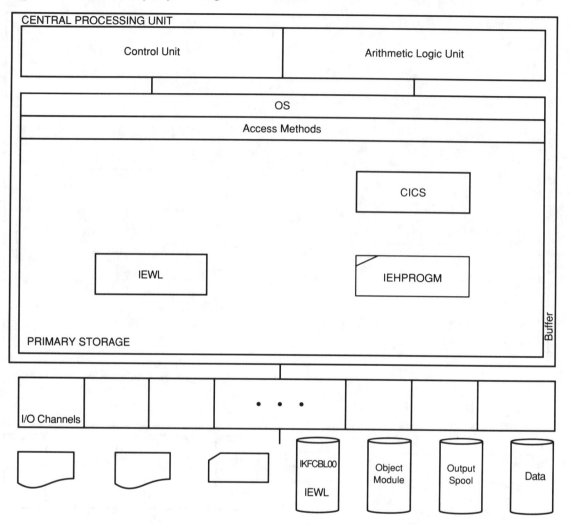

B.21 shows the contents of memory after the physical record (block) has been placed in the buffer area. The access method then is responsible for deblocking the record and subsequently passing the individual logical records to the application program.

The COBOL program will retain processor control until an interrupt occurs or it completes its execution. Each program is allowed a certain amount of time, called a time slice, in which it can use the processor. Once that time has expired, the program is placed in the wait state and another program is dispatched. After the GO step completes, the terminator is loaded which releases the resources acquired by the initiator. Because there are no more steps in the job, the terminator alerts the appropriate output writer that the spool files associated with the EXAMPLE job can be processed.

The output writer, which must compete for processor resources just as other programs, determines whether the needed devices are available. If they are, the spool files begin printing or punching in the order that they were created. In other words, the spool files created in the COMPILE step would be printed before those from the GO step.

SUMMARY

As can be seen from the preceding example, the execution of a simple CLG job requires much system supervisor interaction. This interaction is often referred to as system overhead because the total amount of time a job was in the system is

Figure B.19 *Main Memory—After Linkage Editor Completion*

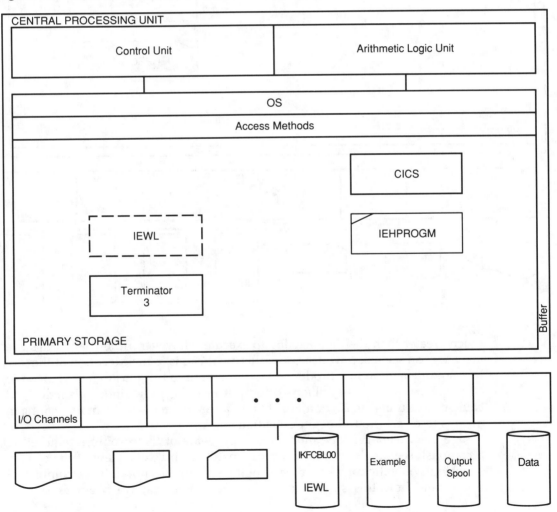

Figure B.20   *Main Memory—Example Program Waiting For Input*

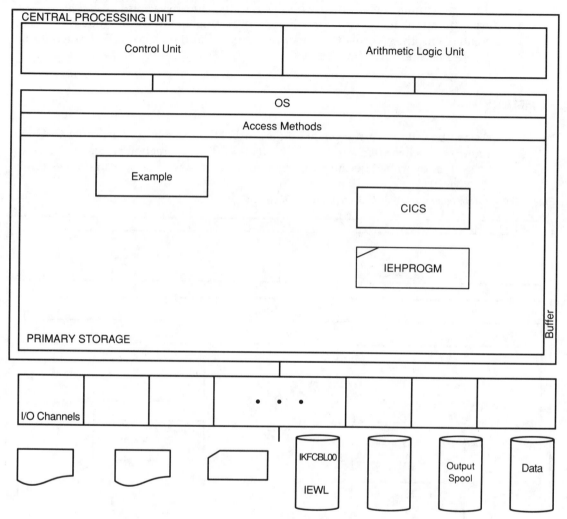

much greater than the time needed to execute. However, from the worm's eye view, we can see just how necessary this overhead is to the execution of the job. It is not uncommon in a production environment to run jobs that contain 50 or 60 job steps, producing millions of output records. In addition, a single CPU could be executing 10, 20, or more of these jobs with many times more waiting in queues to be selected to begin execution.

As a manager, one must be keenly aware of the resources required to accomplish seemingly mundane processing. The bird's eye view of the system showed us only the component parts of the system. It is not until we completely understand how this system interacts as a whole that we begin to see the monumental management task before us. We should note here that this appendix has not even touched on the more complicated operating systems and processing environments. In addition, the complicating factor of human behavior can also make the difficult job of DP management even more frustrating.

The worm's eye view is important because we must see that the system functions as a whole, rather than as a collection of parts. The more sophisticated the environment, the more critical this view becomes. Not only is it necessary for one to understand the rules and regulations governing the posting of accounts payable to the general ledger, but we must also be knowledgeable of the fact that the correct functioning and interaction of a large number of system and application programs must occur before any processing can take place at all.

Figure B.21 *Main Memory—After Physical Read*

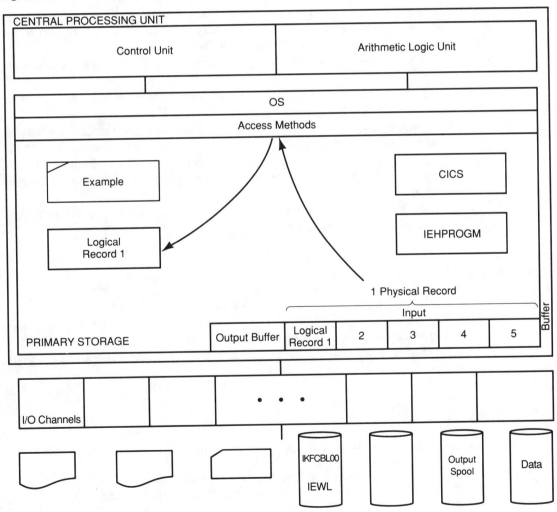

QUESTIONS

1. Using a facility for printing the number of generated lines of machine instructions from a high-level programming language, determine the average number of machine language statements generated per instruction. Which language elements require more statements, arithmetic or I/O? Why?

2. Using accounting records from your installation, determine the average total time in system compared to the average time in execution. Would this be any different at different times of the day? Why or why not?

3. Write an application program that simply reads from a DASD. Change the blocking factor of the data set. How does the number of execute channel program instructions (EXCPs) change?

4. There are several types of interrupts. Many were not discussed here. List them and give examples of each. Which type of interrupt would you think supervisors would use to communicate with each other?

5. List the job classes and resource requirements of each class at your installation.

6. List five different access methods and the advantages and disadvantages of each.

7. Compare and contrast queued access methods to those that do not handle blocked records. Be sure to list the advantages and disadvantages of each.

8. Often, data processing managers feel that they should not be bothered with the technical details of information systems. What do you think? Defend your answer.

9. Should an educational institution use a compile-and-go procedure rather than a compile-load-and-go? Why?

CASE ANALYSIS

Take a program that you wrote in a previous computer class (use one that is at least moderately complex) and run this program on your school's computer system. Relate the ways in which this program interacts with the computer system. That is, relate the specific worm's eye view of the processing on your computer system.

ADDITIONAL READINGS

BERNHARD, R. "More Hardware Means Less Software," *IEEE Spectrum*, December 1981, pp. 30–37.

BOND, R. "XA: The View from White Plains," *Datamation*, May 1983, pp. 139–152.

DAVIS, W. *Operating Systems: A Systematic View:* Reading, MA: Addison-Wesley, 1983.

DENNING, P., AND R. BROWN. "Operating Systems," *Scientific American*, September 1984, pp. 94–106.

DUGAN, R. "System/370 Extended Architecture: A Program View of Channel Subsystem," *Proceedings of the Tenth Annual International Symposium on Computer Architecture*, June 1983.

KURZBAN, S., T. HEINES, AND A. SAYERS. *Operating Systems Principles*, New York. Van Nostrand, Reinhold, 1984.

WEIZER, N. "A History of Operating Systems," *Datamation;* January 1981, pp. 118–126.

INDEX

Notes